We Were So Beloved

We Were So Beloved

AUTOBIOGRAPHY OF A GERMAN

JEWISH COMMUNITY

Gloria DeVidas Kirchheimer &
Manfred Kirchheimer

Foreword by Steven Lowenstein

Afterword by Dan Bar-On

UNIVERSITY OF PITTSBURGH PRESS

Published by the University of Pittsburgh Press, Pittsburgh, Pa. 15261
Copyright © 1997, University of Pittsburgh Press
Manufactured in the United States of America
Printed on acid-free paper
10 9 8 7 6 5 4 3 2 1

LIBRARY OF CONGRESS CATALOGING-IN-PUBLICATION DATA

Kirchheimer, Gloria DeVidas.
We were so beloved : autobiography of a German Jewish community /
Gloria DeVidas Kirchheimer and Manfred Kirchheimer.
p.   cm.
Includes index.
ISBN 0-8229-3997-5 (alk. paper)
1. Jews, German—New York (State)—New York—Interviews. 2. Refugees,
Jewish—New York (State)—New York—Interviews. 3. Holocaust sur-
vivors—New York (State)—New York—Interviews. 4. Washington Heights
(New York, N.Y.)—Biography. 1. Kirchheimer, Manfred. 11. Title.
FI28.9.J5K57   1997
974.7'1004924—dc21   97-4824

A CIP catalog record for this book is available from the British Library.

This book is dedicated to the memory of
Henny and Bert Kirchheimer,
who were indeed beloved, and to our children,
Gabriel and Daniel Kirchheimer.

Contents

❧

Foreword

Steven Lowenstein, University of Judaism

Among immigrants to the United States, the refugees from Nazi Germany had many traits that set them apart from the ordinary. They were more often middle class, older, better educated, and they often came with a complex mix of German and Jewish identities that made their integration into their new country more complicated than usual. Within this wave of German-speaking, mainly Jewish immigrants, those who settled in the northern part of Manhattan in the area known as Washington Heights–Inwood were also far from typical. Washington Heights attracted those within the spectrum of German Jewry who were most likely to be southern German, from small towns, religiously traditional, and of modest social background. They shared the general characteristics of other German Jewish immigrants, but in a less extreme way. Although they, too, shared the ambivalences of conflicting German and Jewish identities, the Jewish side of the equation tended to be stronger in Washington Heights than it was among immigrants who settled in other areas.

Washington Heights–Inwood comprises a large area at the narrow northern end of Manhattan Island. Within its shifting boundaries lived over a quarter of a million people. An area of widely differing subneighborhoods, Washington Heights was the last part of the island to be urbanized. East of Broadway most of the apartment houses were built between 1890 and 1920, whereas in the more prestigious west, overlooking the Hudson River, most of the buildings dated from 1920 and later. At the time the German "refugees" arrived (they hated the word *refugee*), the neighborhood was almost totally covered with five- and six-story apartment buildings, interspersed with a great deal of parkland overlooking the river. It was a middle-class neighborhood inhabited mainly by second-generation Jews and Irish, with some older English mixed in and some newer Greek and Armenian inhabitants. After an ambitious building campaign in the 1920s came the Depression, which left many new apartments vacant. When the German Jews began to arrive in America after 1933, the large cheap apartments overlooking the river were an attraction to a population that came to America penniless, but with middle-class tastes, furniture, and clothing. Most of the German Jewish settlement in Washington Heights occurred between about 1937 and 1940 when the flight from Hitler was at its peak.

Of the 150,000 or so refugees from Hitler who came from Germany to America, about one in seven eventually settled in Washington Heights. This represented the largest German Jewish settlement in the world. The newcomers never made up more than a small percentage of the total population of Washington Heights (though they did concentrate in pockets of settlement around 160th Street and Fort Washington Avenue, for instance), but they gave their imprint to the neighborhood. On weekends, they filled the parks, sitting on the benches, quietly discussing old times in German. Conversational groups also gathered on street corners or in cafeterias where they lingered for hours over a cup of coffee, sometimes to the dismay of the proprietors. They founded their own organizations—social clubs, mutual aid societies, kindergartens, synagogues, even a society of German army veterans from World War I.

Social clubs, which played an important role for younger immigrants in the early years of their immigration, began to fade away after World War II as the younger generation married and settled in. Now synagogues played the greatest role in communal life. German-speaking immigrants founded at least a dozen congregations in Washington Heights and took over a few native congregations as well. The spectrum of congregations ranged from extremely orthodox, through nominally orthodox and conservative, to the reform Hebrew Tabernacle. Although the orthodox made up only about one-fourth of the German population of the neighborhood, they had a disproportionate influence through the well-organized Breuer community, a congregation that

played an important political role, and also created a network of institutions including a school system, a golden age club, and a network of
supervised kosher butcher stores and bakeries. Sabbath and Jewish hol-
idays were highly visible in the neighborhood, with crowds of well-
dressed synagogue-goers and promenaders. German Jewish congregations of all denominations were characterized by formal services, often
with choirs and considerable solemnity. In general the culture of the
immigrants was a formal one, with set patterns of synagogue seating,
greeting acquaintances, serving coffee and cake, proper dress, and defer-
ence to one's elders.

Although old-fashioned in a number of ways, the Washington
Heights immigrant community was not isolated. Most inhabitants
worked outside the neighborhood and often shopped downtown and
visited relatives, friends, and cultural events in other parts of the city.
For vacations they went to the Catskills or, with increasing affluence,
to Florida and Europe. Many German Jewish organizations were city-
or countrywide, and Washington Heights residents participated in
them. An especially important means of communication among the
immigrants was the *Aufbau* (Reconstruction), the German-language
newspaper of the refugees from Hitler, which had an international readership. Some read it for its news and political reporting, whereas others
looked first to see what had happened to former friends and neighbors
scattered throughout the world.

The German Jewish residents tended to socialize within their own
group and were separated from their non-German neighbors by language and social habits. Their relationship with fellow Jews of non-
German background was ambivalent. "Germans" and "natives" recognized each other as coreligionists but often avoided social contact
beyond the perfunctory. This changed greatly among the children of
the immigrants born in the neighborhood. A large percentage of them
married Jewish partners of non-German background and a minority
married out of the faith. In general, the cultural characteristics of the
older generation were not cultivated by their children. Most spoke little to no German and showed little interest in passing on any "German
Jewishness" to the third generation. In their majority, children of the
community integrated into American Jewry without much difficulty or
ambiguity.

Even among the immigrants themselves, there was an ambivalent attitude toward things German. On the one hand, most of them—to the shock of their English- and Yiddish-speaking coreligionists—continued to use the German language on the street, at home, and even in sermons in the synagogue. Many continued to read the German classics, enjoy German music, and eat German foods. Yet most of the German Jews of the neighborhood did not consider themselves German. Their tie to Germany had been broken off by the Holocaust, and they no longer identified with it. One woman characterized her relationship with Germany in these terms: "It feels like being divorced." Although some residents visited Germany on occasion (often just to visit their relatives' graves), many preferred Switzerland or Israel as vacation destinations. Some boycotted German products, and most called themselves "American Jews" or "German Jews" but never "Germans" or "German Americans." Among the first generation there was a split between their very noticeable German cultural traits and their rejection of German ethnic identity. In the second generation the cultural traits, too, underwent rapid replacement by American culture.

The life and culture of German Jewish Washington Heights was essentially restricted to a single generation. This was caused not only by the Americanization of the immigrant children, but even more by the fact that most of the children moved away, attracted by the lure of suburbia. By the 1970s the community was an aging one, with senior activities becoming the liveliest part of communal life. Meanwhile the ethnic composition and social status of Washington Heights was undergoing rapid change. Beginning at the southern border of the neighborhood, which was adjacent to Harlem, the African American and Hispanic population began to increase rapidly. By the 1980s the vast majority of the neighborhood's inhabitants were of Hispanic descent, especially immigrants from the Dominican Republic. Spanish and not German was now the foreign language most frequently heard on the neighborhood streets. Although there was little overt hostility between the newcomers and the German Jews who were now part of the "native population," there was little social contact between them. The German Jews did not rapidly flee the neighborhood, but they did concentrate more and more in the still middle-class pockets near Fort Tryon Park, the northernmost outpost of Washington Heights.

Today the German Jewish community is an aged one. Reduced from its peak of over twenty thousand to between three and five thousand, the average age of its members must be in the late seventies, if not more. A few institutions, including a reduced number of synagogues, butcher shops, and bakeries, are still enclaves of German Jewish life in a largely Hispanic area. Under the leadership of the Breuer community, whose strictly orthodox members were less likely to move out than anyone else, the Jews of Washington Heights have organized politically in order to protect their remaining stake in the neighborhood. They have learned American techniques of political mobilization even if these are used mainly on behalf of their own ethnic group. The remaining communal members, many of them widowed, speak a mixture of English and German and often look with nostalgia to the early days of the community. They are proud of the accomplishments of their children, most of whom live at a distance from them, and they try to carry on with as much of their now somewhat diminished lifestyle as their age and the changing neighborhood allow.

Preface

꙳꙳꙳

Some of the interviews in this book were seen in the 1986 documentary film *We Were So Beloved*, by Manfred Kirchheimer. Because of the constraints of the medium, only a fraction of the original material recorded was used in the film. This book, then, incorporates additional conversations from those interviews and includes new ones as well to permit a further exploration of the questions raised when the filmmaker first revisited his former community.

Several of the people from Washington Heights who appear in the film were interviewed three times and others only once or twice. First, there was a preliminary conversation on audiotape that helped the filmmaker decide which areas to follow up on, in the film, and the kinds of questions he needed to ask. It also served to familiarize the people with the interview process and to put them at ease during filming. Then there was an on-camera interview, and finally, in some cases, an interview in German, the last for use in a German version of the film, which was shown on German television. All the conversations with former and present-day Washington Heights residents were conducted in 1981–1982, with one exception. The people in Saarbrücken were interviewed only once, in 1991, and their words were translated from the German.

Where an individual was interviewed more than once, all the material has been integrated and edited in an attempt to form a coherent account. Unless crucial to the sense of the topic or the emotional point, repetitions and hesitations have been eliminated. At the same time an attempt has been made to retain the flavor and the tone of a personality. For all our subjects, English is not their first language and there were bound to be some awkward phrases; the most flagrant of these have been corrected. Occasionally material has been shifted to provide a more chronological account. Fidelity to meaning and clarity were our paramount concerns. At every stage we asked ourselves if a change in a verbatim account would be a violation of the original sense or if it was absolutely necessary. Questions of "truth" and veracity were ever present as we worked.

Oral history is always subject to the vagaries of memory. Contradictions within an individual's story, especially if recounted more than once, are to be expected. Here the problem was compounded by our subjects' wish to make coherent that which defies all concepts of order—moral, emotional, psychological. Any editorial effort to set the record straight, to fill in lacunae, or to question the accuracy of what was being reported has been placed within brackets.

All of the interviews were conducted by Manfred Kirchheimer, unless otherwise indicated, and he is the one who devised most of the questions. As an editor and writer, Gloria Kirchheimer worked with the raw material to give it coherence, and she wrote almost all the prose sections. Although the first-person voice is Manfred's, his words and thoughts were refined through a process of close collaboration with his wife.

There is a marked contrast between the fortunate Kirchheimer household, where events abroad were discussed openly, and others where people who endured the worst sufferings were unable to recall them at all, or else did so through tremendous force of will. For every person who was willing to speak of his or her experiences, there were many who refused to revisit the horrors they had endured. Some waited decades before deciding to offer testimony. And it did take decades before organized attempts were made to bring survivors together, to form organizations that held regular meetings, to embark on building permanent archives based on oral testimonies. These activities became even more imperative as accounts were published—and continue to be published—denying that the horrific events of the Nazi era actually did take place.

Age also sharpened the necessity to record these histories for children and grandchildren, many of whom were hearing them for the first time. Some of the individuals who spoke to us were impelled by the thought that their willingness to recount these events might, in some small way, help prevent a recurrence. One woman feared that her nightmares would increase as she aged and hoped to hold them at bay by bringing her experiences to light. Although willing to be interviewed, she ultimately declined to appear in this book, like others who had briefly reopened this unspeakable period in their lives.

The point of view throughout, expressed within brackets, is that of Manfred Kirchheimer. The book is thus a quest for an understanding, if such is possible, of the events that shaped his community. At the same time, he seeks to comprehend forces at work within himself as a product of this community. The questions asked in this book we may ask of ourselves. For example: Are there lessons in survival? Do people change? Does a survivor have special obligations? What of collective guilt? These questions are perhaps rhetorical. Lacking definitive answers, we can only hope that somewhere in the responses of these individuals may lie some illumination.

This book is by no means intended to be a comprehensive account of pre- and postwar German Jewry nor of the Nazi period. There are many excellent works on these subjects and readers are urged to seek them out.

Acknowledgments

᛭

Our first debt of gratitude must go to the people who told us their stories and generously consented to appear in this book. Financial support came from the Lucius Littauer Foundation, the Maurice Falk Medical Fund, the Cultural Ministry of the Saarland, and the Landeszentralbank-Mainz. We also thank the New York Foundation for the Arts for serving as the project's sponsor.

Oskar Lafontaine, state premier of the Saarland, was unfailingly gracious and cooperative; Hans-Jürgen Koebnick, former mayor of Saarbrücken, took time from his duties to conduct us around the region and provided us with important material. Steven M. Lowenstein, who chronicled the German Jewish community of Washington Heights in his book *Frankfurt on the Hudson* (Wayne State University Press, 1989) was an invaluable source. We are also grateful to the staff of the Leo Baeck Institute, particularly Frank Mecklenburg and Dianne Spielmann for their availability and help. Renate Stein deserves many thanks for her sensitive translations. Wendy Henry was our diligent researcher.

We wish to express our gratitude to Louise De Cormier, Faye Geiger, Helen Lane, Rosalyn Manowitz, Michael Riff, and Phyllis Tobin for their encouragement and assistance. Time and funds were made available to Gloria Kirchheimer through the professional development policies of the Social Science Research Council, primarily under the presidency of David L. Featherman, now director of the Institute for Social Research at the University of Michigan at Ann Arbor. The School of Visual Arts provided active encouragement by giving Manfred Kirchheimer a sabbatical to work on this project.

Other individuals were interviewed and although they do not appear in the book, their contribution is gratefully acknowledged: Dr. Theo Kron, Auguste Leeser, Rabbi Robert Lehman, and Rabbi Rolf Neuhaus. In Saarbrücken, each of the following contributed to the progress of our work: Albrecht Stuby and Ewald Blum of the Max Ophüls Preis Film Festival, Michael Beckert, producer for Saarland television, and Gabi Koepnick.

This project had its origins in Manfred Kirchheimer's documentary film, *We Were So Beloved: The German Jews of Washington Heights* (distributed by First Run Features, New York City). The following individuals contributed ideas to the film that carried over into the writing of this book: John Converso, Jean Bethke Elshtain, Walter Hess, Leo Hurwitz, Sybil Milton, and Stan Salfas.

We Were So Beloved

Introduction

❧❧❧

My dad woke me up at 12:30. He couldn't wait until morning to tell me that the good guy had beaten the bad guy. Joe Louis, the American, had defeated Max Schmeling, the German. It was June 1938, two years after my arrival in America from Germany. I was seven years old.

I had been primed for this event for months. We were all rooting for the American, even though my dad had met Schmeling in 1930 and drawn his portrait for the *Saarbrücker Zeitung.* To us in 1938, anybody and anything German was bad, despite the nostalgic mutterings of some of our fellow refugees who seemed unable to connect the sufferings inflicted on them with their former homeland.

Growing up in New York City during the war years, we refugee kids were sheltered from the worst of the Nazi horrors abroad, but there was no ambiguity about who was good and who was bad. I, of course, was one of the good guys, although later this edifice of black and white began to crack. My father's unqualified enthusiasm for America had permeated my youth. But during the late 1940s, I began to question it. My America no longer seemed so pure. I had learned that America's Golden Door was only grudgingly ajar, that strict immigration quotas had been in force and not even those were allowed to be filled. People I admired were denouncing their colleagues to the House Committee on Un-American Activities for alleged communist activities. There was an unofficial blacklist in effect throughout the film industry where I began working in 1952. And despite all the hatred manifested against them for simply being Jewish, my people were grumbling about blacks and Hispanics. Was there no carryover from their own experiences as victims? The certainties of my youth gave way to a skepticism that intensified as I grew older.

Walk along Fort Washington Avenue in upper Manhattan at three o'clock in the afternoon. The street rises gently from 157th Street to 192nd where it culminates in Fort Tryon Park, the highest point in Manhattan. The park commands spectacular views of the Hudson River, a vista so like the Rhine that it was one of the main reasons that led my people, when they fled Germany, to settle in Washington Heights. During World War II, the Swedish liner *Gripsholm* was anchored right off 161st Street, our street, in the middle of the Hudson River. My father and I often stood leaning on the wall on Riverside Drive to check up on her. Assuring me that there were no ocean liners on the Rhine, let alone great suspension bridges like the George Washington Bridge, he convinced me that the Hudson was far superior.

If the weather is good, you will see elderly people strolling or standing on the sidewalks and chatting. The language here is German, heavily accented and liberally sprinkled with American slang. Mostly in their eighties, the men walk slowly, their backs bent, hands clasped behind them if they are not relying on their canes. As for the women, they might be participants in an outdoor fashion show on Frankfurt's Kaiserstrasse rather than elderly housewives on their way to the supermarket. Elegance prevails; not a hair is out of place, not a smudge on a lapel.

On summer days, the people sit in webbed aluminum chairs in front of their buildings, which are six or seven storys high, made of brick, and of prewar construction. The chief pastime is staring, and anyone who ventures out in a housedress or obviously uncorseted is in for some heavy censure. When I came uptown to visit, I had to be sure my shoes were adequately shined to avoid embarrassing my parents.

Just before four o'clock, the street empties. Everyone has gone indoors for the ritual Kaffee und Kuchen. This is Washington Heights, "Frankfurt on the Hudson," where I lived, along with twenty-four thousand other German Jews, a pretty dull place for me when I was at City College where I had met a faster crowd. But I was a lucky child as I was to realize much later.

My dad's autographed picture of Max Schmeling hangs on my wall today, along with those of other celebrities he drew. In Germany my father, Berthold Kirchheimer, had been a leading newspaper cartoonist and illustrator and, at the same time, held down a job as chief graphic designer at a department store in Saarbrücken where I was born.

The Saarland is an area in southwestern Germany, slightly smaller than Rhode Island, that borders on France. Under the Statutes of the Saar of the Treaty of Versailles, concluded after World War I, this was made an autonomous region to be administered by France under the supervision of the League of Nations between 1920 and 1935, when a plebiscite would take place to determine the future of the region. Prior to World War I, it had been a heavily contested area with Germany and France vying for control over the coal-rich region. Although the Nazis came to power in 1933, they were politically ineffectual in the Saar at that time because of its unique political status. My father recalls hearing radio broadcasts by Hitler and Goebbels, rabble-rousing tirades directed against the Jews, but, given the relative safety of the Jews in the Saar, these were not considered dangerous to us.

My father says they knew of the existence of concentration camps for political dissidents because of reports in the social democratic newspaper. And despite the relative calm of the Saar, they knew that conditions were deteriorating elsewhere. Travel was not yet restricted in any way, so he was able to visit his relatives elsewhere in Germany and they gave him firsthand reports. The boycott of Jewish stores in 1933 took place also in Saarbrücken, and my father recalls that Christians who defied it were reviled and spat upon by Nazi sympathizers.

Between 1933 and 1935 many liberal journalists came to the Saar because of its relative safety. One of them, a famous writer for the *Berliner Tageblatt*, came to my parents' home to visit and to ask for advice about emigrating. My father was nervous about having this man in his home, fearing the neighbors might report his presence to the police. Nonetheless he was given dinner and made to feel welcome.

The political situation in the Saar changed as a result of the plebiscite held on January 13, 1935, to determine whether the Saar would maintain its status quo under the League of Nations protectorate, become part of France, or revert to Germany. The sizable social democratic opposition, led by Max Braun, was confident the Nazis would lose. However, the vote was 90 percent in favor of Germany. Whether the numbers were rigged has never been determined, but there was overwhelming sentiment in favor of Germany.

The Jews of the Saarland began to leave almost immediately. Some went to Strasbourg, others to Metz, some to Luxembourg, and others much further away, like my family. Those who went to Strasbourg and other nearby French cities were among the first to be taken by the Nazis after the invasion of France, because of their proximity to the German border. Only a few poorer Jews who did not have the means to start over remained in Saarbrücken.

A photograph of my parents and me on our way to New York in 1936 aboard the SS *Manhattan* gives no clue to the anguish they must have felt in leaving their homeland. In the photo, we are all wearing party hats and the table is decorated with balloons. We had left Germany early enough to be able to bring our possessions with us, unlike later refugees who could leave with only ten marks or four dollars in their pockets (roughly forty-four dollars in today's money). We had our affidavits of financial support and the names of two relatives already living in the United States. It was 1936 and the worst was yet to come for those we left behind.

Had it not been for my father's dismissal from his job in Saarbrücken and his two brothers already living in New York, I wonder if he would have voluntarily left. So many German Jews outside the Saar remained until it was too late. Their reasons were many, among them the refusal to believe that Nazi policies were not merely a temporary aberration. After all, we were Germans and had been so for centuries. On my uncle Siegfried's hand-drawn family tree, the earliest Kirchheimer dates back to the 1600s, though Jews had followed the Roman legions into Germany as early as the third century A.D. or perhaps before.

My grandfather, Moses Kirchheimer, ran a stamp and coin shop in Bremerhaven, a port city in northern Germany. He knew Goethe's *Faust* by heart and was one of the few inhabitants of the city to own a camera in 1900. Although he was orthodox, he permitted himself one lapse: playing the flute on the Sabbath, even though the playing of music was forbidden. His explanation was that God could not possibly take offense at hearing Josef Haydn on the Sabbath. He revered Kaiser Wilhelm II (as we later revered Roosevelt) and even dedicated a novel to him, which he had written and self-published under a decidedly un-Jewish pseudonym in 1914. Hoping to present the book to the Kaiser personally, he traveled to Berlin and waited outside the palace for three days, sleeping on the steps, before giving up and returning home.

Like a hundred thousand other German Jews, my father had served in the German army in World War I. Assigned to work as a telephone repairman, he was sent to the field one day for some emergency work and returned to find his whole unit wiped out by a shell. A rakish teenager at the time of his service, he was awarded the Iron Cross for bravery. In one photo, he has climbed up a telephone pole, engaged in his detail as repairman. He smiles at us as if to say, "Don't take this seriously, I'll be home soon."

Our names were Siegfried, Otto, Johanna, Elfriede; in our appearance we were hardly distinguishable from our non-Jewish neighbors. We did not live in a ghetto and, like other families on the Schmollerstrasse, we had a breakfront to display our family porcelain and crystal. A couple of our shelves were devoted to religious ceremonial objects such as silver kiddush cups and filigreed incense boxes. Every Monday in winter, like the people next door, we ate green kale and cooked salami, and every Sunday evening cold cuts and pickles. Lack of punctuality was treated as a sin. When I left home at the age of twenty-four, I gradually developed the habit of being late to appointments—one of my unconscious acts of rebellion, probably—except when I had to visit my parents. Then I would rush like a madman and fume with exasperation if we were stuck in a traffic jam. It would not be the end of the world, my wife said, if we were ten minutes late. But it was the end of the world to my parents, a violation of an absolute value that contained no room for flexibility. Stories of people arriving at the opera two hours before curtain time are common in my family.

In Germany we did not stand out like the eastern Jews in our midst, many of whom wore sidelocks and long black caftans. These *Ostjuden*, more visible victims of antisemitism, had come to Germany fleeing pogroms and poverty. They were regarded with disdain by most German Jews: They were "uncultured," and spoke Yiddish, which their coreligionists considered a corruption of the language of Goethe and Heine. Some German Jews still believe that were it not for the eastern Jews the Nazis would never have turned against all Jews.

Our Judaism was discreet. Although a small proportion of German Jews were orthodox, most German Jews were considerably less religious than eastern Jews, restricting their observance to the High Holy Days. We had been enjoying most of the privileges of full German citizenship since 1871, when restrictions on civil and political rights based on religious differences were struck down in an edict signed by Kaiser Wilhelm I and his chancellor Otto von Bismarck.

However, German Jews were always aware of antisemitism. It was a part of our culture. A popular saying had it that "the Jews are our misfortune." During World War I, official policy prohibited Jews from advancing beyond the rank of captain. After the war, it was even asserted that no Jews had participated in the fighting. As a response, the Jewish veterans organization published the names and addresses of the twelve thousand Jewish soldiers who had died in combat. By 1933 there were over five hundred thousand Jews in the country, representing approximately 1 percent of the total population.

In 1918, when my father came out of the army, there were anti-Jewish groups holding meetings and putting up posters: "Germany Awake!" "Jews out of Germany!" To counter them, a group of young Jews met late at night and went around Bremerhaven removing the signs. At a public meeting held in a large concert hall in 1919, ostensibly for the public's information, my father was obliged to listen to one of his former professors blame Germany's defeat in World War I on the *"Dolchstoss in den Rücken"* [the "stab in the back"] administered by the Jews. (It was clear that the teacher had recognized him, one of his former star pupils, though he was sitting in the last row.) The professor's speech was a denunciation of Jews and their "criminal acts." The cantor of my father's synagogue gave a rebuttal speech.

Before assuming power, the Nazi party was not taken seriously by the Jews in Germany, even though Hitler's plans had been made public in *Mein Kampf* (1927), a popular and widely distributed book. After Hitler took over, his early targets were his political opponents, social democrats and communists, who were the first to be arrested and taken to concentration camps. Most Jews did not feel physically threatened, although there were scattered outbreaks of violence against them. The rise of the National Socialists was taken as an affront to the loyalty of the Jews as German citizens. "Within the Jewish community, every organized group replied to National Socialism with resounding affirmations of the right of Jews to be German, to live in and love Germany . . . [T]he right to maintain a Jewish presence in Germany was construed as a legal right, a moral necessity, and a religious imperative by all Jewish organizations, from orthodox to reform, right to left, Zionist and non-

Zionist" (Lucy Dawidowicz, *The War Against the Jews, 1933–1945* [New York: Holt, Rhinehart, and Winston, 1975], p. 174). The Zionist organ *Jüdische Rundschau* stated on April 13, 1933: "Our avowal of Jewish peoplehood has never signified that we discarded or could discard anything that the German spirit bestowed on us."

Unlike some of my Washington Heights neighbors, I never heard the Nazis singing the popular refrain as they tramped down the boulevards, *"Wenn juden Blut vom Messer spritzt . . ."* [When Jewish blood spurts from the knife . . .].

By 1935 German Jews outside the Saar were no longer allowed to enter cinemas, concert halls, or recreation areas. With the 1935 Nuremberg Laws, we were not permitted to call ourselves German. Violence increased against businesses and individuals. Still, most Jews remained staunchly German. This was surely a phase, a temporary aberration. They would sit tight and weather this as they had weathered other antisemitic periods. Jewish teachers, lawyers, musicians, and civil servants were dismissed from their positions. Doctors such as my uncle Siegfried were barred from treating non-Jewish patients, but Nazi functionaries continued to consult him because of his reputation as an astute diagnostician.

Gradually, beginning with a trickle in 1933, some German Jews began to leave the country. The "final solution" had not yet been articulated and Nazi policy was to encourage emigration through all means possible, a policy reinforced through harassment, physical abuse, and the punitive Nuremberg Laws, which systematically stripped Jews of all basic rights. After the *Anschluss,* the annexation of Austria in March 1938, emigration was no longer a matter of choice. A policy of forced emigration, carried out under the supervision of Adolf Eichmann, compelled Jews to leave or face incarceration in concentration camps. Since Jews' assets were confiscated and the process of obtaining the necessary papers often took months, Jews found themselves in a virtually untenable situation.

There were other powerful obstacles. To emigrate might mean leaving elderly parents behind, moving to a country where you did not know the language and where employment prospects were uncertain. For those who had substantial assets in Germany, leaving the country meant financial disaster. Many countries, including the United States, had restrictive immigration quotas. The reluctance of other nations to take in Jews did not go without comment from Hitler: "It is a shameful example to observe today how the entire democratic world dissolves in tears of pity but then, in spite of its obvious duty to help, closes its heart to the poor, tortured Jewish people" (Hitler speech, January 30, 1939, cited in Raul Hilberg, *The Destruction of the European Jews* [New York and London: Holmes & Meier, 1985], vol. 2, p. 396). Even during the war when the extent of the exterminations became known in the Allied countries, few relaxed their immigration policies.

Jews applying to the United States could obtain American visas only on the basis of affidavits of financial support and guarantees of employment, so that a prospective immigrant would not become a financial burden to the government. A sponsor first had to be found and persuaded to put up a considerable financial bond as guarantee—not always easy to do, especially if there were no relatives one could rely on in the United States. Still, there were opportunities for escape that were ignored, particularly before the rampages, synagogue burnings, and arrests of Kristallnacht on November 9–10, 1938.

By November 1938, with the encouragement of the Nazi government, 150,000 of the more than 500,000 German Jews had already left. The shock of Kristallnacht, combined with the policy of forced emigration, impelled another 78,000 to depart during the year that followed. Between Kristallnacht and October 1941, when emigration was cut off entirely, 150,000 Jews left Germany. In German-speaking Austria (now considered part of the Greater Reich), 126,000 Jews had left by the time the war broke out in 1939. Of the quarter of a million German and Austrian Jews who, for one reason or another, were left behind after October 1941, 90 percent would perish.

✵

In 1942 when my religious grandfather died here, I began my bid for righteousness by deciding to become an orthodox Jew. I was eleven years old. From then until I was twenty-one, my way was clear; almost every aspect of human behavior seemed to fall in line with the precepts I was studying. While I grappled with many issues, I stopped short of questioning the role of God during the Nazi onslaught.

Although I later abandoned my orthodoxy, I retained my inflexibility on certain matters. I refused to buy German products and condemned my neighbors and family for succumbing to the lure of the Leica and the imported gourmet foods that flooded some of our local shops where the shelves were filled with products such as *Katzenzungen, Mozartkugeln,* and *Senfgurcken.* These shops were often run by orthodox German Jews who had been in hiding or in concentration camps and continued to speak to their customers in German. (Indeed, non-German Jews would have had no inkling these shops even existed. There were no signs outside, shades were drawn. They looked like deserted storefronts, intentionally misleading to any outsiders, especially neighborhood blacks and Hispanics.) Later I bought a Renault, not a Volkswagen, although the German car was better by far. I would not drink wines with names such as *Naktarsch* or *Liebfraumilch,* and when I became a father, I would not buy German toys for my sons.

As the Vietnam War developed after 1963, the feeling grew in me that now I was the enemy. While I was on the home front, insulated from war, from even the least unpleasantness, my government, in my name, was carrying on a war I opposed. We were targeting innocent civilians, poisoning their food and burning people with ingenious new antipopulation devices. These were being manufactured by companies whose products I used in my kitchen or at my desk. I imagined being confronted years later by a Vietnamese who had lost his son or whose wife had been maimed, putting to me the question I fantasized asking every German: What did you do during the war?

"I demonstrated three or four times a year," would be my lame reply. "I wrote letters to my congressmen, sent money to antiwar organizations, bailed out my students who engaged in civil disobedience." But I made sure I would not be arrested.

My former certainty of the collective guilt of the German people was shaken for the first time. How much was I like the German who just stood by while his government perpetrated its evil? And my parents whom I loved, who were apolitical and timid, how would they have acted over there had they not been Jewish?

In Germany after 1933 you could be denounced and put into jail or a camp just for speaking to a Jew or a socialist (if there were any left). By the start of the war, everyone feared exposure by a neighbor. A vivid example was cited by William Shirer in his *Berlin Diary*.

February 4, 1940:

In Germany it is a serious penal offense to listen to a foreign radio station. The other day the mother of a German airman received word from the Luftwaffe that her son was missing and must be presumed dead. A couple of days later the BBC in London, which broadcasts weekly a list of German prisoners, announced that her son had been captured. Next day she received *eight* letters from friends and acquaintances telling her they had heard her son was safe as a prisoner in England. Then the story takes a nasty turn. The mother denounced all eight to the police for listening to an English broadcast, and they were arrested.

An entire citizenry had acceded to the Nazis, standing by while their neighbors were taken away in the middle of the night; many had taken advantage of their neighbors' misfortune, and most claimed ignorance about the extermination camps.

Germany was a "civilized" country, a Christian country. And yet, barbarism was allowed to prevail. It was difficult for me even now to overcome my hatred and rage. How could an entire people be evil? What accounted for the goodness of those who risked their lives to help the Jews?

And what about the range of responses among the German Jews themselves? One German Jewish economist told me he had felt it his patriotic duty to beat up German leftists during the 1920s as a member of the Stahlhelm, a rabidly right-wing group of former World War I soldiers.

"What did you think," I asked a former Washington Heights neighbor, "when in 1936 you read about a Jew who was picked up in the streets and was taken away?"

"I assumed he was a bad person," she told me.

And concerning the deportations of the Polish Jews in Germany before the war, here is what a family friend said: "German Jews who had lived there for generations and generations said, 'These are Polish people, they don't really belong here. They immigrated to this country, so now the Germans sent them out again to where they really belong. Let them go back to Poland.'"

As a German, how would I have acted in their place? I wondered if I, as an ordinary person, would have acted heroically. I was fretting about myself, feeling scarred for not having been tested. Would I have measured up?

※

Whenever I returned to Washington Heights to visit my family, I was struck with the feeling of timelessness. The refugees were older, more prosperous, but they still took their walk to the park or to the bakery to buy two rolls for lunch. Over time, there had been changes in the population. Hispanics and blacks had started moving in during the early 1960s, and there were new Jewish immigrants from Russia. I heard complaints about the new people: They are loud. They take everything for granted. They are taking over. These complaints had a familiar ring. A generation before, the same words had been applied to the German Jews in New York.

Yet my people were a remarkable group who built a stable, loving neighborhood for their children after having undergone the terrors of persecution and exile. They had found work (often menial), they had set up self-help networks, established numerous congregations, and sent us to college. They were indeed remarkable—and still, many of their attitudes troubled me.

There were so many contradictions. Clearly, I needed to go back to my people in Washington Heights to understand their lives, now and during the Nazi time, which also might help me to understand and evaluate my own. To begin with, how did these Jewish people, these Germans, react to the events that enveloped them? Why had some stubbornly insisted upon staying, whereas others left in time? What had they endured and how had they been changed, if indeed they had been changed? The need to better understand where I had come from and what I and my people had become led me to return to my old neighborhood and to interview family and friends.

I start with my aunt Annie Ostertag, whose first, non-Jewish, husband left her to join the German army in 1934. What had happened? As a child I was forbidden to ask about him, for in my house he was always referred to as "the man who is dead for us."

PART ONE

Jews Out

Annie Ostertag

Annie was my mother's youngest sister, one of four. Their mother, my grandmother, opened a pension in Dortmund shortly after the end of World War I and it was there that my father met my mother. In 1930 Annie married Hugo Krahn, the son of a Catholic father and a Protestant mother. The elder Krahns ran a café where Hugo worked and where she also helped out. It was a popular place that attracted many Jewish patrons who came to play cards and to bet on the horses. Odds were posted on a large board.

AO. We were very happy and we loved each other very much. His parents were wonderful people. It didn't matter that I was Jewish. The whole family was anti-Nazi.

I didn't know it then, but wherever I went, I was being watched. People began to talk about me and my husband. Later on we found out it was a man who came to my in-laws' café every day, a Mr. Metzger. He was always very nice to me. And everybody thought this man was a good friend of the Jews but he was a Nazi and betrayed us. He told everyone that I was Jewish and that I didn't belong there. This was in 1934.

[The Krahns were eventually forced to close the café because it was patronized by Jews. Annie and her husband then opened an outdoor café on their own near a lake on the outskirts of Dortmund.]

AO. It was a beautiful café and we thought we could hide there. We were very successful and made a lot of money. I think I even have pictures of you there. But then this Mr. Metzger found us. He had gotten higher up in the Nazis and we had to close the café. Hugo was forced to put on a Nazi uniform.

MK. How did that happen?

AO. I will never forget it. He was in a swimming hole and the people who knew him took away his clothes and they gave him instead a uniform to put on. He came home wearing it.

MK. And he put it on to prove that he was a good German?

AO. Yes, to show that he was a German, that he had nothing to do with me. When he came home wearing the uniform I said, "Either you keep it and I leave, or you don't wear it and we remain together." But he decided to keep wearing it. Then we had to separate.

[The September 1935 Nuremberg Law for the Protection of German Blood and Honor prohibited new marriages between Jews and gentiles, but did not call for dissolution of existing unions.]

AO. He did not want to separate, but we had no other choice. His parents also were against it. They thought the Nazi situation would blow over in a year. We also thought it would be only for a short time and then we could get together again.

MK. Did you ever meet with him secretly after you separated?

AO. Yes, in Cologne, and in Düsseldorf. And then in Essen. Your father's aunt lived in Essen and I went there and found a job. His parents came to visit me in Essen.

MK. He still loved you?

AO. He still loved me, but he knew they would never leave us in peace as long as he was with me.

[Her husband did not want to leave Germany and go to a strange country as a refugee. He was apprehensive about being able to find work as a pharmacist and he worried about learning a new language.]

AO. Then I went to England to visit Aunt Toni [another sister] and there I was told where he was and that if I went back to him they would bother me all my life or they would put me in a concentration camp.

[Annie was advised to file for a divorce, which was granted in April 1936 on the grounds that her husband could not have children.]

MK. After the war, did you ever hear from Hugo Krahn or see him?

AO. Yes, in 1952 when I went back for the first time to Germany. I was sitting in a well-known café in Dortmund with some friends. Then I saw him come in. I recognized him right away and he looked, and looked again, and he just couldn't believe that I was sitting there until I said, "Yes, Hugo, it's me." And that's how we met again.

MK. How did he react?

AO. He was crying and so was I. He sat down with me and the first thing he noticed was my red nails, so I told him this was the style in America.

[The two corresponded until he died, a year later, in 1953 at the age of fifty-one. Subsequently, Annie renewed acquaintance with Krahn's brothers and visited his father who died at the age of ninety in 1972.]

AO. Thank God I had told Paul [her second husband] all about him.

[Annie had met Paul Ostertag in Göppingen in 1937 after her divorce from Hugo Krahn. She was then working in a hotel owned by a relative and known for its Jewish clientele. Paul was a wealthy Jewish bachelor a dozen years her senior who owned a large men's clothing store and employed a chauffeur. The two became engaged. Annie had already obtained her visa for the United States and she also had a visitor's visa for England where she planned to go first to visit her sister Toni. Although Paul had also obtained a visa for the United States, he was not prepared to leave Germany before settling his business affairs. He wanted to avoid having everything confiscated.

On November 10, 1938, right after Kristallnacht, the huge anti-Jewish pogrom, Nazis roaming the streets shot at the hotel. Bullets were fired into Annie's room. She quickly salvaged a few dresses and an autograph album and found a place to hide. There were no more guests in the hotel. Whatever Jewish men the Nazis found were rounded up in the hotel lobby. Annie maintains that the disorders were fomented by outsiders from Bavaria, and that the local people later came to the hotel to apologize to the owner for the destruction. Paul had managed to get to Stuttgart to his mother's house.]

AO. The day after Kristallnacht, Paul was on the street shopping for his mother and a big truck came along. The Gestapo jumped off and grabbed him and they said, "Are you Jewish? Get into the truck." They already had his uncle. That's how Paul was caught and sent to Dachau.

[Nobody knew where the men had been taken. Annie went to the American consulate and sat on the steps, which, as American territory, provided temporary safety from the Gestapo. Annie was advised by an official to contact the mayor of Stuttgart who was an old classmate of Paul's.]

AO. I was the one who first wrote to Dachau. The mayor of Stuttgart gave me the address of the Dachau jail. Paul was in Dachau from November 10 to December 27, 1938. [He was released because he already had a visa to emigrate.] He came out just two days before I was leaving for England. I had to go because otherwise my English visa would have lapsed. In the meantime, Paul's mother and I always had some poison sewed into our dresses in case something would happen to us. We wore the same clothing day after day. Once in a while they came and checked and asked for names. We also had some money hidden.

MK. Can you describe what happened when Paul came out of Dachau?

AO. His hair was so short and my first impression was—I just fainted when I saw him.

MK. Why?

AO. Why, Manny . . . ? Because he looked so different, he was so thin, he had no hair on his head, and I just fainted and that's that.

[Annie left first for England and then for the United States where she arrived in February 1939. Paul Ostertag was supposed to follow her to England but was unable to do so because he was picked up again by the Gestapo. According to Annie, this occurred because a Nazi official who lived in a building owned by Paul was eager to take possession of it and arranged to have him re-arrested. After the war, Paul was able to reclaim the property.]

MK. Later, did his whole family come to America?

AO. No, nobody came out but Paul. He could buy the visa because he had enough money and he didn't need the affidavit. But when he came to the United States in January 1940 he had only ten marks in his pocket. [He and Annie were married soon after, on my grandmother's birthday in February 1940.]

AO. Paul's mother took her life in 1942 when she was ready to be deported. She took poison. Paul's brother Benno was with her when she did it. He was married to a Christian woman and he went into hiding. He was hidden in the woods by friends of his wife. People took him in and cared for him until the war was over in 1945. He knew good people who never betrayed him.

MAKING A LIVING

[Like many other "rich" German Jewish refugees, my uncle Paul found work at Klein's department store at Union Square in Manhattan.]

AO. His job was picking up the hangers from the ground where people threw them when they were trying on the clothing. I worked first as a mother's helper and cleaning woman. Then I found a job with the costume jewelry designer, Miriam Haskell, and was there for fifteen years.

MK. How did Paul feel about working at the department store after having been a rich man?

AO. He was very unhappy until he started a small leather goods business. He had to carry around four big suitcases with merchandise until he got his first car in 1949. Every morning I had to help him carry the bags to Penn Station or Grand Central Station before I could go to work myself. In 1950 he went back to Europe to get some of his money out of Switzerland and Germany. Then times were a little better for us. But he was always afraid we would run out of money and he never let me buy anything.

He never got the concentration camp out of his system. Loud noises frightened him. He had nightmares and was crying and shouting during the night. Once in the concentration camp he fell down during the roll call and nobody was allowed to pick him up. They all had to step over him. You know they had to stand outdoors in the freezing weather wearing only the striped pajamas. Finally, one of the Kapos picked him up and brought him inside. He was always dreaming that he would fall down and not be able to get up again. He didn't talk much about what he saw and heard in Dachau, but he never got over it.

[My aunt was ninety-one in March 1995 and, until just a few years ago, took annual trips to Germany.]

AO. I have no more hate against Germany. Germany is a wonderful country. I go there and I have a wonderful time. I met new people and they were wonderful. Recently I was invited by the mayor of my hometown [Dortmund] for a visit. I have my husband's niece there. The people I know are nice. I have no bitterness toward them. There's nothing bad I can say about them.

[Annie Ostertag died in December 1995.]

⁂

Sary Lieber

Sary Lieber is the widow of Rabbi Herman Lieber, a man who had a profound influence on my youth. This versatile man served as cantor and gave sermons, taught Hebrew school and conducted funerals, weddings, and bar mitzvahs, visited the sick, ran a day camp and took children on trips, rehearsed the synagogue choir, and lay in wait at the 163rd Street subway station at 7:30 in the morning to collar male congregants into making up a minyan, the obligatory ten men for a service. Aside from being my religious advisor, he also took me and other boys and girls to the circus, to Yankee Stadium, to a play, Life with Father, *and to my first concert, Claudio Arrau playing solo piano at Carnegie Hall. He liked my jokes, we discussed current events, and I played devil's advocate on religious matters. One summer he ran a day camp, with new kids from Germany being added to the group almost daily. I was his unofficial assistant.*

When Israel was on the verge of becoming a state, many young boys I knew were preparing to make aliyah *(become settlers). I was profoundly torn, thinking it was a young man's duty to strengthen the vulnerable new land by emigrating. I presented my problem to Rabbi Lieber who assured me that there was no such religious obligation, that I could serve God as well, maybe better, by staying at home. His advice was good and kind, and I was grateful to him.*

Even when I gave up religion in my last year of college, he made no attempt to dissuade me. He did ask me to continue to maintain the rituals so that I would not be out of practice, should I have a change of heart. Out of friendship I agreed, but I was unable to comply with this false stance for very long.

Originally from Nuremberg, Herman Lieber first worked in Zurich as a Hebrew teacher and cantor (he had a beautiful operatic voice). Sary Pifko, who was born in Zurich in 1915, was his pupil there from age seven to twelve. He was a dozen years older than she. Around 1929, Rabbi Lieber left his job and his studies in Switzerland and accepted a position in Hamburg.

SL. He came back to Switzerland every year on vacation, and one day he came to the store where I was working as an apprentice to learn my father's business—table linens and the like. I was supposed to learn the business, not at my father's place, but in a friend's store. One day, in walked my old teacher, to visit his friend who was my boss. At that time [1934] I was a little more than nineteen. I saw him and recognized him. He didn't see me, so I walked around the table to meet him head on and he was very surprised. He had last seen me as a child of twelve.

He said, "Sary Pifko, you have become a very pretty girl," and I said, "Well, you didn't do too badly for yourself, either." That was the extent of our conversation. Then he went to my boss's office and I went back to my station and that was it. Then he went to visit his parents in Nuremberg on his way back to Hamburg, and when he was in Nuremberg, he thought, that was a good kid. I'm going to sit down and ask her whether she wants to marry me. And he sat down and wrote a letter. [In the letter, dated October 7, 1934, he addresses her familiarly as "Du."]

MK. Were you surprised?

SL. I was floored! I was very young, one of nine children, and I still had an older sister at home who was three years older than I was and not married. At that time in Europe it was unheard of for a younger sister to marry before the older one. And since my sister wasn't even engaged, nobody even thought of me as being somebody to look at, to marry.

[She showed the letter to her parents who counseled her to respond in any way she wished without help from anyone else.]

SL. My father put me into the *gute Stube,* the so-called salon, which was a room reserved exclusively for company and which was never heated in the winter except when we expected guests. I had to sit there all by myself and write my letter. [Her response uses the polite form of address.]

I said it was not easy for me to answer a letter like this because I was completely inexperienced in such correspondence. I remembered him very well as a teacher but was sure that both of us had changed greatly in the meantime. The memories I had of him, I said, were those of a child. [She indicated to him that her quick response was proof that her reaction to his letter was not a negative one.] I said I was ready to enter into correspondence with him to see how both of us have developed and whether we are interested in each other.

[She said that her parents had been surprised at his letter and no longer regarded her as a little girl as a result. She showed her response to her father who approved of it and it was sent off. Subsequently she and Herman Lieber entered into an intense courtship by correspondence, writing every day and sometimes more than once a day. They were married in February 1935.]

SL. Then I went with him to Hamburg, Germany. I wasn't allowed to go before we were married to look for an apartment or anything else, because a young girl couldn't go to where the unmarried man was living. That was not in good taste. Also, before I was married, my parents' friends said it was insane to send a young girl to Hitler's Germany in 1935. We were lucky enough to be living in Switzerland, what are my parents doing? Whereupon my father said, "With a man like Lieber, she will never be lost." And that turned out to be true.

BEFORE KRISTALLNACHT

SL. First of all, the Nazi movement started in Munich and Nuremberg. All these southern German cities were much more affected than the northern part of Germany. Hamburg, which is a port city, had a great many foreign consulates. So we didn't feel it so openly. We knew that every store had a sign in the window: *Juden Unerwünscht* (Jews not wanted here). But in 1935 we still could go to concerts, we could go to the opera, and we did go wherever we wanted. People were thinking of leaving the country, of course, but at that time, 1935, we were still hoping that the whole thing would blow over soon. We didn't believe it would last that long. People said, "That's madness, it cannot last." [Even their gentile friends who were not Nazis could not believe the situation could continue.]

In 1936, 1937, it got worse and we saw that there was no end in sight to this terrible situation. One after another, the Jewish people got very serious about leaving the country. They just didn't know where to go.

[As early as 1935, the Liebers had considered going to Palestine. Mrs. Lieber belonged to an orthodox Zionist group and Rabbi Lieber was also Zionist-minded. They were ready to go as "capitalists," that is, they would transfer a restricted amount of capital to Palestine. However, they never succeeded in obtaining permits. Later they found out that one had to bribe the functionaries at the agency that arranged for visas to Palestine. In 1938, still before Kristallnacht, Mrs. Lieber's father came to Germany to urge them to leave. Sary Lieber was then around twenty-two years old. Throughout the 1930s, Rabbi Lieber had been working as a cantor at a Hamburg synagogue.]

SL. By 1938 there were stores you couldn't shop in, you couldn't go to a café, you couldn't go to an opera or a concert anymore. But somehow it didn't matter that much. OK, so we don't go to a movie, so we don't go to the opera anymore. My husband was a great opera lover.

One day we went downtown and met a friend of ours who said, "Lieber, what are you doing here?"

"Going shopping."

"I just came from the American consulate and got myself a waiting number. Why don't you go there and get a waiting number to go to America? It can't do you any harm."

So we did go there and I got number 2 of the Swiss quota, but my husband got 292 of the German quota, so for me it was a very simple matter. But my husband would have to wait.

[The U.S. Immigration Act of 1924 set the German-Austrian quota at 27,370 a year, which was high compared to countries with less-favored populations such as countries in eastern Europe. However, the legislators could not have envisioned a time when virtually every immigrant from those countries would be Jewish. Antisemitism was rife in the United States and was reflected in deliberate bureaucratic delays at the State Department in processing visa applications from desperate Jews abroad. Only in the year following Kristallnacht was the German quota ever filled. Even during the critical period from 1941 to 1944, a "paper wall" left 81 percent of the quota unfilled. The phrase "paper wall" is from David S. Wyman, *The Abandonment of the Jews: America and the Holocaust, 1941–1945* (New York: Pantheon Books, 1984), p. 124.]

SL. One Friday morning, the Polish citizens were told they would be leaving in the evening and they should pack a minimum of possessions. They had to get ready in the greatest hurry. In the late afternoon, they gathered them together and brought them to the railroad station to deport them to Poland somewhere. They just went from house to house, got these people out into green vans, and carried them to the railroad station.

[Deportations of the Polish Jews from Germany occurred in October 1938. Even those who had lived in Germany for years or who had been born there were considered Polish if their parents had come from Poland.]

MK. How did the German Jewish community react to this?

SL. Of course, everybody was shocked and appalled. The chief rabbi of Hamburg, Dr. Carlebach, a very good friend of ours, said, "Forget about all the Sabbath laws, we have to help these people and do whatever we can do for them. We have to bring them food and clothing, whatever we can, no matter how late it gets, until the trains leave." And that's what happened on a Friday Sabbath evening.

The German Jews who had lived there for generations and generations—who knew nothing else but being German—were shocked, of course. But they said, "This cannot happen to us, we are Germans, they cannot do this to us."

KRISTALLNACHT

[On November 7, 1938, seventeen-year-old Herschl Grynszpan entered the German embassy in Paris and shot a minor diplomat, Ernst vom Rath, in reprisal for the expulsion of his "Polish" Jewish family to Poland. Vom Rath died two days later. This act triggered a massive "spontaneous" pogrom throughout Germany, orchestrated by Propaganda Minister Goebbels. During the night of November 9 and into the next day, mob violence broke out all over the country during which hundreds of synagogues were set on fire or demolished (estimates range from two hundred to twelve hundred, including *Betstuben* or prayer rooms). About seventy-five hundred Jewish-owned businesses were vandalized and looted along with countless Jewish homes. Shattered glass littered the streets, giving the pogrom its name, Kristallnacht (crystal night), the night of the broken glass.

Jewish owners were compelled to repair all damage to their property without the benefit of their insurance moneys, which were confiscated by the state. In addition they were forced to pay a collective penalty of one billion Reichsmarks (or 400 million dollars in 1938 U.S. money) for inciting the action against themselves. On November 10 and in the days following, thirty thousand Jewish men were rounded up and sent to Buchenwald, Sachsenhausen, and Dachau concentration camps. It was the first time violence against the Jews had occurred on such a large scale and the first time Jews were thrown en masse into concentration camps.]

SL. On November 10 at six o'clock in the morning, my husband went to the synagogue for morning services. About half an hour later, he came back, white as a sheet, and said, "The synagogue is burning, we cannot even get near it, it's on fire." He said we should not stay in our apartment. The same thing that happened to the Polish Jews could happen to us. They could start gathering all the Jews and take them someplace.

We had two small children, Miriam and Susie. Miriam was about six months old and Susie about two and a half. We had a maid from Denmark, a Jewish girl. At that time, they left the women alone and they didn't touch any foreigners. They were only interested in gathering the men and taking them to concentration camps. I said to my husband, "You are not going alone, I will go with you."

We left the house about seven and we went to some friends who lived in the area and rang their bells and told them the synagogue was burning. They should get out of their houses and not make it easy for the Germans to catch them. Some got out, some did not. One friend, who is in Israel today, took his passport and the coat over his arm, and he left Germany right then and there. Other people were afraid to leave their homes with all their possessions. Shortly after, the Gestapo came from one home to the other and took these people away.

My husband was not caught. We went home after a while to see what was doing. Our maid told us the Gestapo was just there and they said they will be back. So we packed a little suitcase and said, "We are not going to stay here, you stay with the children," and we left the house again. My husband went to a friend who was the caretaker of the Jewish cemetery and they decided to hide there because the cemetery had a door in the rear that many people didn't know about. They were hoping to get out through the back if the Gestapo should come to the front gate.

We arranged that under no circumstances should my husband come back to the apartment. Now I went home and I stayed there. At two o'clock in the morning the bell rings. I thought it could be nobody else but the Gestapo and I was wondering what I was going to do. I went to the door and said, "Herman, is that you?" and the guys outside said, "Yes." So I opened the door and there were two huge SS men with the black uniforms and the boots up to here. I expected to see something like that but I didn't even let them say a word. I carried on—"What did you do to my husband? where is he? what happened to him? I haven't seen him since this morning when he went to the synagogue."

And they put their arm around me and they said, "Calm down, young lady, calm down, don't worry, we will find him. But first we have to make sure he isn't really in the apartment."

So I said, "Come on in." They came in and looked everywhere. Of course, they didn't find him and they left.

I was shaking because I didn't know how they were going to take this outburst. Are they going to believe me? are they going to believe this phony act—I knew it was a phony act and therefore I was afraid. The next morning when I was out of the house they came again. The maid told us afterwards that they looked at Miriam [the baby who was in the crib] and they said, "If we get your father, you will be the last one in this family."

After that I spoke to the other women. We all kept in touch. Most of the husbands of the women I spoke to were already in concentration camps and we didn't know what to do.

[Mrs. Lieber had found out that there was a German doctor in the neighborhood who ran a small private hospital that accepted Jewish patients. The doctor was a member of the Nazi party. Unsure of whether they could trust him or not, they devised a plan.]

SL. We rolled my husband in the dirt and then we took a cab to the hospital, claiming that he had hurt his leg falling off a bicycle. He had polio as a child and had always had a limp. The doctor looked at his leg and then he put his arm around me, and he said, "Kleine Frau, shall we take X rays or just put him in a cast?"

I said, "No, no, we'll take X rays, we have to know what's what."

They took X rays, and of course they couldn't find much. But the doctor put my husband in a cast from the ankle up to here and kept him in the hospital for two days. But after two days he said, "I'm sorry, I cannot keep you in the hospital because my nurses are all younger than forty-five years old." [At that time, the law forbade German nurses under forty-five to treat Jewish patients.] Before he sent him home in the cast, he wrote a letter with his official Party stamp—*Parteigenosse*—saying that this man is very heavily injured, he cannot be moved, he must stay in bed. It is a matter of life and death.

[I express surprise that the doctor, being a member of the Nazi party, should do this. He had to be in the Party, says Mrs. Lieber, in order to survive. *Parteigenosse* did not mean anything if you knew who the individual was.]

SL. They all had their flags hanging out. In fact our non-Jewish neighbors came in to apologize for hanging out their flag. But it was very dangerous not to do so.

After a day or two at home, the cast started to itch and my husband was going crazy. So he took a pair of pliers and started chipping off one piece after the other until it was so far down that he could slip into it when the bell rang and slip out when there was no danger [laughs].

A few days later we got a card from the Gestapo saying that they have everybody connected with the board and staff of the synagogue in custody, except for my husband. He should come down Monday morning at 9:30 to Gestapo headquarters. I said to my husband, "You are not going anyplace. You stay right here and I'll go." I was not particularly afraid because they left the women alone at that time, there was no danger for them.

I went down to the Gestapo, they looked at the card, they looked at me, and they said, "We didn't call you, we called your husband."

And I said, "My husband can't come, don't you know? You were in my house, you threw him down the steps, and he broke both legs. He's in a cast. How can he come to you?"

And they said, "We don't know anything about this."

And I said, "Well, the trouble is that the left hand doesn't know what the right is doing and the right doesn't know what the left is doing. How come you don't know he's in bed with a cast on his leg?" I kept on talking and talking. I put on a very heavy Swiss accent, which is easily done, and I said, "I'm Swiss, I am not a German." (They didn't know I became German through marriage.) "I will contact my consul and tell him how I am being harassed by you." I just carried on.

MK. Weren't you frightened?

SL. There was such confusion then. You just had to take chances. You couldn't live normally. You had to think that way in order to survive. [Apparently the Gestapo believed her and sent her home.] On the radio we heard that everybody who is not being captured by the Gestapo should give themselves up, because if they are caught and did not report to the Gestapo, they will be shot on sight. Some friends of ours, like one who lives in Israel today, got panicky and walked right into Gestapo headquarters and gave themselves up. They promptly put them into a concentration camp, but my husband said, "I'm not going to walk into the Gestapo office and give myself up voluntarily. I will run until I can't run anymore." After a few days, the whole thing blew over. It was the end of getting the Jews out of their apartments and into the concentration camps and that phase was over. [It was still November 1938.]

DETOUR TO SWITZERLAND

[The Lieber family managed to secure passage to America on a ship leaving from Antwerp, though they were not yet certain of how they would get there because of potential visa complications. They decided to go to Switzerland first where Mrs. Lieber's parents still lived. This was only possible because her father had provided a financial guarantee that the family would not become a charge on the Swiss government. They packed their furniture and other belongings into a "lift," a room-sized container, under the supervision of a customs officer. This man, who was not a Nazi, had been stationed for years at the Danish border and when he came to the Liebers to supervise the packing, he spent all his time in the kitchen with their Danish maid, leaving them free to pack whatever they wished. This included silverware and other valuables that other friends had asked them to transport. The official signed the inventory sheet without looking at it and suggested adding other items as they thought of them. He told them he was ashamed that people like them were being forced out and that they were an asset to the country. He expressed envy that they were leaving and wished he could go with them.

The lift was shipped to Antwerp and put into an open storage area exposed to wind and rain for nine months. Half the furniture was ruined, including a grand piano.]

MK. I've never heard a good lift story. My uncle Paul's lift went down to Genoa and as it was being delivered to the ship, the ship was bombed.

SL. What got here safe were jars. A big box of plain glass jars because we thought in America there are no jars *[laughs]*. Also Persil soap powder, which lasted us for about two years.

MK. Did you leave behind any Jewish or Christian friends?

SL. We were on very good terms with all of our neighbors, and we had good friends right next door who were Christians. The husband was a writer. They were terribly upset that we were being forced to run away with two small kids, and leaving so many of our possessions behind. When the taxi came for us, the wife offered to help us by bringing down our little girl, Miriam, the one who had been told by the SS that she would be the last one in the family after they caught her father. I told her not to, because if someone saw her it could be dangerous for her, even if she was only bringing a child downstairs. Because people who were helping Jews were being arrested.

[The super or concierge of the building was under instructions to observe the comings and goings at the building and to report any suspicious activities, such as Germans speaking with Jews, let alone helping them.]

SL. After the war, we were in touch again with our former neighbors. We sent them packages. The husband was here to give lectures at Goethe House. He told us that the day we left for Switzerland, the super's wife was standing in the lobby crying because the Lieber family was forced to flee.

[After shipping their household goods to Antwerp, the Liebers went to Switzerland with their children and the Danish maid. There was no possibility of remaining because, as a refugee, Rabbi Lieber was not permitted to work and Mrs. Lieber's parents would have had to support them. With her low quota number, Sary Lieber could have preceded her family to America and looked for a place to live. However, her parents would not hear of it.]

SL. They said, "You don't send a young woman alone to America, the country of crime, the country of who knows what. Who went to America at the turn of the century? Only thieves in order to avoid going to jail."

[With their passage secured and their American visas in hand, the Liebers were faced with the problem of getting to Antwerp in order to board their ship. To get to Antwerp, one could either go through Germany (clearly out of the question) or through France, which was almost as difficult. The French did not want Jews entering the country and perhaps remaining there. Consequently they required transit visas. Flying was not an option at that time. The Liebers therefore attempted to obtain visas from the French consulate. Day after day they went to the consulate, which was filled with other refugees seeking papers. After more than two months of sitting in the consular office without success, Mrs. Lieber took action.]

SL. One day I had a brainstorm. Susie was a very beautiful child. She was almost three years old, she was adorable. She had a white snowsuit and blond curls, blue eyes, and red cheeks. I put my passport into her hand and I opened the door marked General Consul. I said, "Go to this man in there and tell him, 'My mama wants a visa.'"

So she takes this passport and slams it on the table and says, "My mama wants a visa!" I heard her from outside.

We were sitting there shivering in our boots. And the man, very distinguished-looking with a little beard, took her in his arms and came out, and he said, "Where are the parents of this child?"

"Here."

"Come in."

It was the first time in two and a half months that we had the opportunity to talk to somebody.

[They explained their problem and assured the official that they would not remain in France. He sent a telegram to Paris and a visa to France was issued to the Liebers within twenty-four hours.]

⚜

Siegfried Kirchheimer

My uncle Siegfried, the eldest of the four Kirchheimer brothers, was a well-known doctor in Wolfenbüttel with a reputation as an expert diagnostician. In April 1933, shortly after the two-day boycott of Jewish businesses, he left his practice in the hands of a colleague and took a vacation in Saarbrücken. I was then two years old. During his absence his house was searched by the police.

SK. I had kept some souvenirs from my service as an army doctor in World War I. My spiked helmet, my officer's saber, my Iron Cross—everything that belonged to an officer. I had been stationed in Oldenburg. They took everything they could find.

MK. They just looted the place?

SK. It wasn't really looting because I saved these things in a special place and, of course, my wife told them where they were. I also had a German revolver from the war. That they couldn't find because I had hidden it away. Later on I took it out and threw it into the Oker River.

MK. Why did they want these World War I souvenirs?

SK. They suspected me of being a communist. An enemy of the Third Reich.

MK. Did they have any reason at all to suspect you politically?

SK. Oh no, never. Of course, my practice consisted mostly of working people, poor people. Not exactly the so-called fine people. They didn't come to me.

MK. Why?

SK. Because, you know, I am a very simple man. They found that out and the workers loved me. Today some are still alive and write me letters. They found me, and they knew I would take the best care of them. Better than other doctors. You know how doctors are.

MK. Why would the finer people go to other doctors? Because they lived in better neighborhoods?

SK. Most of the Jewish people were cattle dealers and rich people. They already had their doctors. For many years they didn't need me. And they didn't want to change doctors just because I was also Jewish. The worst thing was that the SA [Storm Troopers] posted soldiers in front of my house so nobody could come in. That started already when I came back from my vacation in May 1933. I reopened my practice because people knew I was back. At first they thought that I had gone to a concentration camp because they had not seen me for a while. There was some gossip: "They caught a doctor and they found weapons in his house." This kind of gossip. I tried to keep up my practice again.

MK. Did a lot of people stay away because the soldiers were outside?

SK. Sure.

MK. So how much of your practice did you lose? Half?

SK. I still had a few private patients.

MK. How did you feel about all that?

SK. Not too good.

MK. But you must have been shocked. And terrified.

SK. I wouldn't call it shocked. I got used to everything, and I tried hard to stay there. In spite of this Hitler Reich. Because they couldn't chase me out. It was impossible. Not at that time.

MK. But they were ruining your career, and they were ruining your ability to make a living.

SK. I kept trying because I still had enough income to manage.

MK. It must have been a great hardship.

SK. It was a hardship, of course, of course. My brothers here—your father and Herbert and Arnold, they always wrote me, "Why don't you come?"

MK. Why didn't you?

SK. Because I hated to give everything up. I had my house, my garden, everything. You hate to lose all this. And so it took about five years until finally I decided to give up.

MK. But when you say you had your house, your garden, everything, you also had the SA outside your house during the whole time. That's terribly intimidating.

SK. Sure, sure.

MK. Like half an arrest.

SK. It wasn't an arrest. This was almost like prison. But still, nobody treated me badly. No. They all loved me there. They hated this. I'll tell you one funny story. Non-Jewish doctors were required to put out a shingle saying "German Doctor." I wasn't allowed to do that. Some people asked me why I didn't put up this sign. I said, "I don't have to. For me it isn't necessary. Everyone knows that I am a German doctor." The others had to do it because maybe they didn't know they were German doctors.

MK. Which meant they weren't Jewish.

SK. I was the only Jewish doctor.

MK. Didn't some of your patients turn their backs on you or betray you in any way?

SK. Some of them, yes. They wrote me saying, "I can't come to you anymore because I feel like a nationalist now and can't visit you." Even my dentist didn't want to use me anymore for the same reasons. I couldn't lose my practice but I had to give it up because nobody was permitted to come to me anymore. More or less.

MK. Were you aware of any antisemitism before 1933?

SK. Not directly, no. I couldn't say. Maybe *im Stillen.* On the Q.T.

MK. What do you mean "on the Q.T."?

SK. *Im Stillen* [not overt]. They didn't talk about it and they couldn't do anything about it. They had to admit me as a doctor in Wolfenbüttel, too. They didn't like the idea.

MK. You sensed already in the 1920s that one of the reasons they didn't like the idea is because you were Jewish?

SK. Yes, yes.

MK. How did you know this?

SK. It is hard to tell you. Jews are always a little isolated. They always feel unwelcome. Isn't that so? Other people don't like them. But they had to let me practice because I had my license. They couldn't do anything about that. They always tried to get rid of me but they had to keep me because I was very *dickköpfig* [stubborn].

MK. In what ways did they try to get rid of you?

SK. It's hard to tell. Usually with colleagues you have a friendly relationship. I never had that. I never had any connection with the colleagues there.

MK. Not one?

SK. No. Not one.

MK. How many doctors were there in Wolfenbüttel?

SK. Twelve.

MK. Did they turn particularly vicious after Hitler came?

SK. No. No.

MK. Nobody?

SK. No. No. Maybe in their hearts, maybe they were very happy that it happened to me.

MK. But you didn't see any evidence of that?

SK. No. One of the doctors was even in the uniform of the SA. Imagine. He wore the uniform of an SA soldier.

[According to my father, Siegfried continued to treat patients, including some prominent Nazis who had previously been part of his clientele. Siegfried and his family left Wolfenbüttel in July 1938 and went to stay with his in-laws in Drieburg. There they waited for a visa to come through for America.]

SK. I stayed there until November 11. Kristallnacht was on the 9th. Between November 9 and 10, they put me in jail in Drieburg. They burned up the synagogue and all the Jewish menfolk were taken to a kind of a prison in the basement of some old building. We stayed there for two nights until I was able to get out because I had my visa.

[My uncle and the eldest of his four children, my seventeen-year-old cousin Lore, had received visas from Hamburg. His wife, my aunt

Martha, had to remain behind with the other children to await their visas. The affidavit of support for Siegfried and Lore had been provided by Mr. Felsenstein, the managing agent of the building I was living in with my parents in the Marble Hill section of Manhattan, after coming over from Germany two years earlier. Felsenstein proved to be a kind of savior for us because he provided affidavits of support for his "cousins," my aunt Annie, my uncle Siegfried, and other assorted relatives. He was a total stranger, but one of those compassionate people who made the difference between life and death for us.]

SK. When we left, I thought we would never see each other again. You know how it was at that time. It was a terrible, terrible thing to leave them behind. We took the express train to Hanover, and for two hours I was sitting there and crying.

[On November 16, 1938, Siegfried and Lore sailed from Hamburg on the SS *Manhattan*, the same ship that had brought me to the States in 1936, and arrived in New York on November 25. We had a gala celebration to welcome him, attended by my other two uncles who had preceded us to the United States by several years, and other relatives. At one point, my uncle Herbert turned on the radio, a strangely inappropriate thing to do in the midst of this emotional gathering. Herbert had joined the German merchant marine many years earlier and, after enduring the patronizing treatment meted out by his shipmates because he was Jewish, had jumped ship in New York and applied for U.S. citizenship. During one of his voyages to America, he had befriended a poor young German stowaway named Otto Feller.

Now, over the radio, came Otto Feller's resonant voice, first greeting his listeners and then, to the amazement of my family, welcoming the well-known Dr. Siegfried Kirchheimer to the United States. Feller had worked his way up from being a waiter in New York to a position as radio commentator for a German-language program. After delivering his moving introduction, he announced that he was dedicating the music that was to follow to my uncle Siegfried. He then proceeded to play excerpts from Siegfried's favorite opera, Gounod's *Faust*. Uncle Herbert, who had engineered this event, was very proud.]

Rosi Spier

At the age of nineteen, in 1920, Rosi Spier determined to leave her hometown near Wiesbaden. She had completed the equivalent of high school and had taken a secretarial course.

RS. I didn't want to stay in that little town of ours, which was lovely. In the summer it was a resort and many Americans came there. It was interesting. But in the winter it was boring. So I did something secretly. At that time I was already rebellious. I wrote to a German Jewish paper. There was an article saying that secretaries were in demand in the city. I had taken a secretarial course so I applied for a job and I got it. This must have been in 1920 when I was nineteen years old. I stayed in the city for a while. But then I went home—for private reasons. Because of my love life *[laughs]*. I had a friend and it didn't work out. Then I met my future husband through my brother. They had been students together. We were engaged for five years. I had clues during that time [that there would be problems]. But I was easily influenced. Today it would be different. But I was too much of a coward. In Germany, for a Jewish girl to cancel an engagement . . .

[Rosi Spier's marriage proved a difficult one and shortly after the death of her first child, a daughter, she began divorce proceedings.]

RS. It was a terrible thing. My boy was born in Frankfurt while my husband was away in France. Eventually I got divorced. Here I am all alone. My mother had died too. And, now comes the sad story of my life *[laughs]*. What do I do right now?

Well, I took a job in Frankfurt am Main. I wanted to be independent from my father and my brother who took care of my financial needs. I took a job as a secretary in a welfare organization and after two or three months the head of this department said to me, "You know, it's a pity you are just a secretary." (After the war I got in touch with her in Israel through the *Aufbau*. [The *Aufbau* (Reconstruction) is a German-language newspaper founded in 1934 in New York City whose readership was primarily German Jewish. Many refugees were able to locate missing relatives through the placement of ads in its pages.] I found her after forty years.) Whenever she wanted to dictate a letter to me, I said, "Tell me what you want to say and I'll write the letter by myself."

She said, "I have an idea." She told me about a Jewish organization in Berlin that had a course to prepare certain people to become social workers. Seventeen people were accepted. All of them were academically educated. I was the only housewife. I took this course in Berlin and had to bring my child to an orphan home there in the suburbs.

MK. Because you didn't have time to take care of the child?

RS. Right. The girl had died. And today my son, in spite of his life, is—thank God—very successful. In Berlin, I once had a chance to go to the orphan home at night. (This is the interesting story.) They asked me whether I would call for a young lady at the train station who came from Munich. She was pregnant and her parents were not supposed to know. And she was to come into the orphan home where they also took care of young unmarried women who were pregnant. And I jumped at that idea: Oh, then I can see my son at night. I picked her up. She was very upset and I had to calm her down. I said, "I visit my son every Sunday, I will visit you too."

I saw my son lying in bed and I will never forget it. If I were a painter I would paint that. He was lying on his belly, so forlorn in his little bed. What did they do? They took them, gave them the bottle, and put them down. They were not cuddled like a child, right? . . . I went home, I was heartbroken. When I visited him on Sunday—he sensed it, when they moved the chairs, that visitors were coming—he came to the gate and waited for me. When I left, he cried bitterly. And all this was in me all these years. I probably would have profited by talking about it. Lately, my son and I have been talking about it. For years I didn't talk about it . . . Other people's experiences . . . the birthings there were in the concentration camps . . . I have friends who were in concentration camps, they lost husband and child. So compared to them. . . .

[Rosi Spier's divorce came through in 1937, the same year she enrolled in the course in Berlin to be trained as a social worker. Her son remained in the orphanage for a year and a half.]

RS. After I took my exam, this lady from Frankfurt wrote to me: "I have a job for you." And I became the social worker of a school founded in Bad Nauheim by the Reichsvertretung der deutschen Juden [National Representation of German Jews] for children who could not attend the country schools anymore on account of antisemitism. And those children went to that school, which was founded as a boarding school. I lived there with the teachers and children, and by then I had my boy with me. We lived in the same building with a kindergarten teacher and the son of the head nurse of the school. I was there until 1939.

[Even before Kristallnacht, Mrs. Spier had made plans to leave for America.]

RS. An uncle of mine wrote to me and said, "All of our relatives ask for an affidavit, Why don't you?"

And I said, "Yes, you are right. It's about time." And I got a last-minute affidavit from that uncle. That was about 1938.

Between 1938 and 1939 . . . what I'm going to tell you now is very interesting . . . the Nazis from Bad Nauheim came into the school and broke everything and they threw us out into the street with the kids. I think it was right after Kristallnacht. We walked through the town with all the kids. All of us had been thrown out. We went to the police chief and he took me in his office. The children and the employees were in the yard. And he said, "My God, I'm also a Nazi in the Party but I never thought it would come to that point. Who had the right to throw you out?"

He took the receiver in his hands and called the mayor of the city who was a twenty-four-year-old young man. Very big Nazi. And he said "Guten Morgen" instead of "Heil Hitler."

"Guten Morgen Herr Bürgermeister. What happened? How come the Jewish children are thrown out of the school?" The result was that we were allowed to go back. But on the same night, they were throwing stones in the city. And they came to the school with bicycles and made the children leave. It went on and on and it became worse.

It had been such a lovely school and we all were one family. Teachers and their children had felt safe there. But then the Nazis made their raid on a Shabbos—the school was orthodox—and then they came again. And all the children had to leave the school. They packed their things and went home. When they came home—now comes the story that is important—they found their parents deported. Then the German Jewish organizations took care that the children were somehow looked after. Some of them were sent to Switzerland. Some were deported.

This police chief asked me, "Can you leave Germany?"

I said, "Yes, I have an affidavit."

He said, "You are so lucky. I wish I could go with you." He was a Party member, but some of them were against such extremes.

After the war, the former teachers and I came together. This one had been deported and the other one went to Switzerland. Some of them came here and were very successful. That's it. Then I also came, in February 1939.

First I worked as a maid in Brooklyn. I was a maid all over because I had taken my son to live with a Mr. Kutz, a teacher from Germany. He had a laundry at that time. He had one son, Paul. And he had taken in two other boys and then my son. I saw him every Wednesday. After he had been in Berlin in an orphan home! . . . As a matter of fact, my son, who is very successful right now, asked me the other day whether I would write down his life story. He couldn't believe it what he went through when he was small. And what I went through. And I, knowing that the first five years of a child's life are the most important ones . . . I suffered tremendously. He always tells me now, "Mommy, don't have guilt feelings. You did what you had to do." But I was so much aware . . . How can that child grow up? No father and no mother. Mr. Kutz was very fine in his way but a typical German disciplinarian.

MK. What happened to your father and your brother after you left?

RS. My father died meanwhile. But my brother was stubborn. He didn't want to leave. He was a director of a Jewish high school in Hamburg. He's a very impractical man. Highly intelligent but very impractical. He didn't want to leave, even though they took him away for a few days, to a kind of concentration camp. They put him in a jail and threw him down the stairs. He came out and he had no affidavit. Now came again my torture. There was a provision made for professors and priests. They were entitled to a special visa. I worked on that.

MK. You were here by now?

RS. Yes. I had to take a job in Vermont taking care of a camp director's little baby. And my son was with strange people here in New York. Just so I could make fifty dollars a month. I hated myself for it because my hands were tied. I couldn't do much for my brother. At that time, if you would have met me, I was like a hysterical person. People thought I was not very normal. I could see it in their eyes when they talked to me. My nerves were so . . . I said, "I sit here, I make fifty dollars and cannot help my brother to get out."

The thing is, my brother had good connections. The banker Warburg was a good friend of his. He supported my brother's school in Hamburg. When I came to the American Jewish Committee, where my uncle recommended me, there was a Mr. Jaffe, and I told him the story that my brother is a very good friend of Mr. Max Warburg. He looked at me as though—"Ach, she tells stories." I knew I was not myself. I was really very upset and nervous. I could see he was thinking, "This woman tells stories. Sure, her brother is a friend of Mr. Warburg."

To make the story short, one day I got a call from the Warburg house. "Mr. Warburg is here and wants to take care of your brother."

I went back to that Mr. Jaffe and said to him, "Now Mr. Warburg is here and he wants you to get in touch with him." I will never forget the sight of his face when he talked to Mr. Warburg. Everything I had told him was true!

And he put the receiver down and said "OK, Mrs. Spier, now we can take care of your brother." He put, I think, ten thousand dollars in an account and he got a special visa for my brother as a professor. And then my brother came.

MK. So the man was very ashamed?

RS. I could see how a mask fell off his face: "After all she is not *meshugah*" *[laughs]*. But when my brother came, he had no confidence in himself. He had Latin, Greek, and French, but not English. He had to learn English. He had to start all over. Even so, he had ten thousand dollars in a bank at his disposal. I didn't have a penny when I came.

❀

Bert Kirchheimer

A self-taught commercial artist from Bremerhaven, my father found work in Dortmund at Altdorf's department store doing displays and advertising. He took his meals at the pension run by my grandmother and there he met and courted my mother during the brief lunch hours when she ran home from her job in a fashionable boutique to help out at home. In 1927, now a married man, he came to Saar-

*brücken as the chief graphic designer of E. Weil Söhne, a large depart-
ment store. He created newspaper and magazine ads, window displays, special outdoor holiday posters, and, on the side, murals for
clubs and restaurants. At the same time, he did illustrations, comic
strips, and cartoons for several newspapers, including the* Dortmunder General Anzeiger *and the* Saarbrücker Zeitung.

*One of his specialties was caricatures of famous figures, which
were published in the papers. These he drew from life, at concerts
and the theater, going backstage to the dressing rooms when he
could, and engaging the people in conversation. He sketched Fritz
Kreisler, Paul Hindemith, Friedrich Holländer, the composer of the
music for the film* The Blue Angel, *Marlene Dietrich herself, and
many others when they came to town for guest appearances.*

*The family lived at 23 Schmollerstrasse in Saarbrücken, a brisk
fifteen-minute walk to E. Weil Söhne. Until I left Germany in 1936, I
was looked after by young nannies—Else and then Tilly, who was
Catholic and an ardent socialist. Her passion for banners and parades was infectious and when I first saw a Nazi parade go by early
in 1936 I was so overwhelmed with fervor that I raised my fist and
shouted "Heil Moscow!" Never was a four-year-old child snatched so
quickly inside.*

BK. In 1935 we were still under the protection of the League of Nations and nobody could harm us, not before April 1, 1936.

[The Jews of the Saarland enjoyed a certain amount of protection after the 1935 plebiscite as a result of the so-called Roman Treaty. Fore-
seeing that the result of the plebiscite might endanger the Jews in the
region, prominent international Jewish bodies pressured the League of
Nations to enact measures that would protect minorities in the region.
Still concerned about its reputation abroad, the German regime signed
a declaration on December 3, 1934, in Rome, guaranteeing to all inhabitants of the Saar the freedom to emigrate with their assets and goods,
as well as freedom from persecution on the basis of language, race, or
religion. The note was sent to the Italian ambassador, Baron Aloisi,
president of the committee of the League of Nations charged with tran-
sition measures for the Saar and signed by Freiherr von Neurath. The
guarantee was provisionally set to expire in March 1936.]

BK. Some time after the vote, I got a letter from the Chamber of Culture, the office that was under Goebbels, the propaganda minister. If you were not Aryan, you couldn't be a member anymore in the professional artists' association, so you couldn't work.

My new boss wanted me to stay—I had won prizes for my posters—but he didn't want me to be seen by the other people because everything had been taken over by the Nazis. I couldn't go in through the main entrance anymore. I had to go in through the back door and go up in the freight elevator and I couldn't be seen in the store itself. I had to stay in my workroom. So I agreed.

Today I feel very stupid to have done that. Nobody could understand how I could stay with the company but the new bosses asked me to stay on as long as I could. [He remained until mid-February 1936.] I had been there ten years and I did a good job.

[What he does not say is that he needed money in order to emigrate, having made the decision to do so right after he lost his position, and therefore felt he had to accept the humiliating conditions imposed on him.]

MK. Were there any Nazis among your coworkers?

BK. Of course, everybody was a Nazi at the time, some more than others. They gave the orders, they instructed the people about what to do. Even the former boss, Dr. Köster, was not allowed to say anything because he was Jewish. The person who took over the whole store didn't know anything. He had been a packer in the shipping room. And he was given command of the store by the Nazi party.

MK. How did your non-Jewish friends treat you?

BK. They were all nice to me, because most of them were left-wingers. Some people were nice, others avoided us, they didn't talk to us anymore. I had a colleague who was a friend, we used to have dinner with him. Then overnight he became a Nazi antisemite. The neighbors in the house where we lived were afraid to talk to us. The Nazis warned them not to have anything to do with Jews. I'm sure they felt terribly sorry about this because we were so beloved. But everybody was afraid.

MK. How would the Nazis know if they talked to you?

BK. They knew they were being watched. Every building was watched by someone from the Nazi party. Even the children were questioned: "What are your parents doing?" The children were told to eavesdrop on their parents. They spied on them and they betrayed them sometimes. Their teachers told them to watch their parents carefully, and to report if they were communists or if they knew any Jews. They did this for the glory of the fatherland! If we met our neighbors on the street, they couldn't talk to us because other people would watch us.

[One Friday night while they were having dinner at their cantor's house, the Gestapo came to the door and asked for the rabbi who was also a guest. They took him away and held him for four weeks, incommunicado, until he was let go because he had a Swiss passport. My father reports that rabbis were required to hand in their sermons to the Gestapo prior to delivering them. This was a hardship because many rabbis relied on improvising on the day of the service in the synagogue.]

MK. Why do you think the German people allowed this to happen?

BK. Because they were afraid.

MK. Only because they were afraid?

BK. Of course.

MK. Many were happy about it.

BK. But not because they were against the Jews. They were hoping that the Nazis could bring about an end to unemployment. Most of the gentile people I spoke to didn't realize what was happening until much later.

[My father rather proudly says the Jews held the most important positions in commerce and banking and there was a good deal of jealousy toward them. He comments that many famous intellectuals wanted to protect Jewish artists, and he cites the example of Wilhelm Furtwängler who tried to protect Yehudi Menuhin and managed to get him out of prison.

It still took about a year after the plebiscite in the Saar until my father was able to obtain visas because of the quota system. The affidavit of support had been provided by my uncle Herbert in the United States. My father applied to the American consulate in Stuttgart, but because of the overwhelming number of applications there he was advised to try the consulate in Antwerp. There, somehow he obtained a quota number that had been set aside for Jews from Berlin. Since very few Jews were leaving Berlin at that time, he was able to get his visa soon after.

People who had made plans to emigrate were called upon by friends and relatives to smuggle money and other valuables out of Germany. My mother had been asked to take some jewelry back to the Saar by some relatives whom she was visiting in Siegen. From Saarbrücken, prior to April 1936, the valuables could safely be mailed to America. The jewels were sewn into the hem of her dress and she boarded her train home. As she tells the story, she was trembling with anxiety lest the customs officials discover what she was smuggling. Apparently her nervousness was so pronounced that the woman sharing the compartment noticed it very soon after engaging her in conversation. In telling the story, my mother stresses the fact that the woman was quite heavy and had a large bosom.

Upon being prodded by her companion as to the cause of her jitteriness, my mother broke down completely and revealed that she was smuggling some jewelry in the hem of her dress. "That's the first place they look," the woman exclaimed. "Give them to me." My mother extricated them from her hem and turned them over to the woman who stored them in her capacious bosom. At the border, the German customs officials came into the compartment, as anticipated. One of them said to the large woman, "Where have you got the stuff, sweetheart?" The woman patted her chest with both hands and said, "It's all right here." The guards laughed and went on to the next compartment.

We all traveled to Antwerp for the mandatory physical examination by a doctor at the American consulate. My parents were afraid they would not be able to obtain the visa because I'd had an ear operation as a three-year-old during a bout of scarlet fever and this had left me partially deaf. But we were lucky.

My father had booked passage on the SS *Manhattan* for April 9, 1936. Even though Jews were still able to take substantial amounts of money out of the country, my father hid his severance pay from the department store in the sole of his shoe and traveled to Luxembourg where it was deposited in a bank with instructions to forward it to Southampton, in care of the United States Lines. When our ship docked there he found the money waiting for him.

We left Saarbrücken in March 1936 and made stops in other cities to visit relatives before reaching our destination of Hamburg from which the ship was to sail on April 9. In Hamburg, one of my father's greatest fears was whether his camera would be confiscated. Later in the United

States, once the war started in 1941, his camera and those of his three brothers were taken away for the duration since even German Jews were considered enemy aliens. The loss of their cameras left the Kirchheimers inconsolable. Even today, my cousin Lore says she would rather take pictures than eat.

For me, a five-year-old, the voyage was an adventure. When the ship docked in Le Havre, my father showed me the *Normandie* and later, in Southampton, the *Queen Mary*, which had yet to make its maiden voyage. It was on shipboard that I was introduced to the movies, dragged kicking and screaming with fright into the darkened theater, only to emerge transformed after seeing a Marlene Dietrich film. Unfortunately, I had to be escorted out of the theater because, unlike the rest of the audience, I found the film hilarious.

My father was thirty-eight, my mother thirty-three. Bert Kirchheimer claims he did not experience a moment of sadness about leaving. He worried only about his relatives who had been left behind. Though he had been a patriot, he seems to have had no difficulty giving up his patriotism as soon as Hitler came to power.]

BK. When I went up the gangplank on the ship I thought, "Now I am in America." I was so excited I ran around like a madman.

MK. But you didn't know what your future would be like.

BK. No, but I had big hopes, because everybody told me my profession was just right for America. I was not afraid at all. I knew there were more opportunities here. The pay was better here for cartoonists. Of course, I could bring our savings along because we were living in the Saarland with its special status. Everyone else in Germany could only take out ten marks at that time.

MK. Weren't you at all apprehensive about going to a strange country, a strange city?

BK. [He seems surprised that I should ask such a question.] I'm from Bremerhaven. Even when we were there, we were already crazy about America. Because we saw the big ships arriving and we had relatives here. We always longed to see America.

Melitta and Walter Hess

Melitta Hess is the mother of my friend Walter, who also participates in the interview. My aunt Annie Ostertag lived in the same senior residence until her death in 1995. Mrs. Hess came from a fairly well-to-do urban family in Frankfurt. When she married Oskar Hess in 1930, she moved to his farm in Ruppichteroth in the Rhineland. Mr. Hess raised cattle, which he bought and sold, and also produced milk, which was bought by local dairies. Although unfamiliar with country life, Mrs. Hess was happy with her new home. There were perhaps a dozen Jewish families in the area.

MK. Did you also work on the farm?

MH. No. I was anxious to have children. And the first year I did. The second year I did. And four years later the third one came. [Walter was the eldest.] First we lived by ourselves. And I felt lonesome. My husband was away [traveling for his cattle-dealing business]. So we built another apartment over my in-laws' house.

[Walter points out that German farms are different from American ones where there are great distances between the individual houses. In contrast, German farmhouses are clustered together and make up a village while the farmland itself fans out from the village.]

MH. Walter was a little boy and he was hungry. I didn't have milk. None of the men were home. So what did I do? Years before, I had never even seen a cow! I went down to the stables and looked for the easiest one to milk. I picked the biggest one and I started to milk it in a little pot. Then I went away. So Walter had milk to drink and that was fine. When my father-in-law and my husband came home, I heard them yell: "What happened?" I had started to milk that cow, and when you start to milk a cow, the milk runs by itself.

MK. You had a flood in the barn?

MH. Not only that. The next day was market day and I ruined the best cow. They couldn't take it along. In the afternoon a neighbor came and asked me, "You still have that cow?" It was the first time in my life I sold a cow.

MK. Were you making a good living?

MH. Oh yes. We were no Rothschilds, but we were comfortable.

MK. How did you get along with the gentiles?

MH. My husband and my in-laws were extremely well liked. We got along with the whole community. A few were not too friendly.

MK. What changes, if any, occurred after 1933?

MH. In our house there, my mother-in-law had a little store and the people were afraid to come in to buy things. We had to deliver at night and they came to us at night. Some came in the daytime too. There was an SA guard standing in front.

MK. Between 1933 and 1936, what else happened to you?

MH. Personally, nothing. Business got more difficult. It took a while to develop.

[Mrs. Hess became increasingly more aware of the deteriorating situation, her sense of foreboding sharpened from reading the newspapers. A friend of the Hesses owned a restaurant where the SS held meetings and conversations were reported back to them regarding the Jews. The general sentiment seemed to be that they should be driven out. She describes an incident that took place in her kitchen. One of their acquaintances appeared one day in an SS uniform, accompanied by some other men. People often stopped by at the Hesses, either socially or for business. One man bought a cow but then refused to pay for it.]

MH. The SS man got up and he said, "I know the Hesses for years. They are good people." He showed his Party card. He was number nine [in the local Nazi hierarchy]. He said, "If you don't pay right away, then I'll take you to headquarters." So the man paid up.

MK. Did you become increasingly uncomfortable as a Jew?

MH. I, myself, yes! I woke up when I read *Mein Kampf.* When I saw what was written there, I knew that it was time for us to go.

MK. How did you get hold of *Mein Kampf?*

MH. There was a work camp nearby, and I think the people were socialists. They were taken from home and they had to work from Monday to Friday. They had to work but they were not allowed to talk about it.

WH. Road maintenance, and that sort of thing. And they gave you a copy of *Mein Kampf?*

MH. Yes.

MK. After you read it, what happened when you discussed it with your husband?

MH. My husband was a true German. I couldn't convince him or my father-in-law that this could ever happen to us. So they insisted on staying. We had beautiful land, we had a nice house, we had nice friends, and they didn't want to go. In 1936, I already had the papers to go to Palestine but my husband insisted: never!

Later, in 1938 we discussed leaving again and I got so mad. Then I regretted it. I said to my husband: "Oskar, I only wish they would take you once to a concentration camp." And then on November 10, they really took him. I wished I could take back my words. That was a terrible day.

WH. Why did the family feel so comfortable in Ruppichteroth?

MH. Opa [Walter's grandfather] and your Papa were very honest people. They helped the small farmers in the neighborhood get started in business. They gave them a cow or they gave them two . . . They could pay for them slowly. Oskar had a very good name all over the neighborhood and all the friends were very nice. Papa was in the soccer club, he was on the bowling team. When he was in the concentration camp and then in Holland, those people brought food for me and the children at night. They put it at the back door so we had something to eat. The Christians, the farmers. Friends who lived there. The nuns.

MK. Did they do it for anybody or because it was you?

MH. You know, you don't ask many questions! They did it for us, and I'm sure for others too.

MK. Did any of these people become Nazis or SS and remain friendly to you?

MH. Most of them were nice to us. And a lot of them *had* to be Nazis. The kids were the worst. The children were Nazi and they were crazy. Hitler was their god.

WH. You're too kind to them.

MH. What?

WH. I think you're being too kind. You make excuses for them.

MH. No, no! Those girls, Schumacher's Marga and others . . . they wouldn't mind having the Jews killed. Those girls! The parents were afraid of their own children. And some of the kids said, "We'll report you if you don't stop" [associating with the Jews].

MK. Walter, how did you feel, going to the local Protestant public school during that time, before Kristallnacht?

WH. It was both marvelous and terrible, in that I felt that I was the preferred one. I was a bright kid, I did well in school, the teachers liked me, and so on. At the same time, we couldn't do some of the things the other kids did. We couldn't sing the anthem in the morning.

MK. You weren't allowed or you didn't want to?

WH. I wanted to and I couldn't permit myself to do it. So there was this pull. You wanted to identify with everything your peers were doing, but at the same time, I was extremely sensitive to who I was.

MK. How were the teachers?

WH. I think they were remarkably kind. I remember the teacher bringing me and Karl [his younger brother] home from school, and holding his hand. And then he made sure that we got home safely. That's the way I remember it, at any rate. I have a vague recollection that at one point the teacher said that we didn't have to salute the flag. There were a couple of other Jewish kids who were in the same grade, and I think he said, "OK you guys, you don't have to sing the Nazi song, you don't have to salute the flag."

When we left, one of the teachers gave Karl a postcard and there was a picture of two dogs on it. A white poodle and a black poodle. And on it was engraved *Einig.* That means "united." It was a remarkable gesture for that time.

KRISTALLNACHT

[On the evening of November 9, 1938, reports were heard on the radio calling upon all the Jewish men to report to Gestapo headquarters. With other Jewish families, the Hesses spent the night in another house and returned home in the morning. Mr. Hess concealed himself in a haystack but later came home and was taken away.]

WH. I remember that there were two policemen standing there, very awkward and shamefaced. You got Papa sandwiches, and Oma gave him a scarf or a coat.

MH. All of a sudden, in the morning, the synagogue was burning across from our house. The policeman from our town went there and called the fire department to put it out. The police didn't even know what was happening.

[Mrs. Hess claims that it was outsiders, not townspeople, who set the synagogue on fire in the first place, and then reignited it when the fire department attempted to put it out.]

MH. While the fire was burning, they put us—me, the three kids, and my mother-in-law—in front of the burning synagogue. Some of them were screaming, "Burn them, kill them!"

WH. It was a photo opportunity. They put us in front of the burning synagogue and people were taking pictures.

MK. These were not people who were friends?

MH. No, they came from other places.

WH. Mom! Some of them, some of the kids—

MH. It was the Nazis. They already had brown shirts on and they were not from Ruppichteroth, they came from outside.

WH. I have to say that I recognized a lot of people in the crowd who were from the town. They were kids who I thought had been my friends, who were playmates of mine, who threw clods of dirt at us. For me, it was the most traumatizing day of my life. To have seen the place you love and where you have your roots . . . and all of a sudden the whole thing is turned upside down.

MH. You were standing there, I had a little baby in my arms—Peter was two years old at that time. Finally they let us go. But my father-in-law went into the burning synagogue and took the Torahs out. He brought them to our house and put them on the table. Then some Nazis came and took the elderly men outside. My father-in-law had to carry one of the Torahs and something else, an axe I think. They made those old people march through the whole village, with the commands: "Quick! Slow!" It was horrible.

Oskar had a revolver in the house and I had it hidden under the bed. In the afternoon of November 10, our policeman came with a Nazi to search for weapons. I knew where the revolver was so I sat down on the bed and they didn't find anything. They finally said, "Leave the Jews alone, they don't have anything."

[Mr. Hess had first been taken to prison in Cologne and then later to Dachau.]

MH. We went almost every day to Cologne to try and make contact with the prisoners but we couldn't. We brought packages and they took them and then they told us the prisoners are in Dachau. It was a terrible thing. People took their own lives.

WH. My father said the people who were nicest to them in the concentration camp were the Jehovah Witnesses. The Jews would fight among themselves for a crust of bread and the Jehovah Witnesses would give what they had.

MH. The orthodox Jews gave Oskar the wurst and Oskar gave them the herring. They made a trade. Because the wurst was not kosher. [When Mr. Hess was freed from Dachau after about two months there was a Kapo who ordered the Jews to put all their money on the table. It was distributed among all those who were being freed that day so they would have money to return home.] A Kapo had to tell those dumb Jews [how to divide up the money].

MK. He made a little piece of socialism there.

[Mrs. Hess immediately set about finding help for the family. She sent telegrams to America and called a well-to-do aunt in Holland. She could have gotten passage to Palestine but her in-laws were unwilling to go so far. Her aunt promised to try to bring the family to Holland and from there they might be able to go to America.]

WH. I remember you told us that when Pop came off the train from Dachau—what did he say to you?

MH. "When can I go?" This was the first time that my husband wanted to leave Germany! When he got off the train he didn't ask how the kids were, he didn't ask how I was. He said, "You got all the papers? When can I go?"

WH. He looked bloated from all the starch in the food. He had all of his hair shorn. He didn't look like the same person. And it was terrible.

MH. And he was afraid. When somebody came into house and walked with a heavy step, he was afraid.

WH. Dachau changed him from a—

MH. —human being into a coward.

WH. He became very afraid after that.

MK. Did this persist in later life?

WH and **MH.** Yes.

MH. He wanted to leave the next day, but I still needed one document. Two, three days later, I got it. And then he went to Holland, alone. I brought him to Cologne but, on the way, all of a sudden the train stopped and nobody knew why. And he started to yell at me: Now he gets picked up again, it's my fault that he's still there.

[The train did eventually proceed to Holland. In Amsterdam, Mr.

Hess tried to obtain visas for the family to emigrate to another country. He was able to get visas for Holland and eventually for Ecuador. However, the only way the family could get to Ecuador was via ship from Panama. But in order to set foot in Panama, they would need a transit visa from the Panamanian consul who was based in Amsterdam. From Holland, Mr. Hess sent for his family.]

MH. We were happy that we could go. The three kids and I took the train to Zevenaar [a town near the Dutch border]. And there came a guy and he said we have to go out, we can't go on. They wouldn't let us into Holland. And Oskar was waiting for us in Amsterdam. [Presumably their papers were not complete.] We had to go back to Germany.

WH. Did you think that was the end?

MH. Listen, there is a time when you don't think anymore if you are desperate. I had three or four valises and they were opened and some things were stolen. I came back into the train and there the Germans closed our baggage and sealed it.

[Mrs. Hess returned home with the three children and remained there for about four months. Her Christian neighbors continued to bring food for the family at night, leaving it at their doorstep. By now her husband had received visas for Ecuador but the Hesses still needed transit visas through Panama. The Panamanian consul refused to issue them without first seeing the entire family in Amsterdam.]

MH. Bastard! He wouldn't give them to Oskar only.

[Through the good offices of her wealthy aunt in Rotterdam, Mrs. Hess and her children were guaranteed a one-week stay in Amsterdam and, armed with this official assurance, she was able to rejoin her husband in Amsterdam. There the Hesses finally obtained their Panamanian transit visas and left Europe at the beginning of August 1939. They arrived in Ecuador on September 1, the day the Germans invaded Poland.]

EMIGRATION

WH. We traveled first class on this marvelous ship, the *Caribbia* [a German ship]. First class, before the war! Everything was available for first-class passengers, but my father would avail himself of nothing. He just looked around. Anybody in uniform was someone dangerous to him. That's why we couldn't enjoy this incredible trip.

MK. How come you went first class?

WH. Those were the only tickets available to us. I think the Nazis forced people to go first class in order to get the higher rates.

MH. We took what we could get. We had two suites, one for the kids and one for us and Peter.

MK. How were you able to get to Ecuador? Did you take money out of Germany?

[Walter explains that they were only permitted to take ten marks from Germany into Holland. Their wealthy aunt in Holland paid their passage to Ecuador and gave them twenty-five hundred dollars in addition.]

WH. The class aspect of people who left and those who stayed is something that nobody has really gone into.

[I make the point that the Hesses were several classes all in one. Walter agrees and adds that this is the case with many people in Germany. His mother's uncles were extremely wealthy. There were poor Jews and middle-class Jews in Germany but sometimes there were connections to other, wealthier branches of the family.]

MH. There were some really rich people in Germany and if they had a little more sense, six million wouldn't have had to die. If those people would have given money to the poor Jews, many more would still be alive. They could have gotten out. A lot of people didn't have money for the fare.

Ecuador was a horrible place for us, dirty and unsanitary. Oskar worked as a farm manager. The land was beautiful. But that was the only time I worried.

[Mrs. Hess feared they would have to remain there indefinitely. They had very little money left. The Hesses remained in Ecuador for seven months, waiting for their quota number for America to come up. They had received their affidavit from Mrs. Hess's sister who was already in Washington Heights.]

WH. The war had broken out in Europe, the borders were closed, and people couldn't get out anymore. That made our number low enough so that we could come to the United States.

MH. Also Papa got very friendly with the consul in Guayaquil *[laughter]*. That was in April 1940.

Theo and Gretchen Krämer

Theo Krämer is Melitta Hess's brother. His nephew, Walter Hess, conducts most of the interview. Mr. Krämer is proud that he was born on Kaiser Wilhelm's birthday in 1901 in Butzbach.

WH. Your father was a patriot and you were a patriot, too?

TK. Yeah. I'm not ashamed to say that.

WH. How were you a patriot?

TK. Listen, the city where I grew up had infantry, army personnel, barracks, and so on. So I grew up in that milieu. I love the place where I was born. At that time there was no difference between gentiles and others. We grew up together and we knew only one thing: Fatherland! Love of country.

[Mr. Krämer left home after graduating from high school and went to Frankfurt am Main to study economics. In order to support himself he took some business courses and worked in a firm. After hours, he attended college and eventually obtained a doctorate in economics in 1931.]

TK. If you want to see the proof, the book is here. I wanted to get into the tax department, but at this time it had already started that they didn't want to take Jews. I had a lot of good friends and some of them were out of work so they went into the Nazi party. They always said, "I don't mean you." But listen, they wanted to make money, they wanted to get ahead. So they had no choice.

[In 1933 Mr. Krämer went to Palestine for a year to work because it was clear that he would have difficulty finding a job in Germany. But he returned when the year was up because he was homesick and had also contracted malaria.]

TK. The only opportunity I had was to get into a certain Jewish export firm. There was no other chance. They were a well-known firm all over the world.

KRISTALLNACHT

TK. The day it happened, I was at home, I didn't feel well. My wife was at the dentist. When she came home she said, "Theo, don't you know what happened?" Where she was, the windows were smashed. The next day I still was sick, I didn't feel too well so I was still home. A Gestapo went to my office, civilian. He took all the Jewish employees to the Festhalle [convention hall]. Since I wasn't on the job, he came to my apartment and picked me up.

GK. I told them my husband was sick. They said, "Don't worry." The next day I went to the Festhalle to bring him some warm underwear because it was November. They said, "Don't worry," and they chased me out.

TK. At the Festhalle they picked out a Jewish star of the opera house, he should sing. There were thousands of people.

GK. What did he sing? "In diesen heiligen Hallen . . ." [from Mozart's *Magic Flute*].

TK. "In these holy halls, you don't know revenge." I'll never forget that.

WH. Was it a kind of joke?

GK. Not a joke!

[Mr. Krämer was then transferred to Buchenwald concentration camp.]

TK. I was lucky. I was there only five and a half weeks because my wife went with the kids to the Cuban consulate. The main guy of the consulate wasn't there. The assistant sold visas for Cuba, so my wife got a cheap visa, but it was after I had been in the camp for five and a half weeks.

Two or three days after I got to the camp I was put in a barracks and given a uniform. Not that you can call it a uniform. I got a pair of shoes that were about three, four sizes too big. So I went to the SS man and said, "You should give me smaller shoes." He took a shoe and hit me. I had to walk with those big shoes. In the morning at five or six o'clock they woke us up and chased us into the cold showers. In November. They wanted to harm us but what they did was good for us because we got stimulated.

GK. He met my brother there. Theo, tell them about that.

TK. There were thousands of people in the yard. And all of a sudden I saw her brother. It was the day he arrived. Some of us were carrying soup and other stuff, rice and so on, for other people. I walked over to my brother-in-law. I had not seen him for months or maybe for years. So, when I came back, the Kommandant was standing there. You know, usually when they catch someone [disobeying rules] they put him over a plug and whip him. But I was lucky. He didn't say a word.

MK. But he hit you?

TK. Not hard. It wasn't bad. I was so lucky, I don't think another person in the place was as lucky as I was, just this time.

MK. After six weeks, did you look different?

TK. When I came back after five and a half weeks, my kid turned his back and said, "That's not my daddy."

GK. He was sick, he had a high temperature when he came home.

WH. You had pneumonia?

TK. Yeah. I got black toes. Frostbite. One Sunday, it was very cold, there were about ten thousand people sitting on the ground. And there was one very religious Jew. He called out, "Shema Yisroel!" They took him away. He never came back.

[In the meantime, the clerk who had issued the Cuban visa to Mrs. Krämer had disappeared. Mr. Krämer says that the man had partners in the SS and the SA with whom he split the money. Nevertheless, it was on the basis of the visa that Mr. Krämer was released. He was then required to report daily to the SS. He was told that he would have to leave Germany within two weeks. The Krämers wrote to a friend in Liverpool for an affidavit of support.]

TK. Something else. When I came out of the concentration camp, I had frozen feet. And you know German doctors were not allowed to treat Jews. But I had a doctor in the neighborhood and he came over and treated me anyway. Later on, after the war, when I had been here already, I wrote to thank him for treating me. Also, I wanted a certificate stating that he treated me because I had come home sick, and I wanted to make the Germans responsible. But I heard there was an air raid over Frankfurt and he was killed. I got his wife to send me what I needed. I sent it to Germany. They didn't even acknowledge it. I went to a doctor here who worked for the German government and told him what I had. He said, "What you had, that's nothing. Everybody got that." So they didn't do anything.

LEAVING GERMANY

TK. I left on a train, May 1, 1939. Before we arrived in Holland, they had the flags out in the villages we went through and I started to cry and cry. I cried because I had to leave my wife and kid behind. I was even supposed to leave the day before but when I got to the railway station, I went home again. I didn't want to go. But the next day I left. [The family was reunited in England a few months later, thanks to the help of a British friend.] This time the British were nice. Even my mother was lucky. The guy she bought her ticket from for the boat to England went to the German police and got a passport for her. Not a Jewish guy, a gentile. The day before the war broke out.

[During the year that he was in England, Mr. Krämer worked unofficially for a British agency that sold transatlantic tickets. Refugees who came from Germany and were in transit to the United States were forced to pay for their passage, even though they had already paid for their tickets in Germany. The British did not recognize the German tickets. Earlier he had said, about the affidavit for his wife, "This time the British were nice." I ask him when the British were "not nice." He mentions the British Union of Fascists formed in 1932 by Sir Oswald Mosley, the notorious antisemite.]

TK. Sometimes at night, especially where the immigrants lived, they passed by and sang Hitler songs.

[The Krämers managed to come to the United States in the summer of 1939.]

҉

Ilse Kaufherr

Mrs. Kaufherr lived in the same town as the Hess family and knew them well. With so few Jewish families in the community, they all tended to be acquainted. Walter Hess asks some of the questions here.

IK. I had a very happy home life with wonderful Jewish people, quite religious, in a very small town but very beautiful, Ruppichteroth near Cologne. And as a young girl I was denied everything because I had to leave school as a Jewish child because stones were thrown at me. I was about twelve, thirteen years old. [Perhaps she means fifteen, as she says later.] This was right at the beginning of 1933. You want to know the year I was born? I'm not ashamed . . . 1918 . . . June 30th, 1918. I was a very spoiled child, the youngest of five children.

It was a beautiful little town. What they would call in this country a summer resort. We had a health spa there and people from Cologne used to come there for their health. Population, I would say, about one thousand people. Jewish population, I would say maybe twenty-five families.

MK. What about the relationship with the Jewish families in Ruppichteroth?

IK. Very close! Very close to each other because most of them were related in one way or another. But very close. One would fight for the other. One would help the other. We had a synagogue there and a Jewish cemetery. My father was a cattle dealer and he was president of the congregation. We used to go every Friday night to the temple, my father with a high hat. And, we were a happy family until Hitler came to town and then everything was denied to us children. Me especially.

One of my teachers came to my parents and advised them to take me out of school because he no longer could be responsible for me. Children were throwing stones at me and calling me "dirty Jew," and pushing me around as a Jewish child. After five o'clock, I was not allowed to be on the streets anymore. I couldn't associate with school friends anymore. Naturally, it started right away in the small towns because the gentile people who had nothing heard of Hitler and they wanted to become big right away. And those were the ones who punished us few Jewish people right away.

WH. Can you talk a little bit about your relationship with the Germans in the town?

IK. With my parents and my brothers it was wonderful. On Sundays, when the Catholic people came from their little towns surrounding Ruppichteroth to go to church, they had to pass our house. And after church, they would come to our house for breakfast. My father was such a generous man and he was loved by one and all. Until the lower-class people of the town wanted to become big shots and joined the organization immediately. And dominated the small town. Short and sweet.

WH. They wanted the Jews' property?

IK. Sure. Definitely. Like my Uncle Herman. He was sent to jail in 1933 because he had the best butcher shop in the neighborhood. His two children had to live with us then. And I can remember the Nazis coming into our house and inspecting it and taking whatever they wanted.

[Mrs. Kaufherr was compelled to leave school at fifteen, and received no further schooling. She left home and went to live with a cousin in Cologne. She worked first for a family and then in a delicatessen store but was forced to leave that job because, as a Jew, she was no longer permitted to work on the same premises as non-Jewish males. This was a direct result of the 1935 Nuremberg Law for the Protection of German Blood and Honor, which was designed to prevent Jewish females from consorting with Aryan males.]

MK. In Cologne, did you witness any incidents or did you see, for example, the word *Jude* painted on signs?

IK. Oh, there were plenty of signs all over. And they made the swastika all over the steps to the houses. There were big trees in front of the houses and there were swastikas on them. And then [1936] I got my visa to come to the United States. I was eighteen years old. My two sisters and a brother were already in the United States. We had rich relatives here and they sent me a visa. I left on my own in 1937 and came to the United States on the *Deutschland*, the only reservation I could get.

MK. It's a very independent thing for you to have done, to have left the country by yourself.

IK. I had the fortunate opportunity to come here because it was made easier for me. I had a very low visa number. In fact, at the American consulate at Stuttgart, they asked me, "Do you want to take anybody else with you?" [In other words, did she want to register anyone else's name on the list of those applying for visas, which were relatively easy to get at that time, since the quota for the United States was not filled.] Being a little girl in those days, I said no, I don't have anybody, but I should have taken one or two more people who were very dear to me including the brother who was left behind, plus my parents. You were a child, you were timid, you were scared to say anything whichever way.

[Mrs. Kaufherr speaks with bitter hindsight, knowing that exiting Germany later became increasingly more difficult, what with restrictions imposed by outside countries and the huge sums of money needed to purchase fraudulent visas that might somehow convey their bearers to safety. German Jews, frantic after Kristallnacht, their passports now prominently stamped with a red "J" and the name Israel (for men) and Sara (for women) added to their own names, tried their luck at one consulate after another. Only Shanghai, under Japanese occupation, accepted them without visas.]

MK. It was quite unusual for people to come over as early as you did, so you must have made up your mind very early.

IK. There was no future for me there, for us Jewish people. We all had to leave, sooner or later.

MK. So many people didn't realize it. Were your parents at all interested in coming?

IK. At that time, no, because my father was a great believer and he said, "I never hurt anybody, why should somebody hurt me?" And he always figured as long as he could make a good living in Germany, why should he leave and come here?

MK. Did you try to convince him?

IK. We all tried, naturally. My sisters and brothers wrote to them, "Come, come, come while you can." So my father wrote to one of my brothers, "Well, did you make that much money already that you can support us in the way we are accustomed?" It's so ridiculous that my father always said, "I never harmed anybody. Why should they harm me?" Maybe they didn't see any further. They figured as long as my brother was still in Germany, as long as he was not willing to go, they were not willing to go. But once my brother came here, my parents wanted to come. They had a quota number. This was already in 1940. Then they were sent from one camp to another and we were still able to write to each other. But then we lost contact due to the fact that we didn't know what camp they had been sent to. Until my youngest brother joined the American army in 1941 and was shipped from the

United States to Iceland, to England, to Holland, and in Holland he got a furlough. He went to our hometown, Ruppichteroth. [This was after 1944.] There he found a letter which my mother wrote from the concentration camp saying that our father had died . . . of "natural causes" at Theresienstadt. He extended his furlough and went to Theresienstadt, and there he was told that my mother was sent the day before to the gas chamber . . . She could have been a grandmother by now . . . That's the story.

[Mrs. Kaufherr is crying. I wonder about the coincidence of her brother learning that their mother had perished just the day before his arrival. But whether it happened precisely as Mrs. Kaufherr related it or not is almost irrelevant in this appalling context.]

WH. *[After a pause.]* Let me ask you something, to change the subject just a little bit. Coming over, so young, were you afraid of being by yourself?

IK. At the beginning, very much so. Because I never spoke out loud, I whispered, because I was always afraid this could happen here too. You were timid. You were scared. But then, once I was here, and established myself a little bit, it was better. You know, you make ten dollars and you were a big shot. With ten dollars, you went far.

⚜

Max Frankel

Max Frankel and I grew up together in Washington Heights, played ball on the street together, and attended the same public schools. This interview was conducted while he was editorial page editor of the New York Times *(1977–1986). He subsequently became the executive editor (1986–1994).*

MF. I was born in 1930 in Gera, a small town in Thüringen. When I was six months old we moved to what I regard as my hometown, Weissenfels, another small town near Leipzig. As far as the first grade, I had the usual kinds of experiences. Actually, I had a very nice warm-heart-ed teacher who used to send me home when the Hitler Jugend [Hitler Youth] would start parading. I regarded that as a great insult, a great de-privation not to be able to march in the streets *[laughter]*.

My father had a [clothing] store on the main square in the town. We were nominally Polish, that is to say, my parents were born in what used to be Poland during the Austro-Hungarian Empire and which has since become part of the Soviet Union. Therefore, in October 1938, we were rounded up along with all the Polish Jews. We were picked up one night by the Gestapo, most of them customers of ours. They used to come in through the back of the store to buy their suits from my father so they wouldn't be seen buying from the Jews. But they got very good credit from him, so they were "good friends."

And they did it with sad hearts and in a very gentlemanly way. They took my father away to the town jail. They told my mother to lock the store in an orderly fashion, they put their own seal on and promised to protect the store—which, by the way, they did. They gave her a chance to go home and pack a suitcase and then they took us to the town jail. Then they moved us that night to Halle, and then by one means or an-other (we were taken by truck, I think), to the Polish border and dumped there. I was then eight and a half, an only child.

We were in a small group of about twenty-five or thirty people, mostly from our town. That was our little band. It was the middle of the night and we were met by Polish guards who didn't know anything about this thing, and they started shooting in the air. We got scared and started running around in circles in what turned out to be no-man's-land. Got back to the German territory. There were dogs and all kinds of threats that we were going to go to concentration camps if we were caught back in German territory. And so, we just squatted in the mid-dle of this field for about a day and a half. I remember it rained, and my father got something close to pneumonia that night. But the main point was that a lot of people had been put on trains and sent right through. There were furious negotiations back in Warsaw as to what to do with these tens and tens of thousands of so-called Polish Jews—we didn't know any Polish, but we were Polish in the nomenclature of the time.

[Between fifteen and seventeen thousand Polish Jews, including those who had become German citizens since World War I, were shipped to the border. The Poles refused to allow them into Poland or invalidated the passports of those who had lived outside Poland for more than five years.]

MF. As a result of the negotiations in Warsaw and all kinds of other places, we were finally admitted and allegedly cleared for somewhere way off, in eastern Poland. To make a long story short, we had some distant relatives in the city of Cracow and we finally did get on the train via a ruse, with visitors' passes, and got off this refugee train in Cracow. And we stayed there for about nine months. We had been waiting for *years* for permission to go to the United States, always denied on some grounds or other—our sponsorship wasn't good enough, or the affidavits; the relatives in America were not wealthy enough. The papers just never qualified.

At some point my mother got permission to go back to Germany to visit the American consulate [in Berlin] to see about our emigration status. This time we were cleared for emigration to America. After Berlin she went back to Weissenfels and found both our apartment and our store well protected from looting or anything else. She liquidated it all and turned the furniture and a piano into cash, which she sent off to America, blind. And because she had all this excess money, which she couldn't take out of the country, she also bought passage for us on a German ship.

She came back to Poland and there we waited until we finally got clearance to go. We were supposed to sail from Hamburg around September 10, 1939. Mother and I went back to Germany in August. My father was afraid to spend that many weeks in Germany and was going to join us just two days before the boat sailed. On September 1, the war broke out, and now we were enemy aliens in Germany. My father was stuck in Poland. He ran from the advancing German armies and right into the clutches of the Russians who offered him Russian citizenship. When he refused it, they tried him as a German spy or something and sent him off to Siberia. It's quite a tragedy.

MK. A German spy who is Jewish?

MF. Yes. And allegedly Polish. He went to this labor camp though we didn't know it at this point. My mother and I moved to Berlin on the grounds that anonymity in the big city seemed better than a small town where everyone knew us as the only remaining Jews.

MK. You were waiting for him to join you?

MF. No, no. We were now waiting for our documentation to get out of Germany. We were now enemy aliens and our permission to board a ship was cancelled. We now needed an exit permit. It's a long involved story. The exit permit could only be gotten from the Gestapo. The Gestapo was on Unter den Linden where Mother, as a Jewess, was not even allowed to walk. And when she turned to the Jewish HIAS [Hebrew Immigration Aid Society] and the other Jewish organizations, they said, "We can't even visit these offices. We don't know what to do."

Meantime, through boxes of candy, this visa number at the U.S. embassy was constantly being renewed, waiting for us, but with threats, almost monthly, that other people who could get out because they weren't Polish were held up, and that we were squatting on this valuable visa. And if we couldn't make use of it, it would have to go to somebody else.

Finally, in desperation, along about January 1940, Mother just strolled right down this avenue [Unter den Linden], dressed to kill, and walked up to the front door and said, "I want to see the head man of the Gestapo headquarters."

The guard outside asked her for her documents and she produced this stateless Polish passport, which is white with a red eagle on it. And the guard said, "Are you Swiss?" confusing the passport with the Swiss one, which was white with the red cross on it.

MK. He hadn't seen too many of those.

MF. That's right. She said nothing and he called upstairs and said, "There's a Swiss lady here to see you, Mr. Kommandant," or whatever.

And she went up and the fellow smiled when he saw this document and said, "I thought you said you were Swiss."

She said, "I didn't say I was Swiss. Your guard said I was Swiss."

And he took a liking to her and said, "Why do you want to leave?"

She said, "You don't want us here. You threw us out once and now you're making life unpleasant."

MK. Very feisty.

MF. Anyway, this went on, and he finally asked her to lunch, and she said, "I don't think that would be very smart, either for you or for me."

And he said, "I guess not."

Then he said, "Why do you want to go to America? We're going to be there soon."

She said, "I told you, I don't want to go to America, I don't want to go anywhere. I just need to get away."

So he opened the desk drawer and wrote out two exit permits. And we left. All the people we were living with we never saw again, of course. It was only a matter of months and just dumb luck.

MK. Did you hear from your dad?

MF. We heard from him twice during the war. He was in a slave labor camp in Siberia until Russia switched sides. [The Russians signed a nonagression pact with the Germans in August 1939.] The Russians went into Poland as a result of the pact [ostensibly to protect the Ukrainian and White Russian minorities]. When Germany invaded Russia [in June 1941] and Russia switched sides, then, at least nominally, Poland became an ally. The Polish government-in-exile in London negotiated with Moscow for the release of all these alleged German spies that were in Siberian camps, and he was released, although not from Siberia and not from duties, but at least he was released from the labor camp. He bummed around Siberia for the next five years, picking up jobs. He wound up in charge of some German prisoners in a furniture factory.

We heard from him twice in all that time. We tried the Red Cross and all kinds of other communication. And finally, at the end of the war in early 1946, when Poland was not yet communist, this same Polish government-in-exile negotiated for the return of all these people to Poland. He was "repatriated" to Poland. He got to Warsaw before it was fully communist and picked up his American visa there. It was waiting throughout the whole war. Once we came to America and especially after we became citizens in 1945, he had an absolute first priority. Somehow he smuggled his way out of Poland to Stockholm, and we were able to get him over by October 1946—seven years too late.

Hilde Kracko

At the time of this interview, Hilde Kracko was working at the United Restitution Office (URO), which processes Jewish claims against the German government for sufferings incurred under the Nazis. She lives in the same building on Fort Washington Avenue as many other German Jews, a couple of blocks from Fort Tryon Park. My mother-in-law, who is Sephardic, lives right next door to her.

HK. We lived in a city near Düsseldorf with a population of about 120,000 people, where everyone knew everyone else. My husband had a furniture store, and after 1933 Hitler gave help—subsidies—to the young people who were getting married so they could buy furniture. But they were not allowed to buy in Jewish stores. That was already a boycott. And that was the beginning of the end.

MK. How did people know it was a Jewish store?

HK. It was an old well-known business. On April 1, 1933, there were two SA men standing in front of the store so people would know there was a Jewish owner. That was the first boycott day of all Jewish businesses.

MK. But you were not yet married.

HK. No, not yet. We were engaged. I had to learn to cook and I went to live with a Jewish family in Westphalia as a so-called house daughter, and I liked it very much. They had a business and I helped them. I stayed there three and a half years, from 1933 to 1936. I was twenty-three in 1936. While I was there, we already had singing in front of the house. It was a very small village where they knew the people very well and they were singing Hitler songs during the night: "Wenn juden Blut vom Messer spritzt . . ." [When Jewish blood spurts from the knife] . . . I remember that. It was very painful.

[Mrs. Kracko returned to her parents' home in 1936. One of her sisters, who had to leave a position as secretary to a judge, was now working for the Jewish owners of a big leather company.]

HK. They had two gentile housemaids under the age of forty-five and they were not allowed to keep them because there were young men in the family. That was the law. So they hired me and another Jewish girl for the housework. It was a very big house, twenty-four rooms. I was there for only three months, and then the Gestapo came one morning and arrested the husband and the son. This was in 1937.

MK. Were other people in the town arrested?

HK. There was the brother, his wife, and (I think) two sons. His wife took her life in jail. She hanged herself with a corset cord. Then came an amnesty in Germany. Anyone who had money in foreign countries and brought it back to Germany would be set free.

[Mrs. Kracko remained in the house by herself until the end of 1937, when the family was released and went to Holland. They obtained working papers for her so that she could be with them. She went to Holland and worked for the family until her fiancé joined her there, reluctantly, and in 1938 they were married. Mrs. Kracko's parents and her brothers and sisters (there were eight children) also went to Holland at this time. Her in-laws did not want to leave Germany, under the assumption that the crisis was temporary, but after Kristallnacht they realized that they could not stay. The Krackos hoped to find a country that would be willing to take the elderly in-laws as well as themselves.]

HK. We tried to go to the United States but from Holland it was impossible. Not because of the quota. Because of the affidavit.

[They knew no one in America who could provide the affidavit of support. Therefore they were required by the American consulate in Holland to show that they had twenty-five thousand dollars (almost three hundred thousand dollars today), which they did not have. The young couple then went to England and obtained a visa for Mrs. Kracko's in-laws to follow them there. But the war broke out and it was no longer possible to get to England from Germany. In the meantime, Mrs. Kracko and her husband had received permission to emigrate to Bolivia where Mr. Kracko had a cousin. Once there they were able to obtain papers for Mr. Kracko's parents.]

HK. So we all went in 1939 to Bolivia. After the Germans moved into Holland, I didn't hear any more from my family. I had three sisters and two brothers and my parents there. After the war, in 1945, I got a card from my sister saying that one brother and two sisters were still alive. My parents and my other sister and brothers-in-law were all gassed at Auschwitz.

They called one brother [for a work transport] and my other brother said, "Don't go."

But he said, "What other people can do, I can do." And he went and we never heard from him again.

The other brother went underground. He picked up one of my sisters by bicycle and they lived for two and a half years underground. Hidden. By gentiles. They didn't know they were Jews. There was an organization who put them in houses where they could work.

MK. This was an organization for foreigners?

HK. No, not for foreigners. They didn't know my family was foreign. They spoke Dutch fluently. [The organization helped political opponents of the Nazis.] You know, there were political people who had to flee, too.

Then they moved all the Jews to a ghetto in Amsterdam and there were *razzias* [raids] in the streets and they took the Jews—I think they had to wear armbands too. My brother-in-law came home one afternoon for lunch. [Mrs. Kracko's parents lived with their daughter and son-in-law.] They were all sitting at the table and the Gestapo came and took him away. My sister received one letter from him that he threw out of the train and it was delivered to her. It said, "We will see each other again." But they never did. Then they came every night and transported people to the camps. They heard the people screaming and yelling when they had to leave the houses.

One evening the Gestapo came to pick up my parents. My sister couldn't stand it anymore and she voluntarily went with my parents and her two children.

[Another sister managed to live illegally in Amsterdam as a Christian. Prior to going underground, she had retrieved some of the family's possessions and gave them to a Dutch family for safekeeping. They were recovered after the war.]

BOLIVIA

[Mr. Kracko had bought a shirt factory in Bolivia. One day the family returned from a vacation to find that the factory had been robbed. All twelve machines and the merchandise were taken. There was no insurance to cover the loss. In fourteen years of living there, they also experienced fourteen revolutions.]

HK. In 1952 was the biggest revolution. There was shooting and all of a sudden there came a dumdum that came from the roof through our dining room and exploded. I think I can show you the picture of the damage. We had seventy-two broken windows.

I said to my husband, "Now that is enough. We have to try and get out of here." My husband had a cousin in the United States but he didn't want to give us the affidavit because we had an old lady with us, my mother-in-law who was eighty-one, and two children. (We lost one child later on in Bolivia.) It was a lot of responsibility. Then I had a cousin who survived the war in Holland and lived in Texas. I wrote to them, and some strangers—Jewish people in a little town near Dallas—gave them the affidavit for us. And that is how we landed in Texas in 1953.

ᘛᘚ

Louis Kampf

By the time Lou Kampf arrived in Washington Heights in 1942, I had already been living in the country for six years. With other refugee kids we hung out in the streets. Like me, Lou Kampf attended George Washington High School. I lost touch with him after he left the neighborhood but I followed his career through the newspapers and through friends.

Lou Kampf's parents were living in Poland when the Russians invaded the country during World War I. Like many other Jews at the time, they went to Austria, where they hoped to lead a more stable existence. Mr. Kampf served in the Austrian army on the Italian front. At the end of the war, he moved to Vienna and began working, selling clothing from door to door on the installment plan.

LK. It was a hard life, but you managed. My parents were married in 1928 and I was born in 1929 in Vienna. As a kid, I was always aware of antisemitism. When I went to school, I had to defend myself against other kids. In the park, they always knew who was a Jew and who wasn't. [Even before Hitler, antisemitism was rampant in Austria.] You couldn't hold political office if you were a Jew, you couldn't be a policeman or drive a bus. Antisemitism was always strong, but somehow you were able to live. My parents often said, "It was better in Poland."

They weren't very religious, just somewhat. I learned Hebrew and we went to synagogue every Saturday. So I always had an awareness of being Jewish and of my parents being eastern Jews and not really Austrian. When you think of Freud and other intellectuals, for example, they were completely assimilated. They were really Austrian. But my parents, for example, often spoke Yiddish, not German.

In March 1938, Hitler took over Austria in the Anschluss. Kristallnacht occurred on the night of November 9, and on November 10 my father was arrested and taken to Dachau, one of the major concentration camps. I can never forget that because his birthday is on November 10. He was released after six weeks because he was a veteran of World War I. He was very skinny and scared. But then he'd always been scared. He got caught up in this because he didn't hide. The word was "They're arresting people." So he stayed in the apartment because you should do the legal thing. He's always been a big law-and-order man. Then we got kicked out of our apartment. Some party official showed up and looked it over and we were told to move out forty-eight hours later.

In the meantime, my mother managed to buy a visa for Belgium. You could get one if you could pay for it. If you had no money, that was the end. We didn't have much, but we had enough to buy a visa.

Now what they did after that was to send me off [at age nine] to Belgium on my own, to Antwerp, at the end of 1938. They followed at the beginning of 1939. We had lots of relatives there. My parents and my mother's relatives were in the diamond business [laughs]. Naturally, all Jews in Belgium were in the diamond business. So my father began a new life in the diamond business. In 1939, of course, the war started for real and Belgium was invaded by the Nazis. My father, ironically, was interned for being an enemy alien, namely, he had a German passport, since Austria had become part of the greater German Reich. They told all enemy aliens to report for internment, and my father reported, him and other Jews who had German passports. And we didn't hear from him in quite a while. So they shipped him and thousands of other peo-

ple off to southern France in freight cars, cattle cars. Near the Mediter-
ranean, on the Spanish border. They got put into the concentration
camps that the Spanish Republicans had been interned in. The French
government interned the Spanish Republicans who had fled across the
border. My father wound up in a place called St. Cyprien. It's a beach
resort now.

We didn't have the slightest idea where he was. So my mother and I
and a couple of other relatives with loads of other people fled Antwerp,
started going off toward the French border. And we got trapped by the
German encirclement just before Dunkirk. So we were in some little
town in a basement with lots of other people for about a week. There
were shells dropping all around us and bombs. We weren't hiding, it
wasn't all Jews. It was the basement of a hotel, I think. And people
shared food, people were decent to each other. And then the German
soldiers arrived and they were perfectly nice. They gave us bread and
canned goods, and back we went to Antwerp where life resumed semi-
normally. It was an army occupation. I used to make some money shin-
ing boots for German soldiers who were quartered down the street.

I went back to school and for a while things were fairly calm, except
of course everybody was worried about what might happen eventually.
I was ten years old. I knew something bad was going on and I sort of
missed my father, but on the other hand, things were exciting.

At night occasionally English bombers would come over and I'd
watch the flash of the anti-aircraft guns. Once I remember a bunch of
kids, both Jewish and Christian, went over to a spot to see a British
plane that had been shot down, to see the remnants of it, and all that in
a way was terribly exciting for a kid that age, and you don't really have
the good sense to know yet how dangerous it is. My mother once tried
to keep me from running out of the house—while one of the bombings
was going on—so I could get a better view of it. So it wasn't a terrible
time for me.

Anyway, at one point, through the kind of secret underground mail
system that was going on, we got a letter from my father saying that he
had escaped from the French camp he was in, in St. Cyprien—which
was easy because the French soldiers guarding it didn't give a damn.
But once you got outside, you had to have papers.

It turned out there was this little town, a spa called Bagnères-de-Lu-

chon in the French Pyrenees, on the Spanish border. It was an old-fashioned spa, which attracted a lot of skiers in peacetime and in the summer lots of people taking the baths, some kind of cure or other. The
mayor was selling papers and residence permits to Jews and word of
this had gotten around. So here you had this town which was practically empty because of the war, nobody was there for vacation, but it had
something like a thousand Jews in it, all of them with papers they had
gotten from this mayor who was stashing it away. My father had some
diamonds hidden on him in his shoes as well as some money, and he
wound up there and sent for us. Again, it's the same story. If you had
money, you could get by. If not, it was the end of you. So for about a
year my parents were writing to each other.

My mother and I had gotten fake papers to go to France, to occupied
France, that is. But we had to get from occupied France to unoccupied
France. In Paris we waited for about a month for a guide we'd been put
in contact with. The thing is, we didn't have papers for Vichy France
[where a French puppet government had been set up in 1940]. My father had the papers waiting for us.

So it was kind of hairy, in retrospect, once we got across the border
to unoccupied France. We walked across the border through a farm to
the train station. Sure enough, there was a gendarme there. He asked
for our papers, which we didn't have, but it took about ten francs to
buy him off. For my mother, the trip from Belgium to southern France
was horrible. She didn't know when we might be hauled off to a concentration camp. For me, of course, it was a big adventure. It was like
being in a movie. I was eleven years old and I really didn't understand
what was happening.

At the Spanish border, the French police boarded the train and arrested a Jewish couple. Eventually, through a series of, in my eyes, minor adventures but, in my mother's eyes, major horrors (we almost got
caught at one particular point on the train, and my mother hid in the
bathroom while I stood out there—being an eleven-year-old kid nobody
bothered me), eventually, we finally wound up in this little town, Bag-
nères-de-Luchon. There we just sat and waited for our relatives to supply us with a visa to get to the United States, and that was not forth-
coming for a year. So we were there for a year. I was having a great
time: no school, and I did all the reading and Ping-Pong and soccer play-

ing I could. My parents were going bananas, of course, but I didn't quite realize that at the time.

MK. Why was the visa being held up?

LK. Part of it was my parents' having been born in Poland. The Polish immigration quota [for the United States] and the racist law that got passed in the 1920s were meant to exclude South Europeans and East Europeans because they were considered to be inferior beings. If my parents had been born in Germany or Austria, they would have been OK. But having been born in Poland they were on the Polish quota.

The affidavit was problematic. We had all these relatives in the United States, yet they couldn't get together about who should sign an affidavit for us that would assure that we wouldn't be a burden to the state. I think that was not untypical. A lot of the American Jews and Jews all over the world simply didn't take Hitler quite seriously, to the degree that he obviously should have been taken seriously. They didn't realize how much a matter of life and death it was at that particular point.

MK. And even then, in 1941, you feel that your relatives didn't take things seriously?

LK. I think so. And I'm not sure that they themselves feel that way. I never really talked about it but I know a lot of other people have the same feeling. Anyway, around November 1941 the visa came through. By December 7, of course, the United States entered the war, which meant we couldn't come over on an American ship. We had to find a Portuguese boat. And so we started off for Lisbon. As we got to the Spanish border, to Pau, which was the point where you could catch a train, for one reason or another the Spaniards decided to close the border. It's the only time in my life I had ever seen my father cry.

We found out that the boat we were planning to take [to America] was going to make a stop in Casablanca—which wasn't famous yet because the movie hadn't yet been made. And so we shuffled off to Marseilles and caught a boat from there, which took us to Casablanca. There we spent about a month waiting for our boat. I had a great time running around with various local kids. I was in all the spots that Humphrey Bogart and Ingrid Bergman were in. Unfortunately I never ran into Claude Rains [laughs]. Cops didn't seem to be that nice.

The boat took weeks [to get to America]. It stopped for three days in Kingston, Jamaica; for five days in Havana. I heard that it got sunk a couple of months later.

One should be clear, and I always am in my own head, that in terms of suffering, compared to what happened to people, especially later on (not only people who actually wound up in one of the death camps but people who fled and had to spend time in people's basements and caves and chimneys, like one of my cousins did, for example), compared to that it was nothing. I mean it was a lark compared to that kind of thing, and I try to be sure never to forget that, and not create some kind of mythology about myself about what I went through.

ﾞﾐﾌ

Ilse Marcus

When Hitler came to power, Mrs. Marcus was still going to school in Breslau, now called Wroclaw, a city in Silesia that was one of the formerly German territories ceded to Poland in 1945. As a student in an all-girls school she was still able to complete her Abitur, *the academic degree required for entrance to a university. Her parents owned a small department store where she helped out.*

IM. I wasn't as badly off as my brother because usually girls are not as rough as boys are. My brother had a terrible time. The boys came to school already in their Nazi uniform, they didn't have to do homework anymore. The excuse was, "It's enough that they went to Party meetings." They threatened my brother, so much that he was afraid they might kill him. So one day my brother came home and he said, "Dad, I just can't go anymore. They threatened me. They will throw me out the window, and I just can't go anymore."

My brother was not very husky. But my father just couldn't give in right away. A son, a boy, has to learn. So the next day he decided to go with him to the director. Now the director was a very nice person and he said, "Look, whatever I can do for your son to protect him, I will do. He should just come to school and I will watch the situation."

So when my father and my brother came home, my father said, "I'll get you a new watch, I'll get you this, I'll get you that, but try to finish school." So my brother kept on going for a short while, but the situation really got very bad, and, I mean, how long and how many hours can you live with these rats? So finally he didn't go anymore and he said, "I'm not interested anyway. I would like to learn agriculture and maybe I will become a gardener." So my father sent him to a school in Dahlem, near Berlin.

My father felt very bad. He believed strongly in learning, especially for a boy. He never was so much interested in my grades or my going to school. In fact, I was the more ambitious one. My brother was never much for learning but my father wanted him to learn.

In 1935, I got married. Now there was another incident. In the meantime, my father-in-law died, and you could say he died because of Hitler. He was on the telephone with somebody on a business call and he heard a click. And coming off the phone he was convinced that somebody overheard the conversation and he might have said something and they will come and arrest him. From then on the idea never left him. It haunted him. And he died in March 1935. Now my mother-in-law said she will never leave Germany, she wants to be buried where her husband is buried. So her two sons, being very good sons, didn't want to leave either, and the whole family stuck together. One would not leave without the other. That's how the whole family stuck together, and perished together.

In 1936, my parents went on vacation to Czechoslovakia. At this time you already had to have the yellow star at the windows of the business. There were signs that said, "Don't buy at Jewish stores." When my parents called from Czechoslovakia and asked if everything was all right, I told them, "Everything is all right." People were still buying, unfortunately. If business had not been so good, we would have known enough to leave Germany earlier.

Unfortunately we stayed on. When Hitler came to power in 1933, you didn't feel it that much yet. Business was good, all over. And our leadership, our Jewish leadership, was talking against leaving Germany. The rabbi was preaching from the pulpit, telling us not to leave.

"Hold out, stay." But they were the first ones to leave, the rabbis themselves.

MK. But some stayed, like Leo Baeck.

IM. *[Nods in agreement.]* If people would have traveled more, they would have known what was happening. Our horizons were very limited.

MK. Were there discussions between your parents about leaving?

IM. Let's say we were talking about emigration. We were preparing to go to Israel [Palestine], we were preparing to go to Brazil . . . But the fact was, my father didn't want to leave. My mother wanted to leave right away because she didn't want to remain as a second-class citizen. But you know, usually a man, the father of a family, thinks differently. He said, "Don't throw everything away so fast." My parents had built up the business from scratch, and a man usually feels more of an obligation to support the family and not just throw everything away, not knowing what will be. So my father was the one who was holding back the family.

You see, I wasn't used to having my own opinion at this time. I was used to being sheltered by my parents. What they said was the right thing. Later on my husband took over. I never did my own thinking. Whatever they did was all right with me.

The business was not much affected. Whoever you talked to, all Jewish business people, they all said business was good.

KRISTALLNACHT

IM. All of sudden at night, on November 9—between November 9 and 10, 1938—my parents who lived in an apartment next door to my husband's and mine came storming in: "All the windows—I heard a terrible smashing of all the windows of the business" (which was just below my parents' apartment). "This must be a pogrom." A pogrom was something never heard of in Germany. It was something from Poland. We had a pogrom! I mean, it took time to grasp this idea. We didn't know what to do. Our first thought was to call the police.

All the phones were dead. You couldn't talk to anybody. So, what to do next? Early in the morning, somehow, all the men had the feeling that they should leave the apartment. Nobody knew why, but it was a certain feeling. My mother left with them and I stayed behind with the dog. I didn't know what to do. And why I stayed, I still don't know. But anyway, a short while later there was a knock at my door. Gestapo! They are looking for the men. I said, "There's nobody here." My dog was barking his head off and the Gestapo man wanted me to take the dog away.

I said, "The dog is my protection," so he didn't search the apartment and he left. I was glad that the men really left in time because my uncle had been caught early in the morning. My brother, my father, and my husband thought it might be safe to hide there, at my uncle's, because the Nazis would not come again. And that proved to be the right thing to do. At least they didn't have to go Buchenwald. Because my brother-in-law who was still living with my mother-in-law was caught at home and he was taken to Buchenwald.

Everybody was stunned. Nobody knew what to do, the women were all helpless. So every morning my mother-in-law came to my bed, and she said, "Can't we do anything for Fred [Mrs. Marcus's brother-in-law]? You know Fred has a permit to go to Cuba."

I said, "Look, maybe it will help him." I figured maybe I could get some information from the police headquarters. You might remember, the police were always more democratically inclined than the Gestapo.

So I went to the police and they were very nice. They said, "Look, the Gestapo headquarters is just above us and we have nothing to do with them, we cannot help you with anything, but try anyway." At that time, women were not afraid for themselves. So I went up there and I saw quite a lot of women sitting and waiting and I found my aunt. I asked her what she is doing there. She told me she already had affidavits to immigrate to America and she was hoping this would help her to get her husband, my uncle, out of Buchenwald.

I said that my brother-in-law, Fred, had a permit to go to Cuba and maybe that would help to get him out of Buchenwald too. I asked one of the Gestapo men and he said it might help and asked for the permit. I had a photocopy done of the permit and it did help. I brought it over to the Gestapo and a week or two later Fred came back and he looked, as you can imagine, just horrible. The whole time he didn't get out of his suit, he was bald, and he looked dirty and terrible. Pale and full of fear.

MK. Did he tell you what happened?

IM. No. We asked him right away, after we sent him to a good bath—

we asked him right away if he would tell us a little bit. He said that before he left the camp he was told that if he tells us *anything* about the camp he would be right back. And he believed it! He believed so much that he even was afraid in his own apartment. He wouldn't say a word. "I just can't . . . I can't . . . I can't."

Every morning he had to go to the police station, to the Gestapo to report, and every morning he was asked, "So, when are you finally leaving?"

Because of an incident that happened he had to leave anyway. He went by tram through Breslau, a streetcar, and he was caught jumping off by the Gestapo, which was a terrible crime, evidently. And the Gestapo told him if he catches him again he will be back where he came from [Buchenwald]. So overnight he had to leave for Holland where we had relatives. Then he went to Cuba and he landed there.

MK. What kept *you* from going?

IM. Nobody wanted to leave without the other one. In fact, my mother and I, we decided to send the men. She and I were talking about how they all should go together with friends. They didn't. My father didn't want to leave without my mother and my husband wouldn't have left without me, and my brother wouldn't have left without having the whole family together. That's how we all landed in concentration camps.

MK. How long did it take for you to leave after Fred?

IM. As very often, lousy money was holding us back. My parents had to sell the business, they had to sell the house, and we really thought the next ship will do as well. Then we booked passage on the Hamburg–America Line. The next ship was the *St. Louis,* a German ship, which we boarded on May 13, 1939, and sailed to Cuba, and everybody was happy. I mean there was entertainment on board and Friday night services; everything was nice until we arrived in Cuba and anchored just off the coast where my brother-law was waiting for us. With the little money we had sent, he had furnished an apartment for us. Every day he came in a little boat to greet us. It was then I heard my first mañana. Whenever we asked when we would leave the ship, we heard "Mañana." And this mañana never came. Years later my brother-in-law told me that my mother had sent a telegram to Cuba to welcome me, but he knew already we would not be getting off the ship, so he never gave it to me. Everybody who was in Cuba knew from the very beginning that we would not get off the ship. There had been demonstrations in Cuba against allowing the ship to land.

MK. By Cubans?

IM. By Cubans. By the authorities. Look, the whole thing was probably managed by the Germans. Already before getting on the ship we had to pay double fare, for going and coming back.

[Mrs. Marcus implies that there was a conspiracy between the Germans and the Cubans to prevent the passengers from landing and to return them to Europe. Paying round-trip fare was common, however, for the simple reason that it put more money into German pockets. Would-be immigrants therefore had to have enough to pay for either round-trip tickets or first-class fares.]

MK. Why would the Germans be in collusion with the Cubans not to allow anyone to land? German policy at that time was to allow people to emigrate if they had visas. That's why they released people from the concentration camps, after Kristallnacht. It would have been to their advantage to send people out at that time. They didn't yet have the "final solution."

IM. I think they did have it. I'm pretty sure that if we had all read *Mein Kampf,* nobody would have stayed in Germany.

We stayed in the harbor for at least a week, I think. And then we were not allowed to remain anymore. Then we had to get out of the— what is it—the two-mile zone, I think. This was just terrible. I mean the way this already turned against us. The food was scarce already, they were not prepared for all this. So standing there in the harbor and standing outside the two-mile zone, we really didn't know what will be. Now the first thing we heard was the ship has to go back to Germany. Then someone committed suicide. That's when everybody was up in arms, because everybody was afraid to go back to Germany. Because they knew right away that would mean going to the concentration camp. Then there were telegrams going back and forth between the Joint Distribution Committee and the committee which had been formed on the ship.

[The American Jewish Joint Distribution Committee, known popularly as "the Joint," was the major American Jewish organization that provided overseas assistance.]

IM. The Joint Distribution Committee was a Jewish committee and evidently they didn't have any influence for bringing the ship to America. After all these telegrams back and forth, finally four European countries promised they would let us in, with certain conditions. We were about 970 passengers. And you know, what amazed us, and we really couldn't understand: four small countries in Europe wanted to take us in. But we couldn't understand that in the big America there is no room for us, for 900 people! By this time we were cruising off the coast of Florida and we could see the lights of Miami.

MK. Was there ever a thought, since there were so many of you, of taking over the ship?

IM. Unfortunately, no. I tell you, I still cannot understand. There is only one excuse: German Jews were just used to obeying authority. We were used to doing what we were told. We were sent to gas chambers and we went. If we hadn't been German Jews we would have been rebellious. We would have gone on a hunger strike. But we were obeying authority.

I'm pretty sure if there would have been Polish Jews they would rather have killed the captain: "Either go to America or we take over." But we didn't understand. We were too used to doing what we were told.

England took in the people who had short-term visas, Holland took people with small children . . . And the rest of the people who didn't have a chance to go to England and Holland were sent either to France or Belgium. So we went to Belgium. And you see, in fact, the only Jews who were saved were those who were lucky enough to be in England.

We arrived in Belgium in June 1939, and we were there together until May 10, 1940, when the Germans came in. The Belgians regarded us not as Jews first but as aliens, as Germans. And they were very much afraid: Germans are coming in and Germans are sitting in their country . . . So they sent all the German Jewish men to France. My husband, my father, and my brother. The Belgians made no distinction between the Germans and the Jews. Belgians were not the friendliest people.

The men were taken first to a camp called Gurs. But for at least six months we didn't even know where they were. We couldn't correspond, we had no idea where they were. The situation among the women was just terrible, you didn't know what was happening. Then my husband wrote, and then my father: They are pretty well-off in the camps there, they have nothing to worry about, but they need money. We were only allowed to send a hundred francs from Belgium, which isn't very much. So all day long, my mother and I went from one post office to another, and from each post office we sent a hundred francs. I might have forgotten to tell you, my parents took money and gold, whatever they could, in a lift van when we left Germany. After we couldn't land in Cuba, the lift vans came to Belgium. But they left everything standing there because we had only one furnished room for all of us. But they took out the box with the valuables. And then when we needed the money, little by little we sold things. And we sent the money to France.

The whole time, we were living in Brussels with false ID cards, which were even registered in city hall. I had just come back from city hall when I was stopped by a Gestapo man and he asked me where I was born. Since I had just received the ID card, I didn't know where, I didn't know when. But I just kept telling him, "It's all on the card, just look on the card!" And there was no doubt about it, he recognized my accent. And he said, "All right, come with me to city hall." Halfway there he said, "All right, here's your card, go home." So this was my first and last chance to meet a Gestapo man who let me go home. The card, in general, did not help me much because it wasn't very hard to recognize my accent.

My mother and I entrusted our valuables to a Belgian family, unfortunately. You know, for money, everything is done in this world, so they tried very much to get rid of us. The minute after my mother gave the jewels to the Belgian family, she was caught while I was away from the apartment. And then I was caught in my working place. They just walked in; they took me, and that was it. But . . . let's say, after my mother was caught a week or so before, I had that feeling: How much longer can I run from them anyway? Because there were *razzias* in the street, day and night. You walked in the street and somebody jumped out of a car, picked you up, and brought you to the gathering camp. And there you stayed for a while and then we were all brought to Auschwitz. And I even met my mother in the gathering camp in Belgium because she was caught only a week or two earlier.

PART TWO

Frankfurt on the Hudson

In our new homeland, my parents were cheerful and even-tempered. As a boy of five, I knew nothing of my father's struggles to find work as an illustrator, nothing of my mother's fears about his livelihood, her loneliness, or the self-consciousness she felt about her poor English. Despite my father's optimism, my mother had been very fearful about going to a new country.

My parents never brooded in my presence, never complained or otherwise made me feel burdened by the upheaval in their lives. At the same time, there was no attempt to hide from me whatever news came from abroad. At the edges of adult conversations during coffee klatches I would hear about relatives who were still unable to leave Germany or about others who had been sent to camps or disappeared without a trace. But somehow all my aunts and uncles arrived, along with my mother's mother and my Opa (my grandfather on my father's side), though I didn't know then what extraordinary efforts had been required to bring them to the States.

My family's first home was in Marble Hill, a neighborhood at the confluence of the Hudson and the Harlem Rivers in northern Manhattan and just bordering the Bronx. Two of my uncles lived there with their families and were able to find us an apartment very quickly. There was constant visiting back and forth, by prearrangement as was our custom, and usually for Kaffee und Kuchen punctually at four o'clock in the afternoon.

One May afternoon in 1937 I saw the giant Hindenburg airship sail over our neighborhood. I had just earned my first nickel by helping a neighbor carry three freshly slaughtered chickens home from the butcher shop. A bunch of us kids chased the dirigible until it disappeared into a cloud. One of my playmates was unimpressed; she was, in fact, crying, having lost the nickel her mother had given her to buy something at the corner store, and threatening to kill her, as an informant told me, if she lost it. Chivalry suffused me and I offered to lend her my nickel, at which point the group turned on me and accused me of stealing it from the girl. Calling me a "little Heinie," they snatched it from my hand and ran off.

That night, when my father came into my room just after I had gone to bed and told me that the Hindenburg had exploded in New Jersey, I burst into tears. My father consoled me by saying that it was sad to see the great ship destroyed but that, on the other hand, it served the Nazis right.

There were not many Jews in Marble Hill where we lived from 1936 until 1942 and my mother was unhappy about having to travel to Washington Heights for synagogue services. By the age of eight, I was traveling alone on the subway from Marble Hill to Washington Heights to attend Hebrew school. My mother determined to find us an apartment there where most of our friends lived and where we could walk to synagogue. In a rare display of independence, she visited a number of buildings and finally settled on an apartment on 161st Street and Fort Washington Avenue.

The refugee children I played with in Washington Heights never spoke about the terrors they or their families had undergone. It was as though it never occurred to us to talk about how we had arrived in the neighborhood. One would have thought that for us there was only a normal childhood—stickball in the streets, homework, the Jack Benny show on the radio, and always enough to eat. "The Wall," lining several blocks of upper Riverside Drive, is where we teenage boys and girls hung out on summer *nights and where, if we were lucky, we met our girlfriends and boyfriends. The one block from Fort Washington Avenue to the Drive often took me a half-hour to negotiate, as I would stop to greet friends, their parents, and other members of our congregation. Folding chairs were lined up armrest-to-armrest. People sat, stood, or played skat, a card game. Sometimes I went four blocks out of my way, describing a peninsula around 161st Street to get to The Wall more quickly.*

　　Later I realized that a great democratization had taken place in Washington Heights. People of different classes, from cities and farms, professionals and manual laborers, those with Ph.D.'s and those who had not gone past grade school, lived as neighbors. This was a situation that could never have existed in Germany where social differences had been rigidly maintained.

Alice Oppenheimer

The Oppenheimers owned two factories (cigars and chemicals) in Mannheim, described by Mrs. Oppenheimer as a beautiful city full of Jewish life. It had two synagogues, one orthodox, the other liberal. Mannheim was rich in culture, and residents were able to attend the theater and concerts. "Jews and gentiles lived very well together until 1933," Mrs. Oppenheimer says.

Mr. Oppenheimer had been an officer in the German army in World War I and among his acquaintances then was a noncommissioned officer who was not Jewish. The two had lost touch after the war. One day, the ex-officer showed up at the Oppenheimers' door in Mannheim. It was Saturday, April 1, 1933, the first day of the boycott of Jewish businesses throughout Germany, though the Oppenheimers were unaware that it was taking place. The man asked what Mr. Oppenheimer was doing that day. Upon learning that Mr. Oppenheimer was planning to go and check on one of the factories, the guest advised him not to go out and to remain at home. That was the day that many beatings of Jews were taking place. The man remained with them through the evening and returned the following day. When he left, he gave them his business card and urged them to call on him if ever they needed any help.

AO. Everything started then and it got worse every year until 1936. There were signs in all the restaurants and cafés: "Jews are not wanted here." So Jews couldn't go anymore to restaurants or cafés. The children had to leave their Gymnasium or high school, and even the public schools. We had to form a new Jewish school, an elementary school. At that time, Jewish students were not being accepted anymore at the university.

[In Mannheim, as elsewhere, Jews were forced to form their own societies since they were excluded from regular German ones. Jews who had never been part of a Jewish group were thrown into each other's company.]

AO. My daughter had a very bad experience as a little girl. She went to the swimming pool—it was a beautiful swimming pool on the Rhine. There was no sign saying Jews were not wanted; it was the only place. She went down to the pool and at that moment a crowd of about thirty people arrived. My husband was sitting above the pool in the restaurant with friends and he thought this group was the swimming club. Suddenly these people went to the restaurant and they rang the bell and started to yell, "Jews out! Jews out!" And they started throwing everything that was in the restaurant into the water: glasses, chairs, tables. My husband thought our little girl was in the water but thank God, the daughter of a friend who was ten years old pulled her back into the changing room. The children who were in the water were hurt and some were bleeding. This was such a terrible experience for this child, that even today—she is a grandmother—she never goes into the water. She doesn't swim anymore. She kept this incident in her mind and can't forget it.

MK. Her husband is a skin diver, isn't he?

AO. *[Laughs.]* Yes, her husband is a skin diver, and when they got married they made an agreement: she sits on the outside and he sits inside the water. Yes, she never swims.

We had the chemical factory and a cigar factory that was founded by my father-in-law. It was an old, established factory. We had a very good relationship with our workers and with all the people. But then it changed. We had to put up a big picture of Hitler. And the workers had to become part of a Hitler group. Even though they didn't want to do it because they felt very close to us, they had to. And things got worse and worse. We saw we were not able to live in Mannheim anymore. We had to make plans to leave Germany because we saw we couldn't raise our two children there.

The factory had 250 workers when I got married. But when we left we had about 65.

MK. What happened?

AO. We could not get the tobacco anymore from foreign countries. There were special rules for German Jews. But it wasn't even the financial part; there were several other things that made us realize we couldn't stay in Germany. There were some incidents. We owned a building with a tenant, and one day one of our office workers reported that the man had not paid his rent. So my husband went to see him and he said, "I won't give money to a Jew anymore." He was a young man, his parents were not antisemites, but he was very pro-Hitler. This gave my husband the final reason to leave. Because when he came home he was so furious. If the man had said anything more to him, he could have lost his temper and done something to him.

WASHINGTON HEIGHTS:
STRUGGLE FOR A NEW LIFE

AO. We came to America in 1938, before Kristallnacht, so we could bring with us a little more from Germany than the people who came after.

MK. Why did you come to Washington Heights?

AO. Some people were already here. We liked the view to the river. It was a nice section to be in and the apartments were not too expensive at that time. Even though a lot of people moved right away to Washington Heights, we found out that something was missing. The people really felt like strangers here, they didn't speak English, they didn't have money. My husband thought that if we, the former immigrants, founded a congregation and the German Jews had their own services, they would feel more at home. We thought that maybe all hardship gets easier if you carry it together. We found a group of people who were willing to hold services. We didn't have anything against the American congregation, but we only wanted to be a little bit together.

MK. And according to our tradition.

AO. The services, sure. In this part of Washington Heights, there were only a few synagogues. One synagogue in our neighborhood was very much neglected. They had only twenty-five members left. And the other was very reformed, and we wanted to have a traditional orthodox service. So in 1938, we founded this congregation, the Gemeinde of Washington Heights. We started at the Audubon Hall [on 166th Street and Broadway, where Malcolm X was shot in 1965] and were there for one year. [My parents became early members and my mother and Mrs. Oppenheimer became friends.] More and more people joined because they really enjoyed being together with their own people. Nobody thought that one person was better than the other because we all came out of the same background and the same experience. Even if somebody had a little bit more money, he didn't show it. So this congregation really started to be a home for them. The synagogue was like a meeting place where you met your friends from all over, even people you hadn't seen for years, and you spoke your own language. Of course, this congregation was for religious purposes but it was also a social get-together.

We started with a Hebrew school [of which my father was named principal], and we bought a cemetery right away and made arrangements with funeral homes, because at that time people were very poor and this was a big expense for them. We thought we would make it easier for them, so we made all these arrangements. After one year the congregation split and part of it stayed at the Audubon Hall and the other part, our part, moved to the basement of the Washington Heights Congregation. The second year we changed the name to Congregation Ahavath Torah, which means "love of Torah." This showed our conviction to be more strictly orthodox than before.

First we had a few cantors, and a few rabbis from the other side who gave us speeches on Saturday mornings. One day we decided that we wanted to have our own rabbi, but he wasn't a rabbi, he was only a cantor and his name was Herman Lieber. So he conducted the service. We got a second teacher, Mr. Klein, from Hamburg. Eventually, the Hebrew school had about two hundred children.

SELF-HELP

AO. Our social work started. In the first place we found that we needed English lessons, so I was very happy to find two teachers, free of charge, and we conducted classes twice a week in my apartment for thirty-five to forty people. The people didn't have to pay anything. The only thing we told them was, "If you can afford it, become a member of our synagogue." Most of them became members later.

[As people began to earn money, they donated more to the congregation, which grew stronger as a result.]

AO. Then we started with clothing distribution. We had a *Kleiderkammer*, a special room for clothing. We were the only congregation that did that. At that time, people were still allowed to bring their good clothes with them from Germany and, of course, it was understandable that they brought only good clothes. But since they had to work on the lowest level in America, doing housework for example, they needed work clothes. So we established this office, a room where everybody could come on a Sunday morning and get clothing. We were lucky to find people who had lived a long time in America and gave us this clothing. And everybody accepted it because it was necessary.

I remember one incident on a very cold winter day, when your mother and I were there, as we were every Sunday. My mother, Mrs. Freda August, who was the president of the sisterhood, was also in the building, and when she went to look for her coat, a warm winter coat, she couldn't find it anywhere. Then we realized that Henny and I had given it to somebody! [Laughs.] It was our policy never to write down any names, because it was very hard for these people to take charity. They were very proud. They didn't want to depend on charity even though they were willing to do any work on the lowest level.

The congregation had many speakers to acquaint our members with the American way of life. My husband and I had started a newspaper, the *Jewish Way*. It was founded to preserve Jewish tradition, Jewish religion, and to acquaint people with the American way of life. It was written partly in German and partly in English, but mostly in German. We had some famous writers.

MK. When you were in Germany, were you involved in these sorts of activities? Were you connected in the same kind of way to a congregation or was your husband a leader?

AO. No, no, he had plenty to do with the factories. I only wrote a few articles in Germany for some newspapers.

MK. Why did you assume all those new responsibilities?

AO. We did not start off as poor as some other people. My husband always said, "We were not saved to think only about ourselves. We are saved in order to think about others." That really was his motto. He said, "It is not right that people as good as ourselves had to die in concentration camps, and we were saved. We weren't better. So we have to do something." He really meant it. It was my philosophy too that we wanted to help others who couldn't help themselves and ease the life of more unfortunate people.

MK. So all this was new?

AO. All new.

MK. How did you know how to do it?

AO. I don't know.

MK. How did your husband and you get your training in that kind of social leadership?

AO. I don't know, I couldn't describe it. We had to do something.

MK. But how did you know how to start a newspaper?

AO. First we had only a small congregation pamphlet and then we bought this *Jewish Way* from another person.

MK. And so you learned as you were doing it?

AO. We learned as we were doing it. My husband was the business-man and he was more interested in the business side and I was more in-terested in the editorial.

MK. How did it feel to take on these new activities?

AO. I didn't think; it came naturally. You were so thankful to be here that you had to do something. [This was a time when you didn't take anything for granted and were grateful for everything. It was an exhila-rating time for many.]

ATTITUDE TOWARD AMERICA

AO. During the war our young men enlisted in the army and went overseas. A few of them were killed. Their names are still on a special honorary plaque in the synagogue. The congregation gave blood many times. I still have a picture of the group, about fifty or sixty people. We wanted to do what we could to help America because it gave us a new life.

I must say I felt at home in America and I was fortunate to meet peo-ple who really helped me to do my social work. As I told you, I found teachers free of charge, and I found people who gave us apartments when they moved out and left furniture there. I didn't need it, I had brought already so much furniture from Germany—at that time it was allowed. But other people who didn't have furniture were very glad about this, of course.

Everybody had sometimes a bad experience. German Jews were not so well liked by all American people. Some Americans hated to hear the German language. The German Jews sat in the cafés for hours with a cup of coffee and Americans were not used to it, but that's the Euro-pean way of life.

MK. They didn't tip too well, either.

AO. This I don't know. But they sat in the cafés for a long time because people couldn't afford to go places.

[In 1981 when I was filming *We Were So Beloved,* I took my crew to lunch at the Unicorn Café in Fort Tryon Park. On the outdoor tables there were discreet signs urging people not to linger overlong so that others might use the table. The sound technician asked whether this was a ploy to reduce the time Hispanics and blacks were seen at the café. I told him no, it was directed at the German Jews who would sit for hours over a cup of coffee.]

AO. The congregation sponsored very nice excursions for the people, and we had very nice Purim and Hanukkah parties, and our youth group even put on plays. The congregation grew together like one family. Everybody was happy there because it was a place where they were well-liked. They were among themselves.

MK. But everybody also worked very hard.

AO. Everybody was working hard. I had also an employment agency free of charge. This is how I got connected with American employers. [Mrs. Oppenheimer says that the example of hard work set by the German refugees was a model for my generation, which also worked very hard to make something of itself, with many achieving a great deal.] Today I meet on the street ladies whose husbands are big lawyers or doctors, or professors. These people started with household employment for thirty-five cents an hour at that time, or they were babysitting, or something like this. They made ten dollars a week, maybe. That was not very much to live on with children.

꧁꧂

Bert Kirchheimer

My father very soon became an enthusiastic Manhattanite. He went to the piers often, especially when a ship was arriving. As natives of Bremerhaven, the large port city, the Kirchheimers were crazy about ships. In New York they were finally able to see those liners that had sailed from Hamburg rather than from their hometown.

In 1942, when the SS Normandie *burned at its berth in the Hudson River, my father was plunged into deep mourning. He and his three brothers spent the entire afternoon and evening at the dock, watching the death of the great liner, frustrated that they could not take a last picture of it since, as German nationals or "enemy aliens," they had to give up their cameras at the start of the war. My father knew every detail of the exterior and interior of the* Normandie *as he did about every other great ship. Once, long after the war, he came home in a high dudgeon because a woman at a pier had mistaken the* Caronia *for the* Mauretania. *The night the* Normandie *finally toppled, mainly because of the weight of the water that had been pumped into her, my father caught the first cold he'd had since childhood. I remember him bemoaning the fact that his camera had been confiscated, almost as though he might have saved the ship by seizing it on film.*

In Germany, Papa was not religious at all, though his father was orthodox, albeit somewhat unconventional with his Sabbath flute-playing. Papa often had to work on Saturdays in Germany; his brothers never went to synagogue. My mother, who was more religious, sang in the choir at the liberal synagogue in Saarbrücken.

After their arrival in America, they began to attend services in various congregations in Washington Heights but were eager to find a more permanent place where they could be members. They joined the congregation started by Mr. and Mrs. Oppenheimer at Audubon Hall, led by Rabbi Max Koppel. The split in the congregation referred to by Mrs. Oppenheimer was precipitated by a dispute between Rabbi Koppel and Mr. Oppenheimer, which culminated in either a fist-fight or a wrestling match (accounts differ). My family joined the breakaway congregation.

Although the German Jews had not been, as a whole, especially religious, here in Washington Heights more than a dozen new congregations were established by the refugees, many of whom found renewed faith in their religion. At one point, there was a total of twenty-nine congregations in the neighborhood.

GENTILES WHO HELPED JEWS

MK. If the situation had been reversed in Germany, would you have hidden Jews the way some gentiles did?

BK. I couldn't do it. I wouldn't. Because I'm sort of a coward. I never would have done it. Because of the danger of it. Because I'm a man who is afraid of everything.

MK. How do you feel about the gentiles who did it?

BK. Terrific. It's wonderful. They are real heroes, those who did it. Those were real heroes. Think of Mr. Wallenberg. [Raoul Wallenberg, the Swedish diplomat who saved thousands of Jewish lives, disappeared in January 1945. It was rumored that he was imprisoned by the Soviets and died in 1947 in a Soviet prison, but this was never confirmed.]

Many religious German Christians did it. Especially the Catholics. Many were church people, especially in France, and Italy too. I don't know so much about the ones in Germany.

MK. Oh, but they did it in Germany.

BK. Of course. In Berlin, I know that. Holland, France. I'm sure there are plenty of those people. After the war, the stories came out. There were many heroes. It was the most dangerous thing to do, to hide Jewish people.

MK. You've never been in such a situation. How do you know how you would have acted?

BK. I know. Because by nature, I'm a coward. I'm afraid of everything. That's the reason I would never have done it. I thought of saving my family, first, and my relatives. I would never have taken in any other Jews and hidden them in my own house. I have to admit that I'm not a hero in this situation. I would have done the same as the German gentiles, just turn the other way and be quiet about it.

[In contrast to his life in Germany, Papa became active in synagogue affairs. When asked if he became more religious in the United States, Papa says yes, "out of gratitude" for having escaped from Germany, and out of respect for his parents. Also, he wanted to be sure that his son received a religious education.

This may have backfired when my revered grandfather died in 1942 and I decided to carry on the tradition in his stead and become orthodox. At age eleven I was going to be the standard-bearer for the rest of the family. Overnight my parents had to conform to my standards of orthodoxy. My father pointed out that one of the consequences would be a prohibition against eating hot dogs at Yankee Stadium and I have to confess that my fortitude was briefly shaken. My mother converted our home into a kosher one. My father surely knew he risked my disapproval if I found him smoking on the Sabbath. Or worse, discovering that he had sneaked out of the house to travel downtown to attend an event he simply could not miss—more than likely it would be the funeral of a celebrity. It could not have been easy for my parents to live with a righteous adolescent. In my third year of college I gave up religion.

The move to Washington Heights in 1942 was exhilarating for my mother. "At that time, life began," she says. Surrounded by friends, active in the synagogue as a volunteer in its many activities, including the Sunday clothing exchange, she was completely at home. She later became vice president of the sisterhood. There were constant get-togethers, roof parties, and picnics at Interstate Park across the Hudson River, reached by ferry.

I asked my mother how she reconciled the Holocaust with the role of God. Her answer was that God is a higher being who does not interfere with personal matters. God is someone you believe in but on whom you do not make demands. In her personal prayers, she thanked God for having given her a good day.

And if it wasn't a good day (she was sick a good deal of the time): "If you're sick, then you pray to get well."

What about all the Jews who were not sheltered, who could not say, "God was watching out for me"? One should not look too deeply into these questions, my mother said, because then conflicts will arise.]

MAKING A LIVING

MK. What was different for you in the United States?

BK. It was a free life. Everybody was nice to me. Germans are stiffer in their behavior. And arrogant.

MK. Anything negative?

BK. I wasn't immediately successful. But I kept trying and eventually I made it.

MK. You said you were confident that you would work here. Didn't you bring anything over that you could sell, just in case you weren't able to find a job right away?

BK. Oh sure. I brought over some display fixtures for windows. I was the agent for the manufacturer. He was not Jewish. These were brand new ideas. And some special liquid color—magic fluid—it was used in Germany just for quick advertising and for window displays. You could cover it later with color. But this didn't sell much because people didn't want to buy German products. And, of course, I brought all my drawings from Germany.

I started freelancing, with cartoons. I sold to the leading magazines: *Collier's, Journal American.* To them I sold a whole Sunday page of cartoons in August or September 1936. They were German gags that my brother Herbert translated into English for me. Later on, *Collier's* gave me ideas to illustrate, about fifty, sixty cartoons. I sold one to the *Saturday Evening Post,* to the *German American Heritage,* and other places.

After that I did graphics. Packaging designs. I designed the first logo for Revlon. I designed wrapping paper for Elizabeth Arden and some ads for Estée Lauder and *Vogue* magazine. Also the packaging for Ideal Toys.

[Although he was a well-known cartoonist in Germany, in the United States my father was just another struggling commercial artist. This loss of prominence did not seem to bother him at all. He worked for a display company finishing sketches for ads and also worked briefly for an advertising agency but was fired when he cut a piece of artwork incorrectly. For a while he was doing designs for birdcages for a company in Brooklyn, "every kind of bird you can imagine." He had the unfortunate experience of being swindled by an agent who was handling some of his cartoons, selling them and "neglecting" to inform my father. In 1941 he was recommended to *Forbes* magazine and worked for them for forty years, freelancing, doing covers, drawings, and layouts. He always undercharged his customers, as I was constantly pointing out to him from the time I was twelve.

In August 1944, in the middle of the war, he received a letter from the U.S. Office of War Information (OWI) summoning him to their office on 57th Street in Manhattan.]

BK. How they got my address I don't know. They asked me if I was interested in doing some intelligence work for the government. They asked me if I had traveled to other German cities just before coming to the United States. They were interested in finding out where aircraft were being built. I knew about an underground plane factory in Braunschweig and I told them about it. They knew I was from Bremerhaven and they wanted to know if I knew anything about the Bremerhaven ports. They already had maps of the city but they wanted me to confirm exactly where the harbors were.

MK. Did you give them everything they wanted?

BK. Not really, no. I thought, "It's dangerous," and I refused to answer any more questions. They wanted to bomb the city but they wanted to know *where* to bomb it in order to save the harbors. They already knew they would win the war and wanted to be able to use the harbors for landing.

MK. Why didn't you tell them everything they wanted to know?

BK. Because I had a strange feeling about it. Somehow I felt like a traitor. Inside, I thought, maybe I'll tell them. But I wasn't sure.

MK. Why did you feel like a traitor?

BK. Because I was born in Bremerhaven. It was my hometown. I felt a little sorry maybe about having my hometown destroyed. My mother was buried there. I felt strange about it and later I refused to work for them. I didn't want it on my conscience that I helped destroy my hometown, but I was very happy later to hear it was bombed by the Allies. As far as I was concerned, they didn't destroy Germany enough, but I didn't want to help them do it. Later, after the war when I went back to Bremerhaven for a visit, I thought to myself, "If only they knew . . ."

꙰

Sary Lieber

The Lieber family arrived in America in May 1939 and stayed with relatives in Paterson, New Jersey, for a couple of months. They were curious about New York City and somewhat apprehensive. Their information was based on a talk given in Hamburg by a rabbi from Mannheim, Max Grunewald, in which he described New York in the most negative terms: dark, devoid of sunshine and trees, filled with depressing tall buildings. The most immediate problem was finding work for Rabbi Lieber, preferably outside of New York City. (At this time he had not yet been ordained as a rabbi.) Almost immediately he was offered a position with a Toledo, Ohio, congregation, which he declined because the congregation was not orthodox. For a while, in order to earn some money, Rabbi Lieber sold stockings as a traveling salesman for another German Jewish refugee. But when he became aware of the poor quality of the stockings he gave up the job. He and his wife also sold Jewish newspapers to local stores but that did not last.

SL. We heard that some German immigrants had started a new congregation in the basement of a synagogue in Washington Heights at 161st Street between Broadway and Amsterdam Avenues. Upstairs there was an older established American orthodox congregation. My husband applied for a job and they auditioned him and they liked him. But they said there are other people who have applied, we have to hear them too. But in the end they hired him at five dollars a week for reading the Torah, praying, singing as a cantor, speaking as a rabbi, teaching (he started the Hebrew school immediately), and visiting the sick. He was doing all the things that either a cantor does alone or a rabbi does alone or a teacher. He did all these things together for five dollars a week and after about a year or so, he was raised to seven dollars and fifty cents.

[Prior to their move into an apartment of their own in Washington Heights, the Liebers rented a room from a family for eleven dollars a month, which seemed like a great deal of money to them. For refugees who had moved into large apartments, renting out rooms was a way of supplementing their incomes. The man of the house worked as a dishwasher to earn a living. The Liebers' hosts were extremely thrifty people: You were not allowed to open the refrigerator for only one item, but had to wait until two or three were needed. This was done to save electricity.]

SL. The war broke out and people started to get married and we were quite busy with weddings. Everybody wanted to get married quickly, before they were drafted [and sent overseas to fight]. Most of the weddings were in our apartment on 161st Street. Sometimes we had three or four weddings in one day, three on a Saturday night or four on a Sunday afternoon. People were sometimes waiting in the lobby for their turn. There was room for about twenty or twenty-five people, and we set up chairs and we had a *chupa* [wedding canopy]. We set up a sweet table in the dining room. The whole thing cost them about twenty dollars, including renting the apartment, the rabbi's services, and the sweet table.

MK. That was a lot of money for the people then.

SL. It was still a bargain, even at that time. Nobody expected to get rich on a wedding. And the young people who came here alone didn't have their parents so nobody tried to get rich on that. At that time there were lots of empty apartments. [Landlords were so eager to rent out their apartments that they were offering concessions of two or three months of rent-free living to prospective tenants.] We lived in 1F and the whole F line up to the sixth floor was empty. With the landlord's permission, we set up sweet tables on the second, third, fourth floor. Everywhere there was a sweet table. A wedding at eleven o'clock, reception on the second floor at twelve, and so on.

My children were four, five years old and they were the bridesmaids or flower girls from one wedding to the other, and finally it came to a point where they refused to do it anymore. We had to bribe them to do it. [Blond Susie was apparently no longer the docile toddler who was enlisted by her mother to charm the French consular official into issuing the family a transit visa.]

[Efforts to obtain affidavits of support for friends and relatives in Germany continued unabated. A friend of the Liebers from Hamburg, a Dr. Wertheimer, asked the Liebers to contact a wealthy relative in Brooklyn who had not responded to any appeals for help. Mrs. Lieber traveled to Brooklyn to an elegant town house where the door was opened by a butler. She asked to see Mr. Loew and explained the reason for her visit. He refused to see her and suggested that if she had any business to transact with him, she do so at his office. Undaunted, she went to his office the next day, where, she says, he was in the middle of a board meeting. Evidently impressed by her fearlessness, he admitted in front of his board that he was ashamed of the way he had behaved the previous day. "She can get whatever she wants," he said. They took a cab to HIAS where he provided the needed affidavit immediately for Dr. Wertheimer (who later became my family doctor). Loew made Mrs. Lieber promise that whenever she needed anything, she should go to him. She was also able to obtain an affidavit from him for her sister. Mr. Loew owned an ice cream company, and for years after, he sent the family big cans of chocolate powder and milk powder.

Mrs. Lieber also applied for an affidavit to Arthur Sulzberger, the owner of the *New York Times*, on behalf of her sister-in-law who had been married to a Sulzberger. A financial affidavit for someone with the same last name as the guarantor was the most advantageous kind, but Mr. Sulzberger refused, on the grounds that anyone could claim to be a relative. The Liebers also tried to buy Cuban visas for Rabbi Lieber's mother, his sister, and her two children, but it was too late, and they all perished eventually.]

SL. Our congregation was in the basement of the older synagogue and kept on growing. People came from as far down as 145th Street. The upstairs congregation did not like the idea of the Germans downstairs growing and becoming more powerful (or so they thought). [Mrs. Lieber says that a number of Germans belonged to the upstairs group and wished to become Americanized as rapidly as possible.] You see, when the German Jews came to America they were not welcomed by other Jews. There was an open hostility. They didn't like the German Jews. [One explanation she offers is that many eastern Jews had suffered discrimination by German Jews while in Germany and their resentment had carried over into their attitudes in America.]

One Sabbath, the downstairs congregants arrived for a service and found the doors to the Holy Ark locked. The upstairs people had locked it. There was big excitement. My husband said, "Hold it, wait."

At a certain point, he goes upstairs to the other congregation, walks into the service taking place, opens their Ark, takes out the Torah, and marches out. The situation was saved.

[Rabbi Lieber's congregation grew to such an extent that it rented a hall on top of a supermarket on Amsterdam Avenue between 160th and 161st Street. A sizable Hebrew school was also established there. When Amsterdam Avenue became unsafe, the Hebrew school was shifted to the Lieber apartment. Eventually the congregation had enough money to buy an entire building, the Costello movie house on Fort Washington Avenue between 159th and 160th Street.]

MK. Were you very involved with the congregation?

SL. As far as being active as the rabbi's wife, I really wasn't. I took part in everything but I was not the active person there. The active person was Alice Oppenheimer and the women around her. She had a whole group of women, like your mother and a few others. The sisterhood was extremely active under Mrs. Oppenheimer's leadership.

MK. Did you feel isolated because you were Swiss?

SL. No.

MK. So you immediately made friends? And did you feel comfortable in the community?

SL. I was much younger than everybody else. I was by far the youngest. When I was complaining to this friend of mine that I have some enemies in the congregation and I don't know why, I never did anything to them, she said, "If you were an old *miese rebbetzin* [homely rabbi's wife] you would be very well liked"! So there was a sort of generation gap. Among the German immigrants of this congregation, nobody had small children like we had. It was a middle-aged group.

MK. What were your feelings about it during those early years? Was it difficult for you?

SL. I always liked what I was doing. Whenever I did something, I did it wholeheartedly. I was at my husband's side. My husband was much older than I was. So there too I was so much younger. I didn't really fit in.

MK. How did that affect you? You're saying it very objectively, that you didn't really quite fit, you had some enemies or some people who didn't care for you, and you became aware of that—

SL. Yes, I was aware of that. I remember one particular incident. Nobody made a lot of money at that time. Some made a little more, some made a little less. We bought a new chair, which was twenty dollars, for our living room. And we were afraid to tell people that we bought a new chair. We said we got the new chair from the person who gave us the affidavit in order not to make the other people jealous that we bought a new chair, which we really needed.

Quite a few years later, my husband bought me a pearl necklace, and I was told that they made bets—"Is it real or is it not real?"—when I came to shul with it. I always had to hold back with everything to be the modest rabbi's wife, not to outshine anybody else. I had to keep a low profile, as they say today.

Melitta and Walter Hess

With ninety dollars in their pockets, the Hess family—Oskar, Melitta (Melly), and their three children—arrived in New York in 1940 from Ecuador and immediately went to stay with a family in Washington Heights.

MH. It was during the last days of Pesach [Passover]. The kids got matzohs. They were full of joy. We stayed with Katinka Rosenberg and she gave us to eat. It was really family, like coming home to your own people.

[After ten days, the Hesses moved to a fifth-floor walk-up in the same building. They were able to pay their first month's rent of forty-five dollars and bought secondhand furniture "with bedbugs."]

MH. My husband had a slip of paper. It said, "I'm looking for work. I have three children to support." And he went wherever he was told to go. He worked unloading barges for a few months at the docks in Brooklyn. Then he went to work as a dishwasher at the Eclair [the pastry shop–café on West 72nd Street that was a magnet for émigré intellectuals and more affluent refugees].

One day, it was the eve of Yom Kippur, they asked him to deliver a package. He fell asleep on the subway and missed the station, 86th Street. So he brought the package home to 159th Street. He had something to eat and was going to shul. My mother was very religious, so I said to him, "Don't mention anything, but when you and Oma are in synagogue, I will deliver the stuff."

I was pregnant with Frankie, and Peter was three. So when Oskar was gone I took the package and went with Peter and delivered it to West End Avenue. The lady opened it and looked inside and one of the petit fours was broken. She was furious.

MK. Was that your fault?

MH. Maybe I shook it. *Nebish* [big deal]. I was pregnant, I had one kid on one arm and the package in my hand.

The woman said, "Tomorrow I'll go to Eclair and tell them."

I said, "Please don't do that. We just came a year and a half ago to this country and we depend on that job." She didn't say anything and I went home.

MK. What was so important about one petit four being broken? How many people were there?

MH. "I invited twelve people" and now she had only eleven and three-quarters! *[Laughter.]* When *I* invite twelve people, I have thirteen pieces, not twelve. I didn't tell my husband everything. On Monday morning when he went to work the woman was already there, talking to the owner. The boss said to Oskar, "Don't bother changing, you are fired." And he was fired. West End Jews . . .

[Both Mr. and Mrs. Hess took on different kinds of work in their struggle to support the family. One of Mr. Hess's earliest jobs was as a "kitchen butcher" at a hotel in Long Beach, Long Island. The owner quickly noted, "You are a kitchen butcher like I am a shoemaker," but he kept him on because he was honest and reliable. The arrangement called for him to remain there for the three or four months of the summer season, with occasional visits from his family. On one such visit, they had brought food along and were picnicking on the beach. The owner saw them and said to Mr. Hess, "You are the biggest schlemiel I know. Take them into the dining room and let them have a meal."]

WH. We were afraid to go inside.

MH. Oskar wouldn't take anything that didn't belong to him.

[Eventually, Mr. Hess was taken into a house-painting business. Mrs. Hess worked at a variety of low-paying jobs, cleaning house and scrubbing floors all over New York City, often traveling for hours on the subway. She also worked as a cook in a local kindergarten organized by the Jewish service organization Help and Reconstruction.]

MH. I washed floors, washed dishes for other people. I went to Queens, I went to the Bronx. I got twenty-five cents an hour.

[Pregnant with her last child, she fell asleep on the subway one Friday evening, returning from her job in Queens, and ended up in the Bronx. Her distraught husband who was watching for her on the street had notified the police. It was, after all, Sabbath eve. When Mrs. Hess returned home, two and a half hours late, she was greeted by a great commotion in front of her apartment building. Her eighty-year-old mother reacted to her arrival by slapping her across the face.]

MK. How do you compare the way children and parents relate to each other here and in Germany?

MH. I can tell you a funny story. Frankie, my youngest son, came home from school and told me a joke that was—not so clean. So I said, "Frankie, that's a good one. I'm going to have to tell that to Papa tonight." Then he said "Mama! Don't you have more respect for Papa than to tell him such a joke?" *[Laughs loudly.]*

MK. But he had told it to you!

MH. Yes . . . *[still laughing].* So there was respect but not like in Germany. It was more *Kameradschaft* [friendship, cameraderie].

MK. Is that better or not as good?

MH. Better! We were friends. There was trust between parents and children. Another thing happened in the Bronx. The lady said, "If you come to me, I'll give you thirty cents an hour." So I went there and worked twelve hours. She had some silver to clean. I cleaned it as well as I could, but I didn't read [the instructions saying] that I had to wet the sponge first. So in the evening when she paid me, she said, "I can see you are not an experienced cleaning woman. You didn't clean the silver right." And I didn't fluff the cushions on the couch. So she gave me only twenty-five cents. What could I do? I was glad to get even that.

[She was also employed by a family of German Jews who had come to Washington Heights in the 1920s. Being pregnant and suffering from heartburn she found it difficult to bend over.]

MH. When I finished for the day, the woman said, "Mary, today you didn't do such a good job. You didn't get on your knees, you didn't do the corners."

MK. Why did she call you Mary?

MH. She said "Mary" and I didn't care. Maybe the woman she had before was Mary.

WH. So all cleaning women were Mary?

MH. It was not so easy. Today, I couldn't do it anymore.

MK. Did you always come home bright and cheerful?

MH. When I was home and the kids were OK and my husband was home, I was happy for that.

[Mrs. Hess always maintained that as long as they were healthy and she could work, they would manage, even though they had very little money. One Passover she had bought all the provisions for the week and was left with three cents. She went to the synagogue, opened her prayer book to the "prayer in time of plenty," and began to recite it. Her sister who was sitting next to her thought she was mad. Mrs. Hess responded that she had everything at home with three cents left over, and therefore felt very rich.]

MH. I remember one terrible thing. A friend of ours from Rup-pichteroth offered me a job cleaning house for fifty cents an hour. I took it although my husband didn't want me to. He didn't like the people much. I worked there maybe four, five weeks, and all of a sudden I got a letter from my in-laws in Germany. They were upset that I was clean-ing house for people who used to work for us in Germany. [Her in-laws did not know the kind of work Mrs. Hess had been doing.]

MK. How did your in-laws find out?

MH. Those guys wrote to Ruppichteroth: "Our cleaning woman is Melly Hess." And after they did that, they let me go.

MK. So the whole purpose was to let them know in Germany so that they could be superior to you?

MH. Yes.

WH. How did you feel doing housework for other people? It's not something you were used to doing.

MH. It didn't bother me. I made an honest buck. Then I couldn't go on working when Frankie was born. That was in May 1941. We were still seven people in the house [the Hesses, four children, and Mrs. Hess's mother]. We managed all the time. We didn't take the subway, we walked when we could. And we didn't go to Warner's cafeteria, we drank our coffee at home. If we had a little money, we lived on a little money; if we had a little bit more, we spent a little bit more.

[Even the children pitched in. At one time they worked at home cleaning old zippers, separating them from the cloth that clung to them. The zippers were supplied by someone who collected old trousers.]

COMMUNITY SUPPORT

[Three weeks before their last child was born in 1941, the Hesses re-ceived an urgent request from Mr. Hess's parents in Germany for a thousand dollars to pay their passage to America. With three hundred dollars of their own money and the rest borrowed, they were able to raise the amount needed and sent it off. When Frank Hess was born

(Franklin, named after FDR) they had a grand total of fourteen dollars and some change. As it happened, Mr. Hess's parents never made it to America.]

MK. Was the community helpful when Frank was born, in terms of donating equipment and baby clothing?

MH. My sister gave us a carriage. We couldn't shlep it up five flights so we kept it downstairs. After three days the carriage was stolen. So Oskar asked the superintendents of the houses where he worked as a painter if anybody had a carriage. All of a sudden he ended up with five, six carriages *[laughs]*. And he sold them again. We made money on the carriages *[laughs]*. [Word got around among the women that Mrs. Hess was in need of baby clothes and other supplies.] One of the women was Mrs. Kirchheimer, your mother. She still had Manfred's diapers.

MK. That's me!

MH. She gave me the diapers.

MK. You mean she brought the diapers from Germany?

MH. Yes, yes! Your diapers. [The two women did not know each other at that time.] I got sick and your aunt Annie came and helped in the house like a mother's helper. All of a sudden, Annie saw the diapers with the monogram and she said, "Oh gosh, I know those diapers. They are from my sister." Frankie grew up in your diapers.

MK. Monogrammed diapers? *[Laughs.]* Unbelievable! [Mrs. Hess, my mother, and my aunt remained close friends and card-playing partners.]

OVERCOMING OBSTACLES

[Mr. Hess had become a housepainter and gradually began to earn more money.]

MH. At first he didn't know anything. In Germany he couldn't step on a ladder. He couldn't push a nail in the wall.

WH. My father had vertigo and they would send him up on a scaffold, five stories up to paint outside the windows. [Walter Hess speculates that his father's experience in the concentration camp contributed to his fears in general.]

MH. He was well liked all over and later he started his own painting company.

WH. I think his great dream was to get the contract to paint the George Washington Bridge.

Rosi Spier

A social worker in Berlin, Rosi Spier was a divorced mother with a young son when she came to America in February 1939. Her first child, a daughter, had died at an early age. Much of the time in Germany and then at first in America, she was unable to have her son live with her because of the kinds of jobs that were open to her. She worked for a time taking care of a camp director's child in Vermont while her son was living in New York. Through a connection to the Warburg family, she was able to arrange for her brother's emigration to America.

MK. What happened when you returned from Vermont?

RS. I was a companion to a mentally sick lady. She had paranoia—schizophrenia. She accused me all day long of stealing things from her.

MK. What type of woman was this? An American Jewish woman?

RS. No. She was from a famous Jewish family in Germany, the Sondheimers. She was Dr. Albert Sondheimer's wife. She must have been a beauty in her youth. To take such a job was a challenge to me for two reasons. I'm always interested in psychology and what's going on in people, but also the job paid sixty dollars a month, where other people made thirty dollars. But she made me see a psychiatrist. She accused me of having kleptomania *[laughs]*. That was part of her sickness. She said "You know, Miss Spier, I like you so much. I know you suffer from migraine headaches, I will send you to a doctor for treatment." She tried to make me believe that was the main reason.

[When Mrs. Spier saw the doctor for the first time, he immediately understood the situation and said that she could not be expected to subject herself to this pretense.]

RS. I said, "If I can help her and if you can calm her down by telling her you are treating me for my migraine headaches, that's OK."

[Doctor and "patient" agreed that it was not necessary for Mrs. Spier to actually come to his office again.]

RS. The doctor said to me, "Tell her that I saw you and you can describe me and I can describe you."

Well, this job was a big strain on my nerves, but I went. I was something like a maid, a governess, companion, all in one. She lived on West 81st Street, in the Beresford Building [overlooking Central Park] on the fourteenth floor.

And the elevator man always said to me, "Mrs. Spier, how can you stand it?"

I said, "I know she's sick so I treat her as sick."

FOUNDING A SCHOOL

[Mrs. Spier's brother was living in Washington Heights on 180th Street. She suggested that, together, they start a kindergarten in the neighborhood. (He had been the director of a Jewish high school in Hamburg.) He would supervise the older children and she would work with the youngest ones. In 1942, Mrs. Spier moved into the apartment that housed the school at 436 Fort Washington Avenue. The space was being rented from Help and Reconstruction, the Jewish welfare organization.]

RS. My son came to live with me and his life began to become normal. He had his room there in the kindergarten, the isolation room for the children when they got sick. So when that boy came home from school, he threw his books down in the room and went out and played. He had no real room like other people. [When other children were sick, they had to use that room.] How can a boy like that grow up normally? But he did. He must have had some backbone.

I was with the children till five o'clock. I washed the floors every afternoon when they left, and went to college at night. I went first to Bank Street College. I needed sixty-eight more credits, or something like that. In order to be the head of the kindergarten, to be accredited by the state, I had to go there.

MK. When you and your brother started the kindergarten on your own, did you apply to the community for help?

RS. No. Both my brother and I were not capable of asking for money from the people who had struggled. But we couldn't make a living because we were not business people, so this organization that had started one kindergarten at 95th Street then took over ours. They made me an employee there. With my kindergarten, three others opened in the neighborhood. We had a total of four.

MK. The children were all German Jewish refugee children?

RS. All of them. There was a need for such a kindergarten because their parents, the mothers, went to work and the children had to be taken care of. And we were open from nine to five. I even had children from eight o'clock on.

[Mrs. Spier remained at the school until she retired in 1970.]

MK. Was it still German Jewish children or had the composition changed by then?

RS. Mostly German Jewish, but we also had American children. We had some Americans who wanted to go to work and the school filled their needs. But then we couldn't go on anymore because we were subsidized by United Help and we had to prove that it was still only Jewish children, refugee children, and we couldn't prove that anymore.

CHARACTER OF THE
GERMAN JEWISH POPULATION

MK. How would you characterize the . . . specialness of this community? Or *was* it special?

RS. They were special because I think the German people are very ambitious and overly correct and also . . . bringing up children was a bit too strict. I'll give you an example: I saw an American mother on the street with her child who was crying. The mother did not get so upset like a German mother would. She called, "OK, Alan, you come or you don't come." And she walked on and the child followed. And I give that as an example: Don't be so excited. Don't be such a disciplinarian. Don't be so strict.

I had a very nice letter from two psychiatrists who had their children in our kindergarten, who said, "That was an exceptional kindergarten." Number one, all of our teachers were like one family. And the people had confidence in us. The children felt good with that. The German people have many qualities, as I said: You can depend on them, they are solid people but also in many ways narrow-minded. I felt that when I was still a child. I had not yet seen America.

MK. Can you give an example of the narrow-mindednes.

RS. *[Pauses.]* A part of this is that people do not understand each other and criticize each other for little things. And I always say, maybe the Americans do this too? They judge people, distrust people. For instance, if I have a girl [cleaning woman] in my apartment, I have it open and I don't think she takes things from me. Most Germans would be very careful that nothing gets taken, and they are suspicious too.

[Mrs. Spier describes the children of the refugees as being very ambitious and hardworking.]

RS. Most of them studied. They wanted to be on a higher level than their parents were. They wanted to be part of America and they wanted to be good Americans.

[Although few of the older generation had gone to college themselves, many were able to send their children on to higher education with the financial cushion provided by postwar reparations from Germany.]

LOYALTY AND CRITICISM

MK. The German Jews wanted to be good Germans. What's the difference between our generation's—or even your generation's—nationalism or assimilation here and there?

RS. This is really something I ask myself very often. I'm a good American, but I don't know whether I'm first a Jew. I am, of course, afraid for Israel. That something happens. It's my real country, my home. But I want to obey American laws. I want to contribute to the welfare of America. I am aware of what happened in Germany. We were the best Germans, but in spite of it, it happened to us. I have not lost my feeling for the country that opened up its borders for me. But even so, I am critical. At the time of Roosevelt, many other Jews could have been saved. They could have admitted more people. They would not have had to be killed.

MK. And there are things that America has done in recent times that are not so wonderful either.

RS. Right. We became in the last few years more critical toward America because of the leaders and because of their attitude toward Israel now [1981]. They would not, I am sure, be so much interested in Israel if it wasn't for their own good.

MK. Of course.

RS. They must stay interested because we are the only democracy there. I always tell my friends, "Don't be afraid, nothing happens to Israel." First of all, I believe that they are very strong. They have intelligence. And second, I say, America cannot let us fall. But deep down, if they wouldn't need us, I'm sure they could say, "To hell with the Jews." That's my feeling.

Max Frankel

Max Frankel was able to leave Germany with his mother, whose courage and audacity gained her an audience with the Kommandant at Gestapo headquarters in Berlin. The officer was obviously so taken with her that he wrote out two exit permits for her and her son. Mr. Frankel, however, had been sent from Poland to Siberia by the Russians as an alleged German spy. Mrs. Frankel and her son arrived in New York on Washington's birthday, February 22, 1940.

WASHINGTON HEIGHTS

MF. We moved in with relatives in Brooklyn for three months. My mother wanted to move to Washington Heights because she wanted to be among friends. She felt more comfortable up there. They were giving rent concessions because of the Depression. I don't know what it was then—six months or something like that. It was a congenial neighborhood for her. It was not for me. No problem about the neighborhood and the schools and the friends I made. But I had a thing about becoming American. This full-time association with refugees seemed to me a step back from acculturation. From the day I landed I wouldn't talk German to my mother. She talked German to me but I would reply in English.

I learned baseball within two weeks in Brooklyn. I never realized how intense this was at the time. Looking back on it as I grew older, I realized that I never even dated a refugee girl. I suspect that, as time passed, that's why I even shopped, subconsciously, for a high school out of the neighborhood. I played ball with everybody, I hung out on the streets all day because Mother went to work, and I felt perfectly comfortable and at ease in the neighborhood. But there was something less than fully American about it, and I think that unconsciously this bothered me. I was an assimilationist.

MK. How did those ideas get fixed so fast, when you were just ten?

MF. I don't know. If you want to get Freudian about it, I guess that from age six there had been this uprooting. When I was seven, we were kicked out of Germany. I learned Polish, I went to a Polish-speaking school, devoted myself fully to that. And within nine months, that was yanked away, and we found ourselves back in Germany. While we were in Berlin, struggling to get out, I could no longer go to the regular public schools and my mother put me into a Jewish-run school. Now I had to learn Hebrew to get by in the schools. Six months after that, I landed in New York, allegedly the promised land.

My guess is, I just said, "Well, damn it, if this is going to be it, it's going to be it 100 percent." I remember thinking very hard that I could grow up without an accent. That was very important to me. I wanted to be a super-duper American. I remember fights with all my parents' friends who found this or that to criticize in New York. Everything was fine for me.

MK. German Jews criticized New York a lot?

MF. Of course.

MK. There is a word for these people: *Bei-Unsniks*. [*Laughter.* The term can be loosely translated as Back-home-niks].

MF. There was also a fair amount of prejudice against us.

MK. On the part of Americans?

MF. On the part of Jews who had been here twenty years longer: "Why don't you go back where you came from?" That was sounding in my ears for many, many months after we got here and I resented it deeply.

MK. So, by the time I met you in 1942—

MF. At P.S. 169! [the local public school.]

MK. You may be the one who taught me baseball!

MF. Could be. I never remembered you having an accent, so you must have gotten past that.

MK. I got past it very quickly. I came here when I was five. People who came over when they were eight or older still retain something of an accent sometimes.

MF. I've made an informal study, just an eyeball study, an anecdotal study. People between eight and twelve have a chance to get rid of the accent, depending on how important it is, or how much of the two languages they speak, or how they speak at home. Past twelve, almost no one can fully lose it, I have found. Like Henry Kissinger, whom I've met. It may not be very heavy, but the trace is there. After twelve it seems impossible to lose it altogether. The shock of course was to be told, not too many years after that, that I had an English accent in German! *[Laughs.]*

But I found Washington Heights a marvelous neighborhood. I remember it was very rich in debate. You could even stand on second base in the middle of a game of "curb ball" and suddenly find yourself in a deep argument about who was running for Congress. Yes, it was a very rich neighborhood.

There was fear and tension across Broadway, when you moved up into the Irish neighborhoods, toward Amsterdam Avenue and the gangs. We should say that the gangs in those days meant that they come with stockings full of chalk or something and bop you over the head. There was only an occasional knife. And then beyond Amsterdam Avenue, there were blacks with whom I had some traumatic episodes later on in junior high school. Stitt Junior High. I left Stitt because of a big problem. But on our side of Broadway it was very comfortable. We had the Boy Scout troop, the Hebrew Tabernacle where I went for Hebrew lessons, and "The Wall" [overlooking Riverside Drive] where I hung out at night and met my girlfriends. It was very comfortable and pleasant and convenient. I learned the New York subway system and got around town quickly. Broadway was the great cultural dividing line.

MK. One side was virtually all German Jews, with a smattering of American Jews, and the other side was Irish.

MF. That's right. I left Washington Heights to go to the High School of Music and Art instead of George Washington High School, which was the neighborhood school. This refugee thing may have had something to do with it, but I was quite serious about wanting to be an artist. I would draw for many hours on end, and it was a serious career ambition, briefly interrupted by some people whom I'd met in North Carolina who tried to get me into an opera singing career *[laughs]. That was dead serious.* I toyed with those two things, but then in the middle of high school, things changed because of a rather odd and brilliant English teacher who noticed that I was doing brilliantly in every subject except English—and the only problem I was having was in reading.

She confronted me with the fact that I was faking my reading and wasn't doing it. When she finally forced me to confess, she said, "Is this because you didn't grow up reading English, or is there another problem?" She was being very sympathetic. The problem for me was simply that I read very slowly. I don't know if that would have been true if it had been my native language or not. To this day I don't know. I am still a relatively slow reader. Anyway, she said, "Look, I run the journalism class in this school and your English grades aren't good enough to get into it, but I'll make an exception because I think that the only way to get you to read is to get you interested in writing." And the minute I hit that journalism class I started sneaking out of art class to go to work on the newspaper.

And loved it. I decided right then and there that I was going to go into newspaper work. And never left. Chose my college [Columbia] because it had a good daily newspaper, spent most of my hours at college on the newspaper. I was lucky enough to get a job working for the *Times* while at college and never let go until I worked my way in. I was always interested in international affairs and you know, even when I was an artist, I drew a lot of maps. Maps were very big in World War II and they were big for somebody who came from there and whose father was over there and it was all part of my life. Borders, visas, were a great part of the youthful experience.

In high school I wrote a column called "Globalisms," about international affairs. In college I got interested in American government and political science and took a regular liberal arts degree, but a master's degree in politics.

ASSIMILATION

MF. Our immigration was rather unusual as a whole. It was a group of people who—while they were leaving under compulsion, so to speak—were going lock, stock, and barrel in many cases. Many had a very comfortable journey, well greased. They were either able to trade their belongings into cash or, in many cases, able to get their belongings over here. They would come, if not with the whole family, in large family groups. They came with friends and/or relatives ready to receive them, with a neighborhood staked out, a place where they could feel comfortable, not learning the language for a year or two, with people to take them by the hand and, if not get them the same kinds of jobs in businesses they were used to in the old country, at least show them the ropes of this new society.

Even in the late 1930s, just before we came, although times were tough, people who were willing to work—and this was a hard-working puritan German-ethic kind of population—these people could make their way. And they did, very quickly. I think the very fact that they were so critical of so many things here reflected the fact that they felt very much at home here and were already taking on the aspects of citizenship. Attitudes changed a little bit through the war when the last waves of immigrants were really in a more desperate category. I mean, my mother and I among them . . . We really did get out by the skin of our teeth, and we were a little contemptuous of some of the money-grubbing complaints that we would hear on all sides. But I think the whole community very quickly realized both the horror that was beginning to unfold over in Europe and what it is we'd been saved from.

I think in my own case (but I would dare to generalize), the result is that a fundamental optimism was preserved in a group that nonetheless had its share of trauma and relocation. It's certainly a group that's smart enough to know how things work, and once you get a little money in America you very quickly bump into more money. And you realize, when you have more money, what true money represents in this society.

I don't mean that there is a Panglossian view that all is right with the world. I think they're pretty shrewd, but they are hard-working people who feel that, by dint of their own efforts, a decent life can be staked out. I think that's a fundamentally optimistic attitude and I find it in myself. I think it differs from some of the kind of hysterical, grieving, deep pessimism that I've seen among many of the earliest waves of East European Jews, for instance. I don't know whether it's the fact that they were peasant stock to begin with and were not yet urbanized and were thrust too quickly into an urban and industrial society, or whether there's something more deeply cultural in the Russian and Polish soul—

MK. —there is a class difference—

MF. And there is a class difference, and there was socialism that was encrusted into the culture of the eastern Europeans.

MK. And not knowing how to assimilate.

MF. That's right. It would make a fascinating study. I can't pretend to have made it, but my instinctive feeling is that we were not just a more *contented* group in Washington Heights than in many other such types of refugee neighborhoods, but fundamentally a more optimistic one.

MK. That's really interesting. Here was this group in the middle of the war, hearing day after day about who was lost. Sometimes they didn't hear till the end, but they were on tenterhooks throughout the war. And yet you and I remember the stable, calm, unnervous neighborhood.

MF. It focuses the mind when, in the end, all that's important is that you have a chance to breathe freely and a chance to earn your daily bread. Then the fact that the slipcovers on the sofa are soiling or the windows are broken or the garbage isn't being picked up on time . . . you develop a remarkable sense of perspective about life as to what matters and what doesn't *[laughter]*.

MK. There are a lot of German Jews who are—

MF. Fusspots!

MK. What would you say is the essential difference, or is there one, between German Jews and Germans of the same class?

MF. I think German Jews were very German. There weren't that many differences, and I think many of them would have been loyal German citizens if they had been allowed to be. I think I would have been. As I told you, I felt greatly deprived when I couldn't march in the Hitler Youth parades at age six. I was a prime candidate for being a good little German if they'd only had me.

MK. Taking that one step further, being a good little German can be OK. Why shouldn't everyone be a good little—whatever—in their country?

MF. Right.

MK. Except that it's not OK if what the country is doing is atrocious.

MF. Of course.

MK. Let me ask you then: Why did these good little Germans—who, if circumstances had been different, might have included good little German Jews—why did they in such masses perpetrate these horrors?

MF. You are asking the question that dogs my life. I don't know, but one of the things I am most grateful for is that I was never tested. That, without any choice, I was put on the side of the good people, the suffering people, the wronged people, the murdered people . . . but that I did not have to choose which side I was going to be on.

I was able to see something of Russia, very shortly after Stalin's death. It was still full of the horrors of Stalin's time. And in that society, in a different but no more admirable way, tens of millions of people made their peace with what they knew, just as the Germans did. We knew this German here, and that German there, who could be touched on the personal level and still make sure that even as you were being expelled it was done with dignity, or even as you were being allowed to escape it was done with a sarcastic joke but a human gesture.

I always had this argument with American Jews when I first came here, and later they wouldn't buy a Volkswagen or they wouldn't do this or that, they were going to demonstrate against Germany. And only if you've been through it, at least if you're lucky enough to have escaped—my grandparents didn't and we left lots of corpses behind— but if you escaped, you have to escape with a sense that there are Germans and there are Germans.

How would any society behave if put to that extreme test? Certainly when we lived through the McCarthy era in our country . . . in no sense comparable, of course; I don't even want to begin to equate the few political and economic horrors committed in America with concentration camps and death chambers . . . all I want to show is that with penalties much fewer than any exacted by Hitler in Germany, with the social opprobrium on protest much less, there were very few Americans who were willing to stick their necks out to help a neighbor who got into trouble.

All I'm saying is that, under a truly totalitarian circumstance, when a country really falls into the hands of hoodlums who are willing to stop at nothing and therefore everybody in the community is being tested as to which side are you on? and are you willing to put your life on the line for decency? I would hate to be tested. And I'd hate to see my own country, which I regard as the United States, being tested. So yes, I am harsh in my judgment of Germany, but I regard Germans as also unfortunate for having fallen into a test that they failed as a society.

❧ Hilde Kracko

After fourteen turbulent years in Bolivia, the Kracko family arrived in Texas in 1953, their immigration aided by people they did not even know who had provided the necessary affidavit of support. They remained in Texas for two and a half years. Life there was particularly difficult for Mr. Kracko.

MK. Was it hard for you too?

HK. It was very hard. There was nothing for my husband to do. I learned to sew. I had never seen a sewing machine and I tried, believe me. But I made thirty dollars a week and I brought home twenty-seven fifty. I learned to sew emblems. I never will forget that. So that we had to eat. My husband couldn't really earn anything. But we lived. And then it was too hot for us. And also there were no Jewish people in this town. We were thirty miles away from Dallas. We were not religious, but you want your child to grow up with the tradition.

We tried to do what we could. We drove her every Sunday to Dallas to Temple Emmanuel and she went to Sunday school there.

[With the help of an affidavit from the Krackos, Mrs. Kracko's sister and brother-in-law came to Texas from Bolivia, but soon after, they moved to New York.]

HK. They wrote about how nice it is to meet so many people. And so we took the car and hired a U-Haul and left Texas. We made the trip to New York in two and a half days. That was in April 1956. When we left Texas it was very hot and we came into a snowstorm in New York.

[Some friends who had been in Bolivia had rented a furnished apartment for the Krackos on 172nd Street where they lived for four months. They subsequently moved to a fourth-floor walk-up apartment on Nagel Avenue. Later, in 1973 they moved to Fort Washington Avenue and 187th Street where Mrs. Kracko still lives.]

HK. Right away we were at home. We were around our own people. Nobody could understand it when we said, "You don't know what it means." You know, New York is not America. You have to go west or south and you can see the difference. It was like coming home. We met people we hadn't seen for a long time. People we knew in Bolivia came to see us, and some from our old town. All the friends and the little bit of family came to greet us. It gave us a very good and homey feeling. And everybody was helping. I met only nice people.

A job was waiting for my husband already. [Like many other German Jewish refugees, Mr. Kracko was given a job at Klein's department store.]

When we came, people said, "You don't know how good you have it. When we came in 1938 it was awful." Now they had the union and everything.

[Mr. Kracko enjoyed his work at Klein's because it brought him into contact with people, and he declined an office position there. He remained at Klein's until his retirement at the age of sixty-nine.]

HK. When everybody says New York is awful, I still say, "Don't say that. I love New York." For me it is home. When you come from where we came from—from Texas—then you see the difference. When we saw the food here! There we traveled thirty miles to get a loaf of rye bread. Down there they say they wouldn't come to New York for anything in the world and I wouldn't go down there for anything in the world. People look at me when I say I love New York.

RESTITUTION

[Soon after her arrival in New York, Mrs. Kracko found a job at the United Restitution Office (URO), the agency charged with processing claims against the German government by those who had suffered under the Nazis. The German term is *Wiedergutmachung* (literally "making good again").

Under legislation passed in 1952 by the Federal Republic of Germany, restitution to some of the victims of Nazism had been established. The URO had begun operations in 1949 when legislation was first called for in West Germany to compensate the victims of Nazi crimes.]

MK. It's a very different kind of job from what you ever had before, isn't it?

HK. You know, we all had to muddle through. As long as you could make a living . . . When I got engaged and we couldn't stay in Germany, my husband didn't have a business anymore. And he still said to me,

"You will never have to work" *[laughs]*. But I am not complaining. [Mrs. Kracko's mother-in-law who was eighty-four when they came from Texas to New York stayed at home and so was able to be there when the Krackos' daughter came home from school at lunchtime.] I like working. I could retire already but I don't want to. We helped a lot of people.

Mostly they were poor people who came out of the concentration camps. Polish people and German, Romanian, Hungarian, all kinds. They were all very poor. They could not afford to hire a lawyer. We helped them get the restitution from the German government. Sometimes it took a long time. You know from your parents how long it sometimes took to get the money. People suffered a lot of damage to their health, they lost their business, and so on. There are still poor people who suffered a lot in concentration camps.

Later they had to get used to everything and it was very difficult. They worked in sweatshops and they had families. And they were not the healthiest people. They still have nervous breakdowns and claims for damage to their health.

There was a time when we couldn't take all the people who applied. Whoever could afford a private lawyer, we would not take. They had to tell us their income. We are a nonprofit organization and the fees were very low. Some people didn't like to pay. And then it didn't go fast enough. We had one gentleman who came one day and he was desperate for the money. He thought we had the money and wouldn't give it to him. But we don't distribute the money. It comes from Germany. And he said, "If you don't give me the money I'm going to jump out the window," and he was already standing on the windowsill. We convinced him to come back. We said we would call the police. What could we do? You know, they are in a mental state sometimes.

We suffer a lot with the people. They still come and tell me the same stories all over again. There is an old lady who comes to me every year. She has to make out the form proving that she's still alive so she can get the checks from Germany. I make that out for her and then she shows me pictures of her children and her husband whom she lost. She tells me that one day she wanted to go out and the inmates in the same bunk with her tried to hold her back. Then she went out and she saw her son and her husband hanging from the tree.

[The terms of the German reparation law require the government to pay restitution until there are no more claims, or until all the survivors have died out.]

HK. I see the pension checks we send back to Germany every month, when people die. It always hurts me to see and to have to send them back.

[When Mrs. Kracko joined the URO there were from 160 to 180 employees. At the time of this conversation in 1981, there was a staff of 25 and their activities were primarily concerned with assisting the new Russian Jewish immigrants. A number of Mrs. Kracko's coworkers had also suffered under the Nazis. One man had already made it to Ellis Island—within sight of the towers of Manhattan—and was returned to Holland because of some irregularity in his papers. This was in 1939 or 1940. He spent time in eight concentration camps and was now, in 1981, the administrator of the URO.]

HK. These stories you hear over the years . . . Whatever they get can never make good what the people suffered. I didn't suffer. We moved a lot but I didn't suffer that way.

⚜

Siegfried Kirchheimer

Two and a half years after my uncle Siegfried arrived, my aunt Martha was able to come to the United States with their remaining three children. Her trip had taken her from Drieburg to Frankfurt, Saarbrücken, Paris, and Spain, and eventually to Lisbon where the family boarded a freighter that brought them to New York in March 1941. Had they waited any longer, it might have been impossible for them to leave Germany since emigration for German Jews was cut off by the Nazis in October of that year.

SK. Martha had not a very nice time together with her parents and sister and brother-in-law and the children. They all disappeared, you know. Finally she succeeded in leaving.

MK. During the time that she was in Germany, after you left, was she or the children molested?

SK. No, never molested. But they couldn't do what they wanted to do. They hardly could go on the street. Friends of theirs took care of them. They brought them something to eat and so on.

MK. What about school? Did the children go to school?

SK. Oh yes. The younger ones were sent to school in Detmold and they lived there in a pension. It was not a real school. It was formed only to teach Jewish children who couldn't go to the regular schools anymore. My son Hans was in Dortmund to learn a trade. He wanted to be a metalworker or something like that.

MK. What was it like for you in America, aside from not knowing if you would see Martha again?

SK. Lore [the eldest daughter] found a good job very quickly in a household, because they liked Jewish girls. It was not so good for me so fast. Because I didn't think of taking the examinations again. I was so sick and tired of all the medicine—*medizinerei.* I didn't want it anymore. Already in Germany I had so much trouble with my doctors, my colleagues. They made my life very hard there too. They didn't like me as a doctor or especially as a Jewish doctor. And then because I always had my practice with the so-called small people. And I had a good practice. So the doctors didn't like me.

I didn't want to go through all this again—studying again. Medicine was different here, of course. You had to learn new things. I couldn't use what I learned in Germany, in the German medical schools and so on. I did not feel like starting from the beginning again, so to speak.

MK. How old were you at that time?

SK. Forty-eight, forty-nine. Yes, that was also hard for me. I had a cousin in the hospital that was attached to the home for the aged on 106th Street. And there I worked as a night orderly. I took care of the patients too.

They had house doctors who said, "Why don't you become a doctor since you were one before? Maybe they would respect you more."

I said, "I don't need respect. I take care of sick people and that is enough for me." I had plenty to do with them. Believe me.

MK. So those doctors were friendly, they encouraged you?

SK. Sure they did. But I wasn't interested in that anymore. And I am a man who can do any work. I was never afraid of doing the dirty work. The first four weeks I was a porter in that home. I had to clean up the stairs every morning, clean out the toilets, and all that stuff. But

I didn't mind. I had a job. For almost fifteen years I was there.

MK. Did you ever regret giving up your medical career?

SK. No, no, no. Not at all.

[Unlike my uncle, all the doctors my family knew in Washington Heights had learned English and undergone retraining. One physician worked first as a salesman for a medical supply company and then took a job in a sanitarium for mental patients outside the city, coming into New York once a week for an English course. A number of German Jewish doctors who were already established gave preparatory courses to incoming refugees so they could take the board examination. Some of these were held in rented quarters at the Amalgamated Union Hall at Union Square. There, recent arrivals from Germany studied previous examinations and were thoroughly drilled in the U.S. medical system.

My uncle, on the other hand, always insisted that he enjoyed his work as a night orderly because it gave him the opportunity to work on his memoirs and correspondence, set down in a minuscule hand from one edge of the page to the other. That was something he really loved to do.]

MK. Later on, did you ever meet or speak to former patients who were gentile, who left you during the Hitler time? Did you ever have occasion to meet them again by accident?

SK. No, not directly. Only by writing to them, through my correspondence. They still love me there. They wrote long letters in the local papers, letters about me, and on my ninetieth birthday, they had a big article in the paper. On my wedding anniversary two years ago they had a big story in the papers in Bremerhaven. In Drieburg I was mentioned. Here, the *New York Staatszeitung* had a long article about me.

[Siegfried's voluminous correspondence was legendary in our family. He managed to establish relations by mail with all sorts of notables in Europe, with former prewar patients, even with European royalty. His praise of all things German, however, did not extend to actually traveling there. He was frequently invited to his hometown of Bremerhaven, all expenses to be paid by the mayor's office, but he always declined. He would tell us that there was so much to see and do in New York, and that his correspondence filled so much of his time that he did not see the need to travel. In his nineties, after his wife Martha died, he established a liaison via the mails with an elderly German widow.]

SK. I had visitors from Germany.

MK. Not Jewish?

SK. Not Jewish. I have no Jewish friends anymore. I never liked them anyhow. I didn't care for them.

MK. What do you mean you didn't like the Jewish friends?

SK. You know I am a cosmopolitan. I don't care for any religion. Maybe you know it, maybe you don't know it.

MK. I do know it. But you said you didn't care for the Jewish friends.

SK. I had none anymore. Otherwise I would have cared, maybe. But there is nobody left. Nobody left. All my friends are non-Jewish.

MK. The ones in Europe?

SK. In Germany. Mostly in Germany.

MK. Now these friends you speak of . . . There were instances—for example, the smashing of your windows and other things—where the gentiles were not "nice." Those were terrible people. They were Nazis.

SK. They were Nazis.

MK. Or not actual Nazis.

SK. Well, you know, you were forced sometimes to be Nazis. You know how that was.

MK. But you're not forced to smash windows.

SK. That's right. Those were special Nazis.

MK. OK.

SK. They were glad to follow the leader.

MK. Now those who were your friends—were they people who continued to be true to you before you left Germany? Before 1938?

SK. I had no friends left in Wolfenbüttel. They all were in concentration camps or were dead already.

MK. I'm talking about the gentile friends that you correspond with today, the ones you knew before, before you left.

SK. Yes. They resumed after the fall of the Third Reich. And they found me again. But before that time nobody could write to me. I mean nobody. I had no connection with anybody.

MK. I'm asking whether, when you were still in Wolfenbüttel up to 1938, some gentiles remained friendly with you.

SK. I don't remember any. Not even the neighbors. At least they didn't show it. My neighbors, some of them, liked me very much because we were neighbors. They had their own house beside my house and so we said hello together but they were afraid to be seen together with me. But inside themselves, maybe they were still friends of mine but they couldn't show it anymore.

MK. Did anybody ever give you a tip, like saying you were in danger and should get out?

SK. No, no.

MK. What about the opposite? Did anyone betray you?

SK. No, not directly. Not that I can say.

[Siegfried may have forgotten a story I heard from my father. Among his medical specialties, my uncle was known to perform abortions, which were then illegal, but he did it out of principle. One of his patients was married to an extremely jealous husband and had become pregnant by another man and my uncle performed the abortion. This occurred in the 1920s. Several years later, as an émigré in New York, the woman let it be known to sympathizers to the Nazi cause that a Jewish doctor in Wolfenbüttel was fouling Aryan womanhood. Clearly she was still worried that her husband would find out about her earlier infidelity. The message went through channels and reached its destination. A German officer in Wolfenbüttel who was having his arm set by Siegfried—his family doctor for twenty years—warned him that he was in imminent danger and suggested that he prepare to leave the country.

Once in the United States, Siegfried was visited by the selfsame jealous husband who, still ignorant of his wife's activities, was eager to engage him again as the family doctor. My uncle who was no longer licensed (nor ever would be) put him off with the excuse that he did not want any difficulties with the authorities.]

MK. Some of the people you write to today were people you knew then?

SK. Yes. Neighbors from my street.

MK. The people who were afraid to talk to you at that time. But now you talk, you correspond with them. Did they ever explain what happened?

SK. No they didn't. You know most of them were young people. I didn't have much connection to them anyhow. We knew each other from the street where we lived but that was all. They were more my children's friends than mine, because they had nothing to do directly with me. But later on they found me. Especially through Lore's correspondence with them. They were all school friends. They got to know me again and now they are very good friends of mine, all of them.

MK. In America, you've lived either just on the edge of the Jewish community or now, in these last years, in the middle of it. How do you explain it?

SK. Most of the people I had to deal with in the home for the aged were German refugees or Yiddish-speaking people. I never had much chance to speak with the Americans. That's why my language is not so good. I still love my *geliebtes Deutsch* [beloved German], as Goethe says. When the children are here we speak German together, and with friends of mine. I don't have many friends here. I don't even want to have any here because they're not my kind. I am an outsider in many ways.

MK. Do you think you would be an outsider wherever you lived? Or just in this particular place?

SK. In any place at all. I hardly go out anymore because I don't like to meet people. You know the most dumb questions are, How are you? and How do you feel? and all this doesn't give me anything.

MK. So, what do you think the reason is that you live in Washington Heights?

SK. It's by accident. I like it here in many ways because it's quieter. As I said I don't care much for people. When I moved in here, I thought maybe there are people here in the house I can talk to in my own way. There's almost nobody. So I don't care for anybody. I say hello to everybody. They say hello to me, "Wie geht's?" [How are you getting along?]

I say, "Auf zwei Beinen immer noch am besten" [On two legs. It's still the best way].

I have a lot of interests, you know. And the terrible thing is that I have no time for them. Almost every day I write three or four letters, long ones, not short ones. So the days fly away like nothing. Every day is filled.

Louis Kampf

My contemporary, Louis Kampf, had gone from Austria to Belgium, and then to a spa town in France, where he and his mother were reunited with his father. They set out for Lisbon to get on board a Portuguese ship that would bring them to America, but as they approached Pau, they learned that the Spanish border had been closed. Lou's adventure—for such it was to him at eleven—then took him and his parents to Marseilles, and thence to Casablanca where, after a month or so, they boarded the ship that took them to America.

LK. We finally arrived in the United States in February 1942. We stayed in Brighton Beach for a month with my aunt and uncle, but then we moved to where some of our relatives lived, namely, Washington Heights. The three of us were in a single room at first and we shared the bathroom and kitchen with five other families.

[After about eight months the Kampfs were able to move to a one-bedroom apartment on West 162nd Street, close to the river.]

LK. And that's where I spent the rest of my childhood and adolescence until I left the roost.

Because there was some kind of guild for diamond workers in New York, my father had to go through a three-month unpaid apprenticeship in order to get his papers to work as a diamond polisher. My mother went to work in a garment factory for fourteen dollars a week and that's how we lived. They didn't earn much and life was always hard. I guess they moved from 162nd Street further uptown in Washington Heights in the mid-1960s because the old neighborhood had turned entirely Puerto Rican and black. They moved away from there because my father got mugged in the elevator. But then he also got mugged in the elevator in the building they had moved to, on Overlook Terrace.

POLITICAL AWAKENINGS

MK. You took an ideological road that was different from the mainstream followed by many of our generation from the neighborhood.

Bert Kirchheimer (left) and Siegfried Kirchheimer in the German army, World War I.

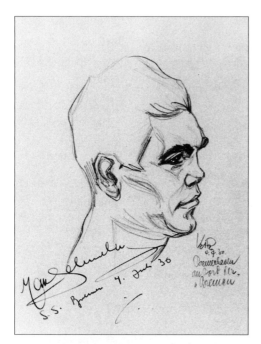

Max Schmeling, July 4, 1930, drawn on board the SS *Bremen* by Bert Kirchheimer, after Schmeling won the world heavyweight championship in New York.

Harry Liedke, film and stage actor. Caricature by Bert Kirchheimer.

Bremerhaven, 1911. The steamship *Kronprinzessin Cecilie*. Bert Kirchheimer is the boy who has turned to face the camera. Next to him are two of his brothers, Arnold and Herbert. Siegfried Kirchheimer, the eldest brother, is taking the picture.

Bremerhaven, August 1925. Left to right: Moses Kirchheimer ("Opa"), his son
Siegfried with Hans and Lore, Herbert Kirchheimer, and Caroline (Manfred
Kirchheimer's grandmother).

German nationalist and Nazi banners hanging from the apartment above the Kirchheimers at 23 Schmollerstrasse, Saarbrücken, 1935.

Illustration from a Nazi children's book. The accompanying text is entitled, "The Sabbath" and speaks of Izzie, who has come home on Friday, having swindled and lied to the gentiles. (From *Stürmer* publication *Trau Kein Fuchs*. Courtesy Leo Baeck Institute, New York)

Manfred Kirchheimer's mother with her sisters, July 1928. Left to right: Aunt Martha, Aunt Annie (Ostertag), Henny Stein, and Aunt Toni.

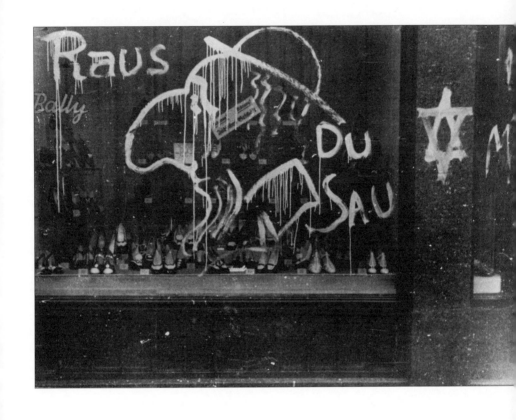

"Out, you swine!" Desecration of a Jewish shopwindow, Frankfurt, 1938.
(Courtesy Leo Baeck Institute, New York)

Hilde Kracko and her husband outside the Amsterdam city hall on their wedding day, 1938. (Courtesy Hilde Kracko)

Melitta Hess with her sons Walter (left), Peter, and Karl after Kristallnacht. Mr. Hess is in Dachau at this time. (Courtesy Melitta Hess)

Melitta and Walter Hess, 1982.

Burning synagogue, Baden-Baden. Kristallnacht, November 9–10, 1938. (Courtesy Leo Baeck Institute, New York)

Jewish men being paraded down the street in Baden-Baden on their way to a concentration camp after Kristallnacht, November 1938. (Courtesy Leo Baeck Institute, New York)

Illustration from a Nazi children's book. The caption says, "The Jewish nose is curved at the point. It looks like a '6'." (From *Stürmer* publication *Der Giftpilz*. Courtesy Leo Baeck Institute, New York)

Illustration from a Nazi children's book. The accompanying text begins "Now it will be nice in our schools/All the Jews must leave/The big ones and the small ones." (From *Stürmer* publication *Trau Kein Fuchs*. Courtesy Leo Baeck Institute, New York)

A group of congregants at a Red Cross blood donation center, 1944, the day
they gave blood (detail). Bert Kirchheimer (with mustache, top left), Rabbi
Lieber (second from right), Max Oppenheimer (light coat, right). Sary Lieber,
wearing a head scarf; next to her on the other side of the Red Cross flag, Alice
Oppenheimer.

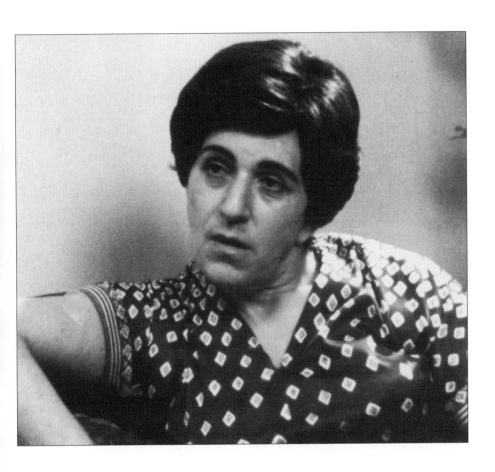

Ilse Kaufherr, 1981.

The young Max Frankel with his mother. (Courtesy Max Frankel)

Max Frankel in his office at the *New York Times*, 1982.

Rabbi Herman Lieber officiating at a wedding in an apartment in the Liebers' building during World War II. (Courtesy Sary Lieber)

The ocean liner *St. Louis,* carrying over nine hundred refugees from Europe, anchored off the coast of Cuba, June 1939. Small boats with Cuban police and soldiers surround the ship to pick up possible suicides. (Reprinted by permission of Dover Publications, from *The Great Luxury Liners, 1927–1954,* by William H. Miller Jr., 1981. Original photo from the Frank O. Braynard collection)

The young Louis Kampf with his parents. (Courtesy Louis Kampf)

Louis Kampf, 1982.

Ilse Marcus (holding dog) with her family in Germany. (Courtesy Ilse Marcus)

Ilse Marcus, 1982.

Jews gathered at an assembly point to await deportation from Frankfurt. (Courtesy Leo Baeck Institute, New York)

Group of Jews about to be deported to Theresienstadt from Frankfurt, 1942.
(Courtesy Leo Baeck Institute, New York)

Hans Rosen in Holland, 1946–1947. (Courtesy Hans Rosen)

Hans Steinitz in his office at the *Aufbau,* 1981.

Bert Kirchheimer with Lilo Lyon (later Kahn), right, and another friend in Saarbrücken, March 3, 1935, soon after the plebiscite that returned the area to Germany.

Gala dinner on board the SS *Manhattan*, April 1936. Manfred Kirchheimer with his parents on their way to America.

Friedel Heilbronner (left) with Lilo Kahn, Saarbrücken, 1991.

Manfred Kirchheimer, conducting an interview, 1981.

What were the beginnings of your political consciousness in Washington Heights?

LK. If I had to choose a particular incident, it would be something that happened when I was around fourteen years old. My mother sent me to a local delicatessen to pick up something. It was on Broadway between 162nd and 163rd Street, I think. I walked in and there was a black man there. Of course, the word was *colored* at that particular time. And he had bought something and he told the clerk that he had been shortchanged by a nickel.

The clerk insisted that no such thing had happened, and the black man said, "Look, I need that nickel, it's important to me, I'm poor."

Whereupon the guy said, "OK, have your nickel."

At that moment, two cops came storming in with brass knuckles on their hands and they just beat this guy into a living pulp. I mean there was blood all over the floor. They then dragged him out, bounced him up and down on the floor as they were dragging him, and his face had disappeared, it simply wasn't there anymore. And I stood there wondering, Isn't somebody going to say something about this? Isn't somebody going to say, "Stop, this is bad"?

Well, nobody did, and I couldn't believe it. I went home and I told my parents. And they simply shrugged their shoulders. I guess maybe they assumed I was making it up since things like that don't happen in America, they only happen on the "other side." And at that particular point I started to ask some questions about what the situation of blacks was in the United States. I started reading the newspaper the *PM*, which carried a lot of articles by I. F. Stone, and I started educating myself politically.

Why I stuck with that is difficult to say, but, for example, one of the first political events, you might say, that I got involved in was at George Washington High School. Since it was named after George Washington, all events were structured around the idea of the United States in colonial times and postcolonial times [the school newspaper was called the *Cherry Tree*].

MK. Right, I went there too.

LK. When we were seniors we wore little hatchets in our lapels, right? And there was an honor guard of girls for all important events, like graduations, who appeared in supposedly colonial robes. Sort of very elegant robes. And one day a couple of us were talking and we realized that there were no colored girls, as they were called then, in this particular honor guard. And we wondered whether we should inquire about this, since one-third of the student body was black. So we went to see the principal, Mr. B——. Mr. B—— was pretty drunk most of the time, you might remember. He used to come staggering out for assemblies. So we went to see him and fought off the breath coming from him and enveloping us.

I was the spokesperson and I said, "Well, Mr. B——, we came to ask you how come there are no colored girls on the honor guard."

And Mr. B—— looked at me in absolute amazement and he said, "Why, they were *slaves* in those days" *[laughs]*. Which left me kind of flabbergasted. What do you answer to a piece of idiocy like that? So we all trooped out and we started organizing a series of protests. We worked up a big petition. We saw that commonsense justice wasn't going to be effective with this particular guy. And we wound up being successful. That gave me a marvelous sense that political activity could maybe get you somewhere. But it also was just so enlightening.

From then on it was one series of fights after another. For example, against the fact that the school newspaper was censored, the fact that the high school administration tried to rig the student election for president, and so on. And I got involved with various political groups that existed at the time, none of which particularly pleased me. And I got more and more political until it reached the point, when I was about sixteen and had become quite left-wing, where my father and I constantly fought. My mother had to feed us separately. I mean, I came first and then my father came, and it's pretty much remained that way ever since, I'm afraid. *[Chuckles.]* I'm laughing about it but believe me, I don't feel it's a joke, I feel very sad about it.

ACTIVISM

[By the time Louis Kampf arrived at the Massachusetts Institute of Technology in Cambridge in 1958, the civil rights movement was at its peak. He participated in the demonstrations that were taking place in support of sit-ins in the South as well as in boycotts of stores such as Woolworths that were known to be segregated. These served to rekindle Kampf's activism. He also became involved with Students for a

Democratic Society (SDS) and antinuclear, anti-armaments activities, as well as efforts aimed at organizing poor communities to fight for their political rights.

With the advent of the Vietnam War, Lou became active in draft resistance, and in 1967 he became associate national director of Resist, an organization devoted to promoting support for draft resisters.]

LK. In 1968 there was a series of protests involved with the Modern Language Association (MLA), the professional organization I belong to, since I teach literature. We had decided to introduce a number of demands at the MLA: supporting draft resistance and opposing the [Vietnam] war, and so on. Eventually, in the process of handing out leaflets I wound up being arrested in a forceful way. You know, a house detective said, "I want you to take that poster down," and I stood in front of it like Jesus Christ and said, "No, I won't take that poster down." And the idiots arrested me. Of course, when they arrested me they assured my election as president of the organization. So, lo and behold, I was president of the MLA, which made my parents very proud, except that they weren't too proud about the events that led up to that.

It became a kind of focus of activity for academics in general because it raised the whole issue of what should be the primary thing in your life at a time like the Vietnam War when people were getting killed, enormous injustices were going on. Do you just keep your head stuck in the sand in your academic haven, or do you see that this is a matter of life and death? It was an important thing.

As far as people like my parents and others like them in Washington Heights, even though naturally I was disheartened by their reaction at the time of the Vietnam War, I also can understand very much what was going on. They were afraid. They had the experience of Nazi Germany, where fighting against a state in the mid- or late 1930s was out of the question. All it could mean at that particular point was winding up in a concentration camp, or being shot in the street, or being shoved off a roof by the Blackshirts. And there was that whole experience of diaspora Judaism whose lesson was that we were powerless and therefore we have to keep peace with the state, with those in authority. You can't fight them.

My father's position was that you never vote for a Jew for elective office because if you vote for a Jew, even if it's for governor (like Lehman, for example), you're just going to be in trouble, they're going to blame the Jews. So you had that mentality which told you: Stay out of it, keep out of trouble. Most of these folks were simply incapable of comprehending that the next generation maybe had enough confidence in itself to take certain risks, to take certain chances. Maybe the next generation learned the opposite lesson from the Nazi experience: If you're going to be stepped on and sent to a death camp, then maybe you are better off fighting against it and seeing to it that the injustice doesn't happen, then maybe you do have a chance. If that's the case, there really are two paths you can take. They're opposite polarities, the lessons that you can learn from that particular experience. I learned one lesson, my parents and people like them obviously learned another one.

MK. You talk about your parents as if they were one. Were your parents' attitudes the same?

LK. Not quite. My mother worked in a clothing factory when we first came over and she became aware very soon, for example, that women were discriminated against in her place of work, that she got less money for the same work. When the issue of women's liberation and feminism comes up, she'll say, for example, "I don't like the fact that the young rabbi who lives downstairs has to help take care of the children, that's no good." On the other hand, she'll go out and vote for Elizabeth Holtzman or Bella Abzug and be absolutely insistent that women should have equal rights and get equal opportunities. And she's very proud of the things my wife is doing, for example.

MK. While working in the garment center, did she have union experience and relations with other workers?

LK. The relationship with other women workers was much more important than the union experience because the International Ladies Garment Workers Union (ILGWU), which she belonged to, discriminated against women itself and didn't really care about the women. Whereas her fellow workers, old women or middle-aged women of Polish or Russian extraction who'd been through the battles, were enormously supportive. It really taught her something about solidarity, and it's a kind of experience my father never had. Therefore my mother was always much more sympathetic toward the kinds of things I was involved in until she really thought it was threatening. When the notion came up that maybe I could lose my job over this or when I started being attacked by the newspapers (the *New York Times* had an editorial attacking me), *that* became scary, and she started telling herself maybe people will go and kill him like they did Malcolm X or Martin Luther King, which was of course a wild fantasy but it was real to her.

THE AMERICAN DREAM

LK. Even though my father was an immigrant fairly late in life, what was still there [for him] was the whole notion of the American dream. You finally came to America, you've gone from Poland, Austria, Belgium. You've run, you come to the promised land, so to speak, where you can get rich, and so it's a land of opportunity. He never became rich himself. The few attempts he made at having his own enterprise in the diamond line cost him dearly. But still it was the land of opportunity and there was the hope that I would pick up at what he failed, that I would become a big success. I'm an only child and a son, to add to that.

So there is this terrific ambiguity. On the one hand, America had failed him, he hadn't made it, and also America became a very threatening place to him eventually. There were the blacks that he felt were threatening, the Hispanics who moved into Washington Heights. They were all objects of fear as far as he was concerned. On the other hand, there was the thought that you really could make it, and he always thought that it must have been his own fault that he didn't.

I was the great hope, the next generation. I was smart, I did well in school, I was enterprising, and there seemed to be every reason to believe that I would make it big. But as far as he was concerned, I took that great opportunity and I chucked it. My parents' dream would have been for me to go to medical school and become a brain surgeon and have a beautiful house out in Oyster Bay, and be the president of my synagogue, and so forth. Well, I didn't do that and that was a terrific disappointment for my father and he did feel betrayed by that. For example, he took whatever opportunity he could to try to compare me to Max Frankel, who is my contemporary in the neighborhood—we played on the same ball team together, and he became one of the bigwigs on the *New York Times.* Max and I stopped being friends in 1948. He went to Columbia University and he became a stringer for the *Times* when Eisenhower was the president of Columbia.

MK. That was the time of the Henry Wallace campaign.

[Wallace, former vice president under Roosevelt, ran for president as a third-party candidate in 1948 with an anti–cold war platform.]

LK. That's right. In 1948 there was kind of the last gasp of holding out against the cold war. In our neighborhood, for example, Paul O'Dwyer who was a Wallace supporter was running for Congress for the House of Representatives and I worked for him. His opponent, running on the Liberal party ticket, was Jacob Javits and Max supported him. That contributed to our parting of the ways.

Anyway, Max was the model of what you should be and I wasn't. Then there was the fear, the lesson learned because of Germany and Austria: You have something to be scared of, so you need to hide . . . and I wasn't hiding. That, of course, was seen as obstreperousness, some kind of craziness, and something done ultimately to hurt your parents. I think this was a fairly universal phenomenon in Washington Heights, parents wanting big important things for their children. Most of the children in fact tried to lead that kind of life and there were a few exceptions. As always, the exceptions are looked upon either as oddballs, "Commie-pinks," or bad children, or people who do things to hurt their parents. I think that attitude was fairly common.

MK. In the United States, was your father a patriot?

LK. He was somewhat patriotic. He was like any ordinary law-abiding citizen. He always assumed that if the government does something, there's got to be a reason for it.

ASSIMILATION

MK. Jews were very assimilated in Germany. Now they are probably assimilated here, the ones who came over. They're patriotic. Many have a totally uncritical attitude toward U.S. government policies.

LK. Let me tell you a silly anecdote. The first thing I felt I had to do when I came to the United States, in terms of assimilating, was to chew gum. So I went around chewing gum, even though a penny wasn't easy for me to come by. So I went around chomping all the time. And here I used to drink orange juice for breakfast. That made me American. Initially I rejected all the foods my mother cooked, and I went on the usual diet of frankfurters, and hamburgers, and shredded wheat, and so on, because that would make me American.

Now if you expand that to cultural and political matters, you wind up with gung ho patriotic Americans, whose motto is "USA, All the Way!" and who cares what happens? Now that's a negative aspect, but assimilation isn't entirely that negative. For Jews who came here from eastern Europe, many of whom were ignorant, practically illiterate, impoverished, whose culture was extremely narrow, being exposed to night school and reading the works of Melville and Whitman, and Goethe—learning the culture, becoming sure of themselves was a very positive thing. You don't want to be stuck in your ghetto mentality for your whole lifetime and generation after generation.

Assimilation here doesn't involve the dangers that existed in Germany simply because, for one thing, in the United States—it's horrible to say so—in terms of groups who are the official victims that everybody can spit on, there are blacks and Hispanics and they are much easier victims and targets than we are. They are much more numerous, they are more obvious, there is a much longer tradition of violent discrimination against them here. Not that for many years there wasn't an awful lot of discrimination against Jews in the United States. A lot of Jews who went to the Midwest and lived in small towns converted to one form or another of Protestantism and simply got lost as Jews.

ANTISEMITISM IN THE UNITED STATES

LK. When I got out of high school, it was almost impossible for a Jew to get into medical school. It was inconceivable to think of a Jew as being chief executive officer of DuPont, for example. Because you couldn't even get to third-level management at that particular time. The Harvard-Yale-Princeton English departments had no Jews at that time. Lionel Trilling, the famous literary critic, was the only Jew in the Columbia English department and it took him years to get tenure. And just simply in terms of day-to-day violence, in Washington Heights where I grew up there were constant battles with the Irish gangs and the antisemitic taunts.

Some of that still goes on, but there's less of it. Something that struck me when I was teaching a couple of years ago was the reaction to a book by Michael Gold called *Jews Without Money* [New York: Carroll and Graf, 1984]. One thing the kids said was, "I didn't know there are any Jews without money."

MK. You mean kids who were not Jewish?

LK. Yes. And even kids who were Jewish. I teach at an elite university and the students come from middle-class or upper-middle-class homes. The experiences described in the book about the kind of ghetto the author grew up in and the constant battles they had with either Italian or Irish-Catholic gangs were very foreign to their experience. It was almost unimaginable to them. All of them had heard people making antisemitic remarks as a joke, and they knew antisemitism existed to some degree, but it's not part of the culture anymore the way it was in Germany or in France. The way it is to some degree in France even now. That doesn't mean one should forget about it.

PART THREE

Left Behind

*Some of my neighbors did not reach America until years af-
ter the war had ended. With escape routes blocked, they were
trapped, shipped to concentration camps, separated from their
families, and (if they were spared the gas chambers) endured
forced labor, torture, starvation, and disease. Others spent
weeks, months, or years in hiding, always a few steps ahead of
the Gestapo. At the end of the war, some found themselves
leading a suspended existence in displaced persons' camps,
waiting for someone to find them. Others had taken up temporary residence in South America or Asia—anywhere that would
accept them.*

*Their relatives in Washington Heights, often new arrivals
themselves, were indefatigable in their efforts to raise money,
search out potential sponsors, and maintain contacts with consulates. News was sparse. Occasionally during the war a tele-*

gram from the Red Cross might locate a parent in a camp. Packages were sent abroad but there was no way of knowing whether they had been received. Word of deportations, concentration camps, and their attendant horrors reached our community but seldom through the newspapers. The children, myself included, had only a dim notion of the massive human destruction being perpetrated by the Nazis.

In our synagogue, memorial inscriptions painted in gilt characters would appear on the tinted windows attesting to a relative's death. With the end of the war, one read with ever-increasing frequency the names of loved ones and, in ghastly apposition, the names of the concentration camps—Auschwitz, Dachau, Theresienstadt, Mauthausen, Bergen-Belsen —where they perished.

⚜

Hans Rosen

Hilde Kracko's brother, Hans Rosen, was an active Zionist and had been part of a group of young people who were being trained to work in Palestine as farmers, mechanics, blacksmiths, and other trades. In November 1938, just prior to Kristallnacht, he was picked up in his hometown of Augsburg with others in his group and taken to Dachau. He remained there for a month. He was then twenty-two years old.

HR. You never forget what happens there. Every day you had the *Appel*, the roll call. And it was freezing. There was snow on the ground. And you were wearing only your pajamas. And I had shoes on but they didn't fit me. After I was released from Dachau, I had open frostbite. And besides that, I never forget when I had to make I think maybe seventy knee bends. And sometimes they were standing there in front of me. And if you do it too fast, you get a kick. Now, he was counting, "Deeper." But that was nothing. We were young, we could do that. We had food. In that time, you could have money sent from your parents. Maybe ten marks, I don't remember. You could go to the canteen. And buy something. What we bought was grape sugar for the energy. Of course I lost a lot of weight.

We had relatives in Holland. I had a brother-in-law who was Dutch and he had called the authorities. He made it possible for me to go to Holland. He had connections with the Zionist organization there. I had the possibility of learning a trade in Holland.

MK. When you first came out of Dachau, were you frightened?

HR. Of course. I couldn't sleep nights. The first night I woke up and I remembered that I had to report to the Gestapo. I was lucky to be going to Holland. From my hometown to the Dutch border is only half an hour or three-quarters of an hour by train. I didn't have a visa, a Dutch visa. My brother-in-law was waiting in Holland at the Dutch border with my visa. It was waiting for me there. When I was on the train from my hometown to the border, the SS came in, passport control. And my hair was shaved. They looked at my passport. And they said, "Where are you going?"

"To Holland."

"Where is your visa?"

I said, "My brother-in-law waits for me in Holland on the border."

And they told me, "No good." They took me out of the train with my luggage. The train went to Holland and I was standing on the platform.

After a while, the man gave my passport back and he told me, "Look, you can go. I'll let you go. You can go with the next train. If you come back, if the Dutch don't accept you, you know what happens to you?"

MK. And you understood what he meant?

HR. I understood I would go back to the concentration camp. But I was lucky. My brother-in-law was waiting for me at the border.

MK. And he really did have the visa?

HR. Yes.

MK. Why didn't he send the visa?

HR. I don't know.

MK. In those days, mail was fast.

HR. I could have picked it up at the Dutch consulate. But I didn't. I didn't know how. But he did it all. When I was standing there in Holland at the border, there were people, a couple. They sent them back.

[The Zionist organization arranged to have Mr. Rosen work as a mechanic and blacksmith for a German employer in a village just outside of Amsterdam.]

HR. My boss was an Aryan. He only took me because the movement paid him for my cost of living. I had to work and got nothing. He had cheap labor. He told everybody, "I got a German Jew working for me." It made an impression. The people, the farmers, came and looked at me as though I was the seventh wonder.

MK. They'd never seen a German Jew before?

HR. Right. [Mr. Rosen had been working there for half a year when the following incident took place.] We had been working, the boss and I, setting water pipes into the ground. It was lunchtime and we came home. I was hungry. I wanted to eat. In Europe this is when you usually have dinner—at noontime. The kitchen was next to the master bedroom. We came into the house. The boss's wife was taking a nap. And she yelled when she heard us coming in: "Everything is ready on the stove. Take your portions." OK, why not? He took his and I took mine. And I was looking around for a clean fork. I opened a drawer, looking for a clean fork. I didn't realize that in the meantime she opened her door. She was behind the door and was watching me. Then she told me, "You dirty Jew! It's not clean enough for you here?" And she hit me in the face. Now, I was not in a concentration camp anymore. That experience was behind me. But I found it there too. I was furious. The boss came between me and her. And he told me, "Get up!" [Go upstairs]. Now I was red, furious.

MK. Did you touch the woman? Did you hit her?

HR. No, I didn't. I was ready to do it but he came between us. Then I took my *Siebensachen*—my clothes and everything I had. At that time I had a bicycle and I went to the inspector for the Zionist organization and I told him what happened. So I wouldn't have to go back there. The organization was responsible to the Dutch government for each of us. If we did something wrong, they got blamed. Now the inspector told me, "I'll straighten it out. I'll go there."

I said, "Look, I am not a dog. I came here, I thought I was free. I came from Germany and have to get the same thing here too? I didn't expect that. And I won't go back."

He tried to convince me because it was very hard to get us placed.

I said, "I won't go back."

[Mr. Rosen bicycled to Amsterdam where his parents were living. Although he had been reported to the head of the organization, the inspector gave him a favorable report. After a couple of weeks he got another job with a blacksmith in the same neighborhood.]

HR. Something different happened over there. He was an excellent tradesman. But he was a drunkard. He didn't have much work, he had no credit. I had to bicycle twenty or thirty kilometers when he needed some iron to make horseshoes or if he needed something from the next city. He went out in the mornings [supposedly] to look for jobs. He gave me some work, a nice guy. But he was a drunkard. They were nice people, they treated me well. But they only kept me for the money. I was a bargain.

[While working there, Mr. Rosen made the acquaintance of an elderly Dutchman, the ex-mayor of a town, who brought his bicycle over for repairs. The blacksmith had told him about Mr. Rosen's history. The man said that there might come a time when he would need help and suggested that he contact him should the need arise.]

HR. This gentleman, he was seventy years old and he bicycled. I'll never forget. He had *rachmonis* [compassion].

One day—it was Christmas [1939] and New Year's—the boss said, "You can take vacation and come back after New Year's." He knew I had my parents in Amsterdam. I bicycled to Amsterdam, 120 kilometers.

I went to the head of the [Zionist] organization and he asked me, "How do you get along with your boss?"

"Good."

"Oh yes? A complaint about you came in."

[Someone had reported finding the blacksmith and Mr. Rosen dead drunk in a ditch. Rosen denied it.]

He said, "If this is true, we cannot keep you. We are responsible to the Dutch government and we don't want trouble. Go back there and sign out at the city hall and come back here."

I said, "Why not? I have nothing to worry about."

[Any move to another town had to be reported. Mr. Rosen's next job was in a factory in Delft where he was an apprentice in a machine shop. When the Germans invaded Holland in 1940, he was compelled to leave and go to one of the provinces where the Jews were still permitted to live. He went to Heligoland where there were other young Zionists. By 1942, Mr. Rosen's entire family was in Holland but conditions for the Jews had worsened. His older brother was summoned to report for transport to Germany. Rosen urged him to defy the order.]

HR. He said, "What chance do we have?"

I said, "I will call this man, this gentleman [the elderly ex-mayor], he will help us." You know, you could not take public transportation as a Jew. We already had the "J" for Jew [on their papers]. I called up the gentleman.

[They met in Amsterdam the following day. Rosen's brother had only about ten days left before he had to report for the transport. The man needed time to make arrangements for the brother's safety and that of Rosen, who expected to be summoned momentarily. He gave them an address, which was to be used only in an emergency and if they had heard nothing from him by the last day. No word came and on the last day, Hans Rosen went to the place where his brother was staying and told him that their only chance was to go to the address that had been given to them. Hans Rosen went there but no one answered. He went to his parents' place (his family was scattered around Amsterdam) and was told that a message had been left by their contact. He and his brother were to travel 120 kilometers to reach a safe place. As Jews, they could not travel by train because the Nazis patrolled them. Their only means of transportation was by bicycle.]

HR. In the morning I went back to my brother to tell him we could go but we had to figure out how to get there. But he wasn't home. He was gone. He had been living with a Dutch family. They told me, "Your brother went to friends to say goodbye." And I never saw my brother again. He left the same night on the transport to Germany.

[Mr. Rosen went immediately to his Dutch brother-in-law to borrow his bicycle. He covered the 120 kilometers in eight hours.]

HR. I could do that because I knew the way. I didn't have to ask anybody where to go. I had nothing, I took nothing, only a little change. I took the "J" off my papers. And I was blond.

In the meantime, you see everything. From far away, I saw people in the railroad yard crossing the tracks. I was cautious, I was worried about it, naturally. Then it was raining when I left Amsterdam. Pouring. I was alone. And suddenly I saw another bicyclist. I tried to make conversation with him. I would have liked to be with him for a little company. He didn't want to listen. He didn't want anything to do with me. That was my luck. At the rail crossing I saw him. He was hauled off by a policeman. They checked his papers. They were busy with him so I could go through. And that was my luck.

MK. You don't know what happened to him? Was he German Jewish?

HR. He was a stranger. I don't know what happened to him. And then I had to cross a river with a pontoon bridge. I knew that when you went over there, the Dutch police were always watching this. And I didn't know how to cross the bridge with the bicycle. There were a lot of vehicles in front of me. Cars, Germans. Everything. I sneaked between them but they didn't see me. I was lucky. I made it. At ten o'clock—I'll never forget—I came to the address and that was the address of the mayor!

MK. That was the same man? The man who said, "Come to me when you need me"? And you didn't know you were going to him?

HR. No. I didn't know where he lived. It was outside the town. He kept me for a week or two. And I was waiting for my brother. I didn't know what had happened to him. I had left a message for him with my parents. Then the mayor had to find another place for me with a farmer *[laughs]*. The mayor did it out of patriotism, out of—

MK. —idealism?

HR. Idealism. And humanism. To help Jewish people.

MK. It didn't matter who you were?

HR. No.

MK. He didn't know you well.

HR. He knew me from the blacksmith's.

MK. And it was a dangerous thing for him to do?

HR. He got in trouble later. Not because of me. He helped a German deserter. And this deserter got caught by the Germans. And this idiot had a black book, a diary, where he wrote down where he was hiding and who was helping him. Then the mayor had to go underground.

MK. In the meantime he found a place for you with a farmer. And do you know why the farmer took you in? Also out of idealism?

HR. No. They knew me from before, from the blacksmith.

MK. So, they did it out of friendship?

HR. Not out of friendship. They helped people who are human beings.

MK. There are a lot of people who didn't go that far. If you asked me, would I do it . . .

HR. I wouldn't do it.

MK. It was a very heroic thing to do.

HR. Of course. Then I was there eight or ten days. Then suddenly the farmer's wife came to me one day and said, "You have to leave."

Why?

"You have to go back to the mayor. The grocer knows that you are here."

[The grocer had a daughter who was a friend of the daughter of the farmer where Mr. Rosen was being sheltered.]

HR. She said, "It's not safe for us and not safe for you."

[Mr. Rosen was taken back by the mayor who found another place for him with a young doctor in the same village. But that proved to be short-lived when Rosen overheard the local mailman talking about him to the doctor's wife. The mailman had known him when he was at the blacksmith's. Once again, Rosen was forced to seek another refuge. The mayor next found a place for him with a local pastor where it was made clear that he could remain only for four weeks.]

HR. At that time I had no identification card, nothing. I couldn't go out. I was locked up for the whole day and night. He gave me books to read.

MK. And they fed you?

HR. They fed me for nothing. That was Christian charity.

[When the four weeks were over, the mayor placed Rosen with a retired railroad clerk. But since there was a cleaning woman in the house during the day, Rosen had to remain locked in a room. Only after she left the house was he permitted to open his door. One day the clerk told him he had a ticket to Amsterdam for him and an address where he would be safe.]

HR. I said, "What happened?" They were looking for my friend, the mayor. They had the German deserter and the information and they were looking for him. But they didn't get him. They came in the front and he went out through the backyard. He was lucky. He was underground for a year. He survived the war and I visited him many times afterwards. Thanks to him I am still alive.

[The mayor had provided Rosen with false papers so that he could travel to Amsterdam. He was now Christian Vandermaas, born in Batavia, Indonesia, which had been a Dutch colony. In Amsterdam he was taken in by some communists. It was 1943.]

HR. But then they threw me out. They told me, "You're a Jew." I told them my name was Christian Vandermaas.

MK. And when the communists found out that you were Jewish, they wanted to get rid of you?

HR. Right. I had to leave Amsterdam in a hurry.

[He returned to the village where he had been staying with the farmer whom the Germans had subsequently arrested for assisting the German deserter. The farmer had been released just two days prior to Rosen's arrival and naturally was apprehensive about assisting him. A neighboring farmhand offered to help and suggested that his employer might be willing to take Rosen in, provided he could work and pay something for his keep. Rosen agreed to do it. He still had a little money from his parents.]

HR. He took me to his farmer and they looked me over. They told me I had to sleep in one bed with the help. But what did I care? It was my life. And I was hungry, naturally. For the first time in my life I ate pork. And lard. And what happens? I didn't sleep. I was walking the whole night, from the toilet to the bed. I was miserable. And the next day we had to do heavy work. The helper told me, "You're not ready for that."

I said, "I have to do it." He told me to stay in bed and I did.

Then the farmer's wife came in. She says, "If you are sick we cannot keep you here. You have to go back where you came from." I tell you, I was healthy right away. I made it through the day.

[After four weeks, Rosen told the helper that he did not mind working but did not want to have to pay for the privilege. He asked if there was somewhere else he could go. The helper made an appointment for him in a neighboring village. All he told Rosen was that he was sending him to two women who were retired schoolteachers.]

HR. I went there and opened the door. And they were sitting down to eat. "Sit down, come and eat. You haven't eaten?" You were accepted right away. I didn't know what to say. I didn't expect that. There were six people sitting around. Jewish people sitting around the table eating dinner. And they told me they would help me and they did. But they got caught later. They went to Ravensbrück, the concentration camp. And they didn't come back. I put a plaque on their house to commemorate the people. I can bring you the picture. They helped other people besides Jews. Everybody in the village knew they had people there. They had a chance to go into hiding but they didn't.

[In the course of moving around, Rosen established connections with the underground. Through their efforts, he was placed with various people until he was forced to move on. He continued to use false identification papers and was forced to lie many times about being Jewish. Mr. Rosen says that in three years he was hidden in eleven differ-ent places.]

HR. I went to every faith: atheists, communists, orthodox, Protes-tants. One wanted to convert me. And another one tried to find out what I was, in the sneaky way. [Just before the Allies arrived, from 1944 to 1945 Rosen worked for another farmer who suspected that he might be a Jew.] I told him, "How can I be a Jew if I was working for you in the fields?"

He said, "Yes, I'm surprised. A Jew generally wouldn't have the nerve to do that. Let me see your papers." So I showed him my [false] papers. [A couple of weeks later, Rosen was changing his clothing in the bedroom he was sharing with the farmer's son.] I was standing there in my underwear.

MK. He saw you were circumcised?

HR. He didn't see anything. He runs down the stairs yelling, "He's a Jew!"

I was angry. I said, "Is this the way to find out? What are you looking for? I told you three weeks ago that I am not a Jew. You don't trust me? I'll go. It's no good for you and no good for me."

Then he tells me, "Look, I like to know who I have in the house."

I say, "You're right. I would do the same thing." [Rosen was forced to leave once again.] I could tell you stories. I had more luck than *sechel* [sense].

MK. And these people were all willing to help you?

HR. All willing. Nobody forced them. They did it to help.

MK. There was great danger involved for them, death or deportation. And they knew this.

HR. I had to fight for my life. I had to lie to them. Aside from the farmer, the mayor, and the retired teachers, the others wouldn't have helped me if they knew I was Jewish. Maybe the priest. But the other farmers wouldn't help me. They were scared. I understand that.

MK. Yes. Were they also antisemitic?

HR. No. They didn't want to get into trouble. As long as they didn't know I was Jewish they could say, "I didn't know." I tell you, so long as I live I will never forget the people who helped me. I still have friends from the war.

MK. So you go back and visit many people?

HR. We go next week to Holland and Germany. I go to my hometown and to the cemetery. Besides, I have friends there. Aryan.

[Mr. Rosen was asked by people in his hometown to write a short history of what happened to his family between 1933 and 1945, to be used as teaching material in the local high school.]

AFTEREFFECTS

MK. You said that what happened during this whole period is something that doesn't leave you. In what way does it not leave you?

HR. You have seen—maybe you feel it too. I am a nervous person. I have a complex. And I would like to get rid of it.

MK. What kind of complex?

HR. Maybe an inferiority complex. And I am suspicious. It's very hard for me to trust somebody. Because in that time, the underground time, every word and everything I did, I had to think about.

MK. But did you also find that having gone through all that has made you stronger in any way?

HR. Look, at that time when I took chances I had no alternative. I traveled with a bicycle. I had the strength and the power and the hope to stay alive.

MK. But then after that period was over, didn't you continue to feel that strength?

HR. No. I don't know. This is very hard to explain. I couldn't do it today. I'm not only too old. I would be too scared. If you're young you don't realize what you're going into. I had a girlfriend in that time, a shiksa. Maybe I didn't realize, I was too careless. Now I know that if the Germans had caught me it would be the end. So far ahead I didn't look. I always survived on hope.

[I ask him about his feelings concerning Germany.]

HR. The first time I went over the border to Germany, I had to restrain myself when I saw the first German person . . . I tell you, I have a friend, a school friend. We were brought up together. He was in the German army. I saw him after the war when I came to Germany for the first time. He told me to come back to Germany. To live. You could give me gold, I couldn't live there.

MK. How do you feel about Washington Heights?

HR. Look. Where can I get this view? Where can I have the park? Where can I get an apartment like this with cheap rent?

MK. And what about the people here? Are you comfortable with them?

HR. They don't bother me. We live our own life. So long as they don't bother me, I go my own way.

[His wife, Marion, whom I interview later dislikes Washington Heights intensely.]

⁂

Hans Steinitz

Dr. Hans Steinitz became a well-known figure among the German Jewish refugees of Washington Heights because of his position as editor in chief of the German-language newspaper, the Aufbau *(Reconstruction), founded in New York City in 1934 as the primary source of information about German Jewish life.*

In 1933, as president of the union of socialist students at the University of Berlin, the twenty-year-old Hans Steinitz knew that he was in imminent danger of arrest because the Nazis were targeting their political enemies. He had, in fact, already packed a small suitcase in case he would need to decamp at a moment's notice, which turned out to be the case.

HS. I left in 1933 with the Gestapo coming up the staircase and me going down the fire escape of the building where my parents lived and making my way over the next national border, which was, at that time, Czechoslovakia.

[The day before Mr. Steinitz ran away, the regular police had visited his home and spoken to his father. They wanted to see the kind of books there were in the house and what newspapers were read. It was clear to the elder Mr. Steinitz that his son was not safe.]

MK. Yours was one of the organizations that Hitler immediately clamped down on?

HS. We were on the target list from way back, of course. There were a number of incidents—or confrontations as you would have called them in the 1960s—which was bad enough for me. I preferred to leave the country. I am glad I did though they caught up with me later.

MK. Were you in touch with the Jewish leadership later when you were outside of Germany?

HS. Actually, I couldn't care less. I don't think I gave the Jewish leadership any thought. I had to give a little bit of leadership or guidance to people who entrusted themselves to me—socialist students and related people. Most likely, as much as I can reconstruct it, I didn't even know what the Jewish leadership did at that time [prior to Kristallnacht].

There's the benefit of hindsight, of course. When I came to this country and found out that all the U.S. organizations of German Jews, the congregations, mutual self-help associations, and what have you, all had been founded and created in 1938–1939, I kept wondering, "What the hell have you been doing until 1939? Why didn't you do it before?"

And they said, "Well, we came only at that time."

I said, "Why, why, did you stay that long? You could have come earlier. In fact it would have been much easier to come earlier because there were more national borders open there, more immigration visas available, less difficulty obtaining passports and other documents."

The answer was, "Well, nobody did us any harm at that time."

So there is this shortsightedness for which many, many thousands of people had to pay with their lives in the most atrocious way. I will never stop blaming the German Jewish leadership [in Germany] for waiting until 1938 until they recommended that people emigrate.

They said, "Oh, it will not last, it is not so bad, the wind will blow over. Just stick it out, don't be conspicuous." I think the German Jewish leadership of that time is very much to be blamed for the fact that until 1942–1943 there were still 150,000 Jews left. They could have been out much earlier.

MK. You landed up in Gurs in France. How did that happen?

HS. Now you are jumping years and countries and criss-crossing over time and geographical scale, but that's all right. My country of refuge was France. I volunteered for the French army, was demobilized, and shortly thereafter, the Vichy police had me detained in Gurs. They knew I was a newspaper man, I was connected with a Swiss newspaper agency. [Dr. Steinitz had been writing for French newspapers, having begun with sports articles.] A little after the French defeat, Vichy France decided that an independent newspaper man of German Jewish origin should not run around freely, so they locked me up.

[On June 22, 1940, Marshal Pétain signed an armistice with Germany and set up a new regime in Vichy, in the south of France, with the understanding that this would be the unoccupied zone of the country. At first French Jews, native or naturalized, were protected, but refugee Jews could be turned over to the Germans. The Vichy government's policy was one of active collaboration with the Germans. On October 3, 1940, and June 2, 1941, it promulgated its own anti-Jewish laws, the *Statuts des Juifs*, which legitimized a systematic policy of deportations. By November 1942, all of France had come under Nazi occupation.]

HS. Gurs was a camp created in southern France, Vichy France, not the part of the country that was occupied by the German army, even though the German army ran the unoccupied part by a kind of remote control. It had been created originally for the elements of the Spanish Republican army, which, after their defeat, were pushed over the border into France and had to be accepted somewhere, however miserably. And when they gradually were removed to other parts of France or repatriated to Spain, the barracks were three-quarters empty. Then, conveniently enough, World War II had broken out. When France was attacked, the empty barracks were conveniently filled, first by the German women who had been left around. The men were transported elsewhere.

MK. Jewish women?

HS. No, German citizens, because they were enemy aliens at that moment. I don't know if they have learned better by now, but the French at that time made no difference between German gentile and German Jewish. In fact, no Frenchman has ever been asked his religion on any police record or passport or anywhere else, so they didn't make any distinction between the Germans and the Jews. It took a while until they separated German Nazi internees from non-Nazi internees, Jewish or otherwise.

They called Gurs a "Center of Reception" for various kinds of people. Even some French criminal elements were locked up there because the jails were filled, or it was more conveniently located, or there was a transport going there, so they lumped them in. It was an odd crowd. But very soon the majority were German Jewish refugees; the ones who had been in Belgium were transferred there because Belgium was overrun.

MK. What did you do there?

HS. Well, I waited for the next meal, which was sometimes on time and sometimes not. And when it came, it was usually a cupful of mostly watery soup, so watery it was transparent, and a small slice of bread. Now Gurs was not an extermination camp, there were no gas chambers, there were no executions, no shootings, and no nothing. But Gurs was a camp in which we had our enemies. One was hunger and the second one—the more important, the bigger one, the more consistent one—was vermin. We were literally eaten up by vermin, and I challenge any survivor who could claim that coming out of Gurs he was free from vermin on his body. There was no such case.

MK. Did this stop you from doing anything there, or were you able to do—

HS. —Yes, we were very active there with all kinds of activities. The French guards who were in charge of us benefited us by their neglect: They didn't give a damn, they did the minimum of what they had to do. Some of them were secretly Gaullists. In other words, politically in sympathy with us. We found out very fast who was and who wasn't. So there was quite an active cultural life. I gave political lectures about the military situation and about what was doing on the eastern front.

MK. Did you do any writing?

HS. I continued to write for my Swiss newspaper agency.

MK. How did you get your material out?

HS. This was my trump card in the camp: When I was locked up there I had my little portable typewriter with me. It was more or less the only typewriter in the camp, I believe. How did I get my writings out? Very easy. We bought off the censor.

MK. With what?

HS. With sardines. Sardine boxes, sardine cans.

MK. Where did you get them?

HS. We had to get them on the black market. Once we had them, the temptation was very great to keep them for ourselves because we were hungry. But I knew I had to give them to that guy from time to time because he let the mail go through.

MK. It's astounding that you were able to be in this camp with your typewriter, smuggling out documents, political documents.

HS. They were newspaper articles usually dedicated to contemporary political topics. The typewriter broke down from time to time, and under the pretext that I had to have it repaired, I often got a one-day permission to go to the next city, Pau. There was a bus twice or three times a day connecting us with Pau, a delightful, beautiful city in southern France. Usually I could smuggle out mail or get in contact with people outside. The typewriter problem was quite a problem because at one point the letter "a" broke off. I could not have it repaired properly, not even by a welding man who was in the workshop of the camp. He messed it up. So I had to operate the typewriter without the letter "a" which is not very easy. My worst case—a footnote to history—was when I had to write a story about the Panama Canal. Can you imagine what that means without the letter "a" available?

[Dr. Steinitz also kept a diary while at Gurs and when he came to the United States he thought of publishing it. But then came the stories of Auschwitz and Treblinka, and he said, "How can I? How can my experiences compare with these horrors? If I publish this now, in 1947, knowing what went on elsewhere, I am a nobody, I am nothing. I don't have a story to tell by comparison."]

HS. What is important is that there was a great deal of political activity in the camp. There was a strong Gaullist resistance faction working closely with some of the French supervisory personnel, among them the chief of the medical services who got a decoration after the war from the de Gaulle people. And among the internees there was one civil engineer who built an illegal radio station, a shortwave, which was hidden under the floor of the barracks. Every night, the guy sat there and received the BBC or London or, even better, whatever orders the French Resistance command in London was giving to Resistance forces in France.

We were not only well informed in the camp, we were actually a link in the underground chain, the Resistance chain. That worked quite well even though, once in a while, it blew up because some Vichy French were suspicious and investigated and searched the place. So it was not easy.

MK. Did you stay in Gurs throughout the war?

HS. I stayed in Gurs for about two years.

MK. How did you get out?

HS. I liberated myself. I had been transferred to another camp, Les Milles, and there I climbed over the wall and underneath the barbed wire. If you ever have to crawl underneath barbed wire, I will give you some advice. Most people who get caught and don't make it crawl on their belly and get their backs caught on the barbed wire. So you have to crawl on your back, which makes movement very difficult because you can move only with your heels and your shoulder blades. That's the only way to move forward, but you can do it because this way you know how high the barbed wire is.

I had cut into pieces a torn bicycle tire, which I had found in the garbage somewhere in the camp. I cut out a piece of rubber the size of my hand and used that as a rubber glove to push the barbed wire over me. This would have aided in case the barbed wire was electrified— which it wasn't, but I didn't know that. It would have neutralized me and it would have saved my hand.

I escaped on Yom Kippur, 1943. I didn't plan it that way. Actually I couldn't care less that it was Yom Kippur or any other day. I didn't have anything to eat in the first place. Yom Kippur didn't have much meaning.

Somehow I got to Marseilles, where I was hidden in a little hotel. I got false identity papers from a Gaullist police commissioner. This took a long time. It took a little bit of money, it took connections, political connections, and eventually I made my way over the mountains into Switzerland. I am a mountain climber by passion and enthusiasm, and so I could climb mountains that many other people unfortunately could not. Many others could not have chosen the same way to safety that I did.

꙳ꙮ꙳

Martin Spier

Martin Spier and I have known each other for years. We were in the same athletic club, Maccabi, in Washington Heights. He continues to live in the neighborhood in the same building as his younger brother,

Walter, and runs a thriving painting business. His concentration camp number is still visible on his arm. Born in 1925, the second youngest of five children, Martin grew up in Holzhausen, a town of perhaps seven hundred people, with about ten Jewish families, one hundred kilometers from Frankfurt. His father was a cattle dealer and the family owned a farm. Martin's exposure to antisemitism began as early as 1934 when his best friend joined the Hitler Youth and would have nothing further to do with him. He and his brothers and sister were continually harassed by formerly friendly children. "We were in fear all the time. There was not a day when something didn't happen."

Like many others, Martin Spier's father believed that Hitler and his policies were an aberration, one that would be short-lived. Even the closing of the local Jewish school in 1937, which necessitated sending Martin away to Frankfurt to attend a still-functioning Jewish school, did not appear to alarm his father unduly. However, just before Kristallnacht, he was tipped off by a local police officer that he soon would be arrested and would be well advised to go into hiding. He did so in another town where he was hidden by a friendly gentile farmer for a couple of weeks. Martin's fifteen-year-old brother was not so lucky and was arrested and sent to Buchenwald for three or four weeks.

MS. There was a baker next door to the synagogue. He took the Sefer Torahs from the building and put them in his oven, to burn them. The story is that [later] he was very good to my mother. He gave her extra bread. Didn't give her coffee but in a small town you don't need much. Food was very hard to get.

MK. Were some of the other neighbors decent?

MS. Yes, certain people were very nice. But we had one neighbor on the left side of us, he was no good. And in back of us, he was no good. And we had one tailor who was very good to us. I had an uncle who couldn't walk. He was in a wheelchair, so that man took my uncle and put him in the front of his house to do some tailoring. [The uncle died in 1935.] Just before we left for the camp, that tailor—he came in the middle of the night, without shoes, to bring us food to take along.

THERESIENSTADT

MS. We were picked up by truck in Holzhausen and sent to Theresienstadt. September 1942.

[Three years earlier, Martin's elder brothers and his sister had been fortunate enough to be sent to England and Scotland on a *Kindertransport* (a "children's transport"). Between December 1938 and September 1939, ten thousand Jewish children from Germany, Austria, and Czechoslovakia had been shipped to safety in Great Britain and taken in by mostly non-Jewish families and institutions.]

MS. Everybody who was left in the town was picked up, in different trucks, on the same day. Everybody. Also my grandmother who was living with us for a year because her son was picked up in Kirchheim where my mother comes from. Nobody knows where that transport went. We had three transports from our neighborhood. The first transport went to Riga and some people came back. Very few. The second one, nobody came back, not even one child. Nobody knows where it went. The third one went to Theresienstadt. Some people came back.

MK. You packed something for the trip?

MS. We packed but we never got the stuff back. We thought we were going someplace where we could use everything. Clothes, linens, whatever. We put two suits on, three suits on, even though it was hot in September. Theresienstadt has no train station and we had to walk. I would say it was roughly five kilometers, so we walked from Bautzen to Theresienstadt. Of course, for some people like my grandmother who was eighty years old, it was a lot for her.

MK. How many of you went to Theresienstadt from your family?

MS. From my family, five, including my grandmother. And only Walter and myself came out. I remember the last Saturday [at home], we were eating and my father said to us: "I will not come back, but you will come back." And he said, "Do me one favor. Take care of the people who bothered us." He said that. And, "What you have to do is, you will meet here." And that's what happened.

MK. In Theresienstadt, the five of you were separated?

MS. We were separated in different buildings, yes. But Theresienstadt was not that big. We were in different barracks. It was like a military installation. You couldn't get in and out. There was water all around Theresienstadt [a moat] and a wall too. The first job I had was for about two weeks. I was picking up the dead bodies in the basement and burying them outside of Theresienstadt. They put about thirty people in one grave. We did that for about two weeks. We were busy all day. We had a wagon where we put maybe fifty people. We had no horse. We had to push it and pull it to the cemetery.

MK. How did these people die, the ones you had to bury?

MS. The old people died from hunger. You got one piece of bread for three days. So if you ate one piece of bread in one day, you had nothing left for the other two days. At noontime, the people were staying in line for two hours for one cup of soup. It was water soup. There was nothing special in there. The people died from hunger. The younger people—like I was working later on outside of Theresienstadt on the land, picking potatoes, picking cucumbers, whatever. Of course that didn't go to Theresienstadt. It went outside, maybe to the military.

Sometimes, what we could do, we could bring one cucumber home. We knew the guards, who was the good guy and who was the bad guy. Most of the police in Theresienstadt were Czechs. When you came back from the field with a potato or cucumber, if you didn't know who the guards were, you threw everything away before you went in. You couldn't put anything in your pocket. You carried stuff in your legs, under your arms . . . You're hiding it. It was always a danger to bring it in.

MK. While you were picking, could you also eat something?

MS. I think you could. Nobody bothered you. That's why what I took home I didn't keep for myself. I gave to my parents. Maybe I got a potato or two. That would help.

MK. When you got a potato, you ate it raw?

MS. No. My mother could cook it. My parents lived in a three-story building, about twenty rooms, with maybe a hundred people. My mother was in charge of the kitchen and she could cook there or warm up something.

Later on, when I had typhus, I couldn't work anymore on the farm. I was in the hospital for about two months. And later on I was working in the post office. A lot of people got packages. Not the German Jews, but the Czech Jews who were mostly from Prague. There were already a lot of mixed marriages at that time and they got a lot of packages. Some of them went through and some of them didn't. Packages for people who had died were put on the side. Sometimes you could take a piece of bread [from the package] or something like that, if you got away with it. Most of the packages were already partly open, from knocking around.

MK. Did you share with other families?

MS. Oh yes, nobody was selfish. Everybody gave to somebody else. Like my mother was in charge. If she had two potatoes, she shared with somebody else. But then, of course, when we came to Auschwitz, that was the end.

MK. When you were in Theresienstadt, did you think that this would go on forever or that it would be over?

MS. In Theresienstadt they say it was [set up as a model camp] for the Red Cross. When the Red Cross came in, they made a big phony . . . they opened up coffee shops . . . It was all nonsense. You had no coffee shops there. It was just a show for a couple of days. You cleaned, you painted the barracks, you cleaned the streets . . . when the Red Cross left, everything went back the way it was. The SS was riding around in cars and trucks. They gave us phony money. Theresienstadt money. But that money was only good for a couple of days when the Red Cross was there.

The one thing we could do was play soccer on a Sunday afternoon. There were some professional soccer players. The ones who had the strength to play were the ones who were working where they could get food.

Some people got killed even in Theresienstadt. I remember one day on Yom Kippur, we were staying outdoors the whole day, from early in the morning until late at night. For what reason, we don't know. They said some people escaped. So we stayed the whole day outside. Why they picked Yom Kippur I don't know. Some people were picked up and sent away on that day.

MK. Were people killed in Theresienstadt itself?

MS. There were some hangings there, yes.

MK. Not regularly.

MS. Not regularly. But, in fact, in Theresienstadt they were building a gas chamber too. If the war had lasted another half a year or a year, they would have had a gas chamber in Theresienstadt. They were building it right where we played soccer.

AUSCHWITZ AND AFTER

MK. From Theresienstadt there were always transports?

MS. All the time.

MK. Did you know what those transports were?

MS. We knew. But we didn't know what happened to the people. When we came to Auschwitz [in May 1944], and they opened up the door . . . it was nighttime . . . the SS had the dogs. My father said right away, "Here the people came a long time ago. And here we don't get out." This was the first minute they opened up the doors of the cattle cars. I was a young kid [nineteen] but things like that you never forget.

We all went to Birkenau [part of Auschwitz]. Maybe forty barracks. The women went on one side and the men went on the other. I could see my parents once in a while. Auschwitz was bad, bad, bad. We had nothing to eat whatsoever. If you could sell your shoes and get a pair of wooden shoes, you sold for just a piece of bread—anything. We had nothing there. There were the Kapos. Every time you walked on the sidewalk, wherever you walked, he took a stick and hit you left and right. They cut your hair, they took your clothes away, and gave us the uniform.

When we were taken there in 1944, it was the biggest transport. They came from all over: Holland, Belgium, Hungary. Most of the Hungarian Jews didn't even see daylight. They went right into the gas chamber. We were still lucky that we went in the barracks.

We could see when the trains came in. You could see where the gas chambers were. You could see the people from our barracks. As soon as they came into the train station, they went right in the gas chamber. You could see the smoke all day long. In May 1944, every half-hour a new transport came. We were lucky, some of the ones who came from Theresienstadt were still alive. Very few.

I was in Auschwitz for one week, and then we were sent out to Schwarzheide [a forced-labor camp]. My parents were killed in Auschwitz two days after I left. Walter [Martin's younger brother] saw my parents when they died. He was there. I left with a thousand young fellows my age to work in a factory. What they made there I don't know. It was for the army. We were working in the factory at night. We were building bunkers above ground for the bombs.

MK. Did you get food there?

MS. We got food in Schwarzheide in the camp. Not too much. But enough to survive.

MK. Better than Auschwitz?

MS. Better than Auschwitz.

MK. Better than Theresienstadt?

MS. Less than Theresienstadt. What happened in Schwarzheide is that the Russians bombed the factory. Where we lived was less than a half a mile away from the factory and they bombed our camp. Half of my barracks was completely knocked out. And the ones in that part of the barracks were killed. We were just lucky. The whole camp was very lucky. The longer you were in camp, every day was lucky.

We were working at night. There were different shifts. It was better at night. We took the paper that was around the cement and wrapped it around us to keep warm. In the daytime, you couldn't do that. If they would see that, they would rip it off or shoot you right away. It was cold, but we had that paper. We got used to it. We had only very thin uniforms. We had no sweaters. Maybe we had an undershirt.

MK. You had bad supervisors?

MS. Some of them good, some of them bad. Especially the SS, the Polish SS, the Romanian SS. The German SS was bad too. But the Romanians and the Poles were ten times worse than the Germans. They hit you . . . One time I was loading coal and I wanted to stretch just for second. And one of the Romanian SS came with his rifle and hit me, I don't know for how long. Just for stretching for a second.

MK. You didn't get sick during that time?

MS. You couldn't afford to get sick. Otherwise you got shot. As long as you worked you were OK.

[Martin Spier was in Schwarzheide for half a year, from June to December 1944, when the Germans evacuated the camp in order to escape from the advancing Russian troops.]

MS. We were on the march from January on while the Russians came closer and closer. We were like cattle in the field. We were eating grass. Anything we could find. We had no food whatsoever. If you passed out, you got shot.

[The forced march was headed back toward Theresienstadt.]

MK. Were they moving you to a new place to work?

MS. We don't know. Outside of Theresienstadt was a *Kleine Festung* [small fortress; in reality a killing facility]. Most people got killed in the Kleine Festung. It was about ten kilometers from Theresienstadt. Most probably they wanted to bring us there to kill us. Definitely, they didn't want to bring us to Theresienstadt, they didn't want to save us.

MK. In Schwarzheide, there were no killing facilities?

MS. In Schwarzheide, people just died. Died from overwork. On the march, one night I went in and took some potatoes from the place where the SS had the food and they caught me. One SS man wanted to take me out to the woods and shoot me. Another SS man—he came from Frankfurt and he knew I had lived there—he said, "Untie him." And he let me go. So I went back on the march. I could tell you more stories . . . *[long pause]*. It's hard, it's tough . . .

One time we were working in Schwarzheide. I'll never forget. The SS's name was Shuster and he said to a couple of fellows, "Wir Deutschen haben den Krieg verloren" [We Germans have lost the war], but "Japan wird den Krieg für uns gewinnen" [Japan will win it for us].

MK. What did that mean to you?

MS. We lived from day to day.

MK. This was a way of taking your hope away?

MS. No, no, once you gave up hope that means you were finished. We never gave up hope. We wanted to survive. We knew that maybe some day something would happen. Once you gave up, forget about it, you couldn't survive for one hour. We always had hope.

MK. When you started on the march from Schwarzheide, did you know it was because of the Russians?

MS. No, we found out later on. We were hearing the shooting already. I remember we went to Cottbus. There were big farms there, big cattle farms. The SS shot every cow so the Russians shouldn't get the cows. [The march lasted several months, from January to May 1945.]

The way we got liberated, I still don't know today. I have a good friend in Hartford and he tells me (in fact, he was at my [seventieth birthday] party last Sunday) we were liberated outside of Leitmeritz. Leitmeritz was the next big city near Theresienstadt. All Czechs. We were liberated in the middle of the street. All of a sudden we found no more SS. We knew that Theresienstadt wasn't too far away, maybe five, six kilometers. We walked there.

If the war had lasted another day or two, this was May 6 or 7, we would have landed up in the Kleine Festung. In Kleine Festung everybody got killed, nobody came out. It was a little concentration camp. There were no Jews there, only gentiles. Political people.

We left Auschwitz with 1,000 guys of my age. And maybe 250 or 280 people were liberated. We went to Theresienstadt and, when the Russians came in, they gave us heavy food and half of the [former prisoners] died in Theresienstadt after the liberation. From eating the heavy food. Beans and all that heavy stuff. I was sick, but I survived. I have a good friend who was working with me the whole time in Theresienstadt before I went to Auschwitz. He didn't even recognize me. I was maybe, the most, seventy pounds. From Schwarzheide to Theresienstadt we were marching, marching. Maybe I wouldn't have made it, but my friend from Hartford pushed me along. He was a little bit older and he guided me. That's why my wife said last Sunday that I was here because of my friend. Today he's a sick man himself. He can't walk anymore. He doesn't see, he doesn't hear. He's in bad shape.

MK. You lost track of your parents, so you didn't know if they were alive or dead.

MS. I didn't know until I got back home to Holzhausen where I was born. I was in Theresienstadt for six weeks [after liberation by the Russians]. I didn't want to come to America. I went from Theresienstadt to Prague. I wanted to go to Palestine. I had no intention of coming to America. But everything was closed [emigration to Palestine]. It was very hard. I went back to Theresienstadt. One day I hear there's a bus coming from Bad Nauheim picking up people to go back there. I thought I'll get on the bus and once I'm in Bad Nauheim, I can get home from there. The Russians didn't want to let us go. They wanted to bring us to Russia. We were lucky that most Russian officers at Theresienstadt were Jewish. Otherwise, they wouldn't have let us go.

MK. Were they friendly to you?

MS. They were good to us, but they tried to talk to us. I remember one woman officer—she was Jewish—came to me and she said, "I'll take you as my son, come back with me to Russia, you will have it good, I'll send you to college . . ." Yes, they were good to us.

[From Bad Nauheim, Martin took a train to Marburg that was so crowded passengers had to lie on top of the railroad cars. In Marburg he sought out an acquaintance who used to live in Holzhausen and borrowed a bicycle so he could get home.]

MS. I was too weak to walk. Once I was in Holzhausen, of course, I couldn't get into my parents' house. A woman whose sister used to work for us took me in. Then my brother Walter came too.

[He recalls his father's instructions to meet at home afterward, "and that's what we did." The two had been separated a year before the war ended. Walter had remained in Auschwitz with their parents, while Martin was sent to Schwarzheide.]

MK. Do you remember the meeting with your brother?

MS. I was sleeping and he went like that [shows how his brother shook him]. I was in bed and, of course, we were happy, we cried . . . And then he told me the story of my parents. They got killed in Auschwitz. [Their grandmother had died in Theresienstadt.] And then later on, we went back to our house—the house was never sold—we got two rooms back. We let the other people live in the house. People told us where our furniture was. [Neighbors had appropriated it when the family left and had sold it.] Like the bedroom set was here, the living room set was there . . . We picked up most of it again, with the Bürgermeister's [mayor's] permission. He gave us two horses and a wagon and we picked it up.

[In 1940, Martin's father had packed up some of the family's effects, including silverware, linens, Hebrew books, and a Sefer Torah, "whatever he could carry on his bicycle"—and took them for safekeeping to the farmer next-door and to former business acquaintances in the next town.]

MK. He left these things with trusted people.

MS. Yes. In fact, when we came back after the camp, we got everything back, including the Sefer Torah.

The people who had the furniture were all Nazis. The people in the house were good. He was the brother of the tailor who had been very good to us and who came at night to give us stuff to take along [when the Spier family was about to be taken to Theresienstadt]. So, of course, we couldn't kick him out. The tailor was still there. In fact, I went to Holzhausen once in 1969 after I was here in New York. And he was the only one I visited.

MK. When you came out you encountered a lot of people who were Nazis?

MS. The first couple of months we didn't do anything. But later, when we had a little strength back . . . There was one especially, who had bothered my father. We bothered him too. We had a lot of young boys living with us because they had no place to go. When he went out to the field, we followed him and we took care of him.

MK. You beat him up?

MS. Beat him up. But, of course, we couldn't do it too long because otherwise they would have arrested us again. We didn't break windows like they did to us. And we didn't hit the women either. Just the men.

MK. Did you have relatives in the United States?

MS. My cousin was in the U.S. army in Bad Nauheim. [He visited the Spier brothers in Holzhausen.] We went to the HIAS, in Frankfurt, and got papers to come to America. We found out that both brothers who went to England were in the British army. Julius was stationed in Italy and Alfred in Germany.

MK. Eventually, did everyone come to the United States?

MS. After the war my brother Alfred married a German girl and took her back to England. He couldn't make a living there and he went back to Germany with his wife. She became Jewish. Very nice woman. My other brother who was in the British army came here in 1962. He's still here. My sister is here. She didn't like England. She came here during the war.

[Martin speaks of his gradual return to religion.]

MK. You came back to religion after all you went through?

MS. I asked a hundred rabbis and they said, "Don't ask any questions."

MK. How do you feel about that?

MS. You can ask questions. Sometimes if you ask questions you can [come to] believe. Why did six million get killed? OK, we gained the state of Israel. Maybe if six million hadn't gotten killed we wouldn't have it today.

MK. How did your experiences change you psychologically?

MS. You appreciate life more than other people. If somebody asks me, "How do you feel?" I say, "I feel *good*." I get up in the morning, there's something to eat . . . Even today I have a big argument with my wife when she throws something out.

Ilse Marcus

Brought up as an obedient, unquestioning girl, it was only during her voyage on the ill-fated St. Louis that Ilse Marcus began to realize that it might have been possible for the passengers to take matters into their own hands and compel the crew to land in American waters. So close to safety off the coast of Cuba, the ship and its passengers were turned back to Europe where most of the Jews on board eventually landed in concentration camps.

AUSCHWITZ

IM. From a human being to an animal, I think, is a very short step. Our human being [identity] and our behavior as a human being depends on the atmosphere, on the surroundings. The minute we are treated as an animal and put in animal-like circumstances, the animal is there.

How fast . . . from one minute to the other. In Brussels, for instance, when I was caught by the Gestapo, we were brought into a cellar and locked in. Whoever needed a bathroom, they brought in a pail, and there you do whatever you have to do, in front of everybody. And, I mean, with the smells and everything, not going any further . . . How much more can you do to humiliate a human being?

The minute somebody has a power over somebody else and uses it— uses it as we have experienced under Hitler—he will be worse than the wildest animal. When I came out of the camp I figured I would rather go to a jungle than ever live among human beings again. *[Long pause.]*

Even before we went to the concentration camp, the Germans were telling us there are "labor camps" where they take us. And people went voluntarily to labor camps. But those who were more suspicious didn't believe in labor camps and very often I reminded my mother. I said, "Look, if we are caught and go to a concentration camp, you will never have a chance. I am young, I might have a chance."

[Mrs. Marcus had tried to persuade her mother to go into hiding in a convent, since many had opened their doors to Jewish women. Her mother refused to go without her. "Today I don't understand why I didn't go. I told my mother that I couldn't stand to be inside the whole time."]

In the camp, it was very seldom that one would consider the next one [person]. Everybody was thinking of himself. You could steal from somebody. You did it if you needed to. There was nothing left of a human being anymore. I saw mothers and daughters . . . I mean, the daughter couldn't care less for the mother anymore. Everybody for himself. And really, everybody was, in fact, capable of doing everything that's cruel . . . It didn't matter anymore. I lost all confidence in human beings.

MK. Do you think this happened accidentally or was it planned by the Germans?

IM. I think it was planned. *[Pause.]* Because the minute we came to the camp, the clothing was taken away, everybody was sitting naked, one next to the other, then the hair was cut off. I mean, what was left? Then the number was put on, so what else is left?

MK. That was their policy, to dehumanize you.

IM. That's right.

MK. You and your mother went together . . . So who went left and who went right?

IM. My mother went to one side and I went to the other side.

MK. And you knew right away what that meant?

IM. I knew . . . That much I knew.

MK. Did you ever see your mother again?

IM. No, how could I? You didn't have to know *when* they burned the people because the whole camp was smelling from human flesh.

The worst experience I had right away, the second day when I was there. I was still stunned, I was in a daze. There were still lots of things I just couldn't grab in my mind. I looked out of the window and I saw hundreds of people, all naked, walking. And I asked somebody and they looked at me.

They said, "You don't know what it means?"

I said, "No."

"They are all going to the gas chamber." And people were just *walking*. I mean there was no fighting, there was no nothing, they were just walking to the gas chamber. And then a soldier came into our block and called some numbers. Even that I didn't understand. I had just arrived.

So I asked somebody else, "What does it mean?"

And that girl said to me, "You don't know? You are lucky if they don't call your number. The number they call—they go right to the gas chamber." That's what they called "selections."

MK. Do you have a number?

IM. I had it taken out, but my number was—I can still tell you— 74,560. You may be sure I wouldn't forget it.

MK. You arrived in Auschwitz in 1944?

IM. January 1944.

MK. And by that time, were things worse, as far as you could find out, or were things better? Or had things become more organized or less organized?

IM. Now I found it terrible and horrible. But the Polish Jews who were already there since 1940 or 1941 and survived . . . they said to us, "You don't know how well-off you are." Because they were brought there just into open fields. They were standing in snow and ice, without shoes. They had no barracks, they had to build them themselves. There was no water and there was a minimum of food. So when they were brought out in the morning to stand in the cold, people were just dropping dead, left and right.

When I arrived, there were already barracks, we had our shower every day. We were standing outside for hours, but we had shoes. Even if we didn't get much food, we got enough to survive and things were more organized. We had to do this stupid work right in the beginning, just to keep us busy. We had to pick up big stones and carry them a few miles; then we put them down there and then we brought them back again, six times a day.

MK. When you first arrived there, did you . . . keep your will to live?

IM. In the beginning I had the will to live. I was young and I saw middle-aged people who really had a problem, health problems, and they tried very hard to live. I think it's kind of human, everybody wants to live. But after a while, you lose strength because you are undernourished. Then, from what you see every morning . . . Every morning we came out of the blocks and we saw the skeletons lying sky-high in front of the blocks, uncovered . . . I mean it's amazing how a human being can take all this and continue to live.

[I ask if anyone committed suicide, or whether they tried to. Mrs. Marcus herself reached a point of such despair that she considered the best way to die. She had seen people try to electrocute themselves against the electrified barbed wire, but that did not always work.]

IM. The soldiers were watching all the time from high poles. And they turned off the electricity so the people continued to live. So that's when I figured out it's not a sure way to die either. Then I figured another way, because I knew everybody who went into the hospital for health reasons never came back. So I decided I will go to the hospital and be done with it. And then one day I was standing near the hospital, which only had very small windows on top, and a terrible smell came out of there, so I didn't like this either. You learned that nobody ever came back from the hospital so you never let on when you were sick. I even had typhus. I knew it. I had the symptoms. There was a sort of nurse who checked everyone to see that they were healthy enough to work. Whenever she came around, I went the other way.

Sometimes it came to the point where we were jealous of those people who had the whole thing behind them already. Because we figured in the meantime we are working and suffering and the end will be the same. [Somehow, gradually, Mrs. Marcus's will to live reasserted itself.] Evidently, as I was young enough, I figured I want to live, though nobody imagined they would ever come out.

Then we worked. We were digging trenches. Not that it was very necessary but it was a different kind of work. We had very nice soldiers who accompanied us. Older soldiers who were not interested in the war anymore and they always let us sit in the trenches, as long as no overseer came. Then we had to get up fast and start digging. But when we were sitting in the trenches, we were talking. What were we talking about? We were all very hungry and we were talking about recipes. We were cooking! The women were exchanging recipes, the best recipes. And we were thinking, in case we ever get out of here, if we would all have enough to eat, we will try out all the new recipes. It's very hard to imagine what people think about if they are very desperate. We were very hungry and we were thinking of recipes. This shows that people continued to act according to their old habits.

There were always people who tried to behave humanly and not be degraded to [the level of] a beast. For example, there were four French girls. You could tell they came from very refined families. Every day they managed to find some white paper and set a table, though you couldn't really call it a table. It was on the floor of where they were sleeping, but they set it with white paper and everything they had to eat. And they cut it in little pieces and the whole thing looked a little bit different. They were not eating like beasts, at least.

MK. Where did they get the white paper?

IM. All these things you could manage. It was called "organizing." For instance, you knew where they had paper and for a piece of bread you could get paper, you could get a piece of thread, you could get scissors.

There were four girls who came with me in the transport from Belgium. We also tried to make everything as nice as possible. For instance, we were all given the same prison dresses. But one was too big, and one was too small . . . And since I was short, whatever I wore was too big. In the camp, I had a reputation for sewing. I shortened things or I made them tighter. For instance I would eat only half of my bread and then use it to buy some thread in another block. I had a pair of scissors. I was always sewing. Now I was in the camp in the wintertime and it was terribly cold. And for me it was less important to eat than to be warmly dressed. I went without bread one day so I could use it to buy a sweater. I always said, "When I get out, I want to come out healthy and not with frozen glands."

One day we got the honorable offer to work in a munitions factory.

MK. What do you mean, "honorable"?

IM. That is what the *Gauleiter* [section commander] called it while we were in the shower—the "sauna" it was called. There we were, a hundred girls at least, stark naked standing there. That's when the Gauleiter picked the moment to come in and talk to us about the honorable offer to us, because so far they had never taken Jews into a munitions factory, but we should try to do an accurate job because a lot depends on it. If we are doing sabotage, we will be hanged. So next day we started. There was a day shift and a night shift. I was on the night shift, which was considered better because then we didn't have so much supervision. The overseers were occupied with their love affairs and they didn't bother so much with us, so we had a better time.

I was working on hand grenades. Evidently you screw them on top of something because they had the screw things inside. There were, I think, twenty-four or thirty-six in one box. After I was working for a while, I heard that a few girls there had been in the underground and now they are doing sabotage. It was very hard to get their confidence. They were very careful, but I got their confidence and I told them I would like to find a purpose in my work here, to work against the Germans, not *for* them. And they told me, the first twelve we put on the bottom of the box. They should not be done the right way—only halfways—and the good ones we should put on top. That's what I did. And that went on for a while.

One day we were all called together and we were told a whole truckload which came from this factory was defective and we must have done sabotage. If that happens again, they will send us all to the gas chamber. But we never stopped. We did it again and again and again, and sometimes they caught it and sometimes they didn't. But there were girls who tried to steal dynamite. They wanted to blow up the whole camp and they were caught, unfortunately, and two girls were hung in front of the day shift and two in front of the night shift. Despite the hangings, we didn't get intimidated because we didn't expect to get out anyway, so what's the difference how you died? We wanted to have a purpose, to work against the Germans.

If anyone was found out, they cut everybody's hair again. We all were without hair. It hurts a woman very much to have her hair cut. But they were so systematized. They knew exactly when the end of the war was approaching so that by the time the camps were liberated, the hair had grown in. They didn't cut the women's hair just prior to the end.

MK. How do you explain the fact that you survived?

IM. You know, it's amazing with how little you can survive. You needed luck and willpower. I couldn't have gone on much longer. By the time I came out I weighed only seventy-five pounds.

THE END AT AUSCHWITZ

IM. I was in Auschwitz [and then at other camps] for sixteen months. From January 1944 to the end of the war in May 1945. [They knew the end was imminent because of rumors that were circulating in Auschwitz.] Everybody talked about it there because the soldiers who accompanied us to the trenches sometimes gave us moral support. From them we got reports of the war and they told us the war is coming to an end, Germany is losing. They said, "You will have it better afterward than we will." And every so often they gave us cigarettes, which we exchanged in the camp for soap, for bread—all the nonsmokers. And this helped a little bit to survive morally.

We had to leave Auschwitz [in January 1945] because the Americans and the Russians were coming closer. They had encircled Germany and so we were chased toward the middle, toward the center of Germany. This we did by walking "the Death March" . . .

MK. The Death March was in order to clear out Auschwitz so that the inmates wouldn't be found, I think.

IM. We were walking for quite a few days on the Death March. [The weather was freezing cold.] Whoever wasn't strong enough couldn't survive . . . It was quite strenuous and more women did survive than men. I think women in general are tougher and can take more.

And whoever couldn't march along was shot on the spot. After three days we came to another camp, to Ravensbrück. We stayed there for a while. We heard later that the minute we left Auschwitz all the crematoria were all destroyed. *That* they didn't leave behind. What I heard much later, when the restitution started, was that they had all the documents. You see, this is typical German. You wouldn't believe it: When the restitution started, I told them I was in Auschwitz, I was in Birkenau, I was in Ravensbrück, I was in Neustadt. I need not have told them that; they had all the documents. They knew my mother was in Birkenau, that she went right to the gas chamber. They had all the documents, from A to Z.

I mean, the Nazis had to run too, right? They had all the documents. Nobody could have told them [the authorities] I was in a concentration camp when I wasn't. In the meantime they put us on a railroad and we were taken to Neustadt. That was the last camp. There we met some girls from the German underground. They came to our train and they told us, "The war is finished, you survived until now, you have a chance. In a few days, the whole thing will be over. Just keep going. Nothing will happen to you anymore." And by the way, when we passed Berlin we saw it burning. That was the nicest moment I was dreaming of for a long time. It was burning on all sides. It was a pleasure to see.

LIBERATION

We were liberated on May 10, 1945. [The usual routine was for the inmates to stand outside every morning for hours until they had been counted by a German soldier.] One day, all of a sudden, the soldier was throwing around cigarettes. And we couldn't understand what happened.

The next morning we woke up and we didn't see anybody. Unfortunately, one girl was so curious, she couldn't wait. She jumped out of the window and she was shot in the last moment. Somewhere, somebody was still there. We still heard shooting. So we waited. We were all afraid. We waited a while and then we left our block and we went outside and nobody was there. And you know, the first moment you saw the gates of the concentration camp open, you thought it must be like when the criminal, all of a sudden, leaves the prison. Only he deserves the prison and we didn't.

Then we left the camp. Evidently there was one German soldier who didn't make it in time to leave with the others. And I still cannot excuse ourselves that we didn't kill that guy. Because the first thing he said was, "Why were you here?" I mean, I think it's impossible to think that people, especially soldiers who were stationed nearby, didn't know that there was a concentration camp. I mean, he only deserved to be killed on the spot.

We were hungry and we didn't have anything to eat yet. And there was a dead—can you imagine—there was a dead horse lying there. I went over with my little pocket knife that I always carried and I cut a piece from that horse. I brought it back to the camp to my friend who was the cook and she cooked it. But you know, when you cook horse meat, it turns dark. I couldn't eat it, as hungry as I was. I cut it from the dead horse and when I saw it cooked, I couldn't eat it. And you know, in Belgium, horse meat is a delicacy.

And then we were looking around for food. First we wanted to be away from the camp. We didn't know where to go but there were a few Polish girls who were really smarter than we were because of the pogroms and their life in Poland. And they were running somewhere to find food, so we ran too. As weak as we were, we still could run. We followed them to the next village. You would not believe it. The Germans were prepared for another ten years of war. Wherever we went, the cellars were full of meat and canned foods.

Then we wondered: How are we going to transport all this food to the camp? We wanted to cook, we wanted to eat. We found a little carriage with two big wheels. There were four of us girls, we kept together all the time. There were always cliques . . . So we put all the food in there and brought it halfway home and the whole thing broke down.

We had forks, and knives, and spoons . . . We wanted to live like human beings again. We took candles because there was no light, and whatever clothing we could find because, in the meantime, we had lice all over. If we had gone back to Belgium right away, we could have infected the whole country. Because in the last two camps, there was no water anymore, and no chance to keep clean.

MK. You didn't have lice in Auschwitz?

IM. No. In Auschwitz they kept you alive or they gassed you. But as long as they kept you alive, they kept you clean. They sent you clean to the gas chambers. But after Auschwitz, everything was topsy-turvy.

So halfway home the carriage broke down and we found another one with four wheels and we finally arrived home [back to the camp area]. Where did we go? We wanted to be outside the camp, we didn't want to see the barbed wire anymore. So we went to the small SS houses outside the camp. There were four beds in one room, a big stove in the middle. We started cooking, we started eating. The Belgian woman with us was the cook. We made hot water.

We had our candles, we lit the stove. We had wood, we washed ourselves. We changed clothes. But you know, to get rid of lice nothing helps. We washed with hot water a hundred times a day. We burned all our old clothes. We couldn't get rid of the lice. But in the meantime we were sleeping in beds, we had a ball. So we started little by little recuperating, and we figured we'd stay there a while and then go back to Belgium when we looked like human beings again.

ENCOUNTERS WITH GERMANS, RUSSIANS, AMERICANS

[Mrs. Marcus was having stomach troubles and needed some medication—charcoal—for her stomach. This was a common remedy for stomach ailments.]

IM. We went to a pharmacy and we asked for some medication. And he asked us if we had money. I said, "Where do you expect us to get money? We have come from the concentration camp. You have no choice. You give us the medication or we will take it. And you are lucky if we don't kill you, if we don't do to you what they did to us."

That was the end of my patience and my obedience. So he was kind of very subdued and he gave us whatever we wanted. Where should we have gotten the money from?

So one night, Russian soldiers came in. It's good we had this one Polish girl with us, she could understand them. They told us that everyone had to go back to their original country or they would take us to Russia.

The Americans offered to take all those from the West and the Russians would take those from the eastern countries. The few Germans who were left were running not from the Americans, but from the Russians.

Our first experience with the American soldiers . . . They didn't know if we had food, and they were throwing little packages at us that we thought was chocolate. But it was chewing gum. I mean, they had to consider that we don't have anything to eat. What are you going to do with chewing gum on an empty stomach? We were very disappointed.

MK. Did you know what chewing gum was?

IM. No. We opened it up and then we saw what that was and we didn't like it.

I will tell you another incident. We didn't have very much food left so we went to a house where German civilians were living and asked for a few eggs and candles, whatever we needed. On the way back, we met some American soldiers. Oh, they were very angry. "How could you do that to the Germans?" Taking the food from them. They really didn't have the least understanding.

Look, even in Belgium they didn't know how to behave. When I was in Brussels after the war, before I came here, they would go to the movies and put their legs over the seat in front. When I came to the States I went for a job interview. I didn't see anybody sitting, I saw a pair of feet. Who is putting feet on the table in Germany or anywhere in Europe? They don't know any better.

I was once in Europe on a tour and I was very much ashamed to see how they [Americans] behaved. We were in Germany on the tour and we were in some kind of hall [in a public building]. There were museum pieces in the hall, sofas with silk and brocade. A woman from the tour goes to the sofa and lies down on it with her shoes on. I went over to her and I said, "Look, this is Germany, this is Europe. You don't do these things. It is not your sofa. This is a museum piece."

[I point out that Americans may have lacked culture but that many Nazis were listening to Bach while smoke was coming out of the chimneys. Mrs. Marcus agrees and refers to Churchill's saying that democracy may not be ideal but it was the best system we had. She adds that the United States, with all its faults, is still the best country. "Where do you find a better one?" she says. She does make reference, however, to the fact that the United States did not take in as many refugees from Nazism as it could have.

After liberation, the Americans took Mrs. Marcus and others by truck to Holland, where they received a great welcome.]

IM. The Dutch are very hospitable people. We arrived there and the table was all set in white. Everybody got a Red Cross package. Right away we got noodles and white bread. The priest was there. It was a terrific welcome. [From Holland they were taken to Belgium.] Now I will tell you the reactions of the Belgians, which I gradually found out: "Too many Jews have come back." Because they had taken right and left [what the deported Jews had left behind].

[Asked if she tried to recover the jewelry she had left with some Belgians, Mrs. Marcus says she went to the police but knew she would not succeed. She no longer had the strength to pursue the matter and did not go directly to the people themselves.]

In Brussels I hoped my husband would come back. But nobody did. Not my husband, not my father, not my brother, not my mother. You see, every day another transport arrived from the camps. For weeks and weeks, every day there came other transports from somewhere. I kept hoping until the last transport from different parts of the country came back. Then you just assumed they didn't survive. That my parents wouldn't survive I was practically sure. Elderly people wouldn't have a chance. But I hoped very much that the young people would survive. And I heard from somebody who came back who knew my brother that he had lived almost to the end. He told me an SS man advised my brother to stay inside for a few days because he had a very bad cold. And my brother said, "I'm not taking any favors from an SS man." And . . . he died.

AMERICA

MK. When did you decide to come to the States?

IM. I never wanted to stay in Belgium. As soon as I came back, I knew I didn't want to stay. I couldn't stand the people, I couldn't stand the city, I couldn't stand anything.

[Mrs. Marcus had an uncle in New York. Her brother-in-law Fred, who had been in Cuba, was also in New York working as a photographer.]

IM. I tried to contact my brother-in-law and the answer I got to my first cable was, "Where is Kurt (my husband)?" And he was very nice from the beginning and offered to put together an affidavit for me. I knew I had an uncle here, too, but I was very afraid. I always heard from American people they can change their names and as he had a very funny name, "Adolf," and "Rosenberg," maybe it was too German. So he might have changed it. But fortunately he didn't, and I sent a cable, and he said right away he would try everything to bring me over.

It took me four years to come over because I needed four affidavits. I had one cousin who was, let's say, smarter than average. She went to her congressman and she asked him. She said, "I have a cousin in Brussels, she wants to come over, she is young and healthy. Something must be wrong or crooked that it needs four affidavits to come over." And sure enough, a few days later I got a request to come to Antwerp to pick up my papers at the consulate. Now I knew what happened from a previous case: Whoever paid for the affidavit got the papers right away. Whoever could not pay went back to the bottom of the list.

MK. How did you feel about America and what were your impressions?

IM. New York is a unique city, dirty as it is. I would never leave it. I still love it despite everything. What New York can offer no other city can offer. Don't forget, when I came over, New York was marvelous . . . You could go out at night. Not like it is today.

[Mrs. Marcus worked in a factory for a time but was dissatisfied with her job, given her educational background. She wanted to become an accountant and went to business school at night in the Times Square area. The school would have given her college credits, but it would have required six years of night school. She still regrets not having done it.]

IM. I picked the business school in Times Square. I tell you why. I worked all day and I was very tired at night. But when I saw all the lights, I woke up. I love Times Square. I love lights. So I became a book-keeper.

[Her first job was with a Viennese Jewish firm. She was terrified of answering the phone because of her poor English. Mrs. Marcus had learned grammar and spelling, but not conversation.]

IM. Whenever the phone rang, I ran. My boss said, "Don't run. In an office you don't run."

PART FOUR

Attitudes

I came of age in Washington Heights among the German Jewish refugees at a time when the events and traumas they have described were mostly past. In the introduction to this book I described my feelings of ambivalence toward the neighborhood that, along with other factors, eventually led me to move away. On the one hand, I admired my people's resilience in overcoming the wounds of loss and their ability to build a solid community with a loving atmosphere for their children and a nurturing one for their neighbors. On the other hand, I was dismayed by their complaints about eastern Jews, minorities, and new immigrants and by their unquestioning patriotism for America and political timidity.

Their present-day attitudes are what I now wanted to investigate and penetrate: what they learned; how they changed, if at all; how they felt—about Germany and Christian Germans, about Jews from the East, about "God's role," antisemitism, minorities in the United States, resisting authority, and helping victimized people under conditions of duress.

I approached my father first, knowing I could count on his directness and honesty, which would make it easy for me to bring up searching questions.

≈ひく

Bert Kirchheimer

My father, a passionate enthusiast about all things American, appar-
ently never doubted that he would be able to establish himself in
this country. Despite many reverses in his professional life as a free-
lance graphic artist, he did indeed manage to attain a comfortable
life for the family. Some nostalgia for Bremerhaven was always pre-
sent, fed by his three brothers who continually exchanged newspaper
and magazine clippings about the city, as well as information about
the great ocean liners, both past and present. During the war, when
approached by the U.S. Office of War Information, my father was un-
able to bring himself to help them with their plans to bomb the city.
In a strange way, he said, he would have felt like a traitor to his
hometown.

EASTERN JEWS: JEWISH ANTISEMITISM

[My father wonders whether, if he had been Christian, he might
have been antisemitic.]

BK. Maybe I would have been against the Jews for some of the things
they did. I'm not so sure. [He complains about "bad Jews."] Most of
them came from the East. I'm sorry to say this.

We were always told that the Polish Jews were not as good as the
German Jews. That's a kind of arrogance, right? German Jews didn't
talk Yiddish and they hated the Polish Jews. The Polish Jews were religious and they wore caftans. They looked different. We didn't like that
in Germany, because they caused prejudice among the gentiles.

MK. So you were ashamed of those Jews?

BK. Sometimes, yes. You would see them on the streets, begging and
trading door-to-door. On the other hand we felt sorry for them because
they had no money, they came from Russia and Poland where there
were pogroms. They didn't make much money there and they lived in
ghettos. They were suppressed there so they came to Germany and

they started businesses. They tried everything to make money. They cheated and then . . . they were not honest men and that makes *risches* [antisemitism]. Real Germans never did that. They were patriots and never dared to do that. They were educated in a different way.

MK. Do you think that Hitler needed the excuse of the Polish Jews?

BK. Of course he needed it.

[He describes newspaper campaigns even in the 1920s in which Jews were depicted as criminals. Some stories reported that shady Jews were running bordellos and enlisting German women to work in them. There were also reports of embezzling on the part of Jewish financiers.]

MK. Alice Oppenheimer says that after they saw Jews being arrested in the street in Mannheim (this was before Kristallnacht), they read in the paper that these were bad Jews and deserved to be arrested. She believed it.

[My father claims he never believed the newspaper accounts though he knew there were Jews who engaged in illegal activities. The misdeeds of the few, he says, made it bad for the rest of the Jews. I point out to him that when Jews do something wrong, it makes for Jewish antisemitism, or self-hate.]

AMERICA

BK. Even when we were in Bremerhaven we were crazy about America. Because we saw the big ships arriving and we had relatives here. We were always longing to see America.

MK. What happened when you came here?

BK. I was happy. It was terrific.

MK. How do you feel about it today?

BK. The same. I agree with many things and I disagree with many things, but I'm still enthusiastic. I like the way they live here, and the ideas they have. I love the beauty of the country because I'm an artist, and I love Americans. There is no comparing them with Europeans. Americans are more polite, they are nicer, they are helpful. All these things combined make me a happy American.

[He says he has always hated the concept of the "chosen people." He claims to see no differences between Jews and gentiles.]

BK. All the hatred came from jealousy because Jews were prominent. Look at the Nobel prizes. How come? Because Jewish people study more. Why were the most famous people—the writers, the musicians, the artists—Jewish in Germany? And in the United States also. Percentagewise. Many political figures are Jewish—Kissinger, for example. I'm always proud when I read about famous Jews. Like Dr. Salk who invented the polio vaccine.

[My father always worries about Jews running for office. He has always felt that Jews should keep a low profile. On the one hand he is very proud of them, on the other hand he worries that their mistakes will reflect badly on Jews in general. "If he makes a mistake, they'll blame the Jews." Louis Kampf reports a similar attitude on the part of his father.]

AFTEREFFECTS

MK. How were you changed as a result of having to leave your country and change your life?

BK. I was always an enthusiast. I had big hope.

MK. Didn't you become more mistrustful of people as a result of your experiences?

BK. No. I knew it would never happen here.

MK. Did you change at all?

BK. I started to hate Germany.

MK. Do you dream about Germany?

BK. At least once a week. About jobs I didn't finish at E. Weil Söhne [the department store in Saarbrücken where he worked. He also dreams about his old boss. Will he be punished for not having completed a job?]

MK. Do you dream about Nazis?

BK. No.

[He dreams about criminals, being shot. But not about Nazis. Someone at the apartment door is trying to get him and he's trying to keep the door shut. Incidentally he was held up at gunpoint in the lobby of his apartment building at 720 Fort Washington Avenue a few years after this interview.]

OFFICIAL VISITS TO GERMANY

[The Kirchheimer family had long been in the public eye in Bremerhaven after the war as a result of my uncle Siegfried's years of correspondence with the city's newspapers and various chroniclers of the city's history. As a result, my father was invited by the mayor to exhibit his caricatures of well-known figures of the Weimar era. The exhibit was to be mounted in the foyer of the Bremerhaven Stadtheater (where he used to sneak onto the stage with his brothers when they were children, pretending to be supernumeraries during an opera performance). This was one of the most thrilling events of my father's life.

In January 1978 he spent a week in Bremerhaven, where he was treated as a celebrity. Speeches were made in his honor; he was interviewed by the press and television and invited to the mayor's home. One of his chief pleasures during that week was to eavesdrop on opera patrons as they milled around in the lobby, discussing his work—and then to break in and introduce himself. This visit led to three other exhibits in Germany, including another one in Bremerhaven of his graphics and commercial work, one at the Stadtheater in Saarbrücken (August 1980) where he exhibited caricatures that had appeared in the *Saarbrücker Zeitung* when he was living in the city, and another in Dortmund, my mother's hometown (January 1983), where he showed some of his caricatures, many of which had previously been published in the *Dortmunder Anzeiger*.]

MK. When you go back on a visit to Germany, do you think about what the people were doing during the war?

BK. Always. Everybody I talk to. The waiters, anybody. People I was introduced to at the reception for my work in Bremerhaven. Dr. this and Dr. that. They were all Nazis. You can't get rid of this thought. Right away I always introduce myself by saying I'm Jewish. I tell them: "In my family forty-six people were murdered." I counted them.

And then the Germans say they regret it, and "We are different now. We were different. We didn't like it at all. We didn't know about it . . ."

[My father's responses and the attitudes he reflects in this interview were mostly familiar to me. Even though my questions elicited firmly held opinions, and even though he was a talented and intelligent man, he was clearly not able to recognize his own contradictions; for example: There is no difference between Jews and gentiles, but Jewish people are disproportionately famous. He relishes hearing about Jewish achievements but wants Jews to keep a low profile. He believes he would have acted like other Germans who were Christian and turned away from helping Jews, but he hates Germans of his generation— "They were all Nazis!" He himself is able to sympathize with some of the reasons for antisemitism.

As a father he was kind, loving, and really my closest friend. Of course, I realized he was imperfect. But reflecting on this interview, I came to appreciate his extraordinary candor. He has no qualms about admitting that he was "a coward," and reluctant to aid the U.S. war effort against the Nazis. My father says outright that he would not have helped others if there was any risk. I wonder. Despite his fears, my father entertained a fugitive journalist at his home in Saarbrücken. He always behaved decently. I think he may have underestimated himself. He died in October 1985.]

ᢍᎵᏓ

Siegfried Kirchheimer

A well-known diagnostician in Wolfenbüttel with a large practice, my uncle Siegfried never attempted to resume his medical work once he arrived in the United States. He seemed to take pride in his withdrawal from professional life to work as an orderly in a home for the aged while devoting all his energies to his memoirs and to a vast correspondence, primarily with people in Germany. His disillusionment with the forces that drove him out of Germany seemed to pervade his feelings about humanity in general.

MK. How do you feel about Germany today?

SK. I am only interested in the part of Germany where I lived, where I knew everybody, the northwestern part of Germany and Westphalia, because all my ancestors—your ancestors too—came from Westphalia. But the other Germany I don't care much about. It's not the *Vaterland* anymore. As it used to be. My *Vaterland* is only where I was born, where I learned to speak and to walk, and went to school to Gymnasium, to high school and the university. The German culture—that's what is mine. All my books are still full of German poems and German stories and so on. That's what I still like. Nobody can take that away from me.

MK. You get very attached to that.

SK. That's right. Because I still have my friends there and they still love me and talk about me and write about me.

MK. Do you have a lingering sense of anger that Germany rejected you?

SK. No, never. I never hated anybody there because I know history. It is not the first time that things like that happened to a country or to a people. If you know a little history, go back two thousand, three thousand years ago, it's more or less all the same thing. That's why I don't care much for religion. Because they hate each other too and fight each other, like in Brooklyn, the different [Jewish] parties. When the rabbi from Israel came, they had to protect him and all this stuff that I don't like.

MK. In other words what you're saying is you've seen it all happen before and it repeats itself and it continues to happen.

SK. Yes, yes.

MK. But this happened to *you* in Germany.

SK. Yes, but still—

MK. The country spat on *you*.

SK. That's right, but I never blamed anybody for that. Maybe for a short time I did because I was in the middle of it. Because of what happened to me, being forced out of Germany. But after that I never could blame anybody for this. Because you know how people are.

MK. Would you have done such a thing?

SK. No, I never would have done that.

MK. Well, if you wouldn't have done such a thing, how could you not blame people who did it?

SK. Because people are like sheep. They follow the leader. I would like to cite something from Goethe's *Faust*. It's in there already . . . "den entrollten lügen Fahnen" [conveying the sense that people are deceived by banners waving in the breeze even though they proclaim nothing but lies]. They follow like sheep. They always follow a leader, the good one or the bad one. Do you know the story of the Pied Piper of Hameln?

MK. Yes. But it seems to me that everybody is capable of making an individual decision. Some people make a bad decision because they're selfish. Because they think it's better for them. I have a different attitude. I blame people who do that.

SK. But you feel very, very sorry for them. Because they did it. Because they know they didn't do good, right? That is why Germany,

West Germany, is the only land that sends you money for that. *Wiedergutmachung* [reparations]. No other country does that. They know what happened. You know when you do something wrong and are punished for that; after that you get better. You say, "Well, I did wrong." So that's why I don't blame anybody nowadays. They had to follow the orders. They were military persons.

MK. They didn't have to.

SK. I know that. But they did it.

MK. There were many Christians who helped Jews.

SK. I know.

MK. There are many Christians who did not follow orders, who secretly defied them.

SK. Sure. There are always people—

MK. Now there's a difference between those people and the others.

SK. I know, I know.

MK. You have to make a distinction.

SK. It's why there are good people and bad people.

MK. Some people were heroes and some people were bastards.

SK. Some people don't like to be heroes, and some people like to be heroes and to be famous even if they have to die for that.

MK. *Like to be heroes?* I heard stories . . . Jews would run out with a bicycle to the country and they would go up to a farmer and say, "Can I stay in your barn?" And the farmer said OK. I don't think that farmer was thinking about being a hero. He was just a good person.

SK. Of course, there's a difference.

MK. There are some people who are just good people. Otherwise it's too cynical.

SK. I know, I know. I didn't have anything to do with those other people. I only know people from my hometown and the place where I lived. At that time there were no bad people.

[He points out again that there were always people who were ready to be seduced by a false leader.]

MK. They smashed your windows in and you don't blame them?

SK. I blame them for that, yes. They are all dead already. I can't blame them anymore. It was the times. They were part of history. As I always say, they talk too much about the Holocaust and all about this. They didn't know that these things happened before.

MK. They talk about the other things too. The Holocaust is just the most recent event. They still talk about the . . . the slave trade and the Hundred Years' War. So why shouldn't they talk about something where 40 million people died?

SK. Yes.

MK. Forty million. That's the most that ever died in one operation. Forty million. That's a lot to talk about.

SK. I know, I know. They will talk about it for a long time. As long as I live. But after they are dead then they won't talk about anything anymore. The people after them forget everything very fast. Unless somebody makes films or writes stories in books if they are interested . . . Of course, then people know about it. But in their hearts they don't care so much about that. They can't imagine what happens to people. How they can be murdered.

MK. Do you think that there are lessons to be derived from history?

SK. There is always something.

MK. Let's say for yourself. Did you learn lessons from history?

SK. In a way I don't know if I needed lessons because I'm a self-made man and I already learned it.

MK. But once, when you were only nine years old, you weren't yet self-made.

[Siegfried then goes into the story of how he was sent to live with two elderly aunts in Essen who treated him harshly and included beatings as part of his training. He talks of being unhappy at school where others made fun of him and called him a greenhorn. Even when he was in the army in World War I as an officer his aunts put him down and undermined any self-confidence he might have had. He tells of visiting his aunts for the last time prior to being sent to the front. "The old aunt, when she saw me, said, 'You call this the face of an officer?'" Despite his rank, he remained extremely timid in his relations with others.]

MK. Those years with them still affect you? They gave you a bad self-image.

SK. Yes. Not enough self-confidence. You can't change me.

MK. Would you say that your early experiences affected you more than everything else, more than the experience under Hitler?

SK. Yes. That's why I like to be alone. I have always avoided people. During the war [World War I], I had a high position. I was somebody.

But I never felt important. Not even when I was a doctor in Wolfenbüt-tel. Sure, I was somebody, people respected me—not my colleagues, but the people.

[He recalls again the ten years he spent with his aunts.]

SK. I could learn nothing in that house. It was nothing like my fa-ther's house. My father played the flute. My father collected stamps. My father collected pictures from magazines and so on. He loved Goethe's *Faust*. In spite of that, he was a very religious man. *Faust* usu-ally means nothing to very religious people. My father took his flute and his *Faust* into his grave. They are still in there. And *Faust* is my bible, as he called it. I still read it.

[Siegfried Kirchheimer died in January 1991, just a few weeks short of his hundredth birthday. The newspapers in Bremerhaven were full of stories about him and a street was named after him in Wolfenbüttel where he had lived and practiced medicine. The ceremonies were at-tended by two of his daughters. Although he abandoned medicine after his arrival in the United States, he kept all of his medical instruments, which were integrated into a collage of his life and exhibited in a new museum in Wolfenbüttel.]

꙳꙳꙳

Ilse Kaufherr

Ilse Kaufherr lived in the same village as the Hess family. Forced to leave school at an early age, she is still bitter at having been deprived of her education. She came to the United States by herself at eigh-teen and still appears to feel guilty that she did not know enough to avail herself of the opportunity, offered to her by the American con-sulate, to apply for additional visas on behalf of her family. Both of her parents were lost in the camps. Mrs. Kaufherr worked for years as a check-out clerk at a supermarket until her retirement.

IK. I fell in love with this country immediately. I wanted to forget all about Germany and the Hitler time and I said, "This is my future home for ever and ever, God willing." There's only one country: the United States.

[Mrs. Kaufherr lived in Newark for a few months with one of her sisters and then went to Rutland, Vermont, to stay with another sister and her husband. He was from Vienna and had come over at the end of World War I.]

IK. He said to me the day I arrived, Tuesday, "You are most welcome in my house. Today and tomorrow you can speak all you want to in German to your sister. From Thursday on, only English in my house." Which made me feel not too happy. I had money to go back to my sister in Newark, but how in the world do I get back to Newark? I didn't know how because I didn't speak the language and there was no transportation like there is today. So naturally I cried.

My sister said, "Don't worry, when he goes to work Thursday morning, we can speak German all we want to." But at eleven o'clock, she had to go to the store to bring him lunch and I went with her. He was a watch repairman and he had a jewelry store. He made me sit in the back room with a pencil and paper. I looked at him like an idiot with this paper and pencil and all I could say was, "How do you do?" "Good morning," and "Good night." So he made me write the ABC.

He said, "You sound it out in German and I'll sound it out for you in English," and that's how I learned English.

When I came to New York a year later, people did not believe I was in this country such a short time. Speaking such a beautiful English without an accent. Then, meeting German refugees here again and marrying into a refugee family, speaking German all over again, against my better wishes, I lost my good English and speak a lousy English today. Also a lot of Jewish people you meet on the street speak only German to you. You feel like an idiot if you want to answer them in English. [They'll say] "Oh, she wants to show off already. She can speak English." Which I really did at the beginning. They said, "Oh, look at her. She's showing off."

[Mrs. Kaufherr worked as a nursemaid to a family with small children, first at a summer resort in upstate New York and then in the Bronx. In 1939, she was married to another German Jewish refugee and moved to Washington Heights. Her life was a difficult one because of the instability of her marriage coupled with financial problems. She was living with her mother-in-law who looked after her first child, a daughter, while she held down two jobs, working five days a week at a bakery and three nights a week as a cashier in a restaurant. She was unable to count on her husband who was absent much of the time. Her straitened circumstances were particularly painful because she could not easily socialize with other mothers.]

IK. In the summertime when it was brutally hot and you met the women on the street with their babies, they said, "Let's go for a Coke" or whatever. I had to be allergic to everything because if I did have a nickel I wanted my child to have a Coke or an ice cream or whatever the other children had.

[After her second child was born she stayed at home to look after her children. She made very few friends in the neighborhood.]

IK. I was busy working either in the house or taking care of my mother-in-law and didn't have the money to commute when they wanted to go to a show or a movie or just entertain. I could not entertain in my house as much as I would have loved to because, if you are being entertained at someone's home, you would like to entertain too. So I had a very small social life. I could not go to theaters or operas, which I would have loved to go to. Movies I didn't care too much for, but I would have loved to go to the opera and to shows.

MK. Did you see any of the people you knew from your hometown?

IK. Very few, until one day I received a postcard from my dearest family from Ruppichteroth saying they had arrived here. It was the Oskar Hess family.

[Unlike today, postcards were frequently used as a mode of communication, even if, as in the Hess family's case, people lived just a couple of blocks away. They were cheaper than telephone calls and would arrive the next day, without fail.]

It was one of the happiest days of my life when I saw the family again.

GERMANY

MK. Do you think that you would have had a better life if you hadn't been chased out of Germany?

IK. I don't ever, ever regret coming to the United States. I would never, never want to leave it. It has given me a home, it has given me all the opportunities, especially if I had been smart enough to use them. I could have gone to school here had I used my brain. I would never, never go back to Germany, even though they tell me it's beautiful today, but nobody could pay me to go back for a visit.

WH. You've never been back?

IK. I've never been back, and I never would go back. No matter what anybody would offer me. That's the sour feeling I have about my childhood. Just picture yourself being pushed around and robbed, and called, "Dirty Jew!" and you had never done any harm to anybody. We weren't raised to be harmful or disrespectful toward a child or toward any adult. We were brought up to be honest, nice people.

MK. Do you feel the same way about buying German goods as you do about going to Germany?

IK. If I can help it, I will not buy German. I will not. I have no good memories from Germany so why deal with them? All my parents' jewelry was taken, and people have gone back to inquire about it, and the ones who had it denied it. Why not give it back? It belongs to us. No, I wouldn't go back. Bad memories. There are other people who have suffered much, much more, who have been in concentration camps. Thank God, I never was.

And only one thing I'm sorry about: that they ever built Germany up again to something so beautiful like everybody says it is today. I resent that. The money that this country sent out to build it up . . . they should have kept it here and helped poor people. They should have demolished it and demolished it more.

[Though not as drastic, the Morgenthau Plan—devised by Henry Morgenthau Sr., secretary of the Treasury under Franklin D. Roosevelt—called for converting Germany from an industrial economy to an agrarian one to forestall any military potential. The plan had many advocates but was never approved.]

IK. And if they would start demolishing Germany today, I would give my last dollar for it.

America has so much to offer. So many beautiful places that I've only heard of but have never seen. My wish is that some day—and this is a wish I had as a little girl—I will own a car and drive through the United States. Stay as long as I want to and keep on going. And see every little bit of every big bit of the United States.

Theo and Gretchen Krämer

An ardent patriot trained as an economist, Theo Krämer had difficulty advancing in his profession in Germany because he was Jewish. While employed at a Jewish export firm, he was sent to Buchenwald concentration camp. His wife worked frantically to arrange for his release and their subsequent departure from Germany. His nephew Walter Hess asks some of the questions here.

WORK IN AMERICA

GK. The first day I was in the United States, I made seventy cents. I made a necklace. My husband helped, my mother, my sister—the whole family helped. They came over on Saturday and then on Sunday. I got seventy cents. I was so happy, I made money! I was rich when I got the seventy cents.

TK. Even my three-year-old kid helped a little bit.

GK. That's what I did every day.

[Mr. Krämer's first job was in a hardware store where he earned seven dollars a week.]

TK. After I was there four, five weeks, I went down to the cellar to bring up some stuff. There were so many spider webs, spiders. I got an infection in the arm. The boss sent me to a relative of his, a doctor, who treated me so nobody had to pay. After it was healed I was out of a job because I couldn't go back there [to the store]. My boss let me go because I had trouble with the arm. And he didn't send me for workman's compensation or anything. Only to his relative for treatment.

WH. Since you were university trained and had a doctorate, did you think of getting work in your field?

TK. I couldn't do it. We came over in the summer, it was so hot. My wife had work and sometimes she took the kids with her. She worked on Saturdays too. But she couldn't take the bus or subway because she's religious. We lived on 159th Street at this time and she was working on University Avenue in the Bronx. So she walked from 159th Street and

Amsterdam Avenue, in that heat, on Saturday, with the kid. And she walked back. [This would be a good two-hour walk.]

MK. She worked on Shabbos?

TK. My wife did, I didn't.

GK. It was for a very old lady. It was not a hard job. I got eight dollars a week.

MK. You were telling Walter why you didn't go into economics even though you already had a doctorate.

TK. I didn't want my wife to work too hard while I would be studying. I wanted to work too, I had to make some money. And I was nervous again. I couldn't read the paper. When I saw people in the subway reading the funnies, I couldn't believe they could sit down there and read and read. I knew what was happening in Germany. I didn't lose my nerves, but I was nervous. I wanted to work and make money because we didn't bring anything over. We wrote to Germany to get our stuff shipped. It was in a lift. They told us, "Send some money." Then they told us it was bombed out. So if we had sent money, we still wouldn't have gotten anything either. We came here with just a pillow.

GK. With a pillow?

TK. Yes, because I wrote to you before you came to England, "Bring the pillow with you."

WH. So you felt the need to work overrode the possibility of studying again.

TK. I didn't have the brains anymore for studying.

WH. Since you already had your degree, why did you need further study?

TK. I had to start over. Because what I did in Germany, they wouldn't recognize here as a public accountant. The laws are different and you have to take an examination to prove that you studied here too.

MK. Just like doctors had to do to be licensed here.

TK. Sure. In Germany I studied not only social economics but all about taxes too. Everything is entirely different here.

WH. How do you feel about Germany today?

TK. I'm grateful that they did a lot for Israel.

MK. You never went back?

TK. No, no. I probably could have been invited to go to Frankfurt or maybe to Butzbach.

MK. Can you describe your feelings?

GK. I hate them. If you had seen them in Germany ... "Wenn juden Blut vom Messer spritzt ..." [When Jewish blood spurts from the knife ...], when they sang that song ...

TK. A couple of years ago I was in Israel and I met a German boy, a tourist. He was about twenty, twenty-one. He said he doesn't know anything about what happened in Germany. I don't think he was lying. He was a very, very nice boy.

I had really good friends in Germany. Once I was walking on the street in Frankfurt, and all of a sudden the SS came along. The officer who was on a horse looked at me. He was a friend, we were in school together. I cried. I know exactly what he thought about me. He had been in World War I and had an Iron Cross. He was a good friend. But he didn't have a job and he was a good soldier. So what should he have done? He joined the SS. I had other friends, but when I passed them on the street they turned away.

AFTEREFFECTS

MK. Do you think your experiences changed you in any way?

TK. You became more careful about other people. *[Long pause.]* When I was about ten, fifteen, sixteen, seventeen, I had no contact with antisemitism. When Hitler came, you found out you were Jewish. That other people look down on Jews. And that never left me. That gulf between gentiles and Jews. So when I have to deal with gentiles, I don't just want to do good—I want to do double-good. I want to show them that the Jew is not worse than the gentile.

MK. The Hitler experience made you more cowardly or more afraid?

TK. No, no. The first couple of weeks after you came out of the concentration camp and you walked along the street you always heard the heavy boots behind you. That's logical.

MK. You said before that when you were in the subway here and saw people reading the funnies, it disturbed you that people could carry on such a normal existence.

TK. Yes. I thought to myself, "Why can't you sit down and do the same thing?"

MK. How long did it take you before you could do it—sit down and have a normal existence?

TK. I have been here in the States for forty years.

GK. Forty-one.

TK. Forty-one years. I don't think I read ten books all the way through from beginning to end.

GK. He can't read a book!

MK. Did you read books then, in Germany?

TK. Sure I could do it.

WH. You mean you can't concentrate on that kind of work?

TK. That's it.

MK. How do you explain that, even today?

TK. The nerves.

⚹

Ilse Marcus

Brought up in Breslau in a comfortable middle-class family to be a docile and obedient young woman, Mrs. Marcus can scarcely recognize her former self. The example of the Polish Jews she met at Auschwitz and the resistance of the Warsaw ghetto fighters has marked her. She returns often to her belief that the ship, the St. Louis, *would never have returned to Europe after being denied permission to dock in Cuba had there been Polish Jews among the refugee passengers who might have taken over the ship. The* St. Louis *sailed back and Mrs. Marcus and her mother were eventually shipped to Auschwitz from Belgium. She survived the Death March and two other camps, and, rather than remain in Belgium where she had last lived with her mother, she opted to come to America.*

MK. It's many years later and you've lived in America. Is this like the home you used to know?

IM. I am very unhappy to say that I lost one fatherland and I didn't find a second one. When we needed America badly, it was closed to us and that's why I lost our family.

MK. So Roosevelt is not the hero for you that he was for other German Jews?

IM. Definitely not. And it's hard to believe that his election depended on letting us in or not. People who lived in America before World War II probably know that antisemitism in America was bigger here than it ever was in Germany before Hitler. Because there was never a restricted area in Germany, and here you had restricted hotels, for example. I remember I was told what it meant when you saw a sign: "Church nearby." And I heard of the case of Senator Lehman, when he wanted to go to a hotel and they didn't want to accept him. All these things never happened in Germany before Hitler. There was no such thing as "restricted hotels" or a "restricted area." So I would never build too much confidence in any country but Israel. First of all, we know we have a country, and we know we have a country that would take us at any time.

I could never understand how in all of America there was no room for nine hundred Jews [from the *St. Louis*]. But now there is room for—how many thousands from all over the world? German Jews came with a very good background, they brought culture, they could immediately be put to work. Even though we started, let's say, under our level. But we did any kind of work, nobody took unemployment, nobody needed welfare. The people who are coming in today are starting with welfare right away, they don't know the language, it's hard to put them into the working process, and they are the biggest problems.

For instance, the schools have to be at least bilingual. We were told right away, "This is an English-speaking country, you have to learn the language if you don't know it. If you know it you have to improve it," and nobody was bending backward to understand our German, as we have to do now to understand the others' Spanish. In my neighborhood I have a problem finding an English paper. It's all Spanish papers around me. And I think this is a mistake in our system. Why shouldn't the children who come here learn English in school? Why should schools teach Spanish?

GERMANY

MK. Many Germans say they didn't know about the camps. Do you believe that?

IM. No, it's not true. It's unbelievable that no one heard about them.

MK. Even if they didn't know, they saw enough going on. The deportations, for example.

IM. It's really amazing that the mass of German people all went along with it. All right, the political situation was bad, unemployment was high . . . all this worked for Hitler.

MK. How do you feel about Germany today?

IM. I would never go back to Germany. Because I have the feeling that every stone is covered with blood. I might be wrong. In the meantime, it's another generation, which probably, definitely, has nothing to do with Hitler. For them probably the whole period is history. I see a German and I see red! I don't want to talk to any of them. The minute I have a chance, I explode. I am, in general, very controlled, but that's beyond my control. I just see a Nazi in every German. That's something I can't overcome. It's probably wrong, but that's how I feel. It's an emotional feeling. Whenever I am in contact with Germans there is a collision.

[Despite her refusal ever to fly in a German plane, Mrs. Marcus found herself in a situation while traveling in Spain where she had no alternative but to take a Lufthansa flight. At that time airlines were very strict about baggage limitations. Anyone who had overweight luggage usually took it on board as hand luggage, which did not have to be weighed. However, at the Lufthansa counter at the airport Mrs. Marcus was asked to put her hand luggage on the scale. The particular bag she was carrying had been with her to many places around the world and she had never been asked to weigh it by any airline.]

IM. I'm standing there with the bag over my arm and the German Lufthansa woman says to me, "This has to be weighed too." I said, "Over my dead body."

MK. In German?

IM. In German. My friend from Colombia who was with me was fluent in Spanish and English. So we repeated everything in all three languages—English, German, and Spanish. In the meantime there was a whole crowd around us and everyone understood one language or another. I would have thrown that bag at her head! She would not have gotten me to put it on the scale. Finally, a German man next to her said in German, "You'd better let her go."

MK. There are some Germans who hid Jews.

IM. Yes, I know, because I had an aunt and a cousin in Berlin who were hidden the whole time by Germans.

[She adds that it was easier for German Jews to survive underground in Germany than in another country. First, they were helped by German clergy, and second, you could not tell German Jews apart from the rest of the population.]

IM. I mean it is wrong, it's always wrong to generalize, but the mass of the people were Nazis. They had to join or they did join, but just the fact that something like this could happen in Germany . . . one of the countries highest in culture. It's unbelievable. We just didn't want to understand the situation.

We were all so German. I remember in 1933, in school, we talked about our family tree. My family went back to the sixteenth century. Who could imagine these things? It just didn't click. And that's why most people just didn't leave in time. Because everybody thought that it was impossible for this to happen in Germany.

MK. Of course, the German Jews were very assimilated.

IM. They called themselves "Germans of Jewish faith." First they were German and then they were Jews. American Jews are Americans first and Jews second. I am against any kind of nationalism.

MK. Because it's dangerous?

IM. Yes.

MK. How about Israeli nationalism?

IM. That's a different story. *[Laughs.]*

MK. Now that wasn't true of the Polish Jews. The Polish Jews were Jews first.

IM. They were Jews first.

[Mrs. Marcus grew up in a religious, but not orthodox, home. As a result of her experiences during the war, she lost whatever little belief she had, and for a long time after her liberation she did not set foot in a synagogue. However, she was drawn to Israel and all it symbolized and continues to be a staunch supporter.]

IM. If Israel had been another country, the whole world would have supported it. But because it is Israel, it's Jewish, and everybody hates it.

The Polish Jews were the only ones who put up a fight against the Germans and they really tried to defend themselves while we did nothing. They always had to struggle and fight their whole lives in Poland. They never had rights like everybody else and they had a lousy life in Poland.

MK. Isn't it true that many German Jews tend to have contempt for the Polish Jews?

IM. That's right. Unfortunately, the Polish Jews we met were of a lower class in Germany. So we were kind of snobs.

[Breslau was close to the Polish border and many Poles who were fleeing from Poland passed through there. Mrs. Marcus describes her mother as being very socially minded. For a time, a Polish family stayed at the Marcus home where they were clothed and fed.]

IM. When they came through on their way out to immigrate to another country, we helped them but our heart was not with them. I have to admit that. I mean, education is not everything. We were lucky, we could get the education, but Polish Jews couldn't.

MK. Do you work for Jews at present?

IM. I work at present at Fordham University for the Jesuit order *[laughter]*. I do bookkeeping, and they are awfully nice. They are highly cultured, highly educated, and it's a pleasure to work with them and for them.

LOOKING BACK

MK. Did you ever marry again?

IM. No, unfortunately. Whenever I met someone, I compared him with my husband and the other one couldn't measure up. I have seen a lot of second marriages that are not very good and where women make a lot of compromise just to find a companion. I am not too much in favor of compromise. I am willing to do fifty-fifty. But not more than that. I would never have married a man, let's say, below my standard, below my level. Maybe I am a snob, I don't know. But in order for a marriage to hold there are a lot of things you have to have in common.

MK. Do you think about the past with your husband?

IM. I think a lot about the past. And mostly at night. That's where my sleepless nights are coming from. In daytime I am busy enough, but at night I cannot fall asleep right away. I twist around a hundred times. My nerves are really very bad, and at night, it's my past. I think about my husband, about the whole family. These are wounds that never heal. I never got over it.

MK. What do you think you learned from all this? Have you changed?

IM. I think I changed. First of all, I wouldn't just blindly obey any authority anymore. I wouldn't trust any authority. It made me a lot tougher. For instance, as most girls probably are, I was very sheltered by my parents, I was sheltered by my husband, and I didn't even think for myself. Nowadays, I would think: "This is right, this is wrong, this I want to do, this I don't want to do. And there I will obey and there I will not obey."

MK. Do you think you would seem strange to your mother today?

IM. Probably. Nobody—my parents, my husband—nobody would recognize me. I was the most timid girl you can imagine. My mother always said, "You will never be able to stand on your own two feet." But I have learned to fight.

I walk around with a knife. I walk around with my old tripod—it looks like an umbrella. I would hit somebody over the head if he attacks me. I would try to defend myself.

MK. Do you think other German Jews also learned what you have learned?

IM. I think so. From this experience everybody should have learned. I mean, they should have learned this: Who can you trust, just blindly?

⚹⚹

Alice Oppenheimer

Well-to-do owners of two factories in Mannheim, the Oppenheimers arrived in Washington Heights in 1938, before Kristallnacht, and then almost immediately established themselves as community leaders. They founded a newspaper and became prominent members of a new congregation. Mrs. Oppenheimer refers to the common perception that German Jews were German first and Jews second and did not take their religion as seriously as other Jews.

AO. I think there is a wrong attitude toward the German Jews. Some German Jews were very assimilated and some were still very religious.

When I came over and became an editor of a newspaper, I was invited very often to big affairs where I was the only German. And I was told that the German Jews didn't want to be Jews anymore—but I was the only one who kept the dietary laws. And everyone talked about me because, out of forty or so newspaper editors from Jewish newspapers, I was the only one who said I wouldn't eat there unless I could keep the dietary laws. And they would sometimes order something special for me.

MK. How do you feel about Israel?

AO. Since my early youth I was always Zionist-minded. Always. I have the biggest admiration for the Israelis and for what they did. When you go to Israel, you can see. I was there in 1936 and later in 1959. There was a big difference. I was there in 1972 and there was a big difference again. You must admire what these people did. They really made it a cliché, the desert blooming. But when you are there, you can't believe what they did.

I went back to Germany a few times. I had to go because my husband passed away and I had things to attend to. I didn't feel at home anymore in Germany. My home is America. I got acquainted with the life in America and too many memories came back to me. Everybody I met told me that he wasn't a Nazi. I couldn't believe it, so I never would go back again. I had to go then, but I never would return.

MK. In general, before Hitler, the Jews were not critical of Germany.

AO. Yes, they were uncritical and they felt very much as Germans. I mean my own father was such a patriot. During World War I, they had to give everything. We had very big copper pots and other things and we had to give them up to help the government.

MK. Do you think that the Jews would have voted for Hitler if he hadn't been antisemitic?

AO. No, no.

MK. It's a harsh thought.

AO. I think there were people who wanted to vote for Hitler, of course.

MK. Jews?

AO. Jews too, but you have every kind of people. Where there are people there are different opinions, so there were people who were for Hitler and people who were strictly against him.

IN AMERICA

MK. The Jews from Germany seemed to me to become very uncritical of America once they came here.

AO. Sure, but you must always take into consideration that these people went through so much that they felt it was their duty to support America. They took us in at that time and our best people came to America. I think that America didn't lose anything.

MK. But America *didn't* take in many Jewish refugees.

AO. Unfortunately they should have taken in more. I will never forget that we could have saved many more Jews if America would have taken them in.

Today they take in everybody and they go right away on welfare and they don't work and they even kill people and so on. But in our immigration there were people who wanted to do something and they were refused.

MK. What about the new Jewish refugees? Are they like us when we came over?

AO. What do you mean? From Russia? No, I think the Russian Jews take everything for granted as far as I can see.

MK. Can you give me an example.

AO. You know, I can't really say, I don't know too many, but I work in this center where they come to eat in the luncheon club. I see these people are satisfied with their life without working. I don't know from what they live, they must live from something. It's a different kind of immigration from ours. But I wouldn't give an opinion about them because I don't know too many Russians.

MK. Looking back, how do you feel about your last forty, forty-five years in America?

AO. I feel that we survived, and I am very happy that I could help other people to survive too. And that gives me a feeling that I have not lived in vain. It was a big shock for me when my husband died when he was only fifty. The only way I survived was that I had a lot to do. I was editor of this newspaper and I did a lot of social work and I was president of a few organizations.

[Mrs. Oppenheimer remained active in the Jewish community until her death in 1990.]

Gabriele Schiff

Even before she left Germany in 1938 at the age of twenty-one, Gabriele Schiff had already been actively involved in trying to smuggle Jewish children out of Germany and in attempting to persuade young people to emigrate to Palestine. Her primary interest was in becoming a social worker but it was evident that she would never be able to obtain a degree in Germany. Her father was a physician in Hamburg and she had many relatives in the United States, but she did not want to be "the poor European relative who had to be supported." Although she was a member of the wealthy Warburg family, she determined to make it on her own. She was fortunate to land a job in Philadelphia taking care of children in the household of a University of Pennsylvania professor who encouraged her to apply for a scholarship to college.

During the war she worked in a psychiatric hospital in Maryland and then was sent by the War Relocation Authority to Oswego, New York, to help administer a refugee camp.

At the time of this interview, 1981, Dr. Schiff was one of the directors of Selfhelp Community Services, the nonprofit welfare organization founded in 1936 by a group of German émigrés to assist Jewish refugees in finding homes and work. My friend Walter Hess is present and asks some of the questions.

GS. Oswego was the only camp that ever existed where President Roosevelt brought a thousand refugees to live in this country behind barbed wire. They were predominantly Jewish refugees who had landed up in Italy. The secretary of the Interior, Harold Ickes, had sent his assistant, Dr. Ruth Gruber, to Italy to look over the Italian camps and she came back with a thousand people.

It was a wild mixture of nationalities and religions, though predominantly Jewish because the Italians had put the Jews into camps. They were not concentration camps, though people always say they are, but you can't compare them. They were detainment camps, I guess. And when we unpacked our package, the first thing that happened was a wild fistfight between a Lithuanian and a Russian who both thought they had a claim to a nonexistent crown of Lithuania. That type of thing [laughs].

They came from Italy and they had been in various camps. And right away you had different nationalities fighting each other. European men are not very much used to doing the cooking and so we had very many fights. And also many good times. We had to set up a hospital and we really didn't have any doctor with a medical degree. We had Yugoslav doctors [who were trained but were lacking degrees]. I worked there for two years and then the camp was dissolved. Many of the people ended up in Washington Heights because they already had relatives or friends there. So some of my Oswego gang ended up in the Heights and some a little further downtown, say from the eighties up on the west side.

MK. They were not German, predominantly?

GS. They were the second-largest group. The biggest group were the Poles, and the second-largest were the Germans.

WH. Oswego is quite far north and it must have been cold.

GS. It was ice cold and terrible things happened. People had to shovel coal and one man froze to death. It was not all roses . . . Anyhow, that was that. I had been waiting eagerly for my papers to come through because I wanted to work in Europe as soon after the war as possible. In the meantime I worked at the children's court for adolescents here in New York, which I loved. I am by training a psychiatric social worker. Then my papers came through and very early in 1947 I went to Europe and worked for three years in the displaced persons camps.

[By the end of World War II, several million people had been uprooted from their home countries and were stranded throughout Europe as "displaced persons" (DPs). The work of repatriation took years and was conducted by a number of agencies including the Joint Distribution Committee ("the Joint") and the U.N. Relief and Rehabilitation Administration (UNRRA). Even after most DPs were returned to their homelands, approximately one million still needed to be placed in other countries.]

GS. I was constantly on lend-lease from the Joint Distribution Committee. In the camps, of course, you had German Jews but they were surely not the majority. I tried to get them into this country. I worked with people who had tuberculosis. I got them right out of Bergen-Belsen—they were the first ones. I got them into rehabilitation centers. This was in 1947.

MK. They were still in Belsen? In 1947?

GS. Yes, because Belsen had been changed into a sort of relocation camp. It wasn't a concentration camp anymore.

[Back in America, Dr. Schiff resumed her social work, with the New York Association for New Americans (NYANA).]

GS. I returned to NYANA because I wanted to welcome my displaced persons whom I'd gotten out of the camps. I wanted to see how bad a job we had done in retraining them because we had trained them in all sorts of trades that they couldn't use here, such as bookbinding and mending shoes. That was something of a failure. In the early 1950s, with NYANA and HIAS [Hebrew Immigration Aid Society] you were very much in demand if you had the experience of having worked in the camps abroad. And I had to get people resettled, some in Washington Heights, some in Williamsburg [in Brooklyn].

MK. What were your first impressions of the community in Washington Heights and when did you first encounter it?

GS. When I came in 1938 I knew people in Washington Heights whom I visited. I had a cousin there. I liked the landscape. It reminded me of Europe. It wasn't too crowded and people were talking German. There were some intellectual people I knew who invited me in the evenings. We talked about philosophy—it was nice. But I didn't want to be caught by it because I felt that if I was going to live in America, I better live in *America*. There was a temptation [to remain in Washington Heights]. In later years I could afford that temptation, but in the beginning I had to make it on my own in the American community.

SELFHELP

GS. In Washington Heights they had begun a German-Jewish *Landsmannschaft* [organization of fellow countrymen] in the 1930s. It began as an employment agency, people trying to help each other find jobs. So many of the early immigrants were professional people where the men all had to study again. And the women had not really been trained for anything, but they were very good housewives and that's how the job of homemaker came into being. Today we have thousands of homemakers at Selfhelp but they are not the German Jews anymore. But that was our beginning.

[The organization adapted to the changing needs of the group].

GS. When there were small children part of us split off to help reconstruct the community and started a kindergarten [see the interview with Rosi Spier in part 4]. Of course, now we don't need that anymore. Now we are a geriatric agency.

[With the help of unclaimed restitution money from Germany, the agency built three residences for aging citizens, open to all ethnic groups. The agency continues to expand its activities, particularly in finding and helping elderly survivors of Nazism in the Brooklyn, New York, area—thanks to new funding from the German government.]

MK. Who are the Hitler victims who still need your help?

GS. The people who are now seventy-five and over, who are sick and who never quite adjusted to this country. They moved here but they never emigrated, if you know what I mean. They are still living on Berlin's Kurfürstendamm or wherever. They find it very hard to fight for their entitlements or even to accept them. Medicaid is something shameful to them.

WH. What about cultured people or educated people who were wealthy?

GS. Yes—people who had a very different living standard in Europe. We were trying to use some of our restitution money to help those people live a little bit by the same standards they had in Germany.

MK. Did they become financially secure after a while with reparations? And was the adjustment you speak of more of an emotional adjustment than a financial one?

GS. It's both. On the whole the German Jewish group did rather well financially, better than the other groups. They had the big advantage of much more schooling behind them. They really knew how to work. The others knew it too, but in a different kind of work. Emotionally, the German Jews had a more difficult adjustment because they had a more pleasant life in Europe. If your life was worse in Europe then you thought this was paradise.

What we have now in Washington Heights are the people who could not move out of there. Because what you see again and again is that the children of the people in Washington Heights who did very well are in Scarsdale or Great Neck. And they have brought their parents along, if not directly there, then somewhere in the vicinity. What is left in Washington Heights are the financially more limited, some highly educated, though this has nothing to do with it; many are lonely, because these are the people who often had no children to bring them somewhere else. Many, many widows.

I've always had a leitmotif for this agency (for some time now, I was the director of Social Services): We are our clients' last surviving relatives. And that is how I see the special challenge of this agency. Our clientele does not have the family support system that many elderly people have.

[Walter mentions the strong "hometown" support system in Washington Heights. When his mother was widowed, many people in the neighborhood rallied to her. There was a continuing infrastructure of relationships.]

GS. That is true. And you also have the many congregations in Washington Heights. But there are always people who are not being caught by any of them. You have so much sickness with old people, and Washington Heights is not the most secure neighborhood. People don't want to visit except during daylight. We have to see that people get fed. We did run a trip program—we are out of money now—where we would take people to Macy's by bus, or wherever they wanted to go shopping. That has died out right now. But we do a lot of counseling. We have quite a staff of trained social workers who go into the home and do everything from helping to write a will and getting a lawyer, to seeing that people get to the hospital and making sure funeral instructions are being carried out. But in Washington Heights, we find that the children have really moved out of the neighborhood and that leaves this isolated elderly community.

In the beginning Washington Heights was such an attractive community. Do you remember? Fort Tryon Park was lovely. On Memorial Day I thought that would be a nice day to go to the park. But the people have changed there, too.

MK. The poorer Washington Heights people have moved closer to the park too.

GS. Yes, that's so.

[Dr. Schiff had married a Polish Jewish physician in 1952 who, like many other professionals, had to undergo retraining in the United States.]

GS. When my husband came over, he and his old mother lived on Audubon Avenue, around 181st Street. Well, that has changed so that I would not want to walk around there after six o'clock. In the beginning when I got the room there, it seemed to be a little bit like home and there were people who spoke German. And they called me Frau Doktor in the store. It's this type of thing that makes for a cohesive neighborhood.

But in a way, and I think we have to keep this in mind, Washington Heights isn't so different from other communities in this city. Communities change completely.

EASTERN JEWS VERSUS GERMAN JEWS

MK. How were the Jews changed by the Nazi experience, if they were changed at all?

GS. Some were and some were not. I think human beings are human beings, and you run also into the very difficult (to me unsolvable) problem between eastern and western European Jews. I find that people have not changed very much. And I hear myself very often say: "Hitler did not make any distinctions, why do we have to?" I've been to one conference after the other. I have been quite active with the children of the Holocaust. They are good enough to ask me in as an advisor and also to the psychiatric meetings. The split is just among the older generation. I think the children have overcome it. When I look at the marriages or nonmarriages—the lifestyles these days—I really think for the first time many problems have been overcome, whereas some of the [organizational] boards still feel the differences very strongly. A good bit of snobbism on both sides. I think it is time that changes human beings more than anything else.

MK. It's usually a good deal of snobbism by the German Jews and resentment by the eastern Jews.

GS. Yes, and the resentment is then compensated by another type of snobbism. You know, "We are the intellectuals, we are the people of the book. What do you know? You are virgins."

Marion Rosen

Marion Rosen is married to Hilde Kracko's brother, Hans Rosen, who spent the war years eluding the Nazis in Holland. Mrs. Rosen was born in a small village near Kassel, a city in Westphalia.

MK. Listen, I was brought up in Washington Heights—

MR. —Isn't it a horrible place, especially when you've come from Ohio?

MK. Is that where you came from? Tell me why this is a horrible place.

MR. I'll tell you why. You come from Shaker Heights, Ohio, from a beautiful house to Audubon Avenue and a lousy three-room apartment, and you feel like you're in jail. And that gives you a lasting impression.

MK. This place is beautiful. [The Rosen apartment is on Fort Washington Avenue.]

MR. It's not bad *[laughs]*.

MK. Did you have a better view in Ohio than the Hudson and the Palisades, the eighth wonder of the world?

MR. No, but we had wonderful, nice people.

MK. Tell me about that.

MR. What do you want to know, doctor? *[Laughs.]*

MK. Well, what about the people in Washington Heights?

MR. I'll tell you what I think. No, I'm not angry. I'm disappointed. Because I feel they're not together, they're very clannish. If you don't belong to a certain group, you're out. If you are a middle-aged woman, like I am, and you wear dungarees, you are either an idiot or they think you want to be in your twenties. Or they're just jealous because you don't conform. You see? You understand what I mean? I'm taking it very, very personally.

MK. That's one of the reasons I left the Heights. As a matter of fact, I changed out of my jeans before coming to you, not knowing who you were.

MR. Well, that's all I wear is jeans. What else can I say? . . . If you don't belong to a . . . if you are an atheist, don't belong to a temple, you're certainly out. If you voice your opinion, you're out altogether. You must have one opinion, and that's their opinion.

MK. Now you're talking generally.

MR. I'm talking in general.

MK. You must have gotten specific reactions from individuals rather than groups of people.

MR. Well, from individuals, yes. Who belong to groups . . .

MK. Give me an example.

MR. Yes, I'll give you an example. I was born in Germany, but my parents are eastern, from Russian Poland. So you are excluded right away. Because that already makes you an outsider.

MK. But how did the people know that?

MR. Because of my actions. Because I don't act like a *Yekke* [a sometimes derogatory term for German Jew, derived, according to one theory, from "Jacke," the German word for "jacket" and indicating the alleged formality and "correctness" of German Jews. I have been called a Yekke myself. My family believed that the term had originated in Israel after the war, and was meant to describe the German Jews working in the fields with their jackets on.]

MR. You know what I mean? I don't act like a German Jew.

MK. Can you give me an example?

MR. *[Very agitated.]* I'll just give you one example. I overheard a couple in our elevator, quite an elegant couple as a matter of fact—if money makes you elegant, I don't know. But they seemed to be elegant-type people. They come from Frankfurt, right? So they're talking in German and I was standing next to them and they thought I could not understand German. So they were saying, in German, "Die Frankfurter Juden sind immer noch die besten" [The best Jews are still the ones from Frankfurt]. They have the most class. They're classy people and any Jews who don't come from that region or from Frankfurt itself are low-class people. OK?

So I went up to her and I said, "Excuse me, Madam," and I was furious. "I was born in Germany. I am a Jew. And do you know something? My parents died because of you. You are living in style. My mother was twenty-eight years old when she was gassed because she was Jewish and did not have the money to get out of Germany. That doesn't make me or us a lower class because we don't come from your region. My parents died because of you. People like you should have helped people like us. People don't stick together."

MK. You said this in German?

MR. That I said to her in English because my German is grammatically terribly poor.

MK. How did she respond?

MR. Well, she hasn't spoken to me since. Which, of course, I can't blame her for because I was fired up. I could have throttled her. That's one example. You see, if you don't have money, if you don't come from a certain region, and you are not a religious person, and you don't belong to, let's say, Breuer [known as the most orthodox German Jewish congregation in Washington Heights], you are nothing, you're a nobody. You're not even a Jew. But yet, Jewish people could not get out and these people could, and these people could have helped poor people like us in Germany. You understand? It makes us inferior. A Jew is a Jew. I just gave her a piece of my mind and I think I'm right.

[I point out that the majority of German Jewish refugees were not wealthy. Many of them had great difficulties, first in finding financial sponsors and, later, in struggling to make a living. They were not financially secure until after they began to receive reparation payments from Germany.]

MR. I am bitter that people go around saying, "I had this and that in Germany" and saying that there were no poor Jews in Germany. That's a lot of . . . I don't want to say it . . . that's garbage. Because there were a lot of poor German Jews.

At least I admit it. At home we had absolutely nothing. We had bread for breakfast and sometimes we had margarine on it. We were lucky. Did you ever meet a poor German Jew who admitted being poor?

I'll tell you something else. They don't even talk to us on a Saturday because, maybe, we dress differently. But yet, we are Jews, our hearts are Jewish. We are more Jewish, maybe, than they are. If it were not for our home here, which I'm trying to keep nice, according to my tastes, I would have moved long ago. I hate Washington Heights. I think this is an obnoxious place.

The people are not pleasant and they are terribly unfriendly and very German. I wouldn't even say they're Jewish. Really German. No wonder they call this the Fourth Reich. I can see why. Very arrogant. I'm very unhappy up here and I've lived here for thirty years. Thirty years and I cannot get used to this. I cannot get used to Washington Heights. I can't.

MK. Why have you stuck with it so long?

MR. First of all, because of my first husband who passed away. I was a widow. We had a business in Harlem. And he said, "It's easier to commute from this area to 128th Street. Why drive around? Why move to Jersey or Riverdale?" Right? And I thought it would be easier for his health. So I did it for him, I didn't do it for myself. My children never liked it either. They think it's a horrible place, Washington Heights. They hate to come and visit.

MK. But there are other areas, like West End Avenue or other sections.

MR. Yes, but that's too expensive. We have a bargain here, we don't pay that much rent. I've been in this apartment for fifteen years. If I could move this apartment, let's say, a little further uptown . . .

[The preceding Monday had been a Jewish holiday but Mrs. Rosen wasn't aware of it and had gone to work.]

MR. I didn't even know it was a holiday.

MK. Neither did I.

MR. You see!

MK. I should have known. I was dressed inappropriately when I came up here that day.

MR. Me too. When I came home from work I put on dungarees. And I said to my husband, "Oh, my gosh, we cannot go to the park because I am not wearing the uniform." The gloves, with the hats, with the right shoes. You know what I mean? I feel uncomfortable.

I went to temple here once at the Fort Tryon Jewish Center. And somebody came to me and said, "Welcome aboard!"

I said, "Aboard what?"

"Well, you're Irish, aren't you?"

So I said, "No, I happen to be Jewish."

"I could have sworn you were Irish but we accept all faiths here." She didn't believe I was Jewish.

MK. But are they German, the Fort Tryon Center?

MR. It's mixed. It's American, Russian, Jewish. You know, a lot of Russians are in this area also.

MK. Yes.

MR. Very clannish. I liked it mixed more with Americans. You know what I mean? But I never liked Washington Heights. Why my husband's family moved here, I can't imagine.

MK. When did you leave Germany?

MR. It was in 1939. I left with my parents. I was about ten years old.

MK. Where did you go?

MR. To Theresienstadt [the concentration camp]. For six months.

MK. What was that like?

MR. It was OK. It was fine. It was nothing. It was like a big camp. At that time it was still all right.

MK. But it must have been a shock to you after they took you from your home.

MR. The only shock was that you're separated from your parents. Because then I didn't see them anymore. There were thousands of kids. Thousands.

MK. How did you get out?

MR. They formed children's groups to go to Holland. Underground. And from Holland to England. In fact Hans [her husband] was in Holland, underground. There were three thousand children who went to Holland, to Haarlem.

I met one woman on the street here. It was years ago. She recognized me by my walk. She said I walked like my mother. She stopped me on the street. An old woman. I had noticed there was a woman walking behind me, very fast. And I turned around.

She came toward me and she said, "Your walk looks familiar. Is your mother so-and-so?"

And I said, "Yes."

She said, "You walk just like your mother." By that time I was older than my mother because she was twenty-eight years old when she died.

MK. So you left your parents in Theresienstadt. When was the next time you heard anything about them?

MR. In 1942, 1943. I was in England. We used to correspond by official postcards. Never with their signatures. I used to send them packages. We had food coupons in England and I used to sell them so I could buy canned foods to send them. I would get a "Thank you very much for your package," but never in their handwriting. It was a preprinted card. Whether they had gotten the package, I don't know.

You interviewed my husband. He has a better story than I have.

MK. Everybody's story is unique.

MR. But it's all the same.

MK. That's nonsense. It's not all the same at all.

MR. Yes it is. The outcome is the same: You come to the United States.

MK. But if you say it's all the same because we all get born and live and die, then yes, it's all the same.

MR. It is!

MK. It isn't. And you even prove it by saying you're so different from the other people in Washington Heights.

MR. Well, you're born the same, you die the same. That's it!

MK. That's not so.

MR. Some die with a silver spoon—maybe. In the long run maybe it depends on your values. What your values are or your expectations, or what you put into life is what you get out of life. Maybe that's the real McCoy.

MK. I think everyone's sorrows are unique also. Even if they can be understood in a common way.

MR. I think people our age will never be understood. Because we all got a little, what shall I say, "ein kleinen Klopf." You know what I mean? That's German for saying "a little nuts." Something got loosened, something happened. You can't get rid of it. It sticks with you. You have a guilt complex.

MK. You do?

MR. I do. Because I come from a very poor home. I feel that I have so much here. If my parents could only have had half of what I have. I feel guilty about it.

MK. You feel you abandoned them?

MR. No. I just feel guilty that I have so much and they had nothing.

MK. But material things aren't everything.

MR. No, but it helps. You can sleep well at night.

MK. But you have other sources of unhappiness. Like the neighborhood and your inability to make friends.

MR. No, we have friends. I just feel bitter that my parents didn't have what I have. Going back to Washington Heights, it's not Washington Heights any more. It's called Upper Harlem.

MK. It is?

MR. Yes. I don't mind. It doesn't matter to me. People are people. As long as people are good, a little integration won't do any harm. If there would be a nice black family in this house who might be my neighbor, why not give them a chance, like we were given a chance, right? It wouldn't harm me. But I think most people would be opposed to it in this area.

I said to my husband, "If we ever move out of here, maybe I would contact a black family and say, 'Here's an apartment.' *[Laughs.]* 'Take it.'" Or Spanish people, it doesn't matter.

MK. Do you find no one at all who is sympathetic to your views, to your way of life?

MR. No.

MK. No one at all?

MR. No. I think maybe it's jealousy also. Because we live differently, we think differently. I'm very opinionated. If I don't like something, I say it. If I like it, I say it too. You know what I mean? My best friends are in Ohio. Unfortunately, they live there. Or maybe fortunately. They're better off.

MK. Do you ever think about your Theresienstadt experience?

MR. No.

[This surprises me. I ask if she's deliberately trying to put it out of her mind and she says no. Does she dream about it?]

MR. I don't dream about it either. I don't dream at all. At least I don't remember if I do. I also don't take tomorrow for granted. I live each day as it is, as though it were my last day on earth. You cannot look back into the past because that's done with. But you can't look into the future either because you don't know what the future holds. So it's today. You can go to bed tonight and not wake up.

MK. When you clean the house [she seems to pour her energies into keeping it immaculate], that's an investment for tomorrow.

MR. No, that's for today. Because if something happens to me, my husband will have a clean house *[laughs]*. You will not find any dirty laundry anywhere. Or socks under the sofa *[laughs]*.

I did have a traumatic experience when my dog passed away, a Yorkshire terrier. I had him for thirteen and a half years. And that was a traumatic experience. I couldn't live with that for a long time. I couldn't leave the house for a week because I was crying day and night. That,

I think, was the love of my life. My dog. He's right there in front of you with a rose on top. *[She points to an urn.]*

MK. Is it possible that loss had an echo in your past?

MR. Maybe it had an echo because my first husband passed away eight years ago, at home, in my arms. Fifty years old. And that, of course, you can never forget. Now I can talk about it. I couldn't talk about for several years because . . . you get a lump in your throat. From this man I learned how to live. I learned what life was all about. That there are better things in life than what I had experienced before. We were married twenty-three years. Never long enough. Right? You have children by this man, so that was a traumatic experience. But I can talk about it. The second experience was my dog. I hope not to have a third experience like that.

MK. How do you avoid a third experience?

MR. I don't know. I don't think about it. That's why I don't think about tomorrow. It's today. Today was fine.

MK. Until I walked in, right?

MR. You're fine to me. If you are single, I have a very nice daughter . . .

Sary Lieber

Rabbi Lieber worked indefatigably for his congregants, not only ful-filling his official duties as rabbi, but also extending himself to help neighbors and neighbors' children who had gotten into trouble. On occasion, the Liebers were called upon by a distressed congregant to intercede with school authorities on behalf of a child.

SL. The German-Austrian immigrants were hard-working people. They did not ask anything from anybody, they took all kinds of jobs, no matter what. There was no job too low for them to accept. They were dishwashers, they were people who picked up clothes from the floor at Klein's department store on 14th Street, the women went out to clean for thirty-five cents an hour. Many were educated and this was not the kind of work they were used to, but they did it. They did not take any support from anybody, there were no demands made on the people who brought them here [those who put up the financial affidavits] or, God forbid, on the government. There was no such thing where they said, "I need twelve dollars a week to make a living, give it to me." They worked day and night. They came here with their "lifts" with all their furniture, they rented big apartments. They lived in one room and everything else was rented out. That's how they supported their families. It was one important way of making a living.

MK. Nowadays [1981] there are many new immigrants coming into the United States and we have to assume that conditions are very bad for them—Russians, Cubans, Haitians, people from Latin American countries and Asia. What's the difference between this immigration and ours?

SL. There's a great difference. At that time, I never heard of "illegal immigration." There was only legal immigration, which was very hard to attain. You had to have financial guarantees so you wouldn't be a burden to the American government, a visa, a quota number. You had to show all sorts of credentials before being considered. You were asked all sorts of questions by the American consul to ascertain your loyalty to America: for example, whether you belonged to the Communist party, whether you intended to assassinate the president. We were asked about matters that were absolutely foreign to us.

Today I don't know if these people ever needed to visit the American consulate in their country in order to get a visa to come here legally. There are hundreds of thousands of immigrants living and working here illegally. There was nothing like that in our time.

MK. What about the new Russian immigrants in the neighborhood?

SL. You know there is a natural barrier between people who are settled and others who come and want a job and want an apartment and want this and that. Our demands were very small. The refugees who come today have a different attitude—the Russians and the others. I have heard this from quite a few people. If you want to give a Russian family something, a piece of furniture or drapes or something, they will look at it ten times before accepting it, it's not good enough. We wouldn't have dared to refuse something that was given to us (though nobody offered us anything). We are offering these people a lot.

[She describes the Sunday morning clothing exchange, the *Kleiderstube*. "They would look over the things and if they fit, they would take them."]

MK. Once the German Jews were settled and confident and secure, and no longer in fear of their lives, what were the aftereffects of their experiences? What had they learned?

SL. That is a very individual matter. Some people never forgot what they went through, others wanted to forget. They didn't even want to talk about it. I don't believe that people became better because of this experience. One cannot generalize, but I do believe that experiences like these do not make better people if they were not good people before they came here.

MK. Would you ever go back to Germany?

SL. I would not go back to Germany to live, that is out of the question. Nor would I go there on vacation. I could only consider going to visit the grave of my father-in-law in Nuremberg. It is an unbearable thought for me to live among people with blood on their hands, not knowing who has and who hasn't. If you ask them, most of them say they didn't know anything, they had no idea of what was happening, which is not credible to me. They saw how people were hounded and rounded up and transported, that people had to leave in order to survive. That Germans knew nothing of this strikes me as totally unbelievable.

⚜

Melitta and Walter Hess

Walter Hess is with me during this conversation with his mother. He is hearing some of these stories for the first time.

POSTWAR GERMANY

MH. When I heard that they were in need, the people who helped me in Germany, I sent packages.

WH. Did they write to you?

MH. A lot of letters. I still get letters today from friends in Germany.

[Mrs. Hess returned to Germany for the first time in 1967. Asked why she went back, she says that she wanted to visit the cemetery in Butzbach, in Hesse, where her in-laws and her father were buried. She also was looking forward to seeing some friends. In addition, Mrs. Hess wanted to find out what had happened to their land.]

MH. I met one woman in Ruppichteroth. She was from one of the poorest families. They had the fewest things and the most debts, and they were the biggest Nazis. She was a girl then. She was a married woman now and I didn't recognize her at first. She tells me her maiden name. Then I got mad.

And she said, "You don't know me."

I said, "I know you. I never forget when you were standing in front of the post office with Marga Schumacher the day after the synagogue burned. And you said to her, 'That's nothing. It's going to get much better. We're going to burn many more. The Jews have to leave.' You had just come back from Cologne where you saw the Führer and were all enthusiastic. You had never encountered a lovelier human being."

And she said, "I think you're mistaken, I didn't know you."

And I said, "You knew me. Often enough you bought goods on credit from my in-laws' store."

She said, "We were children, we didn't understand. We also suffered a lot." She told me she lost two brothers in Russia.

I said, "How many of my people were lost? More than yours. My in-laws were gassed." Then she left because she said she had things to do.

[Mrs. Hess visited the cemetery in Butzbach and was dismayed to discover that her father's gravestone had been removed. She paid a visit to the mayor's office to complain.]

MH. That bastard—he said, "Here is a Jewess who claims her father's gravestone is gone."

And I said, "I don't claim it, I know that is where my father is buried." I had a terrible argument with him and my husband wouldn't let me stay there any longer. That guy was such a Nazi. We never said anything to my mother. We didn't want her to know the gravestone was taken away. We always said to her, "The stone is standing."

[On a later visit to Ruppichteroth after her husband Oskar died, she visited an old friend.]

MH. She told me once in a letter that she has dishes from my in-laws, I should pick them up. I didn't remember anything, and now after forty years, when I sat down, all of a sudden she showed me a whole set of china. I was so shocked that she kept the dishes for me. It was dangerous for her even to keep them for me through the war.

So I said to her, "You keep them." I didn't know what to say.

And she said, "But they are from your mother-in-law, she wanted you to have them."

So I went back to my cousin in Limburg and I couldn't sleep the whole night, I was so upset. This was the last memento from my in-laws and I left them there. I thought, if Oskar would have been alive, he would have been very mad at me. He would have said, "If they came from your side of the family, you would have taken them. Since they are from my side, you are leaving them there."

So I said to my cousin, "I'm going back to get those dishes." So she drove me all the way back to Ruppichteroth again.

My friend said, "I told you to take them home." So she packed them in a big bag and everything was fine until I came to the airport in Amsterdam to fly home to America. [Mrs. Hess had been visiting a cousin in Holland.] At the airport the girl said I have to pay a hundred dollars for overweight baggage for those dishes.

I said, "I will not. This is hand luggage and I am allowed to have two packages with me."

She said, "Maybe that's so in America but we don't do that here. If you don't pay, we have to confiscate it."

I said, "That's the last thing I have from my parents' house and I will take it back to America without paying a penny."

She said, "No, no, that's impossible."

So I asked to talk to an officer. The woman officer came and asked what was the matter.

I said, "That is a bag. My husband was in a concentration camp, my in-laws died in a camp, and this is all I have from them. People kept it for us so we would have something to remember of our parents." I started to cry, I was very upset. Not because of the money, but it was the only thing left from them.

The officer said, "Don't cry, it will be all right. Take it to America and I hope you come back to Holland. We would like to have you here again." I brought the dishes back and I gave them to Frankie [her youngest son].

MK. What happened to your land? Did people take advantage?

MH. Yes! There was one guy . . . My husband trusted everybody. He gave him the signature, he could do what he wanted. [Mr. Hess had signed over the rights to his property.] And he did what he wanted. He sold a lot of stuff for incredible prices. We got money but we should have gotten more.

MK. When you went back, you saw your old land?

MH. Yes.

MK. And who had it then?

MH. Neighbors. I was very shocked when I saw the beautiful land parceled out in pieces. He took a piece, and he took a piece, and the other neighbor took a piece. When I saw what they did with our land, how everybody took part of it and grabbed it, I got so mad. It hurt.

MK. Were these Nazis or were these friends?

MH. I don't know. They were Germans. They all took when they could.

MK. How do you feel about the Germans?

MH. In general, there were a lot of good guys. If there wouldn't have been some good ones, we wouldn't be here. The day Oskar left [for Holland], the pastor came to the train and said, "Mr. Hess, I wish I could go with you." Also, a lot of people had to be Nazis. They were afraid for their lives.

WH. Do you forgive the Germans for what they did?

MH. *[Hesitates.]* Uh . . . Yes . . . I don't know. If I were out there, maybe you would have put on a brown suit and maybe you would have looked pretty good . . . to save your life . . .

WH. Maybe not. A lot of them were Nazis and gladly went along.

MH. Walter, if this means, "To be or not to be . . ." If a father has to be afraid for his daughter or his son, you will act as a Nazi. Inside you wouldn't. I can understand. But they didn't have to kill and do everything else.

WH. "Inside" is all very nice but it doesn't help anyone.

MH. Wolfgang, it was too late! We were all sleeping. That's why the Nazis became so strong.

WH. Were the Jews at fault, too?

MH. Sure. There were very rich Jews and they didn't help the Socialist party. They were afraid. They helped the capitalists, the Nazis. They thought they would be safe with them.

[Her son concedes the truth of this, characterizing his father as a conservative agrarian farmer who did not favor any change.]

WH. Who's responsible, then?

MH. Human beings.

MK. In general?

MH. In general. In 1930, 1933, when Hitler was small, a lot of people defied him, but not enough.

MK. Your attitude is unusual. Many people like you won't go back to Germany. They don't want to shake hands with someone who could have been a murderer.

MH. My Frankie who is born here won't buy a German car. He is named for Franklin Roosevelt. But Roosevelt made a lot of mistakes too.

IN AMERICA

MH. In America we could always work, we always could make a living. Only in America do you have an opportunity like that. Maybe that's why I'm mad. Maybe our background was different from the background of the people who are coming today. We wanted to stand on our own two feet and not look out for gifts. We worked very hard. We were satisfied with what we had. It took us a very long time until we could buy a steak, but we were satisfied with chopped meat too. People have it much easier today. It took us five years to become citizens. The new people get welfare and unemployment benefits right away. Sometimes I can't blame them. For so many years they had nothing and all of a sudden they see that Mr. So-and-So can buy things, "so why shouldn't I?"

[She implies that the Russian Jewish immigrants would never work in menial jobs as the German Jews did. She tells of offering to give a bed to a needy Russian family and having it rejected. They have houses, good apartments, a lot of help, she says. But they complain of having to pay fifty cents for lunch at a Jewish center. For herself, she doesn't like people who "take advantage." She always preferred to earn money rather than be beholden to others.]

MH. It's hard . . . [She is not happy that it is the citizens' taxes that support the new immigrants.] I don't know if later on they [become] better people. If I look at our immigration, and all the children from it, not many failed. They saw it at home, they learned, they studied. When something was wrong in school, I went to school. Today, the father lives here, the mother lives there. The kids have no home. Today there's a lot wrong.

MK. Were you religious when you were younger and did you change your attitude?

MH. I believe in something. I don't know what it is. There is something there. On the other hand, I'm a hypocrite. I go to shul and pray and then I don't believe. But I believe in *Bestimmung* [destiny]. If there is a God then he was very mean to me. On the other hand he was good to me.

For me two things are important: to be healthy and not to need anybody. To be independent.

MK. Are you sure this came out of your experience?

MH. I think so. I learned never to forget.

꙰

Hans Steinitz

Although he could have remained in Europe after the war ended, Hans Steinitz opted to come to the United States in 1947 since most of his family had already come to Washington Heights. He continued to work as a journalist for a number of Swiss newspapers and some German ones as well. From 1959 to 1961, he was president of the Foreign Press Association and was one of the earliest German Jews to try to reestablish links with the new democratic Germany.

In 1966, Dr. Steinitz became the editor in chief of the German-language newspaper, the Aufbau *(Reconstruction), which had a large circulation in Washington Heights among the German Jewish refugees. Aside from its importance as the main source of information about the community, it served a key role in reuniting relatives—or at least in providing information about their whereabouts—through ads placed in its pages.*

Dr. Steinitz died in 1993.

MK. In Manhattan you were surrounded by Jews. Did that affect your manner of living?

HS. Very little. I have always been a very liberal-minded Jew, the opposite of orthodox. You see, I smoke on the Sabbath. I always said that if there had been no Hitler in Germany, I would most likely have married a gentile girl and stepped out of the Jewish community altogether. But since Hitler persecuted me for being a Jew and I am not a coward or didn't hide (assuming that would have been possible with that racial mania), I became a conscious Jew through Hitler, and as an impact of persecution I figured this is my place. This was my position from 1933 on.

[Though Dr. Steinitz lived in Inwood, just north of Washington Heights, the *Aufbau* was located on the upper west side of Manhattan, on Broadway and 75th Street, a more international neighborhood that housed another German Jewish community, those who were somewhat better off financially and tended to be professionals and intellectuals. These were the people Melitta Hess referred to as "West End Jews." The *Aufbau* was a couple of blocks away from the Eclair café and pastry shop from which Mr. Hess had been fired because of the mishap involving the delivery of some pastries.]

HS. The social and psychological role that Eclair has played in the context of this history is tremendous. I have gentile German business friends here—the director of North American Lufthansa, who comes to see me once a year. He says, "OK, I come but only on condition that we go to Eclair for lunch."

MK. You played an important role in building bridges between the German Jews and the German government. I'd like to hear about your attitude and those of other people about postwar Germany and how you tried to carry out your convictions.

HS. First, in Switzerland, it was pretty clear in refugee and émigré circles that once Hitler was out of power and the Hitlerites pushed overboard, the beginning of new democracy in Germany would be made, and that we, the anti-Hitler refugees, would give it all the support we could give. Not to forget the past but to rebuild for the future. And I came here with that conviction in my heart.

By 1947 the war was over, Hitler was wiped off the surface of the earth, his political system had followed him into the depths of hell, and there was at first a very remote attempt to rebuild Germany along democratic lines. I figured that the reason we had all emigrated and left the country was no longer in effect, so why don't we all return? Naively, I thought that. I was completely overwhelmed and flabbergasted to find I was totally isolated, totally alone with that kind of attitude. In fact, I was almost lynched by people who were outraged.

For all of these people, the idea of going back to Germany, for a visit, to try to recuperate lost property, buying German goods, was completely out of the question. They were deadly enemies forever. It took me years—and I take some credit for that—to change that attitude. Eventually people from this country also returned but that was much later, after the restitution program had been established.

LEARNING THE FACTS

HS. It was only after the war that slowly the details about the Holocaust began to be known. So I can plead a little bit of ignorance—not much—because I had known about many angles of the Holocaust while I was still in Gurs. The first rumors were already coming through, and the first vague announcements concerning a holocaust came over the BBC so I was not completely ignorant. But the details, especially the six million . . . that was completely unknown.

At first, people [non-Jews in America] did not want to believe it. Actually it became a matter of public knowledge only when the American army came into those camps and liberated them. Then you had the testimonies of the commanding officers of the U.S. army and others. [Documentary footage was also made at the time.] Then slowly, the magnitude of the catastrophe became known, but it took time to sink into the minds of the people.

A DIFFERENT VIEW OF GERMANY

[Dr. Steinitz says that several factors contributed to a gradual change of attitude toward Germany: the cold war, the Marshall Plan, the establishment of NATO, and a slow conviction that the new German democracy had solid roots. Perhaps a major factor was the policy of restitution to victims of Nazism on the part of the German government.]

HS. Now it would be wrong to say that, because they got restitution money or pensions or compensation out of Germany, the Jews changed their minds and their attitudes. Such crass materialism would be wrong. But gradually, of course, it contributed. With the rather generous and fair handling of the restitution laws [for those Jews who had lived in West Germany] and with the money received, there was a gradual change in attitude. Many people had to go to Germany to represent their own claims directly to the German authorities. They stayed in a hotel, everybody was nice to them and everybody was normal to them—not particularly nice, which would have been suspicious, but normal. They read the local newspapers and noticed that this was a free democratic country where everybody expressed their views and that the Nazis had disappeared and the communists were extremely weak. So gradually that contributed to a change of attitude.

In Washington Heights, Konrad Adenauer [chancellor of Germany, 1949–1963] became a kind of holy hero. It dawned on many of the German Jews that there was indeed a new generation of Germans, the children and grandchildren of Nazis. You cannot punish the grandchildren for the sins of their grandfathers.

When I became editor of the *Aufbau*, there were already some fertile grounds for a change of attitude. In the beginning, people objected to, let's say, advertising from Lufthansa Airlines. But that has disappeared completely over the years.

[Dr. Steinitz became very active in improving relations by working vigorously with German government agencies and organizations.]

HS. Maybe the thing I am proudest of is that I started the big program whereby the city of Berlin—West Berlin—invites former Berliners, Jewish Berliners and their immediate children, to a free stay as guests in the city. The program was later picked up by other cities as well—Frankfurt, Cologne, Munich, and quite a few others. In the field of bridge-building, this is one of my proudest achievements. [The first announcement of the program appeared in the *Aufbau*.] I started that around 1969 and by now [1981] there are about twelve thousand people who were guests in Berlin, with free round-trip flights, a free stay in a good hotel, guided tours, free meals, tickets to the opera and the Schiller theater, which is the number one theater in Berlin. Also receptions in the city hall, receptions by the local Jewish community, attendance at the Friday night service in the Berlin synagogue, and the rest of it. And that program is handled so unbureaucratically and generously and warm-heartedly that it really tore down barriers. They do it in a very fair way. First they took all people who had suffered in concentration camps, and then they went by age [the eldest receiving preference]. There are still a few people who have turned down invitations, and those who do, I am afraid, secretly regret it.

[The program has grown in the intervening years and thousands more have availed themselves of the opportunity to return for visits to their hometowns. On the other hand, many adamantly refuse to set foot in Germany again.]

PATRIOTISM

MK. In Germany the German Jews were very patriotic before Hitler. They came to America with gratitude and they were also very patriotic over here. Do you see differences in the way they assimilated in Germany and in the United States?

HS. This country permits "acculturation," or many cultures. Still they are all good neighbors and respect each other. The American bouquet contains many flowers: roses, tulips, and so on. You have the San Gennaro festival, the Simon Bolivar festival, the B'nai B'rith. The French or Italian bouquet contains only roses, for example.

MK. But there is also an American nationalism where immigrants take a stand that is pro-American, for example, during the Vietnam War.

HS. It has been said by Theodore Roosevelt that the new immigrant tends to overemphasize his American patriotism.

WHY NAZISM HAPPENED — WAS ANYTHING LEARNED?

MK. How do you explain the fact that the entire German nation went along with what was happening?

HS. You will have to live under a dictatorship to find out. Every person who was against it thought he was the only one in the whole country against it. The devilish system of the totalitarian dictatorship is that everybody who is anti-Fascist, anti-Nazi, anti-Mussolini, anti-Stalin, anti-what-have-you, must believe that he is the only one in the whole country because he cannot communicate with anyone else—a neighbor, a friend, a relative, a fellow worker in the factory—because he is afraid of being denounced.

He must come to the idea: Oh my God, I am the only one, I must be out of step with the whole country, and how can I raise my fists and my hands and open my mouth against the whole country? Even assuming there was only a minority of opponents—maybe it was the active minority or close to an active majority (nobody made any count, there was no census and there never could be)—these people had the terrible difficulty of getting in touch with each other. There was always the fear of discovery.

The question of why the German people did not move against the Nazis cannot be answered because nobody knew who else would be moving. I know people personally who were supposed to physically do away with Adolf Hitler during the war using all kinds of hidden machines. All the attempts always broke down in the last minute, because you couldn't be sure of somebody else. The backup people. Would they be available or what would they do? Would it work?

It is a problem that people will be discussing for generations. I mean why did nobody do away with Stalin or King Philip II of Spain? History is full of missed opportunities.

⚔

Hilde Kracko

Hilde Kracko was still working for the United Restitution Office when I spoke with her.

MK. Is this restitution office only for German Jews?

HK. Oh no, it is for the East European Jews too, the Polish Jews who came after the war. Mostly they came out of the camps or were hidden in forests or whatever. Everybody had a story to tell and everybody had a claim on what they lost, in lives and on property and so on. But I think the eastern Europeans don't get the fair share they should have. They suffered the same thing. The Germans came to Poland and took everything over. But it is very difficult for them to get restitution for their businesses. They had to leave a lot behind and couldn't make claims for their businesses. I think that they didn't have a fair trial.

MK. From whom? The German government?

HK. The German government after the war when they passed the laws.

MK. Do you think they make it easier for German Jews than for other Jews?

HK. I think so. The German Jews had the business and they could bring the papers showing what they lost and what kind of business it was.

MK. Do you feel that this is a matter of discrimination by the German government?

HK. Well, they had to draw the line. That was how the laws were made and who are we to say something?

MK. Do you agree with it?

HK. I don't agree with it, but that wouldn't help and wouldn't change anything. Who am I to speak about something that I think is not right?

MK. You're a human being.

HK. Sure, but I don't want . . . You know, I think there is still the difference [antagonism] between the German Jews and the eastern Jews. There was always a difference and I feel very bad about that. And because I think we learned our lesson, we shouldn't think that way anymore.

MK. That's a wonderful thing you've said.

HK. I am not the one who should say it. [People more highly placed] should say it.

MK. I wish more German Jews would say it.

[I mention the comment by Dr. Gabriele Schiff from the Selfhelp organization regarding Jews who speak negatively about eastern Jews: "Hitler didn't make any distinctions."

German restitution policies did not apply to Jews from the eastern bloc who returned to their original countries after the war. As long as they continued to live under communist regimes, they were not permitted to file claims for compensation under the 1952 Luxembourg Agreement between the Federal Republic of Germany and the Conference of Jewish Material Claims against Germany. Only if they left those countries after 1965 were they eligible to apply. With the unification of Germany, provisions for restitution were incorporated in the Unification Treaty of September 18, 1990, and extended to cover some other categories of Jews who had previously been ineligible to receive benefits, including those living in the former German Democratic Republic.]

GERMANY

HK. I still have a very good friend in Germany, and she writes, "Come and visit us." We were very close, we were children together. And they were not Nazis. But I can't. Once I wanted to go but my husband said no, he wouldn't go. He inherited the business from his father and he suffered a lot when he left everything behind and had to start all over again. He knew everybody there and he always said that he once had the biggest business and the competition had it now. He said, "I knew they were Nazis and I know they took my business away. I don't want to see them anymore."

I go to Italy every year and I have been in Europe a few times, but I can't go to Germany. My husband wouldn't go near it and that sits in me too. I can't get myself to go back. Because if I would see the people and would have to shake hands with the ones who could be the same age as the ones who killed my parents, or my . . . I just can't do it.

They say you should forgive but not forget. You can't forget what they did to us. I lost more than twenty people in my family. We had a very big, close family and all of a sudden you are only three. You miss a lot of love. And I suffered because my husband suffered.

NEW IMMIGRANTS

MK. I've been talking to people in Washington Heights about the Russian Jews and heard many negative things about them. Namely, that they complain about everything, "not like us." And that they are unwilling to do menial work. What's your experience with them?

HK. I haven't had bad experiences. The old people speak only Russian and I can't talk to them. We have two young ladies in our office, very intelligent, very nice, very educated. You should see how they adjust. We have one family living here in the house. They speak only a little bit of English but they are working. And the HIAS [Hebrew Immigrant Aid Society] is giving them wonderful help.

The Russian girls in our office speak better English than I do because we speak only German in our office and that is a big mistake. And so I can't complain. You heard that they didn't like it in Israel. They thought that they would find the big jobs right away. Most of them are professionals. It is very difficult for them to scrub floors. It is not 1938 and 1939 anymore. There is a saying in Germany: "Wenn wir Steine klopfen müssen, nur raus!" [When you have to start breaking rocks, it's time to get out.] When they went to Israel and had to construct a house, they called their doctor [to build it].

MK. That's an old story!

HK. When we came in 1956 they told us how much easier we had it than the ones who came in 1937 and 1938. And now our people are telling them how much easier they have it and what the organizations are doing for them.

MK. There's a new influx of Hispanic people in your neighborhood. What is your feeling about that?

HK. After what we went through, we should not be that harsh, you know? They have to live, too, and as long as they keep the neighborhood clean and nice, there is nothing to say. You know we don't have the right to do what they [the Germans] did to us. There are a lot of minorities living around here but there is nothing to complain about. People can still go to [Fort Tryon Park] in the evening until 9:00–9:30 in the summer till it gets dark. We see them going home peacefully and there's nothing to say about it. Should we complain? No, we shouldn't. Isn't that true?

GENTILES

MK. Do you feel that all gentiles are antisemites?

HK. Oh no. I would not say that. You have very good people. There is my very close friend in Germany in my hometown. My brother is going to visit her. It must have been in 1935 when I was walking in the street and I saw her coming with her mother. I turned around because I didn't want to make a fuss and get them into trouble. Her mother came to me and she said, "Don't turn around. We are not that kind of people. You are the same as you always were." And that friendship is still on.

My brother had a friend, a German boy who was the same age and very close to him. He was already in the Hitler Youth when he went to visit my brother in our hometown and he was wearing his uniform. A neighbor denounced him and he had to go to jail for that. After the war he came to visit my brother here and he told us this story. I think my brother went to twenty families in Holland, from one to the other. When they found out he was Jewish, they wouldn't keep him. But they were not antisemites. They thought he and my sister were Dutch and that they had to flee for political reasons.

AFTEREFFECTS, REFLECTIONS

MK. How do you think your experiences of that time affected your present life?

HK. It did not affect me as much as my husband. For him it was very difficult. He could not adjust and he suffered very much. He was brought up as an only child in a well-to-do family, he got a good education and a ready-made business and then we had to give it up. He was past fifty when we came to the United States. I was pretty young at that time. I didn't lose so much in material things as he did. He lost his existence.

But we made a living and we were content. And we always did what we could. We had his mother with us and she was close to ninety-two. We counted our blessings. We had to live for today. We couldn't live in the past.

When I hear some people complain, I say, "What do you have to complain about? You came with your brothers and sisters and we came from a big family. Now there are only two of us left from nine children at home." As I said, I don't complain, but what you feel you feel inside. Others have suffered more and lost more. I still have my daughter, two beautiful grandchildren, a good son-in-law. I have good friends, you know, your in-laws next door. We moved into this house and right away we were welcomed. So I'm satisfied. I don't have any complaints. We are all friends.

≈Ö≈

Max Frankel

From 1986 to 1994, Max Frankel was the executive editor of the New York Times. In an earlier conversation in this book we discussed comparisons between Germany and the United States and the idea of being tested, morally. The question continues to beset him.

WASHINGTON HEIGHTS

MK. Are you in contact at all with people in Washington Heights today? Have you a sense of their interests, values, prejudices?

MF. Only the senior citizens. My parents live a mile away from where we used to live. They live at 185th Street and Cabrini Boulevard [in upper Washington Heights]. But fear stalks their lives and those of their friends in a way that it does most older and less truly wealthy people in New York. The town is not as clean, as efficient, as comfortable, as *gemütlich* as they knew it to be. Part of that is a function of age. Part of it, I think, is a function of their never having truly acculturated. Many of them are underemployed in terms of mind and spirit. They never got into the American tradition of volunteer services. They're helpful to each other and they have extraordinarily close bonds, and they are protective of one another.

I don't mean that they are cruel or hard, but they don't reach outside their own community. And so they can't feel a part of what's going on. They have no sense of the new immigrants, except that some of their youthful members [appear to be] threatening in the streets. How much of that is age and having skipped a cultural beat, so to speak, and how much is peculiar to that group, I don't know.

MK. One of the similarities with their lives in Germany, I think, is their assimilation here, their patriotism, their loyalty, not only to America. The only time they're really critical of America is when America isn't good to Israel.

MF. Exactly right.

MK. And Israel is their other loyalty.

MF. That is right.

MK. So in that sense, they're nationalistic.

MF. Very, very . . .

MK. They were hounded out of Germany, which was their country for over a thousand years. And then they come here and they have their prejudices. In Germany they had great prejudices against the Polish Jews.

MF. Sure.

MK. They still have them. Here they form new ones. What is your explanation of it? That is, have they learned anything? Having been victimized and having gone through this, what have they learned?

MF. I think that the biggest thing they've learned is that nothing is permanent and I think that's the appeal of Israel. Israel to this generation is not just a Jewish home. Israel to this generation is not just a place where some of their families had an alternative at the end of the war. Israel was to them the hope (although that hope is wavering at the moment [1982]), but it was the hope of one permanent place where the Jew could finally belong, whether he lived there or not. It gave you a kind of permanent citizenship, so to speak, so that no one could ever come along again and question your documents, or tell you that you have no right to be here, and that the Jews all over the world would be safer for having a place to which they belonged.

And they act that out and the one thing they now demand of America is that this promise not go soft. And that the one anchor that was dropped in their lifetime and gave promise of taking hold should not be eroded.

MK. And to what extent is that your feeling as well?

MF. I supported Israel intellectually for all the reasons I have just given and continue to do so, and I think I would find its demise emotionally unbearable. But I cannot be Israeli deep inside, and I guess that has nothing to do with being Jewish, and America not being Jewish. I think it has something to do with scale. Having been able to come to this country and join it at a young enough age, I regard myself as a continental person.

I need a big place, a big pool to swim in. I need to deal with big institutions and big power, and to think in terms of bigness. And I think I would find Belgium or Germany for that matter as unsatisfying as Israel for myself. Once you say that to yourself, once you say that something cultural or even geographical about America is more important in your personal life than being at home in a Jewish state, then no matter how close you feel and no matter how emotionally committed you are, and no matter how important the survival of Israel is to you, then, if you are saying clearly, "But it's not for me, I'm not going to make my life there, and I'm not necessarily going to commend it to my children either, other than the usual trip of acquaintance, and so on," then I'm speaking to them as cousins. And that's the way I view Israel.

AFTEREFFECTS IN GERMAN JEWS

MK. You said before that there was something that dogged you, which had to do with "How come the Germans could do what they did?" And there is something that dogs me, which is that these German Jewish people came over, escaping one of the most atrocious things that's ever occurred. And then they began to mirror some of the attitudes that produced that phenomenon, such as prejudices, such as blind nationalism or blind patriotism, such as overlooking any fault that Israel might be guilty of.

MF. Right.

MK. Israel itself was built up of survivors. And I've never been able to reconcile the fact that the experience hasn't produced—not higher morality—just higher understanding of what is needed in this world not to reproduce terrible situations. Do you have a response to that?

MF. I think people behave less than spiritually when they are afraid. Plain and simple. In most cases, the degree of fear—and the totalitarians understand this very well, because they produce fear!—the degree of fear is directly related to the degree of mean-spiritedness in any individual whether it's economic fear or political fear. Those of us who came here in our teens acquired an optimism and we acquired a sense of what really matters. In other words, "Get yourself out of the line of fire and save your body and then go ahead and save your soul and forget about possessions and all the other things."

All this happened to the older generation in midlife. If I were forced, at this moment or even ten years ago, the way my father was forced to go and spend seven years in Siberia and not to see my children, and then to come to a strange place . . . let's say southern Naples, which for me would be comparable . . . and some guy tells me, "The way to make a living is for you to take a suitcase full of stockings and dresses and go through the slums of Naples." And you start selling door-to-door, and give people credit, and then come back at night when they're home and try to collect five lira a week from them . . . That's what my father did. Now, if you come through that and aren't afraid or aren't prejudiced or aren't passionate or you don't feel cheated by life as a result of all that, then you've really got grace.

⊱✲⊰

Rosi Spier

Mrs. Spier and her brother founded a kindergarten in Washington Heights. She attended Bank Street College in the evening in order to complete her training in education and to have the school accredited by New York State. She and her son were finally able to live a normal life together after having endured separations and makeshift living arrangements. Although there was no reluctance on Mrs. Spier's part to be interviewed, she revealed that the former head of her kindergarten was not happy about it. Mrs. Spier felt the woman was being unduly anxious, "like a German."

RS. I said to her, "What can happen even if we would show a film about the kindergarten? There was a need for it when we arrived and it was founded."

But she said, "Mrs. Spier, we have to be careful. That is an order." And she's an intelligent person. You know, we still have this fear in our system. I find it with many of my friends.

[She gives me an illustration. Irritated by the poor bus service in Manhattan, she decided to send a letter to the *Times*. Older people in particular suffered from having to wait at bus stops for long periods of time, often in poor weather. She made the point that older people still wanted to get out of their homes to go downtown to shop, and to attend concerts and the theater. But bus service made this very arduous. She sent the letter first to her brother so that he could correct her English.]

RS. He said, "I wouldn't advise you to do this." And my sister-in-law agreed.

I said, "Why?"

"Well, it's not good to criticize them."

I said, "We live in America. Why can't I? If I could stand on a corner, I would make a petition. But this way I'm writing it to the *Times*."

And, he said, "It wouldn't help you anyhow."

I said, "This is the attitude of most people: It won't help you. If more people would protest about things, maybe we would succeed." He didn't correct it and I let it go.

MK. You didn't send that letter? Did you perhaps agree that it wasn't a good idea?

RS. No. Not me, not me.

MK. It wasn't out of fear, then.

RS. No! It was more out of negligence that I didn't follow it up. I said he didn't correct it. I don't want to write bad English and I still translate a lot when I speak and when I write letters. My letters still sound German.

MK. But your speech doesn't.

RS. Well, but my sentences . . . You know that the German sentences are very long. My brother very early on told me, "Break up your sentence! Make a period and start with something new." So I let my *Times* letter go.

Now, this was a fear deep down in my brother—this fear, which we Germans still have about expressing our thoughts. And they are still handicapped by this experience with Hitler. Not to speak, not to open up our mouths. I am not the type who is afraid. I have to explain to my brother all the time, "We are in America! You can open your mouth!"

MK. What other evidence do you see of this residue of the trauma of being in Germany? That is, among the older people in Washington Heights, or even in some of their children, like myself—is there some evidence deep inside, some scars?

RS. We Jews are always afraid about what Jews do. For instance [*laughs*], I will give you a silly example. I hate it when the synagogues are out and all the German ladies walk out in mink coats. And I say, "Why do we have to upset the other people again and make such a show of ourselves if we are well-off?" But then I think, why haven't we got the right to be well-off? The Americans can buy a mink coat if they are well-off without having this feeling. That might also be a part of it. Don't be conspicuous.

I personally feel awful if someone misbehaves in a restaurant. I have a cousin, she's an American. Instead of asking for more butter in the restaurant, she went to the place where the butter is kept and took it. And I said, "Helen, I think that's awful. It's not ladylike."

Sure enough, the owner had seen it and was very upset. And he said to me, "You can come anytime in my restaurant but not the lady who is with you."

But I had again that feeling, "The Jew!" A Jew cannot allow himself to do this, I think. I also feel a lady shouldn't do this. But I don't know which is more important, the lady or the Jew.

GERMANY, MINORITIES

RS. My grandson asked me, "Would you want to live in Germany?"

No. Because always in the back of my mind, I think, "His father or she or he was a Nazi." But on the other hand, to be correct, you should not judge a whole country, all the people. If I become acquainted with a decent German and I have proof he is not and was not a Nazi, I have nothing against him. I cannot have something against all Germans. I hate generalization. You know that even we Jews generalize. Like with the color. If I have a nice decent colored lady and her husband living next to me, I don't mind it. Why do I think right away they are not good?

MK. Many people would.

RS. But here we are again. I always meet people [who complain about the Russian Jews]. I have a friend who says, "They all are the same."

I say, "You know, you do the same thing that Hitler did, what American people did on Fort Washington Avenue. They moved out when German Jews came in." I get so angry. But this is how the world is built. Prejudice.

WAS ANYTHING LEARNED?

MK. What do you think was learned by the people in the community from this experience with Hitler?

RS. All of us feel that, no matter what we do, no matter how good we are, the Jews are hated in every country. That's our fate. Whatever we do. Of course, we should be the most ethical people, we should strive to do everything as good citizens. But what have we learned? We have learned, deep down, that no matter what we do, we are the scapegoat. If ever an economic disaster hits, we are the ones to be blamed for it. I don't know why.

Because we are the minority, we will be observed more. Everything we do we have to do better. That's part of our character. That's true of me at least: Don't do anything where somebody could say I'm not an ethical person or whatever. That's because I'm a Jew.

MK. Do you think it would have mattered to Hitler whether you were ethical?

RS. You are right. I don't think it would have.

MK. If every Jew had been a saint, do you think it would have mattered?

RS. No. He wanted to have a scapegoat. Why do they all have to have a Jew as a scapegoat? In every country, wherever you look, they blame us. Our faults are more obvious—or they want to find our faults. I don't know why. That's part of our fate.

MK. But then does that mean you have to repress yourself?

RS. Many times, I think.

MK. But even so, it hasn't changed anything.

RS. No. It has not changed anything.

[We have returned to the subject of Israel.]

MK. Now Israel's attitude is "No! We're going to be ourselves." And, of course, sometimes they're much too aggressive.

RS. But they learned a lesson from Hitler. The Israeli Jews would have said, "We wouldn't go [to the gas chambers]." They would fight. They would have another Masada. Right?

꙰

Louis Kampf

The friend of my youth, Louis Kampf continues to teach at the Massachusetts Institute of Technology. Though our paths have diverged, his political thinking and mine are very similar, although he has tak-

en more of an activist role, even putting his professional position in jeopardy on occasion.

LK. What we hear from various American-Jewish organizations about antisemitism has to do with support of Israel. They choose to identify any anti-Israeli sentiment with antisemitism, and I think that is terribly wrong and self-destructive. If there *will* be a wave of antisemitism in the United States, that will be its origins: namely that the big Jewish organizations will imprint it so much in people's minds that being Jewish means you're pro-Israeli and that the two are identical— that any bad feeling toward Israel will just simply spill over onto our Jews. That's liable to be the main source of any major antisemitic wave in the future in the United States. Not the old traditional religious hatred.

[Today there is more diversity among the American-Jewish organizations than in 1982 in the spectrum of opinion they represent in regard to Israel's policies.]

MK. What are your emotional ties to Israel?

LK. The emotional ties were made very real to me by the fact that Israel attacked Lebanon [in 1982]. I got enraged and furious in a way I never got enraged and furious about Vietnam, for example. That really hit me precisely because I identify myself as a Jew, I feel myself to be a Jew in my responses. How can people I relate to, who have the same blood flowing in their veins that I have, do this?

MK. And who went through the same experiences.

MK. Especially those who went through the same things. At a recent demonstration, I went up to somebody who carried a big sign saying, "Children of the Holocaust: How Could You?" And that very much describes my feelings. For thousands of years, we've been persecuted, so we ought to know well enough not to persecute other people. So naturally I feel a very strong and emotional thing about Israel.

WHAT WAS LEARNED? OTHER MINORITIES

LK. Sometimes I wonder just how much was learned by people in Washington Heights through their experiences. For example, I have one cousin who was a real success. He fulfilled the American dream and became a millionaire.

This past year when I was visiting my parents, he showed up and he said, "Louis, I want to have a conversation with you. I know you have been involved in many left-wing and progressive causes. Why is it that our people are as conservative and prejudiced as they are now, why are they so racist, why do they hate people of Spanish extraction as much as they do, and above all, why are they so blind in relation to Israel?"

He has two children who moved to Israel and he feels that he can barely talk to them when he goes to visit them because their attitudes, toward not only Arabs but Sephardic Jews, are as racist as they are. He said to me, "My parents and your parents got thrown out of their apartments in Vienna. We're doing the same thing in Israel."

Here you've got two polarities. On the one hand, the fear about what happened to you becomes internalized so that you become prejudiced against other people, you take it out on whomever it is you're able to take it out on, especially if you're scared of them. Older people in New York are scared of blacks and Hispanics, for example, so those people become identified with the Nazis, the Brownshirts and the Blackshirts. They're the future fascists. My father rants and raves about immigrants, even about the Cubans. He calls them criminals. He feels that students who are demonstrating are like the Hitler Youth. People have a historical context, they have a memory . . . That person who beat you up in the elevator is a Blackshirt.

The same with some university professors, for example, who identify the student left with Nazi Hitler Youth in Germany. On the other hand you can get some academic—for example, I can think of a marvelous man by the name of Israel Shahak who teaches chemistry at the Hebrew University in Jerusalem. He survived Auschwitz and has dedicated his life to the civil rights of Arabs in Israel and has made life very difficult for himself through that. So there are two ways that things can turn. In general, the community I'm from has not turned the way of my cousin, for example. It's turned in the other direction and is paranoid about practically everything around it, even about Jews not of German extraction.

The boat I came over on, for example. There was practically a war going on between the East European Jews and the German Jews. The German Jews looked at the East Europeans as *Ostjuden* who got them into trouble with the Nazis. That was one of the particular myths that came out of 1930s: If it hadn't been for the Ostjuden, the German Jews would have been OK inside Nazi Germany. So, in fact, a lot of the prejudice they experienced in Germany was simply internalized in terms of prejudice against other people.

It's also a sociological matter. Most of the Jews in Washington Heights became basically petty bourgeois, and the small bourgeois invariably feel incredibly frightened about anything that threatens their status. They've got very little space, and therefore the little space they have established for themselves becomes something to hold onto desperately. And so it comes out in that kind of prejudice, since they see every other ethnic group as a threat to themselves. My father hated the Irish, the Hispanics, the blacks, all fairly equally. I don't want to quite paint him as an Archie Bunker. I'm only talking about him this way because there is nothing exceptional about him in that regard. I see it as a very sad and upsetting thing the way my cousin does, but it's also a phenomenon I can understand. It's part of the same phenomenon that turned me into a radical.

GERMANS AND GERMANY

MK. Many people find it difficult to believe that the Germans, with their cultural and intellectual history, could become what they did. On what basis do we condemn the German people and on what basis don't we?

LK. First of all, you don't condemn the German people—you never condemn a people. Period. That's racism. As an American, I'm acutely and often painfully aware, at this time in history, that my country's armed forces and the ruling elites are responsible for some of the worst slaughters in the world, from Vietnam to Chile, for example, to some of what is going on in South Africa and in Lebanon right now [1982]. How many people in the United States do we see protesting against that? The thing to remember is that protesting in the United States is easy. You are not going to get sent to a concentration camp, you are not going to lose your job over it. You might have a few people that won't speak to you anymore as a result, but you wouldn't want those people to speak to you in any case. Being a protester in the United States just takes a little bit of energy and a little bit of careful thinking about the issues involved, and some human feeling! Whereas, if you were in Nazi Germany protesting, you took your life in your hands.

Never mind protesting! Just those people who helped get some Jews out of the country, who got food to Jews who were starving, who hid Jews . . . You need to ask yourself: In how many countries after the Nazi occupation were things really different? To the degree, let's say, that most people in France collaborated with the Nazis.

MK. If Hitler's policies had not been antisemitic, do you think that Jews in Germany, in Austria, would have voted for him?

LK. It's hard to generalize, naturally. For example, many Jews were socialists and communists. They were very political and carried out protests. Just as there were many Germans and Austrians, people with a great deal of courage who had a conscience . . .

MK. . . . who were not Jewish?

LK. Who were not Jewish, of course. Look, when Hitler came to Austria, non-Jews were not supposed to speak to Jews. We know a lot of people who took their lives into their hands by helping us. It's important to remember that there are people like that. But most people are just too afraid to do that. Probably most average Jews would have collaborated with the government.

When I got heavily involved in the movement against the Vietnam War and supported draft resisters and deserters, and helped deserters get to Sweden and France, and was one of the leaders in that movement, my father got really upset. He both said to me and wrote me in a letter that, if it hadn't been for the fact that he was Jewish, he would have been proud to serve in Hitler's army in World War II. Now I'm not sure how deeply he meant that, and to what degree he was trying to impress me to stop me from doing what I was doing. You see, I don't think my father was unusual. Most people live with that fear of the state and the impact the state can have on them. And they are right in a way. Most Germans and Austrians who protested wound up getting killed.

Which one of us can say that with a gun pointed in our face we wouldn't have [gone along with the official policy]? I hope I wouldn't have done it but how do I know?

On the other hand, in my mind, there is no excuse for anyone having become an SS man, joining the Nazi party. I can give you one example. My father had this small business in Vienna with a partner who was Christian. They eked out a bare living selling clothes on the installment plan, going from door to door to people who could only afford to pay that way. After the Nazis came to power in Vienna, this guy took over my father's half of the business and joined the Nazi party. As a result he got all kinds of contracts thrown his way and by the end of World War II he was rich. When I went to visit him after the end of the war, he was driving the longest Mercedes-Benz I've ever seen in my life outside of a war movie. And there is no excuse for that! None. The point is that it's not just Germans who act in this particular way. You find people acting that way everywhere.

MK. What do you feel in your German background, in your German roots, that is still alive in you—or is still good?

LK. Something that's both alive and good is that when I went to school as a kid in Vienna—what I experienced in a German school in Vienna was that whole German tradition of scholarship, of concern for the humanities, of finding yourself immediately when you are plunged into literature as a young person, reading it, reciting it, acting it out, and so on. And always having placed in front of you the importance of it. That's remained with me. I think it's one of the things that led me to being a humanistic intellectual and scholar. That's been important for me all along and it stuck with me. That's the positive part of that tradition.

MK. Do you feel that there is a new spirit also in today's Germany?

LK. The young people I know from today's Germany were very strongly influenced by the American student movement, for example. The Socialistische Deutsche Studentenbund (the initials SDS were based on the American SDS, Students for a Democratic Society), the whole business of direct action, civil disobedience . . . That was picked up from the American civil rights protests, for example. The young German students I've had in classes have basically created a new tradition for themselves, I think. There's really been a break with their past. And they've been very conscious that, in some way, some of the traditional elements of German culture led to the acceptance of Nazism. And they've wanted to make a break with this. I found a lot of those young people very lovely people who I would be proud to have as my students.

Max Frankel

Still grappling with issues raised earlier, Max Frankel and I reached no conclusion—nor did we arrive at a mutual agreement. However, he sharpened many of the questions I had posed for myself.

MK. We were talking about being tested. There was a time in Germany when it was still possible to oppose Hitler. That is to say, before Hitler first moved against the intellectuals and the opposition parties— after all, there were millions in opposition, including millions who voted for the communists. After that, if you demonstrated or voiced dissent, you landed up in a concentration camp. It wouldn't have done you any good. You would have been shot on the spot.

MF. Right.

MK. During the McCarthy time, we were able to protest. Now you're saying how glad you were that you hadn't been tested and you mentioned the McCarthy era as having a kind of seed of what might have been. You also said that you thank your lucky stars that, by accident, you were on the good side. Were we—you and I—Americans on the good side in the case of Vietnam? And how do we compare our behavior with that of the Germans in a comparable situation?

MF. I don't equate Vietnam . . . In the American experience, I think it is the McCarthy terror, small as it was, that is much more apt. Vietnam was a traditional, nationalistic foreign policy debate. It became a debate, the society was certainly open to dissent even in the middle of the war. It was, in a way, the right way to handle an issue. In my view, it wasn't the ultimate test because what was on the table was the fate of others, by and large. We were blind to the fact that we were sending our own lower-class people to fight and get killed, or to be drugged up. Our middle classes were buying their way out by going to college or theology school, or whatnot.

But Vietnam was not the sort of situation where I asked myself: Dare I step out of the house and speak and say something on behalf of a person whom I know next-door to me, who is being pilloried in this society? And who is being made to suffer for reasons of conscience that have nothing to do with his being a threat to the society or community? And dare I speak up at considerable risk to my own livelihood—never mind my life? That's what I mean by "the test."

The real question is, Does a society have the fiber to stand up against injustice when it sees it directly? Not when there is a debate as to what did or didn't happen at My Lai, but [rather] when we *know* the fellow down the street is a perfectly decent preacher or schoolteacher and is being pilloried for no damn good reason, and we are made afraid to speak up?

MK. I am going to debate this with you, Max.

MF. Please do.

MK. The Germans claimed that they didn't know the worst of it. I don't know if they knew or if they didn't, but they knew that their friend next-door had been taken away. They knew that the shop had been closed. They knew a lot. By the time of the Vietnam War, *we* knew a lot. We knew about napalm, we knew about the random tactics. Anybody could find out what *pacification* meant. We knew these things. Our behavior was guided according to what side of the debate we were on. And it is the action of the American government, condoned by many—as a matter of fact, I think condoned by the Washington Heights Jews—that I'm really asking about.

MF. On the German part of your question, I'm sure that's true. When they were cutting off this or that Jew, or putting him out of business, or not letting him go to the swimming pool, nobody expected that this was leading to the gas chambers. The Germans never voted on that question, so to speak, consciously. Nonetheless, there was a profound injustice visible in the lives of almost every German. When they weren't directly eager to profit from that (the displacement of a competitor in a business or in a job), they were silent much too long. In a way, that set their own trap for them.

Whether Vietnam is comparable or not is an interesting debate. Without prolonging it, I would only argue that unless you take the position that all wars, except against an absolute evil like Hitler, are unjust (and they are), they are unjust in the nature of who gets killed and who doesn't, and who gets hurt and who doesn't . . . and in that they almost never achieve the objectives. If I respect the position that says,

"Therefore all wars are the worst expression of human evil, and therefore you are total pacifists" (for a combination of other reasons, I'm not), that leaves you with the difficult question, war by war, of figuring out whether there could have been an alternative. And when there wasn't, whether it was justified to begin with, and whether, even if justified to begin with, it was then fought in the proper way, and whether there were decent enough terms offered along the way to settle the thing, and if not, whether it was given up as a lost cause in good time.

Once you say some wars are justifiable, you face that whole litany of five, six questions down the road. There were lots and lots of things wrong with Vietnam. It was an idiocy and it was a failure, and it was, in the end, a corruption, a corruption of our values, and we are paying for it. I think our society—not just our budgets but our society—has paid profoundly for it. And we may even pay in deeper ways, because we now need to recover from Vietnam, which is yet another question.

MK. Germans were unable to dissent. What I'm proud of is that we did demonstrate while we were still able to. But not during the McCarthy period, except for the real left. But during Vietnam we were able to and did [demonstrate] to a great degree. How do you feel about the value of that kind of activity—not only in relation to Vietnam but generally?

MF. I think it is crucial. It is probably the most profound thing you learn about America. When you come as a stranger to this society and you learn about the *shockingly* radical concept of a First Amendment where, at least in theory, everyone has a right to say and to publish and to meet with anybody at all times about any issue, that is really radical and remains so today. It is the single most important part of American society, not just because I am in journalism, but because it allows for correction. If you believe in the imperfectability [*laughter*] of an imperfect man . . . it allows for a constant process of debate and correction of everything that is wrong. Nothing ever stops, nobody ever says, "When I've decided this question, it is over with. We are going to run our business this way or that way."

MK. The demonstrations are important.

MF. They are important and an essential part of it. I not only believe that they are crucial, but I believe that the battle to vindicate the beauty of that system has to be fought and won in every generation. And the founding fathers of American society, writing one little amendment to the Constitution did not secure free speech for themselves and their posterity for all time. It requires an elaborate judicial structure and legal tradition and every generation will find new reasons why there should not be free demonstrations or free speech. And every generation, sooner or later, is called on to win that battle again.

MK. Of course, I agree very much with what you just said about demonstrations. However, over the years, the *Times*, your newspaper, has not really supported demonstrations. They get more coverage in places like the *Washington Post* or the *Boston Globe*. I don't remember the *Times* ever having supported a strike. Except for Solidarity in Poland. How do you reconcile your feelings and your influence on the *Times* with the paper's editorial policy?

MF. The *Times* is news coverage. The *Times* is a way of doing news. It is not the only way and it shouldn't be. But our way of doing news is not to look upon it as a political instrument. The department that I run [Max was the Editorial Page editor at that time], where we express our opinions and collect the opinions of others (letter writers, columnists), that department is completely separate from the News Department, to which I used to belong. We deliberately do that. That is not the European tradition and it certainly isn't universally observed in America either, but it is our way of doing it. So we don't set out to say, "This demonstration deserves attention because we like what they're demonstrating for. And the Ku Klux Klan or the Nazi party demonstration doesn't deserve attention because we don't like what they stand for."

Demonstrations are just another manifestation of unrest and debate in the society and we have to judge at any given moment whether it is worth ten inches or two. And we make those imperfect judgments day-to-day. Where we are wrong (for instance, the recent demonstrations on the subject of nuclear weapons), the *fire* among the public, even our reading public, was greater than we understood until it was far along.

But we come out every day. And if they don't get heard on their first demonstration or their first ten letters to the editor, we get them a month later. We will pay attention. Ultimately, our kind of newspaper not being a pamphlet, the demonstrations [described in it] have to occur in the realm of ideas.

Since I deal in opinions and ideas on our pages, one lone letter writer with a brilliant six paragraphs on some subject can take precedence, in my view, over a hundred thousand people marching around without knowing very much what they are marching about. They are important, they are a social phenomenon, but ultimately institutions, governments, and societies have to deal with an idea, at least in print.

It's our function to ultimately reduce whatever commotion exists in the society to a coherent set of debatable principles.

MK. I understand that. But strikes, for example, are another form of demonstration. It's another way of saying, "We want this."

MF. You're right. The *Times* has not, in recent memory, supported a strike. Since I've taken over these [editorial] pages, in five years we haven't opposed a strike either, except those that were clearly illegal, as in some cases where public service employees were involved. Like the air controllers who had signed contracts saying they would not strike. But I don't think it's my business to tell somebody in a normal free situation who has a legal right to strike, whether eighty-three cents is too much or eighty-five cents is too little. That's not the function of a newspaper. It is our function when we are dealing with public funds. We might have to say, "New York City can't afford to pay its sanitation workers any more than that." And there we're addressing taxpayer dollars. What's of concern and importance to us is the right to strike. That it be reinforced, and that it be respected, and also that it be used properly and legally.

MK. But editorials are opinions. They fall on one side of an issue or another. And they are very influential.

MF. Sometimes.

MK. The *Times* is.

MF. We try to be.

MK. You have choices in the matter, and as Editorial Page editor you have a good deal of influence, I assume.

MF. Yes . . . But when there are five hundred thousand people marching in Central Park, there is no way that the lead editorial in the *New York Times* that morning cannot concern the subject they're marching about. Now maybe only half the people who are marching will agree with what we then write, or maybe not. But nonetheless, they have forced a debate. They have made the point, as far as we're concerned.

MK. What do you think of the Germans demonstrating today?

Demonstrating against America [because of NATO nuclear installations]?

MF. They certainly have a right to demonstrate. I think they have a duty to demonstrate. I feel very good to see Germans standing up and demonstrating about anything, whether they are right or wrong. Beyond that, I hope they're right. I am past the age, I guess. When you become fifty-two years old, you're past the age when you think that demonstrations do more than help you find people who think like you and help you to organize a political movement. I don't think, in the end, that they achieve what they set out to do, unless you take more deliberate political action.

MK. Such as?

MF. Unless you build the purpose of your protest into law, unless you make the system accept the new values that demonstrations usually want to put into the system . . .

MK. For example, right now the Democrats are trying to put the nuclear freeze question into law. Haven't they been affected by the demonstrations?

MF. The nuclear freeze movement has been very effective. If the Reagan administration's policy had been better handled from the beginning, I don't think any of these demonstrations would ever have occurred.

MK. But would the Democratic move to effect legislation have occurred only as a result of the Reagan administration's ineptitude, without a groundswell against it from the people?

MF. No, absolutely not.

MK. So demonstrations do have a direct effect.

MF. They have a direct effect on law, they have a particularly direct effect in the community. Whether in the end you can cause the Soviet Union and the United States to reduce their nuclear stockpiles by demonstrations alone, I am very skeptical. But it doesn't matter, because I think that even the most thoughtful people in the field realize that without popular protest, nothing will happen. So, I welcome it. I think it is a sign of the public's involvement in these subjects, which until a few years ago were [restricted to] two hundred experts in the world.

Walter Hess

Strange to say, this was the first time I was able to speak to Walter Hess about his experience as a child under the Nazis. We grew up together, we always remained friends, but we did not have this conversation until we were fifty years old.

MK. Walter, of the various experiences you had at a very early age, what was the most lingering, or traumatic?

WH. It's difficult not to sound self-righteous about discussing the past. On the other hand, with something like this, perhaps something on the order of self-righteousness is permitted. For me the most difficult and, I think, the most unforgivable problem as far as the Germans are concerned, is what they did to *me*. The Holocaust is terrible. The war is terrible. But finally, I think, what is it that they did to me? And I think that the most terrible thing was that they made me hate myself—for a long time.

Growing up in the face of their overwhelming power, growing up with my parents seeming afraid and not being able to do anything, growing up and passing the caricatures of Jews, growing up and seeing that everyone else seemed to have a life that was relatively free and easy, and I was living under some kind of burden . . . that I didn't know what the source was and why it should affect me. And so, I think, as a child I came to the conclusion that we were perhaps . . . that *I* was perhaps not as good.

For doing that to me, for seeing Jews, for seeing my parents and myself in this kind of terrible light . . . seeing that we were inferior as the Germans were telling us, as the whole culture was telling us . . . There's no single particular incident except that there are a couple of things that always go through my mind. Our neighbor, Mrs. Schumacher, would, for many years, hide Easter eggs for the children to find. I was one of the children who was invited to find the Easter eggs and I loved that. That, somehow, made me part of the countryside, part of the community. Then after a while that stopped. I wasn't invited to the Easter egg hunt.

Then, when I stood in front of the burning synagogue and I saw the children who I thought were my friends throw mud at me . . . those kinds of things, obviously. I remember one other incident, when I was a kid. The German army was on maneuvers, and I saw this soldier who was operating a field telephone. And he was this blond Aryan. I saw him as a hero, as a marvelous hero. And the next minute I thought to myself, How is it possible that I can see this guy as a hero? And so you walk around for half your life with this equivocal kind of feeling about yourself, about the Germans. You love them, and you wanted to see that guy die in Russia!

And the way you feel about yourself . . . It took a long time for me to come to terms with that. And I don't know if I'll ever, really and truly, come to the bottom of it and come to terms with it. I mean, they had no right to do that to me, that's what I can't forgive them. They have no . . . I mean, they simply don't. Nobody has. *[Long pause.]*

Just one other thing. The other thing I can't forgive them for is the way they made me see my parents, for the longest time, as afraid, weak, ineffectual . . . when, as a matter of fact, they're incredibly strong people.

PART FIVE

Return to Saarbrücken

I first returned to Germany in 1978, having long since called off my private boycott of German goods. The Vietnam War had dissolved my youthful certainties about collective guilt. And there was a new generation of Germans, born after the war. The occasion for my return was the Mannheim Film Festival where I had been invited to show my fiction film Short Circuit, depicting a white man's paranoid fantasy about a violent takeover of his comfortable middle-class home by his black maid and doorman and their children.

I approached this first trip back to Germany with trepidation, worried that, to paraphrase Hilde Kracko, "I might have to shake hands with people who are old enough to have killed my relatives." Instead, those I did meet were of a younger generation and socially engaged. The Mannheim festival specializes in politically oriented and progressive documentary films.

Many of the young people were tormented by their country's past. These men and women did not represent a cross section of Germans. They were very much like people I knew at home in New York. Several of them became my friends. I felt comfortable among them.

But my feeling of being at home went beyond the kind of people I met. I was speaking the language of my parents outside of my ancestral Washington Heights home and I was being understood! It was exhilarating to discover the other half of my roots. In America, my father would never allow me to speak German outside on the street where someone might overhear us. German was the language of the enemy during the war; he didn't want us misconstrued even as late as 1985. I became deeply ashamed of anything German about me, made self-deprecating jokes, and even tried to change the accent with which I read Hebrew.

The rediscovery of my Germanness made me angry too. The Nazis had taken my country away from me. My Jewish forebears had been there for almost two millennia and still I had not been considered German enough to belong there, not even in my own heart. What amount of counterindoctrination would be needed for me to reclaim that part of me?

The Jewish half had always been in place. The denial of my Germanness had been so total that I imagined many of my cultural traits, customs, and expressions to be Jewish ones, when in fact they were German, going as far as to include the Schubertian liturgical melodies in the synagogue.

But contradictions stared me in the face, too, as I found myself fascinated one afternoon in Mannheim by the exquisite display of wrapped chocolates and pastries in the window of a Konditorei [shop selling sweets]. In their midst squatted a marzipan figure of a boy squeezing out a gold coin between his rosy buttocks. And the next day in the marketplace, where the vegetables were proffered in the most appealing and "artistic" manner I had ever seen, I turned to confront the raw blood on a dozen hooked rabbits whose fur still held the designs of life. Brutal and delicate, crude and sublime. Did these paradoxes exist in me as well?

The Mannheim visit also marked my first active participation in an international film festival and I was surprised at the amount of press attention. Hundreds of journalists from the media were present. As I stuffed their mailboxes with my publicity material one morning, I came across the name of a critic attached to the Saarbrücker Zeitung in which my father had his caricatures of famous figures published, almost fifty years earlier.

I wrote the critic a note on my descriptive flyer: "I am a Saarbrücker." The next day I got a call from him from Saarbrücken; he had already returned to meet a deadline but invited me to come and spend a day with him since the city was less than two hours by train from Mannheim. That is how my friendship with Michael Beckert and his family began. In 1980, he helped arrange the exhibition of my father's caricatures at the Stadttheater in Saarbrücken. We met again in Mannheim in 1981 where I showed my documentary film about New York subway graffiti, a subject that entranced young Germans and appalled the people at home.

Michael and I met again in 1986 in Berlin. My film about the German Jews of Washington Heights had its premiere in Berlin in 1986, an event fraught with emotion for me. The audience was comprised mostly of Germans in their twenties and thirties. For many, it seemed to have provided a welcome opportunity to speak of the Nazi era. Some had learned of it in school, others through reading, a few through conversations with family members. A comment I heard over and over again was: "The people in the film are just like my family."

Yes, they spoke the same language; their common culture was apparent in their surroundings—the fine china, the breakfronts with knickknacks— and in their appearance, which was no different from that of the Germans we saw on the street in Berlin itself. How could physical distinctions be made if these people resembled their grandparents, their "Omas" and "Opas"? Discussions went on for hours after each of the three showings, as though the audiences were reluctant to let go of the subject.

Michael Beckert suggested a retrospective of my films, at the theater in Saarbrücken that housed the annual Max Ophüls Preis Film Festival. Ophüls (born Oppenheimer) was a German Jew born in Saarbrücken who had escaped to France just after the plebiscite in the Saar in 1935. He had begun making films in Germany and continued to do so in France, in Hollywood, and later again in France. His films include La Ronde, Le Plaisir, Lola Montez, and Letter to an Unknown Woman. I had known and studied his work and indeed had been reminded many times by my father that I was in good company as a Saarbrücken-born filmmaker. Marcel Ophüls, Max's son, is a contemporary French documentary filmmaker who made Hotel Terminus and The Sorrow and the Pity, both of which deal with French complicity with the Nazis.

Most of Saarbrücken had been rebuilt because of damage during the war. But the house on Schmollerstrasse where I lived until I was five was still standing. It was tempting to ring the bell and announce who I was but I desisted. What would I have said? "This is the window from which I saw the Nazis marching"? I walked the route my father took to go to work at E. Weil Söhne department store and felt at home—once removed.

After the retrospective of my work in 1987, I returned in January 1989 to serve as a judge at the film festival; and the following year, and every year since, I was invited to present a program of my students' films at the festival. I found it moving that this German film festival, which drew entries from all over Europe, had been named after a Jew.

During these visits, I wondered about some of my fellow Saarbrückers, both Jewish and Christian, some of whom had also been born there before the war. I decided to extend my inquiry and, in January 1991 and January 1992, I interviewed the following people: (1) Freidel Heilbronner, Max Ophüls's sister, who knew my father and had settled in Paris in 1933. After her escape from France, she lived in South America and then in Paris for many years. She had recently returned to Germany to live. (2) Liliane (Lilo) Kahn, her friend, who also knew my father when they both worked at the E. Weil Söhne department store. She had come back to Saarbrücken in 1948. (3) Marcel Wainstock was born in Switzerland after the war and tended to the minuscule Jewish community in Saarbrücken. (4) I had also met Dr. Hans Stiff, former publisher of the Saarbrücker Zeitung and honorary Belgian consul. He had served in the German army as a teenage anti-aircraft gunner. (5) Last, Oskar Lafontaine—the charismatic leader of the Social Democrats and state premier of the Saarland (the Ministerpräsident) who had run against Helmut Kohl in 1990—had welcomed me warmly; he seemed to articulate, much better than I, many of the issues that concerned me.

Washington Heights had been my home but Saarbrücken was my birthplace. I might well have been one of the Saarland's Jews who perished or who lived in constant fear of being caught.

Friedel Heilbronner

A native of Saarbrücken, Friedel Heilbronner has been a guest of honor at the international Max Ophüls Preis Film Festival, named after her brother, since the mid-1980s. Often referred to as the Good Spirit of the Festival, she presides regally over the festivities, which take place over a period of a week every January. Known to everyone as Friedel (indicative of the informality of my city, which also refers to the premier of the Saarland as Oskar), she is the center of the parties and receptions that take place in conjunction with the screenings. Friedel is the daughter and granddaughter of entrepreneurs who built a department store empire throughout Germany (Bamberger and Hertz) and knew everyone who was connected to any large store in Saarbrücken, including my father. Friedel was also acquainted with many of the theatrical figures I had heard about while growing up. At the time of this interview (1991) she was an elegant eighty-two-year-old. Her presence at the film festival has enhanced my pleasure at being a participant.

FH. They were a very progressive family—my grandfather had been to America as early as 1900 and all of the sons also went afterward. They were all very broad-minded. My father had been brought up strictly orthodox and he once told us, for instance, when he was learning French as a boy, he was punished in school for not saying a sentence with the name Jesus in it.

My grandfather went to the school and told the director that the word *Jesus* was not allowed to be pronounced in Judaism. That's how strict my grandfather was. My father left home at the age of sixteen. Today, of course, one would call my father a revolutionary. He never went to the synagogue again, wasn't religious any longer, nothing. For example, when my brother was born, Grandfather came to the *Bris Miloh* [circumcision] and only ate a sardine from a can and an egg from its shell because my parents didn't keep a kosher home. Yet, when my children were baptized, that was the only day in my father's life when he said he didn't want to see them.

[One needed a baptismal certificate to emigrate to some countries in South America where Friedel and her children eventually ended up.]

FH. Something in him came back, the memory of his parents' house. He had always been a freethinker. He was very revolutionary through-out his youth. When May Day was celebrated here for the first time, in 1919, my father stood in front of his department store on Bahnhof-strasse and watched the parade. And there in the first row with his school cap was his son, my brother, Max, with a big banner saying, "Down with Capitalism!" *[Laughter.]* As a result, he was kicked out of school, naturally, never got his high school diploma.

My father had very leftist opinions and therefore was an enthusiastic follower of Max Braun [the Socialist party leader]. As early as 1927, when Hitler's coup d'état took place in Munich, my father didn't go back to Germany, never set foot on German soil again. The Saar region was, after all, separated from Germany. Besides, there was an enormous French influence here in the Saar since we were economically au-tonomous from Germany. We had barriers, customs barriers, with Ger-many and were open toward France. People went over for meals [Saar-brücken is less than five minutes from the French border] and many people went to Paris. And so we were oriented toward France business-wise and also personally.

At E. Weil Söhne [the store where my father, Bert Kirchheimer, worked] a certain mood prevailed. For instance they were flying a black, white, and red flag, the Nationalist flag without a swastika. That a Jew should fly the Nationalist flag—not National Socialist, but still Nationalist! My father flew the Saar flag.

He had such a heated argument with the owner, Dr. Köster, that he was finally prompted to say, "For a Jew, this is quite impossible—don't you see what's ahead of us?"

The atmosphere prevailing at E. Weil's was "Well, nothing is going to happen to us, you'll see."

BEFORE 1935

FH. I had studied in Berlin and was there when the first antisemitic riots at Berlin University broke out. To make my father happy, I had enrolled to study national economy, but in reality I studied theater. I met Piscator and others through my brother Max. Max was seven years older than I and was there already, and to me, needless to say, he was a god.

Most of the student fraternities were very antisemitic and didn't accept Jews as members. As a result, the Jews founded their own fraternity. And then there was this unbelievable brawl, so I said to myself, "I'm leaving Berlin."

[Friedel went to London in 1929, and in 1930 back in the Saar, she married Otto Heimann who owned a thriving clothing business.]

I was in Frankfurt in September 1933 together with my two-and-a-half-year-old daughter, visiting an uncle. The child was in the garden playing with other children. Then a boy of seven or eight came in and said, "You mustn't play with that child, that's a Jewish child."

So I told them, "Tomorrow morning I'll leave." And my aunt thought I was out of my mind.

And I said, "No, really, I can't take this. I'm going home!"

And then I came back here to Saarbrücken and the next morning I went to the coal mine management, where you could apply for naturalization [as a French citizen]. My family said I was overdoing it and that I was crazy. We had just moved into a new house six months earlier.

And they kept saying, "Right, you'll leave even if you have to wash floors in Paris."

And I always replied, "I'm leaving and my child will not stay in a German-speaking country."

Apart from my father, all the others said that I was overreacting, but I was a revolutionary in my younger years and very stubborn. And I said, "No, they can't do this to me."

[She persuaded her reluctant husband to go to Paris with her every few weeks to explore the economic possibilities, but they were not promising.]

FH. My husband wasn't really prepared to give up his position and the good life we had. He belonged to the kind of people who thought that nothing would happen to you if you were just a decent kind of a person. "We are German Jews," he said, "and we have a clean slate and we have no reason to worry. We are Germans and we are considered Germans."

[Through sheer luck, a French factory owner who supplied Friedel's father's store with raincoats offered to sell his coat factory in Paris to Friedel and her husband. They agreed, and at the end of 1933 Friedel, her husband, and their children went to Paris.]

Max had made a rather dreadful film in 1930, *The Laughing Heirs*, which he filmed in Rüdesheim. Sig Ruhmann was in it and the sets were made by someone called Benno von Arndt. This Benno von Arndt was an ultra-Nazi and he took Max to an SA meeting at night in some cellar—they were still illegal then.

Max said to me afterward, "If they should ever come to power, something terrible is going to happen to us beyond our worst imagination."

On January 30, 1933, three days after the Reichstag went up in flames, this Benno von Arndt called up Max and said, "Max, I saw you on the street today. You look just awful and you must get away from here [Berlin]. Just go to your parents in the Saar and get some rest there before you go on working. But don't wait, take the sleeping coach tonight and leave."

That's what Max did and the next morning the Gestapo showed up at my sister-in-law's. Max's wife was an Aryan and Max had escaped on his own. That's what an arch-Nazi did, as a friend. Things like that happened many times.

Gustav Gründgens acted fabulously also. He was one of the greatest actors in Germany. He was married to Erika Mann [from 1926 to 1929]. Then later he was Goebbels's favorite. He was what they called Janusfaced. On the one hand he was determined to make a career, but he also helped many Jews.

At one point in 1937 he came to Max and said, "You have such a lovely boy [Marcel], it would be a shame if he were to go to the dogs. There is nothing good in store for you. Give the boy to me and I'll raise him." Which Max didn't do, needless to say. Almost everybody had a Jew whom he protected, everybody had his token Jew.

[At the time of the 1935 plebiscite in the Saar, Friedel was established in Paris. She returned to Saarbrücken, as did her brother, in order to participate in the vote.]

FH. We were very eager to vote because people living abroad, particularly in France, would either vote in favor of France or of the status quo. The Saar region was Francophile but the population was German, the culture was German.

I knew my father was very committed to this vote and I said, "I don't want my parents to stay here when the results come out."

Then we went on to Paris and my parents went to a hotel in Metz with their little overnight suitcases to wait for the results. The next day the results were announced [90 percent in favor of a return to Germany] and Max and I said, "Father mustn't go back, our parents mustn't go back."

Both of us had the feeling he would be in danger, and so my parents never set foot on Saar territory again. They stayed in Metz for about two weeks, then they went to Strasbourg and rented a house there for a year [before moving to Paris].

[Friedel returned to Saarbrücken and liquidated the family's two stores at a loss. Unable to sell the house, she took whatever furniture her parents would need, gave some away, and auctioned the rest off. With her parents living near her in Paris and a successful coat factory, Friedel and her immediate family seemed relatively safe.]

FH. I lost four uncles. Gassed or shot while escaping Theresienstadt, and all because they told us, "Nothing will happen."

In 1938, I said to one of my uncles in Paris, "Now, just do me a favor, stay here."

"No."

So, after Kristallnacht, they were taken to the Leipzig concentration camp. Their store was smashed up during the night. The authorities said, "Our gentlemen arrested arsonists." The front page of the *Leipziger Neueste Nachrichten* reported that the Messrs. Bamberger had been arrested and taken to a camp. The other one was in Dachau, but we got him out. The others perished.

There was the one from Munich. In order for him to be able to keep his passport, our factory in Paris bought fabrics from him just for show. Thus he did exports and that's how he could keep his passport and go abroad. But my husband rightfully told him, "OK, we'll pay, but we won't send valuable foreign currency to Germany. You can sue me, but I'm not going to send you good French francs so the Nazis can produce weapons against France. You'll send me the merchandise and then you can say that I went bankrupt or I'm a criminal."

To which my uncle replied, "That won't do, that won't do, I made a commitment. I'm a German, I have a clean slate, nothing will happen to me here."

German Jews were so German, they really didn't understand that they were considered something else. That was their big mistake.

When the war broke out, Max was working for the Ministère d'Information and he did this very well-known radio program called, "Mr. Hitler, Do You Have Problems Sleeping?" He did it from the Continental Hotel in Paris where the Ministère d'Information was located. He broadcast it in the evenings. And it went like this: "So you can't sleep? There's a very effective remedy for this, Mr. Hitler. Just count. Count: one, two, three, the countries you assaulted." And then it goes on: "Count: one hundred, two hundred, three hundred, a thousand, and so on, all the people you murdered, all the people you deported to camps, all the people you sent to war." And this was broadcast every night.

[Until the Germans occupied France, Friedel's parents lived unhindered there because they were the parents of French citizens, Friedel and Max having been naturalized. Friedel's children were sent to a small hotel in Vichy in the care of a young woman whom they knew from Saarbrücken, Lilo Kahn (at that time Lilo Lyon), since it was clear that an armistice between France and Germany was imminent. Friedel was shuttling between Paris and Vichy.]

FRANCE CAPITULATES

FH. When the debacle came in 1940, when it could be seen that the war was over for France and that the Germans would move on, Vichy was in danger. So I went to the interior, to La Bourboule, a small seaside resort for asthmatics in the Auvergne, and I rented a house there for the entire family in June 1940.

[Together with a Czech immigrant who had escaped to Paris with no assets but a patent for gas-proof clothing, Friedel's husband had obtained a contract from the French Arms Ministry to manufacture the gas-resistant clothing. When the Germans occupied Paris, he fled.]

FH. Then everybody escaped from Paris. All of France was in flight [to the south]. My sister-in-law was eight months pregnant with her second child. Max had been drafted into the Tirailleurs Algériens, the Algerian gunnery unit, stationed in the interior at Camp d'Avord. And these *enfants* were meant to be cannon fodder. The Moroccans, the colonial troops, were mostly sent to the front. Max didn't get into a French regiment because he had been naturalized.

It was a real *drôle de guerre* [a funny war], that's what they called it. It wasn't a real war. The French had no fighting spirit. One day, Max's superior came to him and said, "Max, you really have to do something. These Algerians here, these troops are so lazy and laid back, they don't even march properly. I'm sure you know some war songs or something like that. Teach them a few so they shape up a bit."

And then Max said, "Well, apart from 'La Madelon,' I don't know any, and that one's still from the 1914 war. I know German military songs but no French ones."

And then the officer said, "So teach them the German songs." And then Max went to work on these boys.

"It was so funny," he told us. In the evenings, when the sun went down, the Algerians and Moroccans with their fezzes on, went through the small town singing, "Muss i denn, muss i denn zum Staedtele hinaus," in German. *[Laughter.]*

There was no gasoline then and some really odd things happened. We took a car from Paris—I had this small Citroën. Then my husband came from the factory with a delivery van. We also had a Ford, which he had used to drive my parents and his mother down. He had parked it in some garage. Well, the Ford was stolen, and there was no gasoline for the two other cars.

So we got a barrel of gasoline on the black market, and my father said, "This can't remain in the house, of course, because the Germans are advancing and if they bombard us, the house is in danger. The gas barrel has to go."

So we rolled it to the city park, put branches over it, and then hiked over every morning to see if our gas was still there. On the third or fourth morning, there was nothing but branches, and the gas was gone. That was all very terrible back then.

There was this incredible atmosphere. For instance, one day my sister-in-law went down to Camp d'Avord to see Max. There was a small village nearby with a small hotel. Of course, the soldiers were on roll call every morning in the barracks, and during the roll call an adjutant or some other superior said, "Max, you disappoint me very much. I hear your wife is in town and you slept here last night. What's that all about?" Very French. *[Laughter.]* It really was what they called a *drôle de guerre*.

But then later, it wasn't all that *drôle* anymore, of course. Because when Max heard that he was on the extradition list on account of his anti-Hitler broadcasts, and the Germans were advancing, he had to go from place to place and slept in barns and wherever there was refuge.

[At the end of 1940, with the Germans advancing into the south of France Friedel, her husband, and her children, as well as Max's pregnant wife and their son, drove across France, heading for Bayonne where they were hoping to cross into Spain. Her parents and mother-in-law remained behind in La Bourboule with Lilo Kahn.]

FH. At times we even slept on the ground. I remember once they put down a mattress for the children in a barn. I put the children to sleep there, and then we went out to catch some fresh air, and when we returned one of my daughters, the oldest, cried terribly. She had been afraid that we wouldn't come back. The children were in shock, naturally. Children are used to a regular lifestyle and then suddenly we were living like gypsies, stopping here and there asking, "Can we sleep here?"

The smallest didn't cry at all. She was five years old. And I said, "Irene cried, and you weren't afraid?"

And she replied, "I was."

And I said, "You were very brave, you didn't cry."

And then she said, "I thought, if you're not here by tomorrow morning, I'd still have plenty of time to cry." [*Laughter.*]

We arrived in Bayonne and that was it. There was the sea and we couldn't go on. Spain had closed its border. And during this escape, we had slept everywhere, in barns, in churches. We couldn't stay anywhere, there was nothing but rain and all of France was on the move. And then down there, in Bayonne, we came to a screeching halt. The place was buzzing with emigrants. Some were boarding ships for Casablanca, and that's what was suggested to us.

My husband said, "That's totally out of the question."

So there we were, down there, without gas or anything. Max (whom we had picked up on the way) had managed to arrange for his children and wife to spend the night in a movie theater. The next morning the word spread that the Germans were practically in front of the gates. So I went with my sister-in-law with her huge belly like a figurehead to the French mayor, and we described the situation to him and told him about my brother being on the extradition list.

And he said, "As you see me now in my outfit"—in his black suit and his sash—"I'm waiting for the Germans. Just get out of here. The only thing I can give you are a couple of gas coupons. Try to escape to the Pyrenees to safety. From here you can get to Orléans on these coupons and then you go and report to the next mayor."

We used to be friends with a doctor and I had asked him . . . and he gave me cyanide, and Max always said, "The moment the Germans catch me, I'll take that cyanide. Really, I won't survive that." But, thank God, we ended up in the Pyrenees in a village.

We were ecstatic that we were up there. Things were fine until we woke up one morning to find that the car had been stolen with all the luggage and only the van was left. It all turned out to be very tragic in the end. Max wanted to commit suicide. He was desperate.

[Eventually, the family group made its way to Aix-en-Provence, where they were able to settle into an estate owned by friends from Germany. They were joined there by their parents. In July 1940 the pro-Nazi Vichy government had been formed to govern an autonomous, unoccupied region of France. Laval was not yet in power and the anti-Jewish regulations had not yet been promulgated. By August the family was running out of money and since Friedel's husband still had his gas-proof clothing factory in Paris he decided to return. Once he was there, however, the factory was commandeered to work for the Germans. Though he was able to remain, he was not permitted to send any money to his family.]

FH. In those days one simply tried anything. To begin with, we were young and then we were up to our necks. Human beings are unbelievably capable if need be. So I just went into the lion's den, to the Germans. They had an office of the Ministry of Aviation in Aix in the free zone. So I went there with a notification that I had received from a friend—an attorney, who is still around in Paris—saying that I had an appointment to appear in court for my divorce proceedings. [Difficulties had been growing for a long time between Friedel and her husband.]

FH. I went to an officer, but didn't say "Heil Hitler" but simply "Good morning," and told him, "Listen, I have to go to Paris. I need a *laisser-passer*, a pass that will allow me to go to Paris."

I told him my whole story: that I'm about to be divorced and that there's a court hearing that I have to attend in person, and that the French court system was rather strict. I told this big tale and then the

German officer said, "OK, I'll give you a pass for the journey to Paris, but you'll have to report to the German authorities there every day, and then you'll have to apply for the journey back, otherwise you'll never get out."

I said, "I have to come back here, I have a family, my small children are here," and so forth. He even gave me his name. He wasn't exactly a young officer, and he said "Good morning" when I left.

And I thought, "Aha!" Meanwhile, there was this big Hitler photo on the wall.

So I took the train to Paris. One had to cross the *ligne de démarcation* [between occupied and unoccupied France]. I shared a sleeper with another lady who had gotten onto the train in Lyon. The train had hardly started moving when she said to me in French, "You know your way around here?"

And I replied, "No, I don't." I was very cautious.

Then she says, "You know, this is the first time I'm crossing the ligne de démarcation. You know anything about that?"

I said, "No, for me this is the first time too."

So she says, "I have another problem, may I confide in you?"

So I said, "Sure. What is it?"

"Well, you know, I'm Jewish."

Says I, "Gosh, great, I'm Jewish too. It seems there's something in store for both of us at the ligne de démarcation."

We had agreed to pretend to be fast asleep when the train stopped, so that's what we did, and then the Germans came in asking for papers. I had this pass from the Germans so they called their superior. "What's this?"

"It's OK."

The other woman had a Turkish passport and he said, "The Turks are neutral, let her pass." So both of us arrived in Paris safely.

Now to the journey back. Well, the gentlemen gave me a hard time. They said I'd have to stay there, they had to check my file. And I started getting queasy because my husband was still there. Now there were these *passeurs* who took people across the ligne de démarcation illegally under cover of night. The border was at Moulin, a town near Vichy. I found a passeur and took my money and papers and went off with a friend's fiancée, a young thing of eighteen, a Jewess from Reims. We got to Nevers, which had already been occupied and it wasn't free any longer. So there we were without a *visa de sortie* [exit visa], which was required in order to leave occupied France. We wanted to get to Moulin in order to cross over into free France, but Moulin had also been taken by the Germans.

We came to this waiting room and the Germans were sitting there in droves with their rifles, observing everyone's movements. When I saw this I went to the stationmaster who was a Frenchman and told him about our predicament.

He said, "Go to the baggage claim. There's a man sitting there who's a good guy."

We went to him, and he told us that a train would be passing through around midnight.

He said, "I'll lock you into the baggage claim room and you'll stay there until the train comes. There's a little hut where I'll be standing. When the train's in the station, I'll lift the lantern, and you'll cross the rails—not onto the platform, where the train is, but to the back. That's where you'll get into the train. I'll open the door for you and when I lift the lantern, you'll have to be very careful so you don't fall." There were all these cables there and everything was pitch dark.

So we sat there in this cubbyhole and there were mice and rats and it was terrible, and then the train came. It was pouring. It was a very dark night and everything had been darkened. So we went along and Simone was the first to get in, and I just kept looking on the ground for cables. Just as I was crossing the last rail, a freight train came whooshing in and barely missed me. When we were on the train, the porter on the platform where the Germans were sitting with their machine guns threw our luggage in, and the train started moving. And then two men from the French police arrived. They had observed all of this and congratulated us. The very second we were on the train, both of us collapsed.

[With the Gestapo firmly entrenched in Vichy, conditions for the Jews deteriorated rapidly and Jews began to be deported. The Vichy government issued a decree stating that all French citizens who had been naturalized after 1933 (and this included Freidel) were "déchus de la nationalité française" (stripped of their French citizenship). Friedel and her family were now stateless. Jews in the so-called free zone were required to carry cards stating that they were Jews. Even if they could obtain a passport from the French, it had to be approved by the German authorities.]

FH. That was the Germans' doing, in order to get at potential emigrants. They demanded this of the French and of Laval, this noble gentleman who was the secretary of the Interior under Pétain and who collaborated with the Germans. He was the greatest swine you can imagine.

[Friedel set about trying to obtain the necessary passports and visas in order to emigrate, traveling indefatigably from place to place, jumping at any possibility that presented itself.]

FH. Everything was possible [as a destination]: from Santo Domingo to all over South America, Japan, China. Every day someone came along with a different story and different suggestions and we kept running from one consulate to the next and from one racketeer to the other. You paid and you would meet Mafia people clandestinely in small cafés.

[Friedel's house in Aix became a refuge for other stateless people, including a number of politicians and intellectuals like Walter Benjamin who had been interned in a camp near Marseilles, Les Milles. They were required to be at the camp during the day but not at night, and since they had neither papers nor money, they were unable to go to a hotel.

Max Ophüls was in particular danger because of his anti-German propaganda activities. The actor Louis Jouvet took him under his wing in Aix and was able to bring him to Switzerland where he had an acting engagement. In Zurich, Ophüls directed *L'Ecole des Femmes* by Molière but was not permitted to remain in Switzerland. Eventually, thanks to Friedel's efforts he obtained a passport. Through his connections with an American journalist, Varian Fry, and then through a writer, Leon Feuchtwänger, he received one of the few emergency visas issued by the American government to foreign intellectuals and came to the United States via Marseilles and Lisbon.]

FH. Chasing for a *visa de sortie,* I was told one day that I could get one from a man in Cannes. So I went, from Aix, via Marseilles, planning to stop first in Nice. I wanted to drink something in the dining car but there were no free seats. A gentleman got up and offered me his seat. Really nice, a tall, good-looking man. When I got out of the diner he was waiting for me. He asked me what I was up to and where I was going and I told him I was on my way to Nice. He said he was an Italian officer who had studied in Vienna and was on the Armistice Commission.

He said, "I'm on my way to Cannes and I might be able to help you." If I couldn't get anywhere in Nice, I was to contact him immediately.

In those days, you really tried everything. I got nowhere in Nice, and then I called this man. Well, what can I tell you? I was young then and maybe a little more attractive than today and to make a long story short, this man courted me very much.

Two days later he appeared in Aix and said, "Listen, if you don't get a *permis* to go to Paris, I'll take you by car. I have to go to Paris, anyway. I have the car with a large plate saying Commission d'Armistice. Nothing will happen to you."

I had been to Paris earlier on with that Jewish woman on the train. And this man now took me to Paris. That's how I went two or three times to get money for the family, because we really didn't have anything in Aix anymore and my husband was earning money in Paris.

This Italian was a man—as my father always put it—who was God Almighty himself, who held a protecting hand over many Jews, who took me with him three times to Paris and got me out again with money in his car of the great Italian Commission d'Armistice. The fourth time, things got tricky for him, and he said he would get me an ID card from the Italian Red Cross identifying me as an Italian nurse who had to go to Paris for a week. He took me to Clermont-Ferrand to the Italian consul who was a friend of his and I got my ID. My friend was not coming along with me to Paris. I got on the train at Moulin and in comes the inspector and I show him my ID.

And then this German says, "Now isn't that odd? An Italian nurse from the Italian Red Cross, Friedel Heimann, née Oppenheimer. That doesn't sound very Italian, that sounds more Jewish. You come with us!"

So he took me to an office. I was scared . . . I had been so sure of myself. We were in this huge group of emigrants going back and forth to Marseilles. There were an awful lot of people who said, "Oh, you're going to Paris? Please do me a big favor, could you take this letter?" Or could you do this, could you do that? And I, cocksure of myself, had said, "Just give them to me, I have diplomatic protection, don't I?"

So I had this whole batch of letters. And then someone needed a spare part for his radio and I had taken this tube with me. Also my mother had given me a parcel, a Christmas gift, saying, "You're going to open that on Christmas." (I was to stay in Paris over Christmas [1940]). So I had been very bold and very sure of myself.

They took me to the Gestapo and the Gestapo unpacked the luggage and opened the correspondence.

"What's in the letters?"

I had never opened the letters.

"Who are the letters from?"

"I don't know." Of course, I didn't want to give anyone's name. Then they took my notebook. I had Madeleine Ozeray's address in there, a very famous actress, Louis Jouvet's girlfriend, who also lived in Aix. Madeleine had gone back to Paris and I was supposed to contact her too.

"So, you know Madeleine? That's very interesting. We already arrested her." She was a member of the Resistance, which I hadn't known.

"So, here you have the materials, a secret transmitter."

"I never, in all my life, operated a radio. I don't know how."

Of course, they didn't believe me. And then they found the parcel— I'll never forget that—and asked me what was in it and I said, "It's a present from my mother for Christmas."

"What is it?"

And I said, "I haven't opened it yet. It's a surprise."

"*Délicatesse juive.* That's a Jewish delicacy, very typical." They got so fresh, and as a result I got fresh in return, which culminated in one guy saying to the other, "Pity she's Jewish, we could have had fun with her."

All night long they insulted me, interrogated me in such a way that I thought I would never get out of there again. And then they started on their notes and I had to lie through my teeth. I kept saying that I had diplomatic protection and insisted that they call the Italian consul in Clermont-Ferrand. I really got them to do that in the morning, and the Gestapo said, "We have to let this woman go, she has diplomatic protection."

They took everything away from me, and I was very bold then and said, "I want a receipt." Then they gave me a kick in the butt and threw me out the door. I was very, very lucky.

[At the interrogation Friedel had told a number of lies to the Gestapo. Now she was concerned that her husband would be questioned and perhaps contradict some of her statements. It was imperative that she reach him first in order to brief him. Her Italian knight picked her up once more and hid her with the luggage in the back of his car and transported her across the border to Paris. There she was able to meet with her husband and convey the information to him. He was eventually summoned for interrogation and was able to confirm her statements.

Then, also, some of the family's money had been sent to America via secret channels.]

FH. The Italian turned out to be a crook and a swindler in the end. He got the money over through a connection in New York that really never existed and later when we went over there and wanted our money, there wasn't anything left. But at least he saved my parents, he protected them. During the time we lived in Aix, he did incredible things.

And strangely enough, four or five years ago, he called up a mutual friend of ours in Paris and asked for my address. And the friend said, "I'm under the impression that Friedel has no interest at all in ever seeing you again, after how you cheated the family." But he cheated other Jews as well. He helped them, and he deceived them as human beings— but that's incidental.

[The struggle to obtain passports and visas continued, with no avenue left untried. Through her Italian benefactor, Friedel had been put in touch with a French deputy, a Monsieur Antier, who was said to be willing to assist Jews in getting passports. It was known that upon presentation of a valid passport, the Brazilian envoy would issue a visa for emigration to Brazil. (The envoy was later replaced because it was discovered that he had been giving out visas illegally.) Antier assured Friedel that he would have passports for her.]

FH. After about four weeks I got a telephone call from M. Antier asking me to meet him in Marseilles. He was about to leave France for an assignment to do a scientific study of the sources of Nile. When we met, he told me he was leaving the next morning but that my file was in good hands.

"Go to Vichy next week, then your file will be completed and then you can pick up your passports." I was ecstatic.

I went to Vichy to the Ministère de l'Intérieur and I said, "I come from M. Antier."

Upon which the employee says, "Pauvre dame!" [Poor lady!]

I say, "Why 'pauvre dame'? Hasn't my file been completed? Isn't my passport ready?"

Says he, "No, much worse. Don't you know where Antier is?"

I say, "He's in Africa isn't he?"

"He's gone to join de Gaulle. The worst that can happen to you here in Vichy is a recommendation from Antier."

"Well, now what?"

Says he, "The file must disappear!"

Says I, "What can I do, how can I make it disappear?"

"Well, that's your business."

So I say, "What do you want me to do? I can't burglarize this place. Can't you get my file out?"

"Me? For God's sake, I'm a civil servant, there's nothing I can do."

Well, through umpteen connections, we found the cleaning woman who was cleaning this room, and we bribed the woman to steal our file one night and burn it. There we were again, back to square one!

Well, my husband was now a Frenchman through and through, and he said we were safe in France and nothing would happen to us. "You want to go, I don't. You're hysterical, we'll stay here."

And so I said I wasn't going to stay. We argued, and I said I wanted to save the children and get out of here and that I was leaving.

One day I said, "I've had it! I'm going to Vichy to talk to the secretary of the Interior and explain our case. We're Jews and we've always been Francophile. France is, after all, civilized, and I'll achieve something if I go in person. If they can't protect us in France, at least they will allow us to leave for humanitarian reasons."

So I went to Vichy and sat there at the Ministère de l'Intérieur in a large hall where many people were waiting to get a number in order to see the secretary of the Interior. Beside me sat this rather inconspicuous red-haired man, and he kept looking at me, and suddenly he said, "What do you really want here?"

So I say, "You have three guesses. I want a visa and I need a passport." I explained my situation as a stateless French Jew.

Then he said, "Oh, you're Jewish? Let's go for a little walk. I'd like to talk to you. It might be interesting for you."

And since we tried everything conceivable then—you know there were no limits—I went out with the man.

He said his name was Mr. Wolkovje—I'll never forget this as long as I live—and he was a Polish Jew. He had received an exit visa for his family and offered to give me an address. He asked if I had a little money. I would need to take a cab to the town of La Palisse, forty kilometers away.

"What am I going to do in La Palisse?"

He says, "Go to the sous-préfecture. As you come in, there's a man sitting on the right side at a table. He wears a blue smock and has a wooden leg. Tell him you're one of Mr. Wolkovje's cousins. Tell him that Aunt Alice already arrived in Canada and that I too will sail for Canada in two weeks, and that he should do for you what he did for me."

I say, "What did he do for you?"

"He gave me an exit visa."

"You're fibbing."

"No, I want to help you. Do as I say."

I say, "What does this enterprise cost?"

"You mustn't give him money. He doesn't accept money. If you want to do something for him, go to the Marquise de Sévigné" (that's a very exquisite candy store in France). "Buy a pound of chocolate at black market prices and bring it to him for his children. You mustn't do more."

I thought, "He's telling me a fib," but since we tried anything . . .

Well, he was right. I went to the Marquise de Sévigné shop in Vichy, got my chocolate, took a cab, and went to La Palisse. I get to the place and this man is really sitting there. I tell him my story, and he asks if I have photos of the family, which I do. "Come back in two hours," he says. After two hours he gave me the passports with the exit visas.

[Despite his initial reluctance to leave, Friedel's husband had come around, particularly since he now was provided with a passport. The family's eventual destination was Argentina where some of their friends had preceded them. Lacking visas for that country, they were counting on a law in effect stating that anyone who set foot on Argentinean soil would be permitted to remain.

But first it was necessary to obtain transit visas for Spain where they hoped to board a ship for South America. These could be gotten by showing "valid" emigration visas to Chile. After learning that they were being sold by an enterprising Chilean consul in Marseilles, the family paid five hundred dollars per visa. ("A real crook. He gave out numbers that were from people who had already emigrated a long time ago or had died.")

In June 1941, they left France for Spain. Mr. Heimann traveled separately by train, with a couple of thousand dollars hidden in the soles of his shoes. As holders of French passports, they were permitted to take out only one hundred dollars. Friedel also planned to bring a considerable amount of money into Spain. Once again, her Italian friend came to the rescue—or so it appeared.]

FH. The Italian told me, "No need to be afraid, I'll drive you across the Spanish border. You can take all the money you still have, no problem. And once you're in Spain, you're safe."

And then he took me and the children in his car across the Spanish border. There he had us picked up by his *soi-disant* [so-called] cousin who lived in Spain and he took me and the children to a hotel in Barcelona.

[Friedel planned to meet her husband after three days in Vigo where they would board a ship for Chile.]

FH. In Spain, as is customary during wars or after wars everywhere, there was an official price for dollars and a black market price. Of course, the black market price was much, much higher and this so-called cousin said, "Listen, I'll exchange your dollars on the black market, then you'll get much more." OK, great.

[Friedel needed Spanish money to cover expenses for a couple of days.]

FH. I was very pleased and I gave him the dollars and he duly exchanged them. On the third day, I came back to the hotel to my room and received a call—of course, I didn't know Spanish—"The police are here." There were three plainclothesmen and they wanted to know what we're living on.

"Yes, we exchanged money." I'm supposed to show the receipts, where I did the exchanging. Well, I didn't have any receipts, only a few for the first couple of times. Everything else was black market. Subsequently they said that they knew I exchanged on the black market and what type of money I had. I said I had no money.

To make a long story short, they did a search. They searched everything, the luggage—the children still remember this—they removed the dolls' wigs. The rest of the dollars were in my pocketbook, and I went to the bathroom thinking I'd be immensely clever leaving the pocketbook in the bathroom, but they were smarter than I. They found the dollars and made me sign that I would leave Barcelona within twenty-four hours.

And I said, "At least leave me enough money, so I can get away, so I can take a train with the children."

And so they left me some and I had to sign for it. The rest of it was gone. I just had enough for a train ticket to the ship and then I met my husband in Vigo. He still had the money in his shoe, about two or three thousand dollars.

Later it turned out that they hadn't been policemen. I called the Italian, and he came to Vigo and kicked up a terrible fuss, saying he was going to find the people. He even came to us in Cadiz to let us know he hadn't found anybody. Later on it turned out that it had been a whole gang. I wasn't the only one they robbed. I'm still convinced today that this was another coup by this Italian. We lost over twenty thousand dollars to this gentleman, including the money in America.

⚜

Liliane (Lilo) Kahn

Like me, Lilo Kahn was born in Saarbrücken and chose to return to live there after the war although, as she says, "I have no homeland. The Germans took it away from me."

We are sitting in the elegant lobby of the Pullman Hotel and will soon be joined by Friedel Heilbronner. Lilo has brought me a photo taken in 1935 of her and a friend and my father, pausing during a stroll along one of Saarbrücken's tree-lined streets on a winter day. Like her friend Friedel Heilbronner, Lilo Kahn is descended from a prominent department store dynasty. Her grandfather founded the first department store in Saarbrücken, Wronker's, now the present site of the Kaufhof department store. "It was a sensation at that time," she says. "There was even a food department and a restaurant. It was unheard of at that time, a restaurant in a department store."

Another department store was founded by Lilo's father and two cousins, Lyon and Sons, where the present Sinn department store now stands. By 1932, both family-owned stores had been sold to the Sinn company. Lilo says they already had forebodings that Hitler would come to power.

After the plebiscite in the Saar, which resulted in a vote in favor of returning the region to Germany, Lilo and her brother were sent to relatives in Luxembourg where the family had another store, while their parents left for France. (Under the Roman Treaty, described earlier, Jews in the Saarland were given a year's grace period to liquidate their properties and investments and were permitted to take their money with them.)

In Luxembourg Lilo trained as a nursery-school teacher and in 1937, at the age of nineteen, she went to Paris to live with a Jewish family. Soon after, she was engaged by Friedel Heimann (later Heilbronner) to look after her children in France. The two families had been acquainted for years in Saarbrücken. At that time Lilo's father was working as a sales representative for the raincoat factory in Paris owned by Friedel's husband.

In 1940, a few months after the outbreak of war, Lilo's parents were interned in a camp near Gurs by the French, German Jews being considered enemy aliens (as we were in America). They were later released as refugees from the Saar region.

To escape the bombardment of Paris, Lilo was sent away with Friedel's children and their grandmother to Vichy, which was considered a safe area at the time. There she was arrested and taken to a transit camp but was released when Friedel Heimann interceded. Friedel had become a naturalized French citizen but, more important, was able to convince officials that as a manufacturer of special gas-proof clothing, she needed Lilo to care for her children while she remained in Paris near her factory.

Lilo was again in danger of arrest when she was summoned to the mayor's office in Vichy.

LK. I took the children with me to the mayor's to prove that I was a child-care worker. Then he yelled at me and said, "If I hear one more word from you, you're off to Drancy" [a transit camp for Auschwitz]. Then he let me go home again.

[Shortly after the signing of the armistice in 1940 between France and Germany, the Heimanns rented a large house in La Bourboule, a small seaside resort in the Auvergne. There Lilo continued to look after Friedel's children until the Heimann family left the town. After their release from the camp, Lilo's parents joined her at La Bourboule. Lilo's brother, who was also in La Bourboule, was picked up by the French police and taken to a concentration camp, the first of a total of eleven where he would be imprisoned.]

LK. The French militia collaborated with the Germans. The unoccupied zone was almost as bad as the occupied zone. [When Lilo's father became ill in 1941, the authorities refused to allow her brother to go and visit him from Gurs.] They let him go only after my father's death. And even that happened through a Frenchman whose son I had taught. In La Bourboule my mother, brother, and I went from one hotel to another. We were afraid the Germans might come.

[Finally they hid in a hotel room, protected by the owners who brought them food and looked after them.]

MK. Why did they do this?

LK. Out of resistance. They were against the Germans.

[The Auvergne, which bordered on Vichy, was a center of the French Resistance movement, and consequently many Jews found people willing to help them. Vichy, on the other hand, was full of collaborators.]

MK. Were these hotel owners politically-minded people?

LK. No, they were rich people. They had a rather large hotel.

MK. So it *was* political?

LK. Not at all. This is humaneness. They knew us, they knew me quite well. There were children in the hotel whom I taught. I made money that way here and there. I was known as a teacher and I gave lessons everywhere all the time, either German, or English, or whatever—arithmetic, math.

We were in the hotel for a couple of months. And then the big raids started. We heard that they had raided the large hotels. They went from room to room to look for Jews. And then we had to get out.

[Through a friend, they found a family in a village that was willing to take them in.]

LK. It was all very primitive, but they took you for money, of course—it was always for money. But they took you not as Jews. We went into hiding as Frenchmen. The woman's son was supposed to be sent to forced labor in Germany, and we told her that my brother was also supposed to go and that's why we wanted to be in a village. We didn't tell them we were Jews. We had forged papers. [The family's real name was Lyon.] My name was "Lafarge," Liliane Lafarge. My mother was Lucienne Lafarge. We had to keep our initials, which were on our suitcases. And then we didn't have paper tissues back then, but real handkerchiefs. The elegant ones were embroidered with our initials. The real papers in the name of Lyon were hidden in a deserted farmhouse, which was falling apart. We put them under the hay. And they survived, with my father's photo still among them.

MK. The people with whom you lived weren't particularly good people. They did it for money?

LK. Yes. There's a proverb in French: "Un auvergnat vaut trois juifs" (One person from Auvergne is worth three Jews).

MK. They never guessed you were Jews?

LK. No, they don't even know today.

[Lilo's family made it plain that they were anti-German and since they spoke fluent French, it was assumed by their hosts that they were political refugees. As new arrivals to the town they were required to register with the police. Two days after they came to the town they took their forged papers and ration cards, all in the name of Lafarge, and went to register.]

LK. We were up there in the village on the mountain, and my mother and I had to go down a kilometer to the town in our galoshes. We didn't have any real shoes anymore. My brother never went down, he always stayed in the village. To make things worse, there was this huge cathedral there. It was a place of pilgrimage.

We went to the mayor's office and registered. Before we left I asked his secretary what he would do with those papers. And he told me,

"They go to the mayor's office in Clermont-Ferrand." That was the closest larger town.

When we left I said, "Mother, our forged papers will go there and if they find something, they may come and inquire, and we'll be in trouble."

Then my mother had a fainting spell. We had to go to the bakery, and she sat down and had a glass of brandy to revive.

And then I said, "There's just one thing to do. Either we go back and tell them the truth about us, and he might be decent and not send off the papers, or we leave again because we can't stay here."

Then we went back to the mayor's office. I told his secretary—I'll never forget that—I said, "We've gone into hiding here with my brother because of the Germans."

He says, "Why didn't you tell me right away? I was imprisoned by the Germans, I'm against them too." And he tore up the registration form. That was a real gamble.

After that we stayed. We were Catholics—in our minds only. Every Sunday my mother and I went to mass. When I was in Luxembourg, I had gone to a strict Catholic school. Before and after every lesson they recited the Lord's Prayer and other prayers. When they went to church, I always went with the kids from the kindergarten, and I crossed myself and all that. I prayed with them and God must have heard us, because otherwise I wouldn't have known how and when to do everything the way it's done in a Catholic church.

And once, I even—that was awful—I took communion. At Christmas one has to do communion, but if you do communion you have to confess first. No communion without confession. At Christmastime I was in Clermont-Ferrand—I went there occasionally. I went to the cathedral and I looked at the confessionals. There was one with the name Father David on it and I liked the name a lot. It was Jewish and I memorized it. When the farmers in the village asked us, "Madame Lafarge, where did you confess?"

We said, "We don't go here in the town, he's a friend of the Germans. We went to Father David."

At midnight we went down for the midnight mass, and the farmers gave me a rosary because they thought I was Catholic. When we were in the church I said to my mother, "Just imitate me. Do everything exactly as I do." We always sat in the back of the church. All of a sudden the people in front get up and I say, "Good Lord, they are going to communion." That I didn't know—where would I have learned that? So I told my mother to follow me and we went up front. We knelt down, opened our mouths, swallowed, and went back to the pew with me in front and my mother behind me. Luckily, you kneel down and stay put there, thinking of God.

And then my mother and I had a laughing fit. Can you imagine that? It was just horrible. I said to my mother, "That's the last time I go to communion with you!"

[At Easter, on Palm Sunday, Lilo participated in a ritual in which pilgrims walk around the church, chanting the rosary.]

LK. I went around the church with them, thinking to myself, "What would my father say now?"

[In 1944 Lilo and her mother received word that many of the family's belongings were in storage in Paris under the name of Liliane Lyon. In order to reclaim the property, Lilo's mother would have to prove that she was Mrs. Lyon, an Aryan. Without proof of ownership, the Germans would confiscate all the goods.]

LK. Then I said (in my juvenile enthusiasm, I should add), "I'll go to the Commissaire des Juifs" [the agency that dealt with Jewish matters] and request this for Mme. Lyon. I won't go there as Liliane Lafarge but as Mme. de Grange. That's the name I chose. It didn't matter what name you had. Before I went, I dyed this lock of hair blond—I had dark hair—to look a little more Aryan.

The commissaire was sitting at his desk, like Hitler. I thought, "I'm with Hitler." The same hair, small mustache, and all that. In other words, a collaborator.

I told him what I wanted, and he said, "Lyon is a Jewish name, right?"

I said, "I have no idea. I only know that in Lyon" (where I said I had lived) "my friend always came with me to mass every Sunday. I can't imagine that she's Jewish."

He asked me where she lived.

I said, "She's a saleswoman and she's traveling and has no permanent address."

"Where is she now?"

And I said, "She's in Nice." I've never been to Nice in all my life. He asked what street and house number. I mentioned the first street that came to my mind and a number. I don't even understand myself. He wrote everything down. I didn't know if any such street existed or if Nice itself existed at all.

"All right," he told me. "We'll do some research and if everything is OK we'll let you know."

I can't believe that he didn't notice something wasn't quite right. It was destiny that God held his protecting hands over me.

Then he says, "Where are you and who are you, anyway?"

He could have said, "Just show me your papers." I said I was Madame de Grange—even though my papers were for Lafarge—and gave him the name of the village where we were hiding. There comes a moment when you just black out. So he let me go.

After about four weeks, this letter arrives in our village for Mme. de Grange. There were five farms in the village, and each knew exactly what the other was getting and what they had, and so forth. [The rumor had arisen that there were Jews in the village.]

The letter carrier asked everywhere, "Who the heck is Mme. de Grange?" Of course, they all knew that we were Lafarge, not de Grange.

So we said, "That's an aunt, she's coming here soon, give us the letter."

And it said, "We made inquiries in Nice to find Mme. Lyon but the street is unknown and nothing is known about Mme. Lyon."

Now what was to be done? From that moment on, my mother stood at the window from morning until night and from night until morning, like Madama Butterfly, to see if the Gestapo were on their way. Again it was up to me. I wrote back (as Mme. de Grange) saying I wasn't at all surprised at what they wrote. I hadn't heard from her in a long, long time, either, but I finally had news from her from Switzerland [thereby confirming something the commissioner had told her earlier about Jews who came to him under false pretenses and then disappeared in Switzerland].

LK. "Please don't write me anymore since I am a [traveling] salesperson also and I'm no longer at the address stated." I wanted to divert them and make sure they didn't come to where we were hiding.

[The Allies invaded France soon after, and the family left the village for Paris, "with a slaughtered pig in the rented car." Had the Allies not arrived, Lilo is convinced that they could not have held out any longer.]

LK. We were happy that we survived even though we suffered terrible losses in the family. But later, much later, these things come back, and one is more alert than others and more susceptible to almost everything, both to diseases and everything else.

MK. Did you ever retrieve your property?

LK. Yes, everything was there, including six bottles of oil that could still be used. Cooking oil. After the war that was a real treasure. They had absolutely none here.

RETURN TO GERMANY

MK. Why did you return to Saarbrücken?

LK. First, I worked in Paris for the Americans in the Military Intelligence Service, in the censorship office and the American Red Cross. So did my brother. We came out of the war practically without any money. We had spent everything on forged papers, buying supplies, food, and so forth [paying the farmers who had sheltered them].

[They learned that Lilo's wealthy grandmother had died in Frankfurt and had left a substantial estate. Despite most of her assets having been confiscated "by the cartload," there was still money in the bank in Germany. But there was no way to transfer it to France. In 1947 Lilo was working in Paris for the Printemps department store. With the help of Friedel Heilbronner's first husband, Otto Heimann, she and her brother opened two stores, one in Saarbrücken (where her brother was now living) and another in Neunkirchen. She returned to Saarbrücken in 1948 at the behest of her brother, who needed help with the stores. Business was thriving.]

MK. And since then you've been living in Saarbrücken?

LK. Yes, that's where I got stranded. That is to say, I got married here . . . I have no homeland. The Germans took it away from me. I always say so, even when non-Jews say to me, "You must feel happy again to be in your former home country."

I always say, "Just a second. Hitler took 'home' away from us. It doesn't exist for me any longer, or anywhere." I feel at ease in my store, within my own four walls, and I feel fine with my friends. But that's it, there it ends.

IS THE TRUTH DANGEROUS?

[Friedel Heilbronner has arrived, and now our discussion turns to the showing in Germany of my film about the German Jewish community of Washington Heights. The women surprise me with the vehemence of their objections. In the film (and in these pages), my father reveals his timidity and admits that he probably would not have been willing to take the risk of hiding anyone. The women feel that such an attitude could damage the image of Jews vis-à-vis the Germans.]

LK. If I were a German, I would say, "If the Jew Kirchheimer doesn't want to protect his own people and hide them when he has the chance, then why should we do it?"

[The women also object to showing the German Jews in their comfortable Washington Heights apartments, surrounded by their decorative porcelain and silver objects and their fine china. They feel this might lead Germans to disbelieve the stories of suffering and to assume that German Jews were all well-off. But the very fact that German Jews look and act like other Germans, I say, is an important point to make in order to dispel the stereotypes.]

MK. When the film was shown in Berlin, the young people in the audience couldn't tell the difference between the women they saw on the screen and their grandmothers. They didn't understand how the Nazis could make a distinction, and how they could do this to their own people.

LK. Most of them don't know what a Jew is and what a Jew looks like.

MK. Their idea of Jews had been people in caftans and workers in Israel.

LK. When we were in hiding in France, the peasants said that Jews had ears like asses.

MK. The young people today don't think that way. But they saw many photos of Jews in concentration camps, emaciated, or with black hats. That Jews should look just like their relatives was surprising to them.

LK. Unfortunately that's how the media presents them. All they ever show of Israel are the orthodox Jews in their black coats.

MK. That's a totally distorted picture. My idea was that there is a new German generation out there and that they would ask themselves: "Would I hide someone?" More important than the answer is the need for the question to be posed.

LK. I completely agree with you, but I wouldn't want to show the Germans that I would have been as cowardly as they were.

MK. But Jews aren't on a pedestal. They're like everyone else.

FH. There's one thing you don't understand. Today, as a Jew, you have to sustain a certain standing to make sure that the Germans do not get a wrong idea of Judaism, but rather the right idea: that the Jews are in no way different culturally, as human beings, from anyone else. That's the important point. But we mustn't allow them to say, "How dare you reproach us that we didn't hide anyone when you're saying yourself you wouldn't have done it either?" After all, we're the accusers here and we can't simply say we're just like them.

MK. But only a very few people were heroes. You can't expect most people to be that way.

FH. As you say, not everyone's a hero. But it's difficult to leave it at that in Germany.

[Lilo Kahn mentions a change in attitude on the part of Germans toward Jews, as a result of Israeli military activities, first in 1967 and subsequently.]

LK. They marveled that the Jews, the so-called cowards, were the best air force pilots and fighters.

[This, I point out is a romanticization of the Jews. Showing the present difficulties between Arabs and Israelis makes for a more realistic picture. Friedel is distressed about the treatment of the Arabs. She mentions a woman filmmaker who is trying to explain conditions in Israel.]

FH. She said, "If you live there, you see it differently. This issue with the settlements—it's a problem with the many Russian Jews who are coming over. We have to accommodate them."

I said, "Dear child, you have to understand that time goes on, and a solution has to be found. You can't keep people in camps forever. The roots of all this hatred will keep on growing. The Palestinians must be given a land they can live in."

MK. How do you feel about the new immigrants—the Russian Jews, Romanians, and also the gypsies—who have been coming here?

FH. I'm fully in favor of accepting these people here. That's quite natural after all we've been through. And in Munich, I'm fighting where I can and support everything. But unfortunately, even the young Germans who may not be antisemitic don't understand any of this the way we do. There are few young people today who feel responsible about the Jews. They say they don't understand how something like that could have happened. But they're not very friendly toward foreigners. The young people like going abroad and having exchanges with foreigners, but as for people who come here to settle down . . . I live in Nymphenburg, very close to the Turkish consulate. About the Turks they just say disapprovingly, "Turk." There's no chance of changing that, and I'm very scared that there might be antisemitism again with the Russian Jews coming to Germany. That's my great fear, because there are so few Jews around in Germany.

LK. We really would like to have Jews here, if possible Russian Jews, and if possible, younger ones. Because we ourselves are old and dying out, and we would like to see the community live on. After the war, we started up with roughly 800 Jews in Saarbrücken and now we're hardly 150, I think. We're a dying community. The young people all left Germany. Most of them went to France, some to Israel. We have no young people left. I am the youngster here today *[laughter]*. I'm one of the teenagers. And I am—and I don't hesitate to say it—I'm not like the Americans who are twenty-one and never been kissed *[laughs]*. That's not me. I'm seventy-four.

$$\approx \ddot{\smile} \hookleftarrow$$

Marcel Wainstock

Though trained as a literary scholar in France, Marcel Wainstock chose to settle in Saarbrücken and took a job as administrator for the Jewish congregation. "I am one of the few exceptions," he says. "One of the few from the Jewish community of my generation who has stayed here or come back." Born in Zurich after the war, he was brought to Saarbrücken in 1954 from France, at the age of five. Mar-

cel's father, originally from Poland, had grown up in Düsseldorf. He lived in Saarbrücken for a few years prior to the war and then had escaped to France where he served in the military.

MW. I can't tell you exactly when that was because I didn't concern myself with these matters enough earlier on and now it's too late. Besides, my father didn't like talking about it. He used to have nightmares every night and never slept through one single night. It wasn't exactly a subject one could easily discuss with him. For instance, I learned only after my mother died that he had been married once before. I was twenty-five years old by then. An adult. When I sorted out the papers, I discovered all this in the family record; they had always kept it from me. My father had been underground, in hiding in different places, escaping from the Gestapo over and over again in France.

[Marcel's mother had been living in Zurich with her parents through the war.]

My mother never wanted to go to Germany but my father thought he might get firmly established here again professionally. In hindsight, returning to the Saarland, to Germany, wasn't really justified. He could have done exactly the same, no worse—maybe even better—if he had stayed in France. My mother was never happy here. The main industry in the Saarland in those days was mining. The air was dirty, there was soot on the windowsills . . . She wasn't happy with that, but nobody asked how she felt.

MK. And then you stayed here?

MW. And then I stayed here. And that's when the emotional reasoning sets in as to why one becomes lethargic and remains in one place. Together with many young Jews from Saarbrücken of my generation, I attended the French school [in Saarbrücken]. There is a separation between church and state in France and religious instruction isn't given in French schools. So the question does not arise about whether you are Jewish or Christian.

[He explains that for the generation of Jews who had just experienced the war, it was essential to protect their children from any situation that might give rise to antisemitism. Most of the students went on to French universities and few of them returned to Germany.]

MK. Were your parents at all religious?

MW. Religious in the real sense of the word, no. Both of them came from extremely orthodox parents. But due to the war, or maybe already before the war, my father completely abandoned Jewish practices. But when his mother died, a long time after the war, he started going to services again to say Kaddish and then he continued going to Sabbath services. That's how it really started again. But, for instance, we didn't keep a kosher home. Both my parents had the knowledge but they didn't practice the religion.

[The postwar Jewish community in Saarbrücken was founded in the late 1940s and the synagogue building was completed in 1951. Before the war there were twenty-six synagogues in the Saarland. Now there is only the one in Saarbrücken designed by a gentile architect in the Albert Speer style, there being no available Jewish architect. I happened to be in the city for the fortieth anniversary of its dedication.]

MK. Did you have Christian friends at school?

MW. *Only* Christian friends. Even today, those I call my friends are Christian. Partly because there are so few Jews of my generation. Formerly there were more, but being Jewish isn't everything. It's not enough of a criterion for real friendship.

MK. With the Christians, did you ever feel any antisemitism?

MW. No, because the people I had contact with, the kids, had already been sorted out, so there wasn't a problem. And still today, I have a large circle of good friends and a small circle of very close friends and there isn't a problem with any of them, because I won't even bother with people with whom there might be difficulties. Or if there should be problems, I distance myself. But I have a good understanding of human nature and I usually can tell very quickly.

MK. I know that you're working at the synagogue. Is this for religious reasons?

MW. No. It was purely by chance, but I'm not unhappy about it. I've gotten a great deal out of it in the seven years I've been doing it. Before that, I had a totally different education and completely different plans. I'm a literary critic, a literary historian for Italian and Romance languages, especially for Italian, and I had originally planned on a university career as a professor of literature or as a journalist in this field, or something like that. But through various circumstances these jobs became more and more scarce. And I probably didn't have enough determination. I was spoiled by my parents, their only child, and I slept through parts of my youth. I separated from my parents too late also. I should have moved out much earlier. I became aware of this only later. I missed many opportunities.

[Marcel managed to get by with part-time work at the university and with freelance translating, always hoping that he would be able to establish himself in his own field. But it did not work out. He was urged to apply for the position of manager at the Jewish community. He did so reluctantly and was hired. He was a board member of the community, "out of an interest in Jewish matters, but not because of religion." He emphasizes that his position is strictly administrative and that he does not get involved in religious issues. Naturally, his early training in Hebrew school and his own intellectual knowledge are assets in the performance of his duties, which appear to be extremely demanding. He does express some bitterness that "what really interests me (literature) is nothing more than a hobby and a pastime today, and that's not always enough."]

MW. When the community was founded again, that is, right after the war, the majority were Jews from the Saarland, who had returned. And a smaller percentage were displaced persons who had been liberated from the camps in Germany or eastern Europe and didn't want to return to the East European countries, due to the political situation after the war.

Or they didn't have any families left and said, "I don't care where I am or where I go. I have no home here any longer, I don't have a home there any longer, I'm here, so I'm staying here." It's different with everybody. Some couldn't cope with the language abroad or they didn't feel comfortable. Some weren't able to manage professionally, others believed they really belonged here, emotionally. And some had illusions that it would be better, and then they were here and you don't leave again that easily.

[I tell Marcel that many people I spoke with in my own community of Washington Heights refuse to visit Germany and will have nothing to do with it.]

MW. We have that here too. There are people among the former Saarland residents who still live in Strasbourg, in Metz, in Saargemünd, in Forbach, ten or twelve kilometers from the border, and they just might come to Saarbrücken because they have friends or relatives here, but they would never live here again.

MK. And when the Jews first came back here, were the Christian people friendly?

MW. I can't really tell, because that wasn't my generation. That was earlier, and afterward things kept changing more and more. Probably they weren't unfriendly because those who would have liked to be unfriendly probably didn't dare to be, and the others had a bad conscience or they didn't care, they were neutral. For the Jews, it was probably more difficult to deal with one another internally, rather than with Christians. At any rate I never heard of terrible things. Of course, cemeteries have been vandalized. That happened often during the 1950s and 1960s, when headstones were smeared with swastikas or they were overturned. Later, things calmed down, but sporadically it happens again today, not here, but in other areas. Wherever people settled down, they created an environment in which they could live and they didn't have any contact with the others. Where there are antisemitic sentiments one tries to avoid such people.

MK. But these sentiments are relatively rare?

MW. Yes, relatively rare. Antisemitism certainly does exist. It isn't always that overt. But this exists elsewhere as well—in France, in Switzerland—and it's an illusion to think that it's limited to Germany.

MK. Formerly, when your parents lived here, there was little contact between the German population and the Poles. There was great prejudice against the East European Jews and that's why there was no contact. People were ashamed of the East European Jews. There was this notion that the German Jews were better, more cultured, and so on. What was it like when the displaced persons first arrived, and the Saarbrücken Jews returned, and all of a sudden there was one community?

MW. Right after the war the East European Jews were a relative minority. Today the ratio in Saarbrücken is about fifty-fifty, half Saarland or German Jews and half East European Jews, plus a small enclave of Iranian Jews, and a few Israelis who stay for only a few years and then leave again.

[The numbers are changing because the older Saarland Jews are dying out and Russian Jews are coming in. Asked how the displaced persons were treated at the beginning, Marcel says they undoubtedly received some assistance and were accepted into the community.]

MW. But there have certainly been animosities. Maybe not as strongly as before the war, because the war has been a real experience in this respect. Hitler didn't ask where the people came from, but many didn't learn from that either. On both sides, some have. And as long as problems don't need to be addressed, there are really no animosities today in daily dealings. But when it comes to, for example, whether we should have an organ in the synagogue or not, these problems surface again.

MK. You mean between East and West? Those from the East don't want the organ?

MW. The majority. Very few East European Jews are in favor of having it. There are one or two who say, "Well, yes, it's nice, we can leave it there."

MK. Is this religiously motivated or does it have to do with tradition?

MW. It's because of tradition, and not for religious reasons. We have no orthodox Jews here and whoever denies this would be a hypocrite. On such occasions, the problems reappear a little. But not in business, since the East European Jews are as established today, more or less, as the German Jews. They're integrated as a rule. Therefore the social differences aren't that acute any longer and the educational discrepancies aren't as marked in the younger generation either. But before the war, I imagine, there were great differences.

[As far as orthodoxy is concerned, in Saarbrücken, the prewar congregation was "liberal"—that is, somewhere between what American Jews call conservative and reform.]

MK. Do the younger people leave Saarbrücken and the community?

MW. They don't leave the community. But if they leave, they leave Saarbrücken altogether. We have little reason to appeal to people to "Come to the Saarland and settle down." Economically, the Saarland is one of the poorest regions of the Federation. There aren't that many jobs and the economy has been getting worse and worse. Large companies have shut down or closed their branches in Saarbrücken. And for this reason, we're surviving here only with the core of the community. Occasionally one or two families move here for professional reasons and join the community too. Otherwise, things are a bit stagnant. The group stagnates or diminishes, because people die.

[He seems to be discounting the newly arrived Russian Jews as a significant factor.]

MK. Do you have the feeling that some people were more religious after the war than before?

MW. On the contrary. I don't really see a return of religion here in Germany after the war. There is a clinging to some habits and traditions, but no real strong religious motivation.

[This contrasts with my experience of Washington Heights where many people, including my father, became more fervently Jewish. Marcel believes that among the youth in France there is a return to religion. Those who are inclined in that direction in Germany, he says, go to Israel or emigrate to a country where there is a real Jewish life. On the other hand, there appears to be an interest in conversion to Judaism on the part of some German youth.]

MW. I've been getting inquiries again lately, by telephone or in writing, about converting. I think this has been partly motivated by the Gulf War crisis and it always happens at those times when there are problems in Israel or within Judaism. Then, many young Germans get this idea: "I want to show my solidarity."

Another factor is that young Christians, who are religious, who have been feeling and thinking in religious terms, are realizing more and more that Christianity has taken much from Judaism and has been keeping it secret all this time. And presently, it's being revealed more. Christian theology today freely admits it, and there is a Christian-Jewish dialogue in Germany on a theological level, which has been generating very profound insights. There are seminars where the young people realize, "I see, there's so much Judaism in our religion, but it has been falsified for a long time and they didn't tell us everything, and the Jewish religion and the texts are really more authentic." And they feel emotionally more at home. That's what attracts many people to us. So there are these two factors, the religious motivation with some, and with others it's this solidarity with Jewish history after the war.

MK. That also comes out of guilt, maybe, because they talked with their parents.

MW. Maybe. I don't have deep conversations about this with these people, because either I get the impression they're serious and then I refer them to a rabbi or else I realize that it's just a whim. Of course, some also have very pragmatic ideas. Sometimes people think, "The Jews all do well and if I become a Jew, I'll be economically well-off too.

And the Jews stick together and they help each other and if I want to have a career as an opera singer, I'll be better off as a Jew. Then every opera house will hire me."

[Marcel deplores the fact that there are not enough rabbis to service smaller congregations such as the one in Saarbrücken, which had imported a rabbi from Metz on the day we attended a service.]

MW. The religious side of congregants here in Germany gets very little nurturing, unfortunately. Then you don't have anything to offer the incoming Russian Jews, if you don't even offer it to the members of your own congregation. All of Jewish life in the German communities leaves much to be desired. Jewish life here is diminished. There may be a satisfactory Jewish social life, some cultural events and regular services, but this isn't active living Judaism anymore. It's administrative Judaism.

MK. Do you think that there will be new antisemitism because of the Russian Jews?

MW. It's not out of the question, if you look at the basic problem, that is, the way the German population deals with the asylum seekers and the resettlers. Whether you call this antisemitism or simply general xenophobia, in the final analysis, these are probably one and the same. I could imagine that they might say, "Sure they're treated better because they're Jews. And all the other foreigners and those who would like to come aren't allowed in, but they let the Jews in."

I also heard different opinions, for instance from a Christian acquaintance who knows what kind of work I do. He asked me if we had Russian Jews here already and I said, "No, not yet."

And then he said, "I think it is really OK for them to take Russian Jews into Germany." He sees this as positive, as a compensation for all who perished. And probably many others feel the same way.

MK. There are only thirty thousand Jews in Germany. The numbers are surely growing with the arrival of Russian Jews. [By 1995, the total had risen to fifty thousand.]

MW. Yes, and that's exciting.

MK. Jewish life in Germany used to be very, very rich. This was annihilated, and the whole notion of Jewish life in Germany basically doesn't exist any longer. Maybe it will start up again?

[Marcel is dubious that the influx of Russian Jews will rebuild the community.]

MW. Maybe I'm wrong. But the Russian element doesn't bring in a Jewish element any longer. All of them are people who, with very few exceptions, might still remember how their mothers lit Sabbath candles until some years ago. These are people who not only aren't observant—it's not that serious, the German congregants aren't observant either any longer, or just very superficially—but they don't even have the knowledge any longer. They have to acquire the most basic knowledge, if they're so inclined. If they come to the communities saying, "Yes, I do want to come to services, I want to learn to be a Jew again," you can teach them as much as can still be taught in Germany, and even that's only a fraction.

That's what I meant to say earlier on: I don't think that a new positive Jewish element will emerge again because they don't bring anything Jewish with them. This is also a population with a great culture of its own. And it's exciting to see what will come out of it, once they have become acculturated after a while and learned to speak the language. But I don't think that the religious element is very promising.

MK. It seems to be important to you that others be religious while you yourself are not.

MW. Naturally. Naturally, I'm interested in a vibrant community with Jewish life. I'm not interested in lectures at my congregation on X, Y, Z, most of which aren't on Jewish topics. I could hear them anywhere. And naturally, I wish that this addition of Russian congregation members would also enrich Jewish life or the religious life or endow it with a new spark, but I don't think it will.

MK. But you yourself are not religious and yet you want others to be?

MW. I wish more were religious, at least a part of the congregation.

MK. But how can you dictate this if you yourself don't want it?

MW. I don't want to dictate it, but I wish for it *[laughter]*. I feel that the situation is so frustrating today because the religious element has disappeared. I feel it and I know it.

MK. And you're not a good example of it.

MW. I'm not a good example of many other things either *[laughter]*. Basically, I solved my religious problems when I was fourteen or fifteen and discovered Spinoza. And then I was able to synthesize my doubts and the Jewish education I had until then and the doubts I had about religiosity. Since then, this has remained stable. Spinoza was a great help to me in processing and stabilizing these factors in my mind. I'm not deeply religious in a Jewish sense. But I'm far from being an atheist, even though I'm not observant. It's beneath the skin. But I don't even have a bad conscience, an honestly bad conscience. Sometimes, not always. But I feel that the real basis of Jewish life is the practicing of religion. Practicing it properly, that is with your body and soul, from the inside.

☆☆☆

Hans Stiff

In 1987 I was introduced to Dr. Hans Stiff, publisher of the Saar- brücker Zeitung, *by my friend Michael Beckert who was then working as a journalist for the paper. The retrospective of my films had opened and the paper was running articles about it. During the 1920s and early 1930s, the* Zeitung *had printed many of my father's caricatures and cartoons and when he came to Saarbrücken in 1980 for the exhibition of his work, the newspaper covered the event. During that first conversation Dr. Stiff, a man in his sixties, presented me with a copy of a book,* Feuer Frei—Kinder! *(Fire away, kids!), about the teenagers who served as anti-aircraft gunners with him during World War II. Dr. Stiff was one of the four authors of the book, which carries the subtitle,* Eine missbrauchte Generation—Flakhelfer im Einsatz, *which, loosely translated, means "a misused generation—apprentice flak gunners in action."*

When I met him again in 1991, Dr. Stiff was retired from the newspaper and held a diplomatic post as honorary Belgian consul. Would he agree to an interview for a book about German Jewish survivors of Nazi persecution?

He received my phone call enthusiastically and invited Gloria and me to lunch at Saarbrücken's most elegant restaurant, an intimate place with a hushed atmosphere where the loudest sound was that of silverware against china. Most of the patrons were in their late sixties or older. He chatted in French with my wife while I wondered how and when I would start my interview. I intended to pose some hard questions. It did not seem plausible that he would want

to do it here where every word above a whisper could be heard, but I
was wrong.

HS. My father was a tax consultant. My grandfather built coking
plants in the Saarland and in Lorraine, France, and a couple in America
as well. My paternal grandfather was an executive in a food store here
in the Saarland. My father and all my grandparents were in favor of the
reintegration of the Saarland with Germany without taking Hitler into
account. They would have been for it no matter who was in power. It
took quite a while until my father realized what was really going on.
One of my grandfathers was a supporting member of the SS. In the in-
dustrialists' circle that was a common stance after 1935. And his oldest
son was a member of the civilian SS. Then my father began to be totally opposed to National Socialism. From 1935 on.

MK. After the referendum?

HS. Already a little earlier. But my mother supported the National
Socialists. My father always tried to explain to me that this was a very
. . . that the Germans were facing something exceptionally dangerous.
But it was impossible [not to go along] because you were in a community at school or among your friends. [In 1937, at the age of ten, Dr. Stiff
was part of the Jungvolk, a precursor of the Hitler Youth.] Besides, I
must say, it was fun to be part of a community in those days and it was
impossible to resist the pressure.

In 1941, I joined the *Reiterheimat,* the Cavalry Corps of the Hitler
Youth. I wanted to ride and my parents wouldn't have allowed me to.
As I wrote in my book, there were these special units of the Hitler
Youth: maritime, cavalry, air, motor transport. There was virtually no
National Socialist indoctrination there, because the people were differ-
ent. They wanted something totally different. Basically, they didn't ask
themselves any questions, they simply didn't care. But of course it was
paramilitary training, which nobody was aware of.

MK. You said that your father was against National Socialism. And
your mother wasn't. He wanted to teach you to oppose the ideas that
weren't good?

HS. Yes.

MK. So there was a conflict between what went on at school and
what your father wanted. How did this affect you?

HS. Basically, it didn't interest me at all. Mostly everybody in my class was happy about what was offered to us: sailing, flying, riding, motorcycling, community. Besides, the psychological situation had been preconditioned by the dictates of the Versailles peace treaty. We felt that something had happened that wasn't right. And of course it was easy to convince us that it was necessary to restore Germany's national dignity, and this meant overcoming what we felt were unjust restrictions imposed by the Treaty of Versailles. In those days, a sense of national solidarity had an entirely different meaning than it does today. And for that reason, it was a matter of course that most of us would vote for reintegration with Germany in 1935. Particularly since the other options, the status quo or annexation by France, were no real alternatives. It would never have worked.

MK. In what way did your mother influence you?

HS. She didn't at all. She admired the Führer, but she never influenced me.

[Dr. Stiff says that when he joined the flak unit, his mother changed her attitude and turned against the government. He adds that there are no existing photos of him in uniform when he was in the Jungvolk group or later when he joined the Hitler Youth itself. His explanation is that his parents did not want to remember him in that way, though he himself was proud of what he was doing.]

CONTACT WITH JEWS

MK. Did you have Jewish friends as a child in school?

HS. As far as I remember there were none in my class. But as a tax consultant my father had Jewish clients. And my pediatrician was a Jewish doctor.

MK. Were there also Jewish-owned stores?

HS. Yes, of course. There were these so-called Aryanized stores that had been taken away from their Jewish owners. After the war my father had visitors from New York and France, former store owners, Jewish store owners, and my father worked out the settlements.

MK. My father says that formerly friendly neighbors stopped speaking to us because they were afraid to have anything to do with Jews.

HS. I didn't notice anything like that.

MK. Not from your parents or anyone?

HS. Nothing at all. Which reminds me—a schoolmate of mine who is still my friend . . . He was half-Jewish and he also had trouble. He was still with us in the flak, but after 1944, he wasn't there any longer.

MK. And the doctor, the pediatrician? What happened to him?

HS. I don't know. One day, after 1935, he was gone. He surely, I assume, he . . .

MK. Have you ever talked about this at all?

HS. No. Not that I know of. Well, I wasn't there.

MK. Your parents, maybe?

HS. The parents, surely. But it was not talked about. [He seems eager to shift the discussion.] To get back to my grandfather, he was, as I said, a supporting member of the SS. His oldest son was in the SS. The second son was a decorated infantry officer who had been in World War I. He had suffered gas poisoning and was then committed to a mental asylum because he was suffering increasingly from mental disturbances. And in 1940, when we returned to Saarbrücken from Koblenz where we had been evacuated, my grandfather—I was there when the postcard arrived—my grandfather received a postcard saying, "Your son, Heinrich, died in Hadamar from the complications of pulmonary embolism. You may pick up his urn in Hadamar by paying 130 Reichsmarks." Hadamar was one of these euthanasia centers. They murdered my grandfather's son there. And my grandfather knew that, since his other son, who was in the civilian SS, knew [about the euthanasia program].

My grandfather left the SS. Nothing ever happened on account of this, but he left. The same thing happened in my wife's family to an aunt who had contracted meningitis. She became mentally ill and so she was also sent to Hadamar and killed. Because she was—how would you say it—"a worthless life"? This was the euthanasia program, the destruction of "worthless lives." That was in 1941.

MK. Before you continue telling us about 1941, is there anything you can remember about Jews?

HS. OK. On November 10 [1938] I had to go to a swimming lesson so I took the tram from St. Arnual [the suburb] where you were born, to go to the Emperor Friedrich Pool. I had to pass Kaiserstrasse where the synagogue was. And as I said, an uncle of mine (almost an uncle—he was my aunt's companion) was also in the SS. He had been given orders to meet with the others here by the castle. He was given gasoline containers and was ordered to torch the synagogue. And this man, whom I called uncle, this uncle refused to do so. He got into the worst trouble. Since he was an officer of the reserve, he volunteered for active service at once in an infantry regiment and that's how he averted negative consequences. He then became an active officer right away.

MK. Please tell me about your experience of Kristallnacht.

HS. I passed by at eight in the morning on my way to the swimming lesson and I saw the synagogue burning. Naturally, I stopped. Many people were standing there looking. Like everybody else I was in front of the synagogue, in the front garden, and I took a piece of (as I thought then) a flag, something with gilded fringes. Today I know what it was, but then I didn't know. At noon, after school, I took it home and told my parents, "This is what I found."

And my father, who really always used to be quite generous, said with great determination and solemnity, "This comes from a house of God. You take this and carry it back where you found it."

And that's what I did. I didn't understand why, I really didn't understand the whole thing, but I did as I was told.

MK. So what was that? A piece of the Torah covering?

HS. Yes, something like that.

MK. And then where did you return it, to a Jewish—?

HS. —No, no. I took it back to the front yard in front of the burned-out synagogue, where I had found it.

MK. And afterward? Most Jews left, if they could, in early 1936. Between two and three thousand Jews left Saarbrücken.

HS. Yes, many.

MK. That wasn't something one talked about in the presence of a child?

HS. No, not at all.

[Dr. Stiff tells of his father's heated political discussions with a high-ranking police officer sharing a shelter during the bombardment of Saarbrücken. Mrs. Stiff said to her husband, "Don't argue with him. You could land up in Dachau."]

MK. What did you know about Dachau?

HS. We knew this was a camp for political prisoners.

MK. What about Jews there?

HS. We didn't know about Jews being there.

MK. After Kristallnacht it was known that thirty thousand were sent to camps, mostly to Dachau.

HS. I was eleven years old. I didn't know.

THE WAR IN SAARBRÜCKEN

MK. So then the war started, in 1939. Did the atmosphere change at all?

HS. Saarbrücken was evacuated. In the beginning, we were in Bochum, where my grandparents were. Then we went to Koblenz, and in 1940, after the end of the French campaign, we returned to Saarbrücken.

[In 1941 at the age of fourteen, Dr. Stiff joined the Hitler Youth cavalry unit. In 1942 he volunteered to be an army officer cadet, like all his classmates.]

HS. I wanted to become a professional officer because I considered this the right thing to do. My father was completely against it because of his experiences in World War I. He tried everything [to dissuade his son].

MK. As a matter of principle?

HS. Also as a matter of principle, yes. But when he realized he couldn't change my mind, he at least made sure through his old connections that I would get into the regiment I wanted to be in, the traditional cavalry regiment.

We knew in 1942–1943, since Stalingrad, that you couldn't be drafted into the Waffen SS [armed SS] if you had volunteered for an army unit. So everybody volunteered for an army unit, because nobody wanted to be in the Waffen SS. At least not in my class. [The implication is that the Waffen SS was an elite unit that was always in greater danger than other units.] I still believe today, that the categorical condemnation of the Waffen SS isn't entirely justified. Not the wholesale condemnation. [He makes a distinction between the Waffen SS and the Toten SS—the so-called Death's Head SS—who were used to round up Jews but never fought in the front lines. He adds that if he had refused to shoot someone he might have ended up against a wall, but many Wehrmacht (army) officers would have respected such a decision.]

HS. And then in 1943, the high school classes, those who were fifteen years old, were drafted into the flak, the anti-aircraft artillery. We were very enthusiastic. We believed in Germany, in the cause, in the master race idea. We felt this was the right thing to do. Because we had an opportunity to fight against the English and American planes that were destroying our homes, were destroying our cities, were killing, as we saw it, our parents. We did this enthusiastically.

MK. There was also great camaraderie?

HS. Yes, yes, sure. We were convinced that it was right to fight. So we fought. That's how it was.

MK. Great losses?

HS. Yes. We were one of the first batteries, because we were very successful shooting an attacking American bomber squadron. We shot down four or five planes. Then the commander of this American squadron decided to attack the battery. Sixteen of my classmates were killed, fifteen, sixteen years old. And this of course strengthened our determination to fight, our determination to defend ourselves against American and English planes.

MK. When was Saarbrücken bombed for the first time?

HS. The first raid was in 1941, the next attacks were in 1943. The worst were in 1944, the heaviest raids.

MK. You were there?

HS. I was there. Except for the heaviest night raid. Then I was just returning from Frankfurt. We had been relocated to Frankfurt when the American troops were in Metz, and I was discharged from the flak to be part of the Reich's Labor Front. And during the raid of October 4, 1944, I went through the burning city, home to St. Arnual. The next day I took a train to the Austrian-Yugoslav border, to the Labor Front.

MK. What happened at the border?

HS. Hardly anything. Sometimes, there were partisans, Tito's partisans, some skirmishes, but otherwise hardly anything. Then I was discharged in 1944. On December 7. By then Saarbrücken had already been evacuated. I wanted to get my induction order, to get into the army to defend the fatherland. Then I traveled with a friend through half of Germany, to get to where we could receive our induction orders, somewhere in Baden. And the commander of this military district headquarters tried to prevent us from becoming soldiers, which was a very dangerous thing for him to do. We didn't understand that. We insisted on being given our induction orders and then he gave them to us. He was a lieutenant colonel.

Then in January 1945, I got to the Göttingen garrison, to my cavalry regiment. I received my training there and the Allied troops kept coming closer to Göttingen. Then we were relocated to Czechoslovakia.

Two days after the raid on Dresden, I came through it and saw what the city looked like. And there's something that will certainly interest *you*. We passed through Czechoslovakia at night. Everything had been darkened and then we passed a large lighted complex. We couldn't understand that because everything else was dark.

We asked our squadron leader, a captain, "What's that? Why is it lighted?"

He was an officer who had always been in the East. He said, "I have no idea. I assume, it's an armament plant. Why else would it be lit?"

Then we passed a small station—I'll never forget that—and there was a sign, saying "Theresienstadt." We didn't know anything about it and that's really true. Neither did this officer, nor anybody in the squadron. We didn't know what it meant.

MK. It was a whole city.

HS. The station sign was lit. Everything else was dark.

MK. Dark, so it wouldn't be bombed.

HS. Of course. That was in February 1945, two days after the air raid on Dresden. That's why I know this so precisely. It must have been on February 17 or 18, 1945.

MK. Amazing that you still remember the exact dates.

HS. Because of the raid on Dresden. I've thought about this a good deal. I read books about it.

MK. Did you sense in those days that the war was lost?

HS. We didn't believe it.

MK. Really? It must have been so depressing.

HS. We weren't depressed. That's a strange thing. I still think about it today—why it was that we weren't depressed.

MK. Did you think that you might still win?

HS. Yes, that we might still manage. We would have fought like hell. Until the end. Really. The older ones were much more reasonable.

MK. Really? They heard reports on the illegal radio stations?

HS. Yes. We listened also.

MK. From where, England?

HS. Army station Calais. Why? We weren't interested in the news. We didn't believe the reports anyway. We listened to the jazz music.

MK. Then you knew that we were a little closer?

HS. We weren't interested in that either.

MK. No?

HS. No. The jazz music . . . You might say it was a subconscious form of freedom. Only we didn't understand that then. Today I understand that completely.

MK. And then came May. Were you already out of it by May 8?

HS. Yes, sure.

MK. Was it a surprise that the war was over?

HS. Yes, it was a surprise. I won't forget that either. I was in Czechoslovakia [in April]. And on the day Roosevelt died, I took an oath with my squadron. We had to swear as soldiers. We did it together with a Bosnian SS unit with their gray fezzes, which impressed us very much. "Now, we're going to win!" What an illusion! And then came May 8. My squadron was in the headquarters of the commander in chief of the Central Army Group under Field Marshall General Schaumann. The morning after the capitulation he said, "I'll lead you back home." That was in the morning at nine o'clock. At seven in the evening, we were still standing there, but there was no more field marshall general . . . Well, he had taken off his uniform, put on a Bavarian costume, and escaped to the Tyrol with a small plane that he had kept for himself. His excuse was that he had received orders to meet there with the other field marshall generals to organize the last resistance.

MK. He didn't say anything?

HS. No, he just sneaked out.

MK. Everything was already over. The armistice had already begun.

HS. And before that he had hung every soldier, every officer whom he met without a gun or a marching order, on the spot. And then he himself just sneaked out in the shabbiest manner. Just abandoned us. That made me lose all respect for German field marshall generals. But I regained it afterward.

MK. And was the surprise in itself depressing?

HS. It was depressing, yes. Then we marched through Czechoslovakia, to try to get to the Americans. We didn't want to be imprisoned by the Russians. Twenty kilometers from the Moldau, from the Americans, the Russians caught us because we had civilians with us. We couldn't fight any longer, otherwise the civilians might have been killed. Two days after the armistice we were still fully armed and we would have fought. But as I said, it wasn't possible any longer. And then for ten days the Russians made us go through Czechoslovakia.

MK. On foot?

HS. On foot, naturally. Without anything to eat. To a town. And from Teplechorna, I escaped with two other men from my squadron in the middle of the day. Apparently, aside from me and the other two, nobody from my squadron ever returned.

MK. They killed everybody?

HS. Probably. And then I walked for twenty-six days and after all kinds of fantastic circumstances I finally got home.

MK. Home?

HS. To Ulm.

MK. Your parents were in Ulm?

HS. Yes. My father was in the flak unit then and he had come home several days before me. [Before arriving home] I met the first Americans. It was very interesting. There were two of us and we were trying to get to Ulm via the highway. And on every highway crossing were American guards, you know, Japanese ones, Nisei. Needless to say, they took every soldier to the POW camp. But I had changed from my uniform into civilian clothes earlier. (When we got away from the Russians we were in uniform.)

The Americans were sitting on the street, playing with the children. And when they saw us, they put on their steel helmets, loaded their guns, and asked us to raise our hands. They made us take off our shirts and they looked under our armpits. We didn't know why, we thought they were crazy. It turned out that they were checking to see whether we were members of the SS because they had their blood group tattooed under their armpits. Since we didn't have our blood group tattooed on us . . .

Some officer arrived in a jeep and asked us, "Where do you come from?"

We said, "We escaped from the Russians and now we're here."

They asked how old we were. "Sixteen," we said. Never mind that we were seventeen.

They said, "OK. Just walk down there, otherwise, you'll end up in the camp."

And that's how I always got past the American guards. I had a map with me and we always chose the town behind the highway crossing and said, "That's our home." And they always let us go. Thanks to the generosity of the Americans, with one exception, I finally got home.

I'll say something else that might be important: After the war, we had to return to school to get our high school diploma. In 1946, there was only one movie theater here and they showed a film about Bergen-Belsen. The higher grades, particularly those who had been soldiers, were sent to see it. Now, please don't take this the wrong way, but really, it made us laugh.

And we said, "How stupid do the Allies think we are, to present us with such a propaganda film? Things like this don't happen in Germany!"

It took a while and then we understood it *had* happened after all. That was the moment when I started thinking about what had happened to us and what we had done. Up till then, I hadn't believed it.

MK. The film was shown by the Allies?

HS. Yes, the French made us see it. The second shock was much the same. The headmaster, who had always tried to educate us in the spirit of National Socialism, was giving us a chemistry lesson. One of the former soldiers replied to a question, "I'm sorry, I don't understand this."

And the same teacher said, in front of the class, "I'll drive this Hitler Youth and Nazi spirit out of you guys, by God!"

The same man. And it was the second time that we began to think about what was going on. [He comments ruefully that there have been many holocausts "but we Germans carried it out in an administratively correct way."]

In 1947, I went to France to study. And I realized then that everything I had learned at school about the "archenemy" and all that wasn't true. And concerning what came later, all I can say is, "Thank goodness for telecommunications." The same lack of information that led us onto such a path is no longer possible today.

MK. Did you think that the Jew was the archenemy too?

HS. No, not at all. The archenemies used to be the French. When I got to high school in 1937, French lessons were forbidden. We had English and Latin because the argument was, "One doesn't learn the language of the archenemy!"

MK. But during the war the Jews were put down also, weren't they? The newspapers were full of that. There were big headlines.

HS. Well, if you believe me or not, we didn't deal with that at all.

MK. But you heard about it, didn't you?

HS. No.

MK. No? At school?

HS. Not in school, either.

MK. The teachers?

HS. No, not at all.

MINORITIES IN GERMANY TODAY

MK. Is there antisemitism in Germany today?

HS. I don't think so. I don't think so. At least not to any noticeable extent. Of course, there are always, somewhere, animosities, emotional and irrational ones that can't be explained. And certainly there exists a very small group (and that's certainly stronger in the former GDR [German Democratic Republic] than here), those who have a bit of these German nationalist notions, which, however, are understandable considering the development over there. But militant antisemitism, I don't think that exists here, not to any considerable degree. One that could lead to a similar development I consider completely out of the question. Because these things are so well known today, there is hardly any chance that they could be repeated here.

MK. Isn't it possible that what happened to the Jews could happen again?

HS. No way.

MK. But could it happen to others?

HS. No, what an idea!

MK. But there are the Republicans [the ultrarightists], they naturally would be very . . .

HS. I recently gave a lecture on the Republicans. Maybe I should have brought it. In this respect, they have no political effect. You see that in every election. They are a diminutive minority and all these terms that used to be popular then, such as *Rassenschande* [racial pollution], don't exist any longer. They will never exist again, either.

MK. There is great euphoria right now about Germany's reunification, isn't there?

HS. That has nothing to do with it. That's something completely different.

MK. Then, when the euphoria is over and everybody has to pay for it, maybe then people will feel resentful?

HS. No. Why should they?

MK. So many foreigners are coming.

HS. No. This might be similar to France. The French have a problem with people from the Maghreb, with the Arabs. This problem could only arise if the ethnic minorities were to resist a certain degree of assimilation. But even then, I don't think it would. The problem in France is, there are currently 480 mosques. Legal mosques. Nobody knows exactly how many illegal ones there are and this is really a danger. But this isn't true of Germany. Not yet. But it could be a problem.

MK. With fundamentalists.

HS. Yes. But I don't think that there is any danger of a repetition of history.

MK. Has German consciousness changed?

HS. Oh sure.

MK. Yours too?

HS. Yes. Today I know that I fought for the wrong cause, but I only understood that after the war.

MK. Better late than never.

HS. That's what I said. Without all of today's means of communication, we were never informed of what was happening outside Germany. And to listen to a foreign radio station was forbidden. Punishable by death. For this reason alone, there is certainly no danger of a repetition. General information is so widespread, the ignorance doesn't exist any longer.

MK. That depends on reportage. If the reportage is censored, then you don't get the report.

HS. Sure. But today, you have a mixture of reportage, which prohibits one-sided manipulation of news.

[This comment surprises me because, as I tell Dr. Stiff, a journalist friend on the *Zeitung* had written an article about the many banners and signs she had seen in 1990 at many railroad stations condemning the Gulf War. Her article was rejected by the newspaper—the only one published in the city—and she was told, "We won't print that."]

HS. I don't understand this.

MK. She was very disappointed.

HS. Have you seen the *Welt, FAZ, Welt am Sonntag, Bild am Sonntag?* They're full of ads placed by companies and private persons in support of the United States.

MK. But the movement I'm talking about is anti-U.S. It's against Germany's involvement in the Gulf War.

HS. Yes, I know. It's only a minority.

MK. But one has to report on it.

HS. Regrettably we are about to turn into a St. Florian society. Do you know what I mean?

[He explains that St. Florian is the patron saint of firemen. And when one says "Holy St. Florian" it means, loosely, Let the fire rage in my neighbor's apartment, but not in mine. In other words, he believes that there is a danger of becoming isolationist.

Our conversation is over. My wife and I are aware that a tremendous hush descended over the restaurant as we were talking. People were staring openly—not unusual among Germans as I know from my old neighborhood—and straining to hear. Dr. Stiff graciously thanks us. My wife expresses our appreciation and also compliments him on his candor. This is how he was brought up and trained, he says. At home, at school, and as a Hitler Youth.

As he drives us back to our hotel, he tells us how impressed he was with U.S. army equipment. There is even a collector's shop in the area for such equipment. In fact, his wife bought him a surprise gift for his sixtieth birthday, a 1943 U.S. army jeep. He drives it around to scare the local farmers, he says jokingly, and to his golf course.

Early the next morning shortly before our departure, he telephones us at our hotel to clarify a few points and to say that he has left a book for us in the lobby. We wonder if he had second thoughts about what he committed to tape. After we return to the United States, there is another communication from him enclosing the speech he referred to, in which he condemns the ultrarightists.]

✻✻
✺✺

Oskar Lafontaine

Americans may be known for their informality, for their first-name basis, but the Saarbrückers run a close second. Their head of state Oskar Lafontaine, premier of the Saarland, is addressed and frequently referred to in print as Oskar. In 1990, he ran for chancellor against Helmut Kohl on the Social Democratic ticket and was defeated. During his campaign, a woman in the crowd attacked him with a knife and slashed him in the neck. He recovered from this assassination attempt, and although he was displaced as leader of the Social Democrats, he remained a powerful force in the party. In November 1995, he was reelected as head of the Social Democrats.

Oskar Lafontaine has shown me tremendous warmth (skeptics may attribute this to good public relations), and we seek each other out whenever I come to Saarbrücken. When he came to New York he visited our home and asked me to show him around the city by subway, to the consternation of the people at the German consulate, which had provided an official car for that purpose. He particularly was interested in seeing some of New York's poorest neighborhoods.

Our conversation here is conducted on the last night of the Ophüls Film Festival in a conference room of the enormous Festhalle where the prize winners are going to be announced and introduced by Oskar. As we talk we can hear the entertainment from the stage, which is being televised nationally. My friend Michael Beckert is producing the event.

As though he has all the time in the world, Oskar sits back and invites my questions. His staff, which includes bodyguards, is nervous: he is due to be summoned onstage in a matter of minutes.

Oskar Lafontaine was born in 1943.

MK. Tell me something about your father.

OL. He was killed in the war. Actually, I hardly knew him. I just know a few miscellaneous facts. He went to war as a young man, was in Russia, and later was killed in action in Germany in Bad Brückenau, toward the end of the war. He was in the German army, in a tank unit.

MK. And you were raised just by your mother?

OL. Yes, by my mother and aunt. My mother worked and my aunt was at home. That's how it went for a while and when I was nine, nine and a half, I went to live in this episcopal seminary together with my twin brother—he's an attorney here. My mother talked about the hardships—getting food, finding milk for the children. Also about the difficulties of getting an apartment, because toward the end of the war there was a shortage of living space. And she talked about the air raid alarms. These were the three things then: food, apartments, air raid alarms.

MK. Where was this?

OL. The air raid alarms took place where we all originally come from, Dillingen-Pachten. That was the west front in those days. Whether we also had them in the place where we had been evacuated, as they called it then, I don't know. It was near Bamberg.

MK. Everything started in the Saarland?

OL. I think it really started in the Saarland. There were the air raid warnings and we got evacuated. The closer the Allied forces came, the more the population retreated to the interior of Germany.

MK. In those days and before the war there was little contact with Jews?

OL. I don't think that this was a problem in our street—it was a very village-like milieu. This was an exclusively working-class neighborhood where there weren't any Jews. There may have been some Jews who were members of a congregation in Dillingen-Pachten, but I'm not sure. Pachten used to be very much like a village and very limited. I can't recall any discussions now or things that were said about Jewish citizens. [Oskar says that his first contacts with Jews were through literature: Kafka, Marx, Freud, Anne Frank.]

MK. After the war when you heard for the first time about what had happened, what was it like?

OL. The crimes committed by the Nazi regime were revealed to us in British films, these famous British films that are probably known the world over, where you see the heaps of corpses in the concentration camps. And you see the people lying there in the camps, and you see how those who starved to death are simply dumped there. These films really shocked us as ten-year-olds. We were stunned.

MK. Where was that?

OL. At school. These questions were discussed with the teachers and among the students themselves, of course. It was a shock for us because these things were incredible, inconceivable to us. No childhood experience could serve as a bridge to them. We had discussions with the instructors, and basically two attitudes prevailed: on the one hand a very critical one among those who tried to work through these things with us; and on the other, the attitude on the part of those others from the Nazi times who hadn't learned anything new at all.

And they said, "Well, it wasn't really as bad as all that, the others committed crimes too."

[Oskar adds that some people refused to admit anything negative. "'After all,' they said, 'Hitler built the autobahn.'"]

OL. These were the two positions that we were already confronted with at school. Serious examination of this question really began when we were [older] students, probably because our own judgment had become somewhat more independent by then. It was like the famous generation of 1968 asking their parents, "Why did you hush everything up? Why was this possible? How could this happen?"

The issue was clear-cut in regard to the crimes of the Nazi era, as well as the role played by individuals. There was also a whole series of public debates: "What did this one do, or that one, or that one?"

On the other hand, I made the point repeatedly that one ought to be cautious about being too rigid in passing judgment, because you have to ask yourself honestly whether, as a young person, you would have been capable of resisting the temptations of the Nazi system. And would you have had the courage not to be a fellow traveler as an adult, or at least a silent partner? This question isn't only relevant to the Nazis or the Nazi era, it is one for our time too.

In Germany now, we're working through the events of the past for a second time, in the former GDR. Here we're experiencing the same phenomenon of people "going along," even though you cannot equate this [with the Nazi era]. In East Germany people are going through the same experiences we did in the West as young, critical persons after the war. And in other countries where there have been dictatorships, you can observe similar things. At any rate, in these discussions, you always have to keep asking yourself: "As a young person who was not affected, how would you have acted?"

And then when we heard our parents say, "We don't want to hear any more about a party, we don't want to know anything more about politics," we realized that we had to become more engaged politically in order to prevent such things from happening again. This Albert Speer quote about "a society where people believe that those at the top do everything right and that those on top do what they want, anyway" describes an infantile society. It's fertile soil for fascism.

In today's society, too, many people are apolitical or think that those on top will solve the problems. Let me take just one example—say the ecological problem. Many people believe that ecological problems will be solved by a government taking some sort of action. But really, it's everybody's problem, so societies have to learn to act responsibly. And the core of the responsibility lies primarily with the individual. Every form of responsibility starts with the individual.

Earlier you asked about collective guilt. Responsibility starts with the individual and so does failure. This applies to present-day situations as well, such as the delivery of arms to Iraq, rockets, chemical weapons, and everything. I'm not responsible for this directly. However, as a member of a society in which politics inevitably plays a role and as a person who lives within a community and takes on a certain obligation and whose actions can affect the larger community . . . in this sense, I would accept collective guilt also for myself. But I'm separating this responsibility, this guilt or this concept from individual responsibility, which, to begin with, is decisive for my philosophical way of thinking.

MK. What does the individual, who isn't a government official or a politician, do?

OL. My answer isn't based on my present situation or my present role [as an official]. The individual must act responsibly. This means, for instance, that he or she mustn't be apolitical and just say, "Let them do as they please." Then they *will* do as they please.

[He cites Pastor Niemoller who said, "There was a time when one could demonstrate, but that time passed."]

OL. Nor must the individual be proud of not knowing anything about politics. That's a form of stupidity or abandonment of responsibility. It's also a question of socialization, education, the degree of comprehension, of course. But everybody is responsible.

MK. Would you say that racism poses a danger now because of increased immigration?

OL. Yes. On the one hand, there is an increased awareness resulting from the many discussions about dangerous developments, not only here but also in other countries, in terms of racism and xenophobia. On the other hand, there is a much larger migration of people and it will grow even more. One ought to term this a "migration of poverty." And there is the problem of asylum. Here the problem is not primarily that of asylum, but that of a migration of poverty from the eastern European countries to here in order to attain a better standard of living.

And in this connection the question arises: "How do educated, modern industrial nations cope with other cultures?" Here we now have a catchword, "multicultural society." In response, I can only say that in Germany one must finally create the basis for modern immigration laws. This has something to do with the idea of "nation." (I've written a book on this subject.) Modern immigration policies must state: "We'll accept people based on social, humanitarian criteria, not those of race or religion."

I am even skeptical, for instance, of these discussions about preferential treatment, as in the case of the Soviet Jewish immigrants. Many people say, "We have to give them preference." I would put a question mark behind that because then you are going to the other extreme. There's also the question, "Do we send arms to Israel now?" because of the historic guilt.

I really think one has to try to maintain a truly humane and open-minded point of view. And in immigration policy this means that we'll go by social criteria, by humanitarian criteria. Until now, it was different. The Vietnamese have been accepted here for the longest time, the boat people, because they fitted into the prevailing ideology. Every CDU [Christian Democratic] minister-president [state premier] gladly had himself photographed with Vietnamese. But at the same time, they spoke out against accepting Africans.

By the same token, all of them now declare, "We're supporting Israel." But they don't think twice about turning their backs on blacks. And this is a kind of dealing with the past that I don't care for.

MK. This also has to do with the unemployed, with . . .

OL. Yes. Xenophobia occurs when a society takes in more than it can integrate. That's why I'm in favor of quotas. I witnessed a situation where a village in the Saarland was literally flooded by Romanians, *Sintis*.

MK. Gypsies.

OL. Yes, gypsies. Whenever there are too many newcomers, the native population will back out and start developing defense mechanisms. So you have to develop integration policies that will be acceptable to the inhabitants. A city like Saarbrücken can process a few hundred a year. However, if a few thousand come, there will be unrest and fights. And this, in turn, has something to do with the competition for apartments and jobs.

MK. Has there been some disillusionment?

OL. Yes, there has. The left, too, always saw the question of the Palestinians as a political problem.

MK. As early as twenty years ago?

OL. For me at any rate for the past ten or fifteen years. I can't really tell you when all of this started for me. I became more concerned about communal problems and problems closer to home. I wasn't as active in foreign policy. And certain other issues in foreign politics dominated in those days, such as the Vietnam issue. We didn't concern ourselves as intensively with the Middle East or Israel. But human rights are human rights. They apply to everybody, to Palestinians, Israelis, Arabs, or whoever. My generation—maybe "my generation" is too strong—but someone like me refuses to judge Israel by special standards as far as human rights or the right to freedom are concerned. There are people who won't say one critical word [against Israel] when it comes to the issue of the Palestinians, because one mustn't do that as a German, it's not proper. But I reject that.

You have to look at the historical background, the cultural background, the social background. There were a lot of right decisions in Israel, but there were also many wrong ones. And that's why I am against approaching all questions ideologically. Because Israel is good does not mean that everything Israel does is good.

MK. And yet many think that way.

OL. Right. We're guilty in relation to Israel, so we support all that Israel does—that's the prevailing logic. You can see this now. That there are also critical voices to be heard in Germany now doesn't mean that there is an anti-Israel attitude. That's nonsense. There are critical voices in Israel, too.

[On December 20, 1992, out of a total population of approximately 190,000 Saarbrückers, 55,000 took to the streets to protest the recent neo-Nazi attacks against foreign immigrants in Germany. The demonstration was led by Oskar Lafontaine.]

⚜

Friedel Heilbronner

Through personal and business connections, charm, and audacity, Friedel Heimann (later Heilbronner) avoided being imprisoned—though she was detained—by the Nazis. A naturalized French citizen originally from Saarbrücken, she hoped that residence in Vichy France would protect her and her family but this proved not to be the case. After a series of misadventures, they managed to reach a port city in Spain in the summer of 1941 and boarded a ship bound for South America.

First their ship would dock in Argentina where the Heimanns had many friends. Rather than proceed to Chile (their official destination for which they had purchased visas), the family hoped to take advantage of the law in effect at that time, stating that anyone who set foot on Argentinean soil was permitted to remain. However, during the ship's passage the law was rescinded because of the numerous immigrants who had flocked to that country. This was a severe blow. When the ship docked in Argentina, the Heimanns were informed that they would be permitted to disembark but then they would have to take a train to Chile (flying was rare in those days). Friedel appealed to their friends in Argentina for help.

FH. Our friends said, "We'll straighten this out." And naturally, as good Germans that they still were then, they started with the authorities and followed official procedures. They didn't know that really all you had to do was to give them some cash and then we would have been OK. The Argentinean authorities had taken our passports and were insisting on sending us to Chile. Well, I raised hell, and then I said, "I won't get off the ship and I won't go to Chile," and I faked a severe gall bladder problem.

So I lay there in bed, thinking, "Now they'll have to let me go on Argentinean soil." But far from it! Every day a new friend arrived with different advice and different news, until eight days had passed. And then the captain came into the cabin saying, "Listen, it's up to you now, either you leave now or we'll take you back to Europe."

But at that point, they wouldn't even let us go without a guard. And then came an immigration officer and a man from the Jewish Aid Society and he agreed to vouch for us with the authorities.

They put us into a car with the chairman of the aid society and he took us through Buenos Aires, so we'd at least see what we were missing. Friends had told us, "It's really fantastic and so beautiful there." We drove through and there wasn't even a pedestrian area there yet, and I thought, "They're all out of their minds." There were old-fashioned stores; it was paradise as far as food was concerned, that's true, but all the rest was pretty dreadful. But we were in safety.

And then we were transported in this awful train to Mendosa, in West Argentina. I believe it took fourteen hours and then we were supposed to go on through the Andes to Chile. As so often in life, God took pity on us then and sent us an avalanche. The train was blocked. Two bridges had been damaged and the train couldn't go on.

So we were in Mendosa, and they said, of course, that we had to take a plane—they had this little thing there. You know how it is with these small planes, and so I said, "I'm not going to fly across the Andes, I won't do it, I simply refuse!"

[In Mendosa they stayed in a hotel, under the close scrutiny of an immigration agent. Friedel's attempts to extract their passports from him were unavailing. "That guy just waited for me to give him money. That's what I didn't get, we, with our wonderful European mentalities." She decided to seek the help of the French consul in Mendosa.]

FH. We got to this small house. He was a hair lotion manufacturer. And he said, "What is it you really want? You're here in the country so what do you need a passport for?"

We said we wanted to go to Buenos Aires.

"So, if you want to go to Buenos Aires, just go."

We said we didn't have a residence permit. Then he said that was utter nonsense. "What do you need a residence permit for? You're here in the country, that's that."

We didn't trust any of this but went back to Buenos Aires anyway by train. My husband was in the front of the train with one child and I was in the last car with the other, because we had this idea that all of Argentina was just standing there, waiting to arrest immigrants. But nobody asked for any papers.

[With their physical safety assured, the Heimanns resumed their divorce proceedings. Friedel's husband did not wish to remain in Argentina, preferring to go to Brazil instead. The Chilean visas issued in Marseilles had turned out to be fraudulent. Through various connections, Friedel was finally able to obtain a residence permit for Argentina. However, the family's money was under her husband's control. He was receiving money from his mother who had emigrated from Saarbrücken to Luxembourg and then to Washington Heights in New York. Mr. Heimann made it plain that Friedel would receive nothing from him if she insisted on the divorce. It was clear that she would have to find a job of some sort.]

MAKING A LIVING

FH. I got this position in a large clothing store in Buenos Aires run by an Italian. I didn't know any Spanish but I knew English, French, and German. I knew one sentence in Spanish perfectly: "I have an apartment, I have a bedroom, a living room and a dining room. In the dining room, I have a table with six chairs, and a cage with a parrot." I learned it from an instruction book. I could say that beautifully. I never had a dining room, never a table with six chairs, nor a parrot, but I could say it. Only it didn't help me much in Buenos Aires.

So I stood there in this store as a display object. We had taken all my dresses from Europe. I had lived an entire year in Aix and you could have new clothes made there. And when I went to Paris, I could buy clothes, and I bought whatever I could get. They thought it was very chic, a European woman. Argentina was very backward in those days, there was nobody who dressed elegantly. That was almost unheard of.

[Friedel's European flair was quickly recognized by her boss and he promoted her, putting her in charge of his three clothing stores. This arrangement, while paying well, put her divorce proceedings in jeopardy, because her husband claimed that she would have no time for the children and therefore he was asking for custody. She was advised to establish herself independently so that she would earn enough while still allowing her to control her own schedule. Friedel sought out a lawyer for advice.]

FH. Now there had been an attorney, Karl Hirsch. He was a very renowned attorney. Your parents knew these people in Saarbrücken. Then he had this job in France and that's how he got away from Gurs and they went to live in Buenos Aires. And that's how I met Karl Hirsch again with his wife in Buenos Aires. And this is really a funny tangent—destiny.

Karl Hirsch had been my first fiancé in Saarbrücken. I was nineteen years old then. It would go too far to tell the whole story, but at any rate, while I was still at school, Karl Hirsch fell in love with me and three weeks before graduation it said in the Saarbrücken paper that Friedel Oppenheimer and Karl Hirsch got engaged. Karl Hirsch was already a man then. I was nineteen and he was at least thirty-one. It was a real sensation in Saarbrücken, with all the works, with a reception— you know how it used to be in the Jewish community. Unfortunately, the engagement broke off due to my idealism, for Karl Hirsch was an experienced man, very much an *homme à femmes* [a ladies' man]. And I had this idea: I don't need to be cheated on. It was enough for a man to look at another woman, for me to think . . .

And then Karl said, "Listen, my little darling, you are so young, I don't want to rob you of your illusions. What you expect from a husband, I can't give you, I can't fulfill that." And six weeks before the wedding, it fell apart.

It was the tragedy of my life then. [The man she married soon after, Otto Heimann, had been Hirsch's best friend.] But strangely enough, Karl Hirsch—I'm always saying, people can't escape their destiny— married a *Ruth* Oppenheimer during his emigration. That's what he said, "another Oppenheimer."

[In order to establish her financial independence, Friedel decided to turn her sense of high fashion to use and somehow introduce ready-to-wear clothing, particularly sportswear, to a select clientele. Her friend Karl Hirsch was enthusiastic about the idea and brought her together with a potential partner, a woman from Frankfurt newly arrived from Nice. She turned out to be someone who had taken dance lessons together with Friedel's husband, Otto, in Germany. "He was the first man in her life who bought her lilies of the valley and she still had a photo of the dance lessons with Otto Heimann." Now divorced and sharing custody of the children, Friedel opened a shop in 1942 with her partner and hired seamstresses. With very little money and no actual knowledge of couture or sewing they put together a collection based on patterns of their own dresses.]

FH. We didn't have any money, but in those days, you could get everything on credit in Argentina. The people were very humane and friendly to immigrants. The entire textile industry was in the hands of the Jews—Russian and Polish Jews. Very, very nice and decent. They sold us fabrics by the yard, that is, they gave us credit. We knew an Austrian woman, an immigrant, who could sew. We took the fabrics to her and had our dresses copied. For the opening of the shop I had procured all the addresses of the immigrants and sent out invitations. I had even bought crackers and vermouth, all on credit. That's how it went then. You got credit on an honest face, and as an immigrant you got everything. And then all these people came, everybody felt obliged to buy something from you and the next morning we had money in the till. And I could start paying the debts.

My very first customer, I'll never forget, this German woman came into the store. A very attractive woman. And she said, "Well, you speak German beautifully. You know, my son went back to Germany a couple of weeks ago, he'll become a German soldier . . ." (Oh yes, Mrs. Schmidt, I'll never forget her) ". . . and he has a chance to get into the SS." Well, she had come to the wrong funeral.

But I needed money, and Mrs. Schmidt ordered two dresses, suits, and a coat, and now I had this Nazi as my first customer. It was awful. I told her right away who I was and that's how I got my first tip. When I went to deliver the clothes (she lived in a suburb), I went to the back entrance, the delivery entrance. She had deposited a peso for me with the cook. I was very proud. She never came back.

The boutique was successful once we got through the first tight spots. At other times, it didn't go at all. There are these waves. But I could live. And I was divorced. My husband and I agreed that the two girls should be with him for six months and six months with me. But we both saw the children every day. We both visited each other every day. We thought we had found an ideal solution for the children and today they're telling me it was dreadful, because they always had to move every six months.

[At times, the business was heavily in debt, and Friedel often found herself with barely a peso to her name. She tells of dining with a gentleman friend at the best hotel and being complimented for being "by far the most elegant woman there."]

FH. I said, "You know what? Let me tell you, I am by far the poorest of them all, too. Do you want me to open my purse?" And all I had were ten cents. I said, "Look, if you want to be really nice, loan me a peso for tomorrow."

He said, "That can't be!"

Said I, "If only you knew how happy a person can be, if your life has been saved and you're well and the children are well. It really doesn't matter then."

Well, that's how it was. Somehow one was above that whole situation. As if nothing could happen any longer. One was safe.

And one day, as always fate would have it, an Englishwoman came to the store and she was very pleased that we spoke English. For the English colony in Argentina, that was unusual; they didn't learn Spanish and Harrod's had a branch in Argentina and that's where they all did their shopping. Soon I had all the ladies from the English colony as customers and, of course, they were far easier to handle as customers than the Germans.

[With a solid clientele established in Argentina, Friedel decided to expand her activities to Uruguay in 1944. There she was fortunate to have impressed the American wife of the British ambassador who asked that Friedel not sell to anyone else in Uruguay.]

FH. The whole thing ended with my going to Montevideo four times a year, being picked up from the port by a Rolls Royce and then taken to Lady Veraker. She financed my trips to Europe for years, and with what I made through her, I could go to my father every year after the war.

PARENTS LEFT BEHIND

[When the Heimanns left France, Friedel's parents remained behind near Marseilles, hidden in the basement of a boardinghouse owned by a Swiss.]

FH. In April 1943 my mother died of a kidney disease. Basically, she died because she stopped taking her medicine and didn't want to live any longer, because her brother had perished and we were away. As my father told me, she didn't take care of herself at all anymore.

After my mother died, my father lived on whatever the Swiss man brought him and he lived miserably. Someone must have denounced the Swiss owner because two Gestapo men came to the boardinghouse and searched it. They found my father in the basement where he was in hiding and asked for his papers. Since he hadn't changed his name [from Oppenheimer] and had a carte d'identité with *Juif* written across it, it was obvious he was a Jew in hiding.

They asked what he was living on and he showed them a couple of hundred dollars, saying, "This is all that is left to me after forty years of work."

"What was your profession?"

"I had two stores in Saarbrücken, Welthaus, and Bamberger and Hertz."

And then one of the Gestapo men reached into his pocket and said, "You are the owner of Bamberger and Hertz? I was one of your customers and I'm carrying this with me."

It was a small round advertising gift mirror from Bamberger and Hertz.

Then he said, "Take the money from him but leave him here."

The mirror saved my father. But since he had the mentality of a good German, it didn't make sense to him at all that they should take everything away from him and he demanded that the owner of the boardinghouse be called as a witness that they had taken his money. The Swiss man was so beside himself that they had taken something they weren't entitled to that he made a scandal. So much so that he was hauled off to the Gestapo, and after kicking up an enormous fuss, he was finally released.

That's how my father survived. Miserably, but at least he was alive. When I found him, he was like a wild animal. He smoked leaves, put grass into the frying pan—horrible! But he lived until 1950 and I was able to support him with my work in Argentina. He regained strength. And really he still had some nice years. But he always dreamed that I would go back to Saarbrücken and rebuild the stores.

[Friedel's second husband was another Jewish refugee, from Munich, an art dealer whom she met first in Argentina in 1942. "I had found a wonderful man." For years they maintained a relationship, traveling together frequently after the war to Europe and eventually they established residence in Paris. There seemed no need to marry until he fell ill in 1969 at the age of eighty in Switzerland. Concerned lest there be difficulties with the authorities later on, they were married in 1971. He died two years later. At sixty-four, shattered by her husband's death, Friedel cast around for some sort of occupation. Once again her friends rallied around her and suggested she work with art dealers and artists to set up exhibits both in France and in Germany. One gallery owner proposed mounting a show of French modern artists in Germany.]

FH. I said, "Modern art? I don't have a clue. My understanding of art ends around the fifteenth century. I can't deal with modern paintings, I hate them."

He said, "You'll learn it."

I said, "I'm at the age where you don't learn anymore."

"I'll give you books. Give it a try?"

After a couple of weeks, I returned his books and said, "Don't be angry, but this really doesn't work. Maybe, if I had contact with the painters . . ."

[The dealer sent her to visit a compatriot, Henry Goetz, who was her age and lived near her in Paris.]

FH. He said, "Look around, here are the paintings. Go close." So I take a painting and put it on the easel, *"Chère amie,"* he says, "you are holding it upside down, it is standing on its head."

[After a shaky start, Friedel established contacts with a gallery owner in Saarbrücken and others throughout Germany and put together a number of successful shows. She continued to live in Paris.]

RETURNING TO GERMANY

[At her father's request, Friedel returned to Saarbrücken soon after the war to try and obtain restitution for some property and for the Bamberger and Hertz department store, which had been expropriated by the

Nazis. Lacking any sort of documents, it was nearly impossible for her to justify her claims. She decided to call at Overbeck and Weller, the department store that used to be the competition.]

FH. Old Overbeck had died, but the son is still around. I used to know him when we were still at school around 1929. He had started getting antisemitic then. He stopped saying hello. I had never seen him again and wanted to talk to him. But he wasn't in his store and when I returned to my hotel they said, "Mr. Overbeck called and asks you to call him back."

I called him back and explained why I was here.

Then he said, "Maybe I can help you, I have all of the sales figures, all of our company's documents, and since our companies were almost identical—your company certainly didn't sell less, probably even more than we did—I'd be happy to put all of my documents at your disposal."

Now he had gotten friendly and I don't know why. I never saw Mr. Overbeck again. I wrote him later to thank him. I owe it to him that my father got restitution.

[During that first visit to Germany, around 1948, Friedel was reunited with Lilo Kahn who had been with her in France, looking after her children. Lilo and her brother were managing a store that sold rainwear manufactured in Paris by Otto Heimann, Friedel's first husband.]

AT HOME IN GERMANY?

FH. When I came to Saarbrücken for the first time, I said, "I feel more secure in China and more at home there than in Saarbrücken."

I didn't want to see anybody, meet with anybody. I had been invited to my school's hundredth anniversary.

So I said, "I'm not coming, because I don't want to have anything to do with people who crossed over to the other side of the street in 1933 to avoid greeting me." I took care of what I had to take care of and was lucky with the restitution officials. I had encountered people there who were very nice and understanding, partly from bad conscience, and that ended this chapter for me.

When I went across to Germany for the first time, I said to my husband as we were approaching the border, "Listen, I have a French passport." My husband had a German passport. "As far as I'm concerned, I don't know any German, I'm French, I don't want to speak German here like a German woman." My husband spoke French fluently. I got out of the car at the border. An older customs official was there and I showed him my French passport. He looked at it and said, "Strange. A French passport, issued in Argentina in the name of Oppenheimer-Heimann. Were you a German once?"

I immediately replied: "Yes." Automatically.

And then he said, "Where is your car?"

I said, "Over there, in the back." It had an Italian registration.

He asked me, "Do you have any additional nationality?"

To which I said, "Yes, a German husband."

He said, "Please, pass on." And that made me laugh so much—I found that so funny. But he was a German, a man of about fifty years, or older, so that the little bit of aversion I had felt earlier went away suddenly. And I switched to German right away. I had said, "I won't speak German," but I spoke German fluently and was really amazed at myself.

MK. It's the roots. I was also surprised at myself, when I came to Germany for the first time. Theoretically, we all want to get away from it and then comes this inner warmth and you can't deny it.

FH. Precisely. In 1955 we went to Munich because my husband was born there. And that's where I met Germans. Munich was still very damaged then. I met people who had hidden members of my husband's family during the Nazi time, whose homes had been bombarded, who had been injured, had only one leg. And suddenly I felt terribly embarrassed that we were well, that we were dressed well, that our family had, as it were, survived the other families [though many of Friedel's relatives were lost].

I felt so ashamed in front of these people, that I said to my husband, "I can't take it here. Please, let's go away. I can't be with these people. I feel so ashamed."

LEAVING PARIS

[Friedel had been living in Paris after her husband's death and after her retirement from the gallery world. But during her recuperation from a series of illnesses, and after four muggings and the loss of her apartment, she realized that a new arrangement would be necessary.

She moved to Munich in the mid-1980s where she had a close friend.]

FH. Alone in Paris, most people sit and watch TV in the evening and don't go out. I like going to the theater and to concerts. In Munich, you can still do all these things. And besides, if you are two, there are other things you can do as well. So I went to Munich. But my heart is in Paris! Today, I live in Germany like a foreigner. I have, *au fond,* nothing to do with it. To me this is an alien mentality.

MK. The younger ones too?

FH. The younger ones less. I have more contact with the younger ones in Munich.

MK. But the younger ones here in Saarbrücken, for example?

FH. I have more contact with them. Saarbrücken is different. Saarbrücken isn't Germany. It's a class by itself. They are totally different people. But in Munich where I live, I stress at once, to avoid all mistakes, that I'm an emigrant, that I'm Jewish. I always say that right away, always.

When they ask how long I've been here or why I'm here, or if they ask me, "How come you speak so many languages?" then I say, "I owe all of this to your Führer." Then they look at me stupidly.

And then I say, "Yes, I'm an emigrant and I've been to many countries and had to learn the languages." I always like to let them know where I stand. This way, I avoid many unpleasant situations and whoever doesn't want me can ignore me.

"I hope you're feeling comfortable here and it's all over now and all of that was terrible." That's what I hear wherever I go, whoever I meet.

But if you're listening to a cabdriver, you can hear, "Well, all this crime now—that didn't happen under Hitler. That was the good side of the Nazis." It's not that all are unequivocally against Hitler now.

[I want to know more about the people in Saarbrücken and how they behaved. Friedel says she knows of several who were Hitler supporters or in the Hitler Youth or in the artillery. She is sure that they knew about the destruction of the synagogue, and about Auschwitz, though not about the Neue Bremm, a concentration camp in Saarbrücken itself. She mentions an acquaintance who ran a bookstore in Saarbrücken.]

FH. He was a Protestant. All the Jews bought from him. He had somewhat leftist tendencies. And he told me he had a bad conscience.

In the beginning, he said, his parents hid some Jews. "And one day, the Jews were deported and our friends were gone. And we didn't even think about what happened to them. They were gone and that was that. They were deported and nobody in our family talked about it."

And that still haunts him today. "We knew that the Jews were persecuted and somehow it didn't bother us. We were busy with our bombardments, with our ration cards, and our survival, and we totally forgot about you."

He was very honest. In other words there are those people and there are others. You can't put people in a slot. There are always exceptions in every category.

MK. I read that the Jews in Poland, in Warsaw, would say, "The bad Nazi is the one who can't be bribed. The good Nazi is the one who can be bribed." The good Nazi was the corrupt one, the idealistic Nazi was the bad one.

[Friedel speaks of one of her uncles, Fritz Bamberger, who owned the Munich branch of Bamberger and Hertz and other enterprises and who refused to lie about a business arrangement in order to protect himself.]

FH. He said, "I'm a German, I have a clean slate and as long as I have a clean slate, nothing will happen to me." Then he was sent to Dachau and the scales fell from his eyes. He was extremely German, until they arrested him.

They got him before Kristallnacht, he was sent to Dachau, and then they smashed his store to pieces. Rich Fritz Bamberger, who as late as 1937 still visited us in Paris and I implored my aunt: "At least leave your jewelry here, then you will have gotten something out of the country." No.

They left Munich with ten marks, a steel watch, and steel wedding bands. And I took the children—the English consul had taken them to Switzerland—I took the children from Switzerland to Paris and from Paris to London. Well, that's how idiotic you can be.

I found my uncle, the rich Fritz Bamberger, in Los Angeles in 1948. He was cleaning the floors in a pathetic little clothing store in Pasadena because a former supplier of Bamberger and Hertz had employed him.

[Her uncle had turned over one of his many businesses to the former comptroller at Bamberger and Hertz in Munich.]

FH. This man behaved fantastically toward my uncle. He came to Los Angeles at least three or four times, and took care of everything, and gave large sums to the children and my aunt when she was widowed. When the man died, he left her an apartment in Munich in his will—where she never went—just so she should have the feeling that she could come back to Munich if she felt like it. His conduct was fantastic.

MK. We've spoken of Polish and Russian Jews who in earlier days were often dubbed "rotten Jews" and "garlic eaters" by some German Jews. But some of them helped you, didn't they?

FH. You know what I have been saying over and over again? All of us have become Polish Jews. Simply because, during our emigration, we had to dodge and bribe and everything—to get visas, for instance. We didn't behave any differently from the Polish Jews whom we always condemned.

[She tells the following story about a young Bamberger cousin from Leipzig who was sent to England at the age of nine on a children's transport in 1938, like Martin Spier's brothers and sister. Another Bamberger uncle from Munich had emigrated to England just a few weeks before the child, Steffi, was to arrive at Victoria Station. Relatives of these children had been told not to meet them at the station since this would interfere with the procedures that had been established for easing the children's arrival.

Eager to see his niece and curious about how she would be met, he hid himself at the station. The child came off the train and was greeted by a man. The uncle approached him and asked if he was the person with whom she would be living and was told that the real guardian was waiting at Liverpool Station. The uncle accompanied them and there they were met by an older, white-haired gentleman, the child's new guardian, a Mr. Samuels, who invited them into a waiting Pullman car.]

FH. As they entered the compartment, Fred [the uncle] saw a table set with sandwiches and cakes. Mr. Samuels turned to Fred and said, "So empfängt ein polnischer Jude ein deutsch-jüdisches Kind. Und ich glaube im umgekehrten Fall wäres nicht so gewesen" [This is the way a Polish Jewish person greets a German Jewish girl. Were the situation reversed, I'm not so sure it would be so. (Steffi was accepted into the Samuels family as a daughter. At eighteen she cofounded a Kibbutz in the North Galilee.)]

POSTSCRIPT

In January 1993, Saarbrücken paid tribute to Friedel Heilbronner as one of its leading citizens and she received the official seal of the city. There were ceremonies and numerous press interviews. Evoking her own experiences as a refugee, Friedel delivered a speech in which she pleaded for an open policy in regard to immigrants and urged that all quotas be abolished.

A year later, Friedel Heilbronner turned her back on her native city and refused to participate in the film festival named for her brother. The cause of her withdrawal was a 1993 documentary film, *Beruf Neonazi* (Profession: Neo-Nazi), a portrait of Bela Ewald Althans, a young ultrarightist ideologue. Althans is seen delivering speeches, attending meetings, and relaxing at home and among people. He also argues with visitors at Auschwitz, insisting that the Holocaust never happened (an assertion that is considered a crime in Germany). Althans is young, clean-cut, hard-working, charming, and dangerously appealing.

The film was to have been on the opening program of the 1994 Ophüls Festival, but because of the controversy surrounding it, the program was changed. Upset that the organizers would even consider showing such a film, Friedel vowed to have nothing more to do with the festival. Her nephew, Marcel Ophüls, threatened to sue to have his father's name removed from the event. Because of the storm of protest, the mayor of Saarbrücken banned the film from the festival.

Friedel saw the film in Munich and it confirmed all her fears. I also saw it later and understand why it was thought to be dangerous. The filmmaker had hoped that audiences would be repelled by the character's neo-Nazi ideology and would not be swayed by his appealing personality. But the dispassionate presentation might also have had the opposite effect: some viewers will be persuaded by the man's convictions, including his insistence that Auschwitz was not an extermination camp. Although I believe it is important to get to know one's enemy through documentary exposure, I understand Freidel Heilbronner's revulsion.

In December 1994, Althans was sentenced by a Munich court to eighteen months in prison for fomenting racial hatred. On August 29, 1995, a Berlin court sentenced him to three and a half years in prison.

Friedel Heilbronner was subsequently reconciled with the festival's organizers.]

FH. I don't go to any synagogue and I'm not at all religious. I'm absolutely no atheist, but a good Jew. That's how I've become through Hitler. It's simply a question of character, not of faith. Whether a person is observant or not is a private matter, but as a Jew I feel that we have an obligation to stand up for our convictions.

Epilogue

In returning to my former home in Washington Heights and to my birthplace in Germany, to neighbors known and newly discovered, my object was to better understand the complexities and contradictions that inhere in survival. I also needed to resolve the ambivalence I harbored about my own people, many of whom lived half their lives or more in the relatively benevolent calm of their U.S. haven. The nagging and enduring questions that prompted these interviews have shadowed me for most of my life.

After years of living with the kaleidoscopic responses recorded in these pages, I have only partially absorbed the illuminations they contain. With "ethnic cleansing" in other parts of the world so recent a reality, I ask myself how much others, including ourselves, are susceptible to the seductions and fears that can lead to a condition akin to the Nazi regime in Germany. Could we become victims, bystanders, or possibly even oppressors?

Hitler's most reliable citizen on the home front, the one who never caused him a moment's concern, was the ordinary paterfamilias. This hard-working conscientious man did what he was asked to do in order to support his family and to please his superiors. Perhaps that man is in us, the one who, in a corporate industrial society, kept the trains on schedule, designed and constructed the barracks, bottled the new chemicals.

Maybe even the one who turned in his neighbor for unpatriotic activities is in us. For after all, were there not many, including Jews, who "named names," sometimes those of lifelong friends, during our McCarthy period just a scant few years after the war? Certainly the racist is among us, the one who considers certain groups and classes to be inferior.

A number of people in this testament have averred that they were much liked, beloved by their erstwhile neighbors, patients, or tradespeople. How was this affection measured? Was it by being accepted on the local bowling team or receiving grateful notes from a patient? Was it by being *gemütlich* over afternoon coffee?—or even being best friends? We were so monstrously fooled. The moment fear or opportunity turned friends in another direction that kind of good feeling vaporized.

But as we have read here, despite the extreme penalties in force during the Nazi regime, some rare Germans refused to turn away when it was dangerous to acknowledge a Jew on the street. Some hid strangers. Some brought food stealthily in the dark, or allowed unlisted items to go on shipboard, or overlooked a false identity card, or did as little as write an encouraging note, or stored cherished dishes against the threat of discovery. They did it not so much for the love of a given Jew as for respect for themselves, their decent human selves—less would have been self-betrayal. Would I have done it? To paraphrase Louis Kampf, I hope so, but how do I know? It is the test the vast majority of ordinary Germans failed.

These have been some of the thoughts that have come out of this journey of mine. You will have your own. I thank my neighbors and friends for their candor and willingness to indulge my stubborn and often intrusive probing. The process has renewed warm feelings for them and resurrected inside myself a community that I thought I had lost.

MK

Afterword: Were We So Beloved?

Biographical Reconstructions of German Jews

Dan Bar-On, Ben Gurion University of the Negev

This book tells the story of one post–World War II German Jewish community of a type that is rapidly vanishing. In this Jewish community, social bonding had a special, almost admirable quality, which resonates so beautifully in the pages of this book. One can find it in the stories of people who, shortly after arriving in the United States, began to develop support systems for the next waves of refugees. They developed religious services, organized festivities, and provided for the children, the elderly, and the sick. Most of them could even maintain nostalgia for the good old home, left behind, while restructuring "community wisdom" in New York (Bar-On 1986). There appears to have been no contradiction for them between the two.

This warm sense of being cared for (which could also get on one's nerves because one could easily feel trapped by it) represents a deep sense of social responsibility and concern, which I feel is lacking among the refugee communities of the 1990s. It is difficult to say whether the new waves of refugees possessed the same sense of social responsibility in the first place, whether they lost it while still in their homeland, or could not transfer it to the absorbing country. I myself have no doubt that the low level of post-traumatic reactions among the German refugees of World War II, as reflected in this book, is associated first of all with the high level of social support that communities such as Washington Heights could offer during and after the war.

When one moves away from the community level to the individual stories, one can observe that not all the stories of German Jews were success stories. It is true that many refugees brought with them more "degrees of freedom," in terms of potential absorption into the competitive American society, as compared to other Jewish refugees. Many had obtained higher education and begun professional careers while still in Germany. They brought with them a high level of expectation, self-awareness, and social consciousness. Some were lucky enough to arrive with some money to make a new start. In addition, they had a strong desire to make it, to adjust quickly, and to find their niche in the new setting within a relatively short time.

We also hear about those who were traumatized by their departure from Germany, those who were not able to finish their studies, who never returned to their original professions, who worked manually their entire working life in order to provide for their children. Still, even in those cases, the capacity to build something, objectively and subjectively, to help each other cope with the new social context on a relatively open, face-to-face level, created the vitality of the community and became its real success story. This capacity helped so many in this book overcome the loss of their existential sense of security (which the motherland provided them with, whether in reality or in illusion),[1] and to "rebuild life," as one of my Israeli interviewees stated simply, forty years after the war (Bar-On 1995a).

In our post-Holocaust world, the story of German Jewry is more difficult to tell. After Auschwitz our world became strictly divided into victims and survivors, perpetrators, bystanders, and rescuers. Bystanders could be subdivided into those who knew and saw and did nothing, those who could have known but tried not to, those who may have known something but did or did not care. The survivors could also be subdivided into death and concentration camp survivors, ghetto fighters and partisans, those who survived in hiding, refugees who fled during the war, or those who left early enough, without personally experiencing the extermination process. But who were the German Jews? Were they just any of these subgroups? Or did they bear a special iden-

---

1. In my own imagination, I use the term *fatherland* for pride, very much within the German terminology, whereas the term *motherland* is associated with the emotional bonding to one's homeland. This is my own distinction and I am not sure if anyone has studied it systematically.

tification, different from those mentioned above? And if different, in what way?

Educated people view themselves as people who have almost no prejudices. This does not hold up under testing. For example, Jewish Holocaust survivors could easily be identified as coming from Poland, Russia, or Hungary. When they arrived in the postwar setting, be it in the United States or in Israel, they were identified by their clothing, their way of walking in the street, their way of talking. But the Jews from Germany—were they part of the same identification system? Did they bear these signs? Did they actually want to be part of this community? Were they accepted as typical survivors by their fellow Europeans? The initial answer to these questions would probably be to say that they were different from the survivors from Poland, Russia, or Hungary. They did not look the same, did not talk like them, did not walk like them. So how can we classify them in our postwar terminology and stereotyping?

First, one sore point was that many of the German Jewish refugees tended to look down upon the *Ostjuden,* the Jews from the East who had immigrated into pre-Nazi Germany. This became a complicated issue since the East European Jews were the majority in the Holocaust survivors' community after the war. We can hear in this book that some German Jews persisted in looking down upon those from the East, many years after the war, even though Hitler did not really care where they came from. The German Jews could not accept that, because of the war, "all of us have become Polish Jews," as Friedel Heilbronner states so clearly in her last interview. On the other hand, some survivors among the German Jews developed a kind of self-hatred, combined with admiration toward the Polish Jews. Ilse Marcus, for example, states that had the *St. Louis* been populated with Polish Jews, they would have taken over the ship and would not have returned to Europe (which resulted in her capture, along with her mother, by the Nazis). She later also states that the Polish Jews were the ones who helped the German Jews survive in Auschwitz. But this does not prevent other interviewees from extending their original prejudice toward Ostjuden to the Russian immigrants of the 1990s—a newer prejudice that is sometimes only hinted at.

Second, before the Third Reich, many German Jews tried to assimilate and become "good Germans." When Hitler came to power, they could not grasp that this effort was futile (for the latest accounts, see Dippel 1996; Klemperer 1995).[2] Many years after the war they were emotionally still caught within the German cultural web. They could not condemn either the Germans or the Nazis (insisting that they knew the difference), as they still felt deeply rooted in that culture, "waiting for the Germans to come back." Also in this book there is one interviewee who goes out of his way to justify the Germans for "why they did what they did," putting the responsibility on the Jews! This version of "internalizing the aggressor" (Charny 1982) was difficult for me to digest, even though I too carry in my veins the split love and hate for the German heritage, having internalized it from my parents and grandparents during my childhood.

Third, many of the German Jews were "only" refugees, not "real" Holocaust survivors in the strict historical sense, which became an important post-Holocaust distinction for the survivors.[3] They fled from Germany late enough to know they had no chance there at that point in history but, as a rule, were lucky (or capable) enough to be able to make a decent living somewhere else. They did not go through the horrors of the extermination process and could not therefore count as part of the survivors' community. One may sense the difference in this book by listening to the biographical reconstructions of refugees and of survivors (though both came from Germany), by comparing interviews

---

2. In one of his diaries Klemperer wrote, "This is also my problem: the return of the assimilated generation. But the return to where? There is no chance of coming back, there is no sense in going to Zion. Perhaps our duty is not to leave, but to wait. I am German and I am waiting for the Germans to return. They drove away and vanished somewhere. I am waiting for them to come back here" (my translation).

3. In my book *Fear and Hope: Life Stories of Five Israeli Families of Holocaust Survivors, Three Generations in a Family* (Bar-On 1995a), I distinguish between the psychological and the historical definitions of being a Holocaust survivor. We found that after many years, prewar refugees from Europe were not less emotionally burdened than Holocaust survivors. Although they did not suffer the actual experience of Nazi occupation, many of their family members had been murdered and they were themselves physically uprooted. In addition, they felt no legitimacy in their mourning, because "others had suffered more." It is probably a human tendency, when one has to cope with unimaginable suffering, that scaling it to "more" or "less" creates an "illusion of control" (Langer 1976). It is more difficult to say they have all suffered, but in different ways. Who are we to judge what is more or less?

in parts 1 and 2 with the last two interviews in part 3. Though there are no open accusations, one can sense the undercurrents ("Why did you stay too long?" or "Why did you not do more to rescue us too?"). I myself have experienced some more articulated expressions of these strange postwar relationships. Within one family, at a Passover meal, the Auschwitz survivors sit at the head of the table, near them the partisans, behind them those who were in hiding, and at the end of the table those who left before the war. During these occasions, the latter usually have no right to talk at all about their experiences.

Fourth, German Jews tried to reestablish or maintain their sense of German uniqueness immediately after emigration and immigration by setting up separate communities, be it in Washington Heights in New York City or on the Carmel in Haifa. In those neighborhoods German was the common language, spoken privately during the war years, but publicly thereafter. German postwar communities had their own way of dressing, a certain kind of coffee table with pastries, and a daily schedule. These were just a few characteristics that kept this community apart from its Jewish, as well as non-Jewish surroundings. When I read some of the first interviews in this book, I had to remind myself that the interviewee was talking about a community in New York. I could easily recognize the smells and the furniture color or other familiar characteristics from my own childhood. I was even surprised to find out that the nickname *Yekke* was associated with the word *jacket* (a totally different explanation from the one I grew up with).[4]

In addition to the special story of the German Jewish survivors, we have to recognize an additional difficulty, which stemmed from the general post–World War II atmosphere of not being able to listen to the stories of those who came from there. After listening to one of my lectures, an old lady in the home for the elderly in my community told me that when she arrived at her relatives' home in England after the war (she came from Warsaw), they said to her: "Don't tell us, we do not understand." In addition to earlier sequences of traumatization, the traumatic separation from beloved ones, and the traumatic experiences

4. In Israel, *Yekke* is known as an abbreviation of *Yehudi Keshe Havanah*, which means a Jew who has difficulties in understanding; very much in the spirit of how the Jews from Germany were perceived by the local (East European) "veteran" Israelis.

during the war, came the unexpectedly harsh encounter with postwar reality (Keilson 1992), which could not "contain" the survivors, emotionally, imposing on them the demand to rebuild life while silencing their trauma. The alternative was even worse: flight into despair or craziness.

This may explain why we did not hear many of the stories until two new generations had grown up. The postwar silence was intergenerationally transmitted. I illustrate it as a kind of living "double-wall" phenomenon. The survivors or refugees, unable to find words for their experiences and feelings, built a wall on their side (to protect themselves, their children, and postwar relations?). The children, sensitive to their parents' walls, built their own wall, adjacent to that of their parents. If at any later point in time one side wanted to open a window and deliver or ask something, they usually met the wall erected by the other side. Rarely, in my extensive and intensive interviews with refugees and survivors, have I found a case in which, spontaneously, both sides succeeded in opening a window at the same time. Even when parents wanted to speak, the children could not listen, or vice versa.

In that sense, this narrator's effort and success in opening up so many windows in the walls of his parents' generation should be admired. He tells us about his motivation for interviewing his own father, as well as the motivation that led him to the decision to leave the German Jewish Washington Heights community and to find his own way as a Jew in American society. Only after he had found his place and become rooted in American society could he reflect on his German roots. He then returned to conduct these interviews before it was too late. Several of his interviewees have since passed away. What a loss it would have been had he not initiated this enterprise early enough.

My own experience shows that in the efforts to open windows in the "double wall," the grandchildren had an especially important role among survivors' and refugees' families. In Israel, children of thirteen in school usually have to do a project about their roots. As part of this project they ask their grandparents about their life stories. I have heard many accounts from survivors in Israel about how they told stories to their grandchildren that they had never told their own children. The latter were surprised to read these stories in their children's reports at the end of the school year. Perhaps the only shortcoming of the present account is the absence of the grandchildren's voice. It would have added another dimension to the story of the Washington Heights German Jewish community, a story that is basically intergenerational, similar to many stories of living and breathing communities. But perhaps the author wanted to emphasize his opinion that Washington Heights was a necessary intermediate stage for absorption in America and not an ongoing, intergenerational endeavor of German Jews.

It is common to see the descendants of survivors or refugees as recipients of their parents' unresolved conflicts, be it in the form of some deficiency (such as separation anxiety) or capacity (high-achievement motivation). They were defined, emotionally, as "becoming the parents of their own parents" (Danieli, in press). They were seen as becoming the "total good" for their parents, an antithesis to the "total bad" they had experienced with the Nazis (Hadar 1991). Our three-generation study added an important dimension to these earlier descriptions. Now they were also parents of their own children, not only children of their parents.

One woman, for example, described in detail how she had to learn to navigate between the harsh way she was brought up and trying to do the opposite with her children. This she found to be just as harmful for them, causing her to search for a middle path. At the same time she helped both her children and her parents maintain an especially good relationship because she herself missed so much not having grandparents as a child. The grandchildren became capable of opening the distorted family communication, because some adult figure—their mother—had matured emotionally and could help them develop in this direction.

During my intergenerational study it became clear to me that this was part of any immigration process. It usually takes at least three generations until the stories of the immigrants can be told in their own right, not through the black and white prejudices or judgments of those who absorbed them or through some hasty effort to "tell a heroic story" so that it "will not be forgotten" (Langer 1991). The paradox may be that by the time they were told openly and willingly, the distortions of these biographical reconstructions made some stories sound so different, and even obscure, that it became difficult for the listeners to make up their own minds about how things really were or what had actually happened.

When such deeply conflicting emotions are involved, as in the case of German Jews, this is an even more complex process. For our own convenience, we try to put all of the storytellers' traumatic experiences under the heading of one single word: Holocaust. In reality, the variety of conflicting emotions and the variety of actual experiences have to be told and retold, many times over. Only then do we begin to understand that there was no single Holocaust, equal for all who lived through that era. Whereas one Jew from the village was humiliated dreadfully during Kristallnacht, his neighbor was saved through the heroic intervention of another person. Or, whereas one person remembered the harsh events he went through, the other recalls the positive aspects of the same events.

The experience may have happened as remembered but it may also have been colored by later negative or positive experiences or personal developments. We, the listeners, receive today the product or combination of these different options. This could explain why there are so many versions and why studying the differences between these versions may become no less important than identifying their perceived similarities. The question for us, the listeners, is, To what extent are *we* open to internalizing the complexity of versions, counterversions, or subversions that this book, for example, represents?

Whoever is ready to try will realize one thing for sure: One cannot persist in maintaining simple black and white images, as was the trend, concerning us and the Holocaust, *us and them*. In my own country this is still a major issue. Are we ready to relinquish our "just (both meanings) victim" mentality for a less comfortable but more realistic and complicated version that states: Just as other human beings do, we too have in ourselves the potential for being victims and victimizers (Bar-On 1995b)?

This means that we may also have to give up the more simplified version of the "lessons learned from the Holocaust," lessons such as "We should be strong because we cannot rely on anyone else," or alternatively, "We should be more sensitive to other minorities because of what was done to us." We have to learn to consider more refined versions in which one has to take into account, first of all, how different situations have been (and still are) from one another and how complicated human beings are or can be. The recent Bosnian war has again shown us how, under extreme and unexpected conditions, neighbors can act and become atrocious after many years of "as-if" peaceful relations (even after reaching an ethnic intermarriage rate of 46 percent). My own feeling—after studying the Holocaust and its aftereffects for many years, among both survivors' and perpetrators' families—is that the more I listen to stories and accounts, the less I can make sense of it and understand how it could have taken place in the midst of one of the centers of twentieth-century civilized society.

No less important is the lesson of how memory is different from history. I will not discuss here in detail the epistemological discussion between historical truth and narrative truth (Spence 1982). This book does not try to deal with the issue of historical truth, since it is based on the biographical reconstruction of the events in the minds of the people who experienced them and in the minds of their offspring. Biographical reconstructions have some basic rules: They try to sound coherent and logical, and to conform to the dominant social norm or its alternative counternorm.

Through these reconstructions, the storytellers try to overcome both internal and external contradictions that have occurred in the course of their life history, so that what happened in the past will sound logical and fit in with what they are experiencing today. An individual can tell only one sequence of events, though within the span of this recounted story there may be other, hidden, untold stories that are intentionally or unintentionally left out of the discourse. The descendants are usually the ones who become sensitive to these contradictions and react to them, openly or unwittingly (Bar-On and Rottgardt 1996).

For example, if I considered myself a good German in Germany before Hitler and was confident that the Nazi period would soon be over, how can I explain why I finally left Germany in haste? If I used to look down upon the East European Jews as troublemakers, in terms of the rising antisemitism, how can I account for the fact that they were the ones who helped me more than others when I landed in Auschwitz? Or, if I had some very negative experiences with Nazis during that time, how can I make sense of the Nazi who saved my life? Actually, we all experience such contradictions in our life history, but when we have to put them into a story, we try to make them appear more logical so it will make a better story. It needs some sophistication to understand that the more these contradictions can be revealed, the more reliable the story will sound (Fischer-Rosenthal 1995).

Each of these contradictions in one's life history can create very different versions within one's life story. I may distort the initial fact that I felt good in Germany and believe I already knew very early that most Germans were actually antisemites, or I may play down the importance of my hasty departure before the war and emphasize the fact that there were many "good" Germans and those who conducted the atrocities had no other choice within the totalitarian regime. Probably, I might even have done the same had I been a gentile German at that period. The difference between these biographical reconstructions may be associated with one's life history since then. But even this life history may have been influenced earlier by one's initial responses. I might have refrained from going back to Germany ever since the war, not trusting any of *them* anymore, building up a vicious cycle of hate, or I might have reestablished my contacts there long ago and found many friends who confirmed my initial Germanophile reconstruction.

Therefore, I put a question mark to the title of this book: Were we so beloved? To what extent can we trust this feeling, which many interviewees convey, that Germany was for them a loving homeland? It could be a historical reality but it could just as well be a heavily biased biographical reconstruction. I can recall the way my mother used to speak about her own childhood, which sounded like a dream. She was brought up in noble Hamburg, in a very liberal, almost feminist atmosphere during the 1920s, with classical music and a rich cultural life, student parties, and ski trips to the Alps. Did she ever sense any antisemitism? She could not recall any such incidents. She still held to this love for her hometown when I walked with her along the Alster in the late 1980s while I was interviewing descendants of Nazi perpetrators. It was one of her only visits to her beloved childhood surroundings and she did it for me. I could see, however, that it was also painful for her because, among other things, there was no door she could knock on.

During that sleepless night, alone in my hotel room, I had to ask myself, Was it really so beautiful? was she really so beloved? did she live in a capsule already then? or did she reconstruct it in her mind right after she and my father left Germany, a kind of reconstructed illusion that helped them cope with the unpleasant life conditions they encountered in Israel? I am not sure we will ever know what the historical truth was, and perhaps in the meantime I grew up to believe that it was not so important anymore. I learned to appreciate that fantasies and realities have less clear boundaries than we tend to believe when we are younger, or when we are very strict logicians, at least within certain limits of what is acceptable.

Biographical reconstruction is a new term for what we psychologists discussed earlier under the heading of identity formation. Clearly this book deals with the issue of "Who am I?" especially in relationship to "my relevant others"—other Jews (from the East, or America, or Israel), other (mainly gentile) Germans, or other Holocaust survivors. We can see how difficult it is for quite a few interviewees to clarify, to themselves and to others, who they are, who they have been, and how they have changed. Perhaps, therefore, it is easiest for them to view and describe themselves as part of their own "tribal ego," the German Jewish one. They even play around with this question: Should Jewish or German come first? But the moment they have to move a bit further away, we can hear in a number of cases how the ground becomes shaky and the sky clouded.

The reason some of us prefer to talk today of biographical reconstruction rather than identity is embedded in this very difficulty of moving away from one's "tribal ego" (Fischer-Rosenthal 1995). The term *identity* assumed a permanent and internal construct within a person, something that develops in childhood and sticks around thereafter, the center of the personality. But the experience of the Holocaust has shown us that what we assume may not be there after all. A person is not one thing. He or she is full of contradictory potentials, needs, emotions, wishes, self-presentations, and behaviors. These may not fit into one coherent whole at all.

When we talk about a biographical reconstruction, we do not assume anymore that this has to be so coherent (unless the interviewee insists it should be). We can allow contradictions to appear and these are even more interesting to study and understand. In addition, we do not assume anymore that it is an internal entity. Now, the interviewee becomes an active partner in this process: his or her own verbal reconstruction, rather than our professional lingo, determines the process. It now becomes a dialogue between two parties, rather than an entity residing within oneself.

For many German Jews this dialogue is an internal dialogue, which they held with their German gentile "relevant others." Earlier when I gave the example of the internalized aggressor, I was referring to an extreme example of this process. I believe, however, that many years after they left Germany, Jews continued to maintain this dialogue with their German partners, who no longer existed in the real world but only in their minds, just as many of us go on talking with our parents long after they have died.

There are many ways biographical internal dialogues took place among Germans, Jews as well as gentiles, after the war. In my study I found seven kinds of moral argumentations that descendants of Nazi perpetrators and German bystanders used, to account for what had happened during the Holocaust (Bar-On and Charny 1992). These argumentations helped them relate to the past in such a way that they could live in the present, without bumping again and again into the unresolved conflicts the Nazi past presented for them. These were the argumentations identified:

1. *The Holocaust did not happen, or it was somehow justified.* Though these are two very different arguments, they serve the same function for the person who used them. For that person, the Holocaust was no longer a moral dilemma that one had to continue dealing with.

2. *The Holocaust happened, but the Jews did it to themselves.* This strange argument is congruent with the "just world" hypothesis (Lerner 1975). It was not used very often in my interviews, but it did free the German interviewee from the moral burden for what had happened. The interesting point is that some German Jewish refugees accepted this argument, consciously or unconsciously.

3. *Things like Auschwitz have always happened.* This relativization of the Holocaust reduced the moral burden: "We, the Germans, are not worse (nor better) than any other nation under stress of war or totalitarianism." Traces of this argument can be found in one interviewee in this book.

4. *We suffered too.* This is a genuine description of the reality, since many of that generation suffered from the war. But when the interviewee started and ended with this single argument, it became a de-

fense, a way of not recognizing how the Nazis caused other people to suffer in the first place.

5. *Not my family members.* Within this argument there is a general recognition of a collective German guilt and responsibility for the Holocaust but there is a "boundary of evil" that runs outside the wider personal sphere of one's own family. I believe many young German people would accept the price of collective guilt while keeping their families outside this responsibility.

6. *My parents did it.* Here, the boundary of evil runs between oneself and one's parents. This was a common argumentation of the 1960s, whereby young people accused their parents of involvement in the Nazi regime, thereby viewing themselves as totally independent of these crimes. Only years later did we understand that this counterdependency is very different from psychological independence (Bar-On and Charny 1992).

7. *No possibility of drawing a boundary of evil.* For these very few individuals, the Holocaust was a threat from which they could not defend themselves. If their parents were involved and responsible, perhaps they themselves could have been involved too. There is no clear shelter or psychological shield, only awareness. Peter Thomas Heydrich *[nephew of Reinhard Heydrich, known variously as the Hangman of Europe or the Butcher of Prague]* says in his last interview: "There is no way to be 'done with it.' If one is done with it, we should ask what is wrong with the way he or she has worked it through" (Bar-On 1989).

I never tried to develop a similar typology of argumentations for the Holocaust survivors and refugees or their descendants, but I can imagine that it is possible to develop such a typology even out of the argumentations represented here in this book. One topic that recurs is the special place Israel has gained in the minds of American Jews, perhaps specifically in the minds of the refugees from Germany. For most of them, Israel represents the "total good" that would seem to compensate them for the lost pride associated with their original fatherland, which once symbolized the total good and later became the total evil (Hadar 1991).

Whereas the relationship to the Jews who returned to live in postwar Germany is not a simple one (though this complexity is not discussed thoroughly in this book), the relationship to Israel is clearly idealized. Quite a few interviewees never went back to Germany—although they have been invited by their hometowns and although they were aware that their neighbors did accept such invitations and traveled to Germany, some even several times. Israel is a place that has been visited by many German Jews. Still, I am not sure how many would have liked to live in this complicated Middle Eastern reality. But nonetheless, it became an ideal of Jewish pride and positive emotions. This became something to hang on to, after the roots to the fatherland were poisoned by the Nazis.

The author is one of the few in this book who is willing to consciously question this unconditional love for Israel. Is all that Israel does or represents necessarily "good," even when it is harmful to its Arab neighbors, as has happened during the Lebanon war or during the Intifada? Most of the interviewees speak of Israel as if it represents in their imagination a kind of emotional security, a new anchor, on which they hook their injured feeling of security associated with being German Jewish. Theo Krämer even goes out of his way to thank Germany for helping Israel, though he hates the Germans and would never go back to visit his homeland. But the fact that Germany helps Israel is a positive spot in this unconditional hatred.

Another topic that often reappears in interviewees' stories is their relationship to religion. As part of their assimilation efforts in pre-Nazi Germany, many German Jews did not participate in Jewish religious practices. How did the Nazi era affect this trend? On the one hand, many survivors speak of the feeling that the Holocaust proved for them that "there is no God." Had he existed, this would not have happened to us. We know that the Holocaust caused many survivors to give up their religious practices, at least during the first few years after the war. On the other hand, Hitler also proved to the assimilated Jews that there is no way out of being Jewish. Some, consciously, went back to religious practice, identifying themselves with the Jewish fate on which they had once turned their back. Among these two extreme reactions we find the middle groups who tried to maintain some level of religious practice before and after immigration. Some were even the first ones to reestablish some kind of synagogue or religious community, be it orthodox, reform, or conservative.

During my study on descendants of perpetrators, I found my inter-viewees in five different stages in their own working-through process—how they manage the unresolved conflicts of the past (Bar-On 1990). First, they had to know the facts of what happened during that era and how their parents were involved in it. Second, they had to understand the meaning of those historical facts in some historical, moral, social, or psychological frame of reference. Third, they then reacted, emotion-ally, to this knowledge and understanding, either positively by defend-ing their parents ("he was such a loving person"), or negatively (feeling betrayed by a father who conducted crimes against humanity while be-ing a "loving father"). Fourth, there is an emotional conflict that re-sults from the confrontation with the previous contradictory emotions. And last, there was the capacity to integrate the knowledge, under-standing, emotional reactions, and conflict into one's moral self, there-by becoming independent from one's parents and their social milieu. Only a few of my interviewees reached this final stage of being able to live with it more openly, though still also painfully.

Again, I believe that a similar staging of the working-through pro-cess can be identified among the survivors and the refugees, though the content of the internal unresolved conflicts are different, of course. I had the opportunity to watch these similarities and differences in the working-through processes of descendants of Holocaust survivors from the United States and Israel and descendants of Nazi perpetrators in a few encounters of such a group.[5] Following are illustrations of those as-pects of the working-through process that were relevant for descen-dants of both Jews and Germans (non-Jewish):

1. *The impact the Holocaust still has on my life.* Members of both

5. The German group was composed of my interviewees (Bar-On 1989) and started to work as a self-help group in 1988. In 1992 I asked them if they would be interested in meeting a group of nine descendants of survivors. When they gave a positive answer I ap-proached One Generation After (OGA) in Boston and a few of my students in Israel, which created the Jewish part of these encounters (nine participants). These encounters took place in the course of thirty-seven months. We met in June 1992 at the University of Wuppertal, Germany; in April 1993 at Nveh Shalom, Israel; in July 1993 at Brandeis Uni-versity, Boston; in July 1994 at the Evangelic Academy in Berlin; and in December 1995 at Ein Gedi rest house in Israel. The meetings each lasted four or five days. Except for the first encounter, which was devoted to getting acquainted mainly by listening to each oth-er's personal accounts and stories, the scheduling was planned by the group itself.

groups shared their own experiences—how, when, and in what ways they could trace the aftereffects of the Holocaust within their own lives. For some, this was a daily struggle with sleeplessness, fears, uncontrollable reactions, often associated with the silence, repression, or other difficult reactions of their parents.

2. *Self- and social estrangement.* In many cases acknowledgment of a personal relationship to the Holocaust was accompanied by a strong feeling of estrangement, both internal (from oneself) and external (from one's social surroundings). It took many years to clarify and comprehend how this sense of estrangement was associated with one's personal relationship to the Holocaust.

3. *Feelings of uprootedness.* The Jewish members of the group suffered first of all from physical uprootedness, since their parents had emigrated to the United States or to Israel after the Holocaust. This physical uprootedness was usually accompanied by psychological uprootedness, associated with the fact that their parents could not overcome the loss of so many family members and had difficulty in integrating themselves into the new society. The German members of the group shared this feeling of psychological uprootedness, but for other reasons. They felt that, because of the atrocities committed by their parents, their roots had been poisoned and they could no longer use them as a base. They had to develop new roots, as did the descendants of the survivors.

4. *Difficulty in becoming socially and psychologically independent of one's parents.* Can I allow myself to live my own life, neither dependent on nor counterdependent to that of my parents? This was a major issue for members of both groups. Whereas for the Jewish descendants separation from their parents was more difficult (as the latter leaned on them, emotionally), descendants of Nazi perpetrators tended to counterreact, thereby creating other problems for emotional independence. This problem became more severe over time, especially when the parents aged and the objective justification for caring for them became a daily reality or necessity.

5. *How to live with so much death, within and around oneself.* In many ways members of both groups struggle daily with dreams of death, bearing names of dead people (especially Jewish descendants of survivors), having fantasies of sacrificing themselves for a human cause

(especially descendants of perpetrators). As one member of the group mentioned: "We talk about our feelings, emotions, and ideas, but they all concern the dead people who are in the back of our minds." Perhaps not by coincidence many members of the group belong to the helping professions. Perhaps they are trying to give a special meaning to their lives under the shadow of death.

6. *Dialogue with the victim and victimizer inside oneself.* Members of the group could, quite easily, establish an open dialogue with the victim in themselves. This was easy for both descendants of Jewish victims and descendants of Nazi victimizers. But it was much more difficult for both groups to identify and enter into an open dialogue with the victimizer within oneself and to let the two "figures" talk with each other. Eventually it became clear that we all have this potential role within ourselves, and only by openly acknowledging and entering into a dialogue with it may its uncontrolled potential be reduced in future, unexpected situations.

7. *Assigning a scale to power, suffering, and heroism.* In the group context it became evident that we all tend to create a scale of suffering—who suffered more, who less. It is much more difficult to relate to the experiences of the other as just being different, not greater or less. As we cannot grasp the experiences our parents had during the Holocaust, the scaling helps us live with it. Something similar happened around the subjects of heroism or power. It became an issue for the group—how to maintain the legitimacy of the difference without using the system of ranking, which in itself creates unnecessary pain and humiliation.

8. *Asymmetry among the parents, symmetry among the descendants.* It was difficult but important to bear in mind that while we developed a common feeling of mutual trust and respect, suggesting a new symmetry between parties in the dialogue, this by no means erased the asymmetry that still existed in our minds between our parents during the Holocaust: the victimizers and the victims. These two types of relationships are difficult to maintain simultaneously, but it was very important to find a way to navigate between them.

9. *The capacity to live with the past on different levels.* Through the group experience it became clear that the outcome of this process is not to forget or to be done with the past, once and for all, but to find new

ways to live with it, perhaps in ways that are more conscious but also less threatening and self-destructive. This suggests that by working through such massive trauma one does not end it or let it go but one can find new ways to live with it. The Holocaust will always be there as a presence, but its negative impact on our lives and the lives of others can be reduced through such conscious working-through processes, in groups as well as by individuals.

10. *Doing for ourselves, helping others.* From the outset of the group work there was a dilemma. How much time should we devote to ourselves and how much should we devote to working and helping other people undergoing a similar process? This group first chose to use most of the time for itself (especially during the first three encounters). During the later meetings attention was slowly shifted to activities of members of the group outside the group context. One member of the group started a similar group in Austria last July; another member organized a seminar for German therapists; a few members gave lectures at schools and synagogues, trying to translate what they learned and experienced in our group to the various relevant settings. In our last encounter a few new members were recruited from the third generation of Jews and Germans, thereby extending the scope of our discussions to include this intergenerational aspect as well.

I believe that the relationship between Germans and Jews will be a complicated one for many years to come, because so many unresolved conflicts, emotions, and attitudes are involved. This may be even truer for the German Jews who have an emotional and cognitive bond to the German and Jewish communities at large. With the years, though, the bond may change and new questions may become relevant. The importance of the present book is that it allows us to incorporate the views of those who participated in this major cultural change, mostly unwillingly, within their lifetime.

I will end with a personal story. During one of my presentations in Germany, I was approached by a journalist who wanted to conduct an interview with me. I suggested that she read my book first. When we met in Hamburg for the interview she started by saying, "I have some warm regards to you from a former patient of your father—my mother."

It turned out that while reading the introduction of my book she came across my father's last name (which is different from mine) and it sounded familiar to her. When she asked her mother, she immediately recalled my father as the person who had been their family physician during the early 1930s when she was a little child suffering from pneumonia. "He was a very warm person who took care, not only of the medical, but also of the emotional needs of his patients."

After confirming that it really was my father, I became very excited. Then I suddenly had this strange feeling, which I have heard about from a few of my interviewees: "Now I know it was real. Until now, I was never sure—maybe I made it all up?" I know this sounds strange to someone who has not experienced this feeling. I mean, why should people make up such terrible events and experiences as forced emigration or the threat and acts of extermination? But I believe that the events were sometimes so unpredictable and unbelievable that *reality overran fantasy* and not the other way around, as it usually is, or should be. I am afraid that many of us still live with this feeling of "Could it be true? Did it really happen to us? Maybe it was all a bad dream from which we will wake up in a few minutes. . . ."

REFERENCES

Bar-On, D. 1986. "Wisdom of the Community." *Quality of Work Life* 3: 3–4, 251–61. Shorter version also in *Kibbutz Studies* (February 1985): 18–23.

———. 1989. *Legacy of Silence: Encounters with Children of the Third Reich.* Cambridge: Harvard University Press.

———. 1990. "Children of Perpetrators of the Holocaust: Working Through One's Moral Self." *Psychiatry* 53: 229–45.

———. 1995a. *Fear and Hope: Life Stories of Five Israeli Families of Holocaust Survivors, Three Generations in a Family.* Cambridge: Harvard University Press.

———. 1995b. "Encounters Between Descendants of Nazi Perpetrators and Descendants of Holocaust Survivors." *Psychiatry* 58: 3, 225–45.

Bar-On, D., and I. W. Charny. 1992. "The Logic of Moral Argumentation of Children of the Nazi Era." *International Journal of Group Tensions* 22: 1, 3–20.

Bar-On, D., and E. Rottgardt. 1996. "Working Through the Undiscussible: Facts and Fiction." *Gerontology* (April 1996): 82–93 (in Hebrew).

Charny, I. W. 1982. *How Can We Commit the Unthinkable? Genocide: The Human Cancer.* New York: Westview.

Danieli, Y. In press. *International Handbook of Multigenerational Legacies of Trauma.* New York: Plenum.

Dippel, J. V. H. 1996. *Bound Upon a Wheel of Fire: Why So Many German Jews Made the Tragic Decision to Remain in Nazi Germany.* New York: Basic Books.

Fischer-Rosenthal, W. 1995. "The Problem with Identity: Biography as a Solution to Some (Post)Modernist Dilemmas." *Comenius* 2 (Utrecht): 250–66.

Hadar, Y. 1991. "The Absolute Good and Bad in the Eyes of Holocaust Survivors and Their Descendants." Presentation given at the Eighth Family Therapy Conference, Bat-Yam.

Keilson, H. 1992. *Sequential Traumatization Among Jewish Orphans.* Jerusalem: Magnes.

Klemperer, V. 1995. *Ich will Zeugnis ablegen bis zum Letzten.* Tagebucher 1933–1945. Berlin and Weimar: Aufbau Verlag (in German).

Langer, E. 1976. "The Illusion of Control." *Journal of Personality and Social Psychology* 32: 311–28.

Langer, L. L. 1991. *Holocaust Testimonies: The Ruins of Memory.* New Haven: Yale University Press.

Lerner, M. J. 1975. "The Justice Motive in Social Behavior." *Journal of Social Issues* 31: 3, 1–19.

Spence, D. P. 1982. *Narrative Truth and Historical Truth: Meaning and Interpretation in Psychoanalysis.* New York: W. W. Norton.

Appendix I

Excerpts from Adolf Hitler's *Mein Kampf*

Note: The following excerpts from Adolf Hitler's *Mein Kampf* are taken from the translation by Ralph Manheim. Copyright © 1943, renewed 1971 by Houghton Mifflin Company; reprinted by permission of Houghton Mifflin Company; all rights reserved. The first edition was published in Germany in 1925 (vol. 1) and 1926 (vol. 2) by Franz Eher Verlag. The translator, Ralph Manheim, has deliberately retained Hitler's ponderous style. All italicized sections appear in the original. Page numbers are given parenthetically in the text.

GERMAN HONOR

It must be a greater honor to be a street-cleaner and citizen of this Reich than a king in a foreign state (441).

[W]e National Socialists must hold unflinchingly to our aim in foreign policy, namely, *to secure for the German people the land and soil to which they are entitled on this earth* (652).

UNDERSTANDING THE MASSES

The psyche of the great masses is not receptive to anything that is half-hearted and weak.

[T]he masses love a commander more than a petitioner and feel inwardly more satisfied by a doctrine, tolerating no other beside itself, than by the granting of liberalistic freedom with which, as a rule, they can do little, and are prone to feel that they have been abandoned (42).

I achieved an equal understanding of the importance of physical terror toward the individual and the masses.

Here, too, the psychological effect can be calculated with precision (43).

Terror at the place of employment, in the factory, in the meeting hall, and on the occasion of mass demonstrations will always be successful unless opposed by equal terror (44).

The nationalization of the broad masses can never be achieved by half-measures, by weakly emphasizing a so-called objective standpoint, but only by a ruthless and fanatically one-sided orientation toward the goal to be achieved (337).

Anyone who wants to win the broad masses must know the key that opens the door to their heart. Its name is not objectivity (read weakness), but will and power (338).

UNIFYING THE PEOPLE

Just as a man's denominational orientation is the result of upbringing, and only the religious need as such slumbers in his soul, the political opinion of the masses represents nothing but the final result of an incredibly tenacious and thorough manipulation of their mind and soul (85).

[The organizer] must take people as they are and must therefore know them. He must not overestimate them, any more than he must underestimate them in the mass. On the contrary, he must endeavor to take weakness and bestiality equally into account (580).

The victory of an idea will be possible the sooner, the more comprehensively propaganda has prepared people as a whole and the more exclusive, rigid, and firm the organization which carries out the fight in practice (582).

For this, to be sure, from the child's primer down to the last newspaper, every theater and every movie house, every advertising pillar and every billboard, must be pressed into the service of this one great mission, until the timorous prayer of our present parlor patriots: "Lord, make us free!" is transformed in the brain of the smallest boy into the burning plea: "Almighty God, bless our arms when the time comes; be just as thou hast always been; judge now whether we be deserving of freedom; Lord, bless our battle!" (632–33).

PROPAGANDA

It belongs to the genius of a great leader to make even adversaries far removed from one another seem to belong to a single category, because in weak and uncertain characters the knowledge of having different enemies can only too readily lead to the beginning of doubt in their own right (118).

Hence a multiplicity of different adversaries must always be combined so that in the eyes of the masses of one's own supporters the struggle is directed against only one enemy (119).

All propaganda must be popular and its intellectual level must be adjusted to the most limited intelligence among those it is addressed to. Consequently, the greater the mass it is intended to reach, the lower its purely intellectual level will have to be (180).

The receptivity of the great masses is very limited, their intelligence is small, but their power of forgetting is enormous. In consequence of these facts, all effective propaganda must be limited to a very few points and must harp on these in slogans until the last member of the public understands what you want him to understand by your slogan. As soon as you sacrifice this slogan and try to be many-sided, the effect will piddle away, for the crowd can neither digest nor retain the material offered (180–81).

And this sentiment is not complicated, but very simple and all of a piece. It does not have multiple shadings; it has a positive and a negative; love or hate, right or wrong, truth or lie, never half this way and half that way, never partially, or that kind of thing (183).

But the most brilliant propagandist technique will yield no success unless one fundamental principle is borne in mind constantly and with unflagging attention. It must confine itself to a few points and repeat them over and over. Here, as so often in this world, persistence is the first and most important requirement for success (184).

If propaganda renounces primitiveness of expression, it does not find its way to the feeling of the broad masses (341).

In the morning and even during the day people's willpower seems to struggle with the greatest energy with an attempt to force upon them a strange will and a strange opinion. At night, however, they succumb more easily to the dominating force of a stronger will (475).

When from [a man's] little workshop or big factory, in which he feels very small, he steps for the first time into a mass meeting and has thousands and thousands of people of the same opinion around him, when, as a seeker, he is swept away by three or four thousand others into the mighty effect of suggestive intoxication and enthusiasm, when the visible success and agreement of thousands confirm to him the rightness of the new doctrine and for the first time arouse doubt in the truth of his previous conviction—then he himself has succumbed to the magic influence of what we designate as mass suggestion. The will, the longing, and also the power of thousands are accumulated in every individual. The man who enters such a meeting doubting and wavering leaves it inwardly reinforced: he has become a link in the community (478–79).

USE OF FORCE

The first requirement for a mode of struggle with the weapons of naked force is and remains persistence. In other words: only the continuous and steady application of the methods for repressing a doctrine, etc., makes it possible for a plan to succeed. But as soon as force wavers and alternates with forbearance, not only will the doctrine to be repressed recover again and again, but it will also be in a position to draw new benefit from every persecution, since, after such a wave of pressure has ebbed away, indignation over the suffering induced leads new supporters to the old doctrine, while the old ones will cling to it with greater defiance and deeper hatred than before (171).

If popularity and force are combined, and if in common they are able to survive for a certain time, an authority on an even further basis can arise, the authority of tradition. If finally, popularity, force, and tradition combine, an authority may be regarded as unshakable (518).

Firm belief in the right to apply even the most brutal weapons is always bound up with the existence of a fanatical faith in the necessity of the victory of a revolutionary new order on this earth (533).

A SPIRITUAL FOUNDATION

Any attempt to combat a philosophy with methods of violence will fail in the end, unless the fight takes the form of attack for a new spiritual attitude. Only in the struggle between two philosophies can the weapon of brutal force, persistently and ruthlessly applied, lead to a decision for the side it supports (172).

The young movement, from the first day, espoused the standpoint that its idea must be put forward spiritually, but that the defense of this spiritual platform must if necessary be secured by strong-arm means (534).

THE JEW

There were few Jews in Linz. In the course of the centuries their outward appearance had become Europeanized and had taken on a human look; in fact I even took them for Germans (52).

Once, as I was strolling through the inner city [of Vienna], I suddenly encountered an apparition in a black caftan and black hair locks. Is this a Jew? was my first thought.

For, to be sure, they had not looked like this in Linz. I observed the man furtively and cautiously, but the longer I stared at this foreign face, scrutinizing feature for feature, the more my first question assumed a new form:

Is this a German? (56).

All this could scarcely be called very attractive; but it became positively repulsive when, in addition to their physical uncleanliness, you discovered the moral stains on the chosen people (57).

Was there any form of filth or profligacy, particularly in cultural life, without at least one Jew involved in it?

If you cut even cautiously into such an abscess, you found, like a maggot in a rotting body, often dazzled by the sudden light—a kike!

What had to be reckoned heavily against the Jews in my eyes was when I became acquainted with their activity in the press, art, literature, and the theater. All the unctuous reassurances helped little or nothing. It sufficed to look at a billboard, to study the names of the men behind the horrible trash they advertised, to make you hard for a long time to come. This was pestilence, spiritual pestilence, worse than the Black Death of olden times, and the people was being infected with it! It goes without saying that the lower the intellectual level of one of these art manufacturers, the more unlimited his fertility will be, and the scoundrel ends up like a garbage separator, splashing his filth in the face of humanity. And bear in mind that there is no limit to their number; bear in mind that for one Goethe Nature easily can foist on the world ten thousand of these scribblers who poison men's souls like germ-carriers of the worst sort, on their fellow men (57–58).

I believe that I am acting in accordance with the will of the Almighty Creator: *by defending myself against the Jew, I am fighting for the work of the Lord* (65).

Blood sin and desecration of the race are the original sin in this world and the end of a humanity which surrenders to it (249).

Without the clearest knowledge of the racial problem and hence of the Jewish problem there will never be a resurrection of the German nation.

The racial question gives the key not only to world history, but to all human culture (339).

THE TASK AHEAD

The mightiest counterpart to the Aryan is represented by the Jew (300).

The nationalization of our masses will succeed only when, aside from all the positive struggle for the soul of our people, their international poisoners are exterminated (338).

How many a time the eyes of my lads glittered when I explained to them the necessity of their mission and assured them over and over again that all the wisdom on this earth remains without success if force does not enter into its service, guarding it and protecting it; that the gentle Goddess of Peace can walk only by the side of the God of War; and that every great deed of this peace requires the protection and aid of force (491).

Appendix 2
Chronology of Events Directly Affecting
German Jews, 1933–1945

1933
January 30: Adolph Hitler appointed chancellor of Germany by President Hindenburg

March 23: Dachau established as first concentration camp, mainly for political opponents

April 1: Nazis proclaim general boycott of all Jewish-owned businesses

April 7: Jews ("non-Aryans") denied admission to the civil service and the legal profession

April 21: Ritual slaughter of animals for food is prohibited

April 22: First decrees placing restrictions on Jewish physicians

April 25: Quotas established for admission of Jewish students to universities

May 2: Dissolution of free trade unions

May 6: Jewish faculty excluded from universities

May 10: Burning of books written by Jews and opponents of Nazism

July 14: Nazi party becomes the only legal political party in Germany

July 14, 26: Laws restricting citizenship for East European Jews

September 22: Establishment of Reich Chamber of Culture leading to dismissal of Jewish artists, musicians, filmmakers, and writers

September 29: Laws excluding Jews from farm labor and ownership of farmland

October 4: Prohibitions placed on "non-Aryan" journalists

1934
March 23: Law laying the basis for deportation of East European Jews

August 2: Hindenburg dies. Hitler becomes head of state and commander in chief of the armed forces

1935
Summer: "Juden Verboten" [no Jews] signs appear in great number, effectively barring Jews from restaurants, shops, and public benches

September 15: The Nuremberg Laws are passed by the Reichstag. The Laws for the Protection of German Blood and German Honor include (1) the status of the Jews is changed from citizen to subject; (2) marriages between Jews and German citizens are forbidden; (3) extramarital relations between Jews and Germans are forbidden; (4) Jews are not permitted to employ German women under the age of forty-five in their household. Violation of the last three articles is punishable by imprisonment at hard labor.

1936

October 25: Hitler and Mussolini form the Rome-Berlin Axis

1937

July 16: Buchenwald concentration camp opens

1938

March 13: Anschluss, the annexation of Austria to the Third Reich. Nazis apply antisemitic laws

April 26: Jews ordered to register all domestic and foreign property over five thousand Reichsmarks

July 6: International conference at Evian, France, fails to provide refuge for German Jews

July 23: Mandatory identification cards for Jews

July 25: Jewish physicians permitted to treat only Jewish patients

August 17: Jews required to add the names Israel or Sara to their names, beginning January 1.

September 27: Jewish lawyers permitted to represent only Jewish clients

September 29: Munich Agreement: Britain and France accept German annexation of the Sudetenland, part of Czechoslovakia (Chamberlain's "Peace in Our Time")

October 5: Passports of Jews are marked in red with the letter "J," for *Jude* (Jew)

October 28: Jews of Polish origin expelled from Germany

November 7: Herschel Grynszpan, whose parents were deported from Germany to Poland, assassinates Ernst vom Rath, Third Secretary of the German embassy in Paris

November 9–10: *Kristallnacht:* antisemitic riots in Germany and Austria, hundreds of synagogues are destroyed, shops are smashed and looted, Jewish men are beaten in the streets

November 12: Thirty thousand Jews arrested and sent to concentration camps

November 12: German Jews denied all insurance money due them for damages to their businesses on Kristallnacht and made to carry out repairs at their own expense. Jews fined one billion Reichsmarks for causing the pogrom against themselves

November 15: Jewish children barred from attending German schools

November 28: Jews banned from certain districts; restrictions imposed on hours during which Jews may appear in public

December 8: Jews prohibited from attending universities

December 13: Decree on "Aryanization" (compulsory expropriation of Jewish industries, businesses, and shops) enacted

1939

January 1: The Measure for the Elimination of Jews from the German Economy is invoked, banning Jews from working with Germans

March 4: Introduction of forced labor for Jews

March 15: Germans occupy the remainder of Czechoslovakia

September 1: Germany invades Poland. Beginning of World War II.

September 3: Britain and France declare war on Germany

1940

February 6: Ration cards for clothing are withheld from German Jews

1941

July 31: Göring instructs Heydrich to prepare a "final solution" to the Jewish question

September 1: All Jews over six years of age compelled to wear the Jewish Star of David in public

September 23: First experiments with gassing are made at Auschwitz

October 10: Theresienstadt ("model" concentration camp) in Czechoslovakia is established

October 14: Deportation of German Jews begins

October 23: Further Jewish emigration from Germany is cut off

December 7: Japanese attack Pearl Harbor

December 8: United States enters the war

1942

January 20: Wannsee Conference held by Nazis on "The Final Solution of the Jewish Question." Plans drafted to exterminate all European Jews

April 17: Compulsory marking of Jewish apartments with the Star of David

May 15: "Nuisance" decree: Jews not permitted to keep pets

May 29: "Nuisance" decree: Jews forbidden to use the services of non-Jewish hairdressers

June 19: All electric appliances, typewriters, and bicycles owned by Jews are confiscated

October 9: Jews forbidden to buy books

1943

Last Jews deported from Germany

1944

November 25: Himmler orders the dismantling of the Auschwitz crematoria as Nazis try to hide evidence of the death camps

1945

January 18: The Death March out of Auschwitz begins

January 27, one o'clock in the morning: SS blow up last crematorium in Auschwitz

January 27, afternoon: Soviet army arrives at Auschwitz

May 7: Germany surrenders. End of the war in Europe

Index

Accents, 111–12, 188
Activism. *See* Political activism
Adenauer, Konrad, 225
Affidavits of financial support, after
war, 174; alternative to, 66; difficulty getting, 68, 72; for immigration,
4, 34, 37, 42; for relatives, 98–99;
Swiss, 28
Aftereffects of persecution, 146, 181,
192, 198–99, 207, 233, 234–35, 337;
and appreciation of life, 162; on
children, 264; damaged self-image,
146, 193, 250–51; differences in,
217, 231; and disillusionment with
humanity, 164, 183–85, 193; and
fear, 19, 50, 105, 132, 137, 235, 240;
and guilt, 213; and identity confusions, 340–42; and ill health, 119,
137; and immigration, 131–32; and
lack of concentration, 192–94; and
nightmares, 286; and not being able
to talk about trauma, 336–37; and
sense of homelessness, 282, 288;
working-through processes for,
345–48
Allies: approach of, 158, 301–02; and
Bergen-Belsen film, 304; bombing
by, 70, 300, 309; *See also* Russian
soldiers
Althans, Bela Ewald, 327
America: antisemitism in, 90, 133–
34; assimilation into, 109, 226;
dissatisfactions with, 9, 60, 194–
95, 241; idealization of, 1, 131–32,
180; immigration quotas of, 8, 23,
52, 58, 62, 194; immigration to,
after war, 174; loyalty of immi-

grants to, 90, 109, 132–33, 187–
90, 201, 221, 232–34; mixed feelings about, 172–73; soldiers in
Germany, 172, 303–04; stereotypes
of, 29; visas for, 23, 58, 63–64,
71–72; *vs.* Germany, 241–42,
244–49
American Jewish Joint Distribution
Committee, 78–79, 203
Anschluss (annexation of Austria), 7,
69
Anti-aircraft gunners, German, 294,
299–300
Antier, Monsieur, 271–72
Antisemitism: in America, 82, 133–34,
195, 239–41; in Austria, 68–69; effects of on children's self-image,
250–51; in England, 56; in Germany, 6, 32–33, 230–31, 258–59; in
modern Germany, 289, 305; toward
Eastern Jews, 5, 179–80, 197–98,
285, 292
Apartments, 117; crowded conditions
in, 126; Jews evicted from, 69; renting rooms in, 97–98, 216
Argentina, immigration to, 273,
314–18
Arrests, 154; in Belgium, 79–80. *See
also* Deportations; Kristallnacht;
Transports
Artists, Bert Kirchheimer as, 39–40,
94–95
Assets/belongings: brought back to
Germany, 66; confiscation of, 7,
17, 24, 219; kept by neighbors, 67,
218–19; lifts of, 28, 80, 192; liquidating, 62, 77, 261, 276; and

EL CAMINO FUNDAMENTAL HIGH SCHOOL
4300 El Camino Avenue
Sacramento, California 95821